JOHN GAY

JOHN GAY

His place in the Eighteenth Century

by
PHŒBE FENWICK GAYE

 BOOKS FOR LIBRARIES PRESS
FREEPORT, NEW YORK

First Published 1938
Reprinted 1972

Library of Congress Cataloging in Publication Data

Gaye, Phoebe Fenwick, 1905-
  John Gay; his place in the eighteenth century.

  (BCL/select bibliographies index reprint series)
  Reprint of the 1938 ed.
  1. Gay, John, 1685-1732.
PR3474.G3   1972   821'.5   79-39401
ISBN 0-8369-9906-1

PRINTED IN THE UNITED STATES OF AMERICA
BY
NEW WORLD BOOK MANUFACTURING CO., INC.
HALLANDALE, FLORIDA 33009

ILLUSTRATIONS

Mr. Gay by W. Aikman	*Frontispiece*	
Bust of Pope by Roubilliac	*facing page*	56
Bust of Swift by Roubilliac	,,	80
The first page of the MS. of Mr. Gay's *Mr. Pope's Welcome from Greece*	,,	136
Portrait of Catherine Hyde, Duchess of Queensberry, attributed to Jervas	,,	208
The Honourable Mrs. Howard, afterwards Countess of Suffolk	,,	288
Prison scene from *The Beggar's Opera* by Hogarth	,,	344
A contemporary broadsheet with portrait of Mr. Gay by Aikman	,,	440

CHAPTER ONE

Birth and upbringing, 1685-1700.

I have no name
I am but two days old
    What shall I call thee?

I happy am
Joy is my name,
    Sweet Joy befall thee!

                                   BLAKE

WHEN Charles the Second apologised in 1685 for being such an unconscionable time dying he spoke more comprehensively than he knew. More than the body of the king lay on the death-bed then: the body of romantic poetry was dying too. Poetry has tough sinews and naturally there were to be a few survivors, born out of their time and living on into an era strange to the spirit they had inherited. But in the main romantic poetry, poetry-with-the-lid-off, expired with the last respiration of Charles Stuart. Life had been good for both of them, while it lasted ; Lyric poetry in particular had survived the lean years of the Revolution. Light as a cork, it had bobbed above Cromwell's oncoming waves of disapproval and suppression. Dramatic poetry had not been so fortunate; in that field only Dryden remained of the romantics, and even his art had trimmed itself so skilfully to the storm that it was as easy to say of him that he was the last of the Elizabethan as that he was the first of Restoration dramatists.

But other poets could not do what Dryden had been

able to do. They had been born in and of a certain period and had died in it. There had been the spring of English poetry, with the hedges still thin but pricked with blossom, and Chaucer and Spenser had sung then, clearly, sweetly, lustily like the birds of spring. There had been the early summer of the Elizabethan period, with all the birds singing full-throated—the hedges now hidden by the flowers in the hedgerow, meadow-sweet and the wild roses of May. Then song had stopped in the heat of high summer, except for the warblers, the little reedy song of the "occasional" poets, pleasant though trite, short though limited in scope. They had warbled on, regardless of Revolution and Restoration, and occasionally in the echo of a line had recalled, as hedge-warblers and finches can do, the sublimer notes of the song-birds of early summer.

So the seasons run on: first spring's brilliant soloists —the lark, the mating blackbird, the cuckoo's wooden echo. Second the chorus of blackbirds, thrushes, swallows —everything feathered—with the nightingale to crown them all. Then midsummer with its finches and warblers hidden in the green leafage, echoing from time to time the liquid notes of earlier singers. With the death of the second Charles comes an autumnal hush; Nature's breath held for so long as it might take for the first leaf to fall from the first tree and sidle to the ground. Then even the warblers stop, and the exotics take off again to warmer climes. The annual flowers are scorched away to rotting stems, meadowsweet and fools-parsley turn to horny kexes in the deserted hedgerows with their empty nests; sunlight is thin now, no warmth behind it; mists swathe the fields where sweet lovers once loved the spring. Only the robin and wren in the hedge-row (once wreathed in wild roses but gleaming now with bryony and blackberry) are left to carry on. And not even the most romantically-minded could discover romance in the song of either bird. They should not be despised, however. Ornithologically they represent, to perfection, the poets of the Augustan age. So in 1685 robin and wren together tidily dispose of the body of the late lamented Charles, burying beneath the leaves, spring and summer, and the age of romantic poetry with him. Robin and wren are realists, not romantics. They see life steadily and see it whole. They are small, neat, sententious birds, eminently fitted to cheep the rhymed couplets of Augustan poetry. Their eyes are the beadiest and most inquisitive of all the tribe. They sum one up, from a safe distance, with eyes very like the brilliant eyes of Alexander Pope in the Richardson portrait. Their cocked, considering heads and cheeky rumps imply that they cannot be fooled with salt on the tail, that it is the early bird that catches the worm, that rides the whirlwind and directs the storm, that, in fact, knows a thing or two. There are birds with a deep devotion to family life, like Jenny Wren and Richard Steele. There are birds with a pugnacious regard for correctness, for carefully-defined areas of personal property, like Robin Redbreast and Alexander Pope. These and others like them are the singers in the autumn of English literature; in an eighteenth century dwarfed beside the giants of the seventeenth century, but the brief chroniclers of their time for all that, and so essential, and in their way beloved.

The purpose of this digression is to sketch in the background to a life-size portrait. The man to be depicted, like most theories when traced to logical conclusions, is not to be set down definitely as belonging to one particular school. It has been said earlier that occasional survivors of the earlier romantic period overlapped into the Augustan age. John Gay will always be considered an Augustan though he contrived to live, in the course of a comparatively short life, through five reigns. Yet together with Matthew Prior his "occasional" poetry retained an echo of that earlier time, a hint of rapture (no longer careless, it is true, but out-of-tune for all that in an age so inhibited against enthusiasms of any kind), and what Thackeray has called: "A peculiar hinted pathetic sweetness and melody. It charms you and melts you. It is indefinable but it exists and is the property of John Gay's and Oliver Goldsmith's best verse, as fragrance is of a violet, or freshness of a rose."

Prior preceded Gay into the world by nearly twenty years and Goldsmith followed forty years later, so that this lost-chord quality has no particular chronological significance. It was most understandable perhaps in Prior—contemporary, after all, of Rochester, Etherege and the other Restoration warblers—and least in Goldsmith. But it is there, inexplicable or not, and certainly there in Gay. How it worked in him, and how struggled against the incompatible and yet inevitable spirit of his own times remains to be shown.

"I do not find that God has made you a poet," wrote Lord Chesterfield to his booby son in 1745, "and I am glad of it." He might well make the best of a bad job. (Nobody was ever better at taking things sitting down, always with *les manières engageantes et le je ne sais quoi qui plaît*, than Lord Chesterfield; how fitting, therefore, that his memory should be perpetuated in a sofa.) If he had reflected a little more deeply he might have discovered that though poets, like cuckoos' eggs, are dropped into all sorts of unlikely nests, it is not often that the nests chosen are at the top of the tree. The diet of luxury has seldom been considered a suitable one for rearing poets. (The Elizabethan period is the exception that proves the rule: then the urge to self-expression was so impelling that even soldiers burst into song. . . .)

The cuckoo's egg that was dropped in the Devonshire town of Barnstaple one August day in 1685 was not destined to startle the world out of all countenance but it contained undeniably an embryo poet; and Nature, usually careless of such trifles as nomenclature, was kind enough in one thing. Having selected Barnstaple she made sure that John Gay should be born in Joy Street of that borough. The street itself is almost as short as the name—a narrow thoroughfare running between two of the principal roads of the town. The houses in it were for the most part so closely packed that they can have been of no great significance, but at either end of Joy Street two more imposing houses stood, like watch-houses, and in one of these the youngest child of Mr. William Gay was born.

It was not a year in which—had there been any choice—one would have chosen to be born. The country still heaved spasmodically, like a volcanic eruption not yet over, from the alarms of Revolution and Restoration. Nor were her troubles over. Charles's successor James the Second, of futile memory, had sat his throne no more than a month when Romance threw her last card on the table and made a personal appearance, in the guise of the pretender James Monmouth, at Lympne. Exchanging one Stuart for another may appear to posterity, with its advantage of longer perspective, very much like jumping out of the frying-pan into the fire; but however desirable or undesirable the change was not to be. Sedgemoor, the last *fracas* to be dignified with the name of battle on English soil, followed close on Monmouth's landing, and the most immortal part of the Pretender proved to be Kneller's picture of him in the National Portrait Gallery, painted after his execution on Tower

Hill. There, with the mute eloquence of any slave at a Roman feast (and with a sententiousness that nothing as romantic as a bastard Stuart could ever have compassed in real life), the pale, beautiful face bids us remember Sedgemoor, remember ambition and the worms that eat it—remember that even kings and princes must, like chimney-sweepers, come to dust. . . .

It was during the noise of this civil warfare that that particularly peaceable person John Gay made his entrance into the world, and suitably enough (though then without any such significance) the name of the house in which he did so was the Red Cross. The real significance of the name is lost. At first it would seem to suggest an inn, but inns like the lives of good men usually leave behind them footprints in the sands of time—not to mention documentary evidence—and no such traceable footprints lead up to the door of the Red Cross. As its origin is lost in mystery, so is the profession or occupation of Gay's father. Nevertheless, since the Red Cross was amongst the most highly-rated houses in the whole borough, and since Mr. Gay's father-in-law was that very respectable-sounding thing, a Nonconformist Minister of the Independent Dissenting Church, it is generally conceded that he must have been a gentleman. Indeed, if the Gays had ever cared to delve into their early pedigree they might have been interested to discover how very blue-blooded (in company of course with most of their acquaintance) they really were.

Research has traced an apocryphal beginning to the family as far back as the days of King Arthur; after driving out the Romans from Britain and Normandy, King Arthur, it is said, rested on his laurels, and—as was the custom—handed out presents of land to those supporters whose work had pleased him. One Gaius, the royal Taster, was presented with the Earldom of Anjou—understandably, since they also serve who only stand and taste—especially at the court of King Arthur. The family of Gaius reappeared after that in the Gallicized form of le Gay and, under the leadership of one Gilbert le Gay, came over to England with the rest of the world at the time of the Norman Conquest. They settled in Devon for the most part, though a few became landowners in other parts of the country, and in the thirteenth century a member of the family (anglicized back into Gay), one Phillip Gay, became owner by marriage of the manor of Goldsworthy in Devon. From this Phillip, by way of several Thomases, a John, a William, an Anthonie, a Thomas again, a John again, an Anthony, and another John we come down to 1648 and to William Gay, the father of the poet. The family would seem to have been the usual mixed one of yeomen and gentlemen, farmers and Members of Parliament, with a top-dressing of such glories as the mayoralty of Barnstaple (1638), a yeomanship of the King's Chamber and a stewardship of Keynsham Abbey. But whatever their individual occupations the one undeniable fact about them was that they were the Gays of Goldsworthy. Even Dr. Johnson, whose occasional ignorance was as monumental as his other qualities, discovered this. It is thus apparent that, if Gay ever wished to boast about blue blood there had been local blue blood to boast about. The fact that it is not discoverable that he ever afterwards did so may have been because the blue was not of the deepest ultramarine, or that, having been brought early under the dissenting influence, he held simple faith to be more than Norman blood. Or it may have been merely indolence—always a safe bet where Gay was concerned.

The social stratification of England, at the time of

Gay's birth, was settling into three layers as distinct from one another as heaven, earth and hell. They may be classified as the gentlemen, the merchants and the mob (or, as Swift preferred it, having an ear for cacophony as well as for giving a dog the very worst sort of name before you hang him, the Rabble). Of these, the merchants were the newcomers, a comfortable middle-class beginning to elbow its way between the two extremes and to hold its ground, with an ever-growing assurance, until the present day. It is extremely likely that William Gay himself belonged to the merchants' class. The fact that his house was in the centre of the town and not on the outskirts would seem to preclude any likelihood of his being a farmer—that other possibility—and the fact that the centre of the town was, very naturally in a sea-port, adjacent to the wharfs and customs-houses, might suggest that the occupation of William Gay was one concerned with the import of bales and lades of cargo from Portugal and the Indies, or with the export of the woollen goods which were Barnstaple's staple trade. However that may be, the birth of another son must have seemed to him fair compensation for the loss, in the same year, of his eldest daughter, the eleven-year-old Elizabeth; for the attitude of the seventeenth and eighteenth century concerning daughters seems so like the attitude of the ancient Chinese that one can only suppose that the prevalent passion for order prevented a similar exposure of girls at birth. The Gay family made its appearance at happily-calculated intervals, and John, baptised on September 16, joined the three-year-old Joanna, the six-year-old Jonathan and the nine-year-old Katherine. The parents, however nebulous now in outline, seem to have been clear in one thing at least, and that was in their desire to perpetuate, by hook or crook, the favourite family name of John. In this they builded better than they knew.

The Monmouth rebellion once over, a small seaport town in Devon was an admirable place for the infancy and childhood of the young Gays. There they might breathe the soft balmy air of the west, and play in the safe estuaries and creeks of the river Taw—whose clean tides, sweeping through the town twice a day, carried away the accumulated rubbish. The same sort of rubbish, polluting the air from the open kennels and drains in London, successfully accounted for the fevers and deaths of a sixth of the population there. But the young Gays were being brought up in a county where snow never fell and ice never formed and where, on the hottest day, sea-winds invigorated; a county of red sandstone, and soft marl, whose pastures were grazed by sheep as ruddy as the earth on which they trod; in a town with a quiet wide river with green banks, fringed with the tongues of ferns, planted with elms and crossed by a stone bridge, ancient even then. In these green pastures the after-effects of Marlborough's victory at Sedgemoor, the tender mercies of Kirke's Lambs and of Jeffrey's Bloody Assizes, were too far off to be felt. Even in December the farmers' wives, bringing their fowls and eggs and cream to Barnstaple market, could decorate their wares with violets and primroses. The warmth and mildness which in Devon and Cornwall could draw out the crumpled buds so far in advance of England's other counties, was also kind to young animal and human life. If there was not joyfulness in Joy Street in those early days, when the children were young and the parents ignorant of coming tragedy, then joy indeed is far to seek.

Three years after the invasion of the Duke of Monmouth's forces, a second invader chose a landing-place in

Devon from which to start a similar campaign—marching towards London and gathering followers as he went. Where Monmouth failed the Prince of Orange succeeded. What was that extra weight in the scales, the little more which brought the second invader down on the winning side? One thing was certain, time had been on the side of the Prince of Orange. When he landed at Torquay that summer he had two tremendous advantages behind him—three years of unexampled maladministration by James, and the recent Revocation of the Edict of Nantes by Louis the Fourteenth. The first had filled England with discontented Englishmen, impatient of James's Catholic misdemeanours; the second filled her with discontented Frenchmen—Huguenots and Protestants fleeing from a country whose dictator, the sun-king, setting the example for all dictators after him, put back the clock by revoking a law which for over a hundred years had shown a spirit of toleration towards all subjects who were holders of a faith contrary to the faith of the State. As the German Jews fled when the sun-king Hitler began to purge Germany in the twentieth century, so the French Protestants, prohibited from earning any sort of a living in their native land in 1685, took flight over the Channel to an Albion which though perfidious was still Protestant, at least *pro tem*. Hundreds of French refugees filtering through English towns and parishes, each with a tale of Catholic persecution behind him—these, combined with a genuine dread of France on the part of the English people and a detestation of the Catholic Stuart at Kensington Palace, made the way easy for the Prince of Orange and the Glorious Revolution in 1688. So it was that the best king of England since Queen Elizabeth came to the throne, and James II. and his warming-pan associates took refuge under the very wide wings of *le Roi Soleil*.

The history each man is most ignorant of is the history of his early childhood, and John Gay at no age concerned himself tremendously with national affairs, except in so far as these affected himself or his friends, and certainly not in youth. Such momentous happenings as the Bill of Rights or the battles of the Boyne and La Hogue never kept him or his brothers and sisters awake at nights. The massacre of Glencoe would have seemed to them, busy about their own entrancing childhood occupations, as remote as the continental rebellions under Louis XIV. They cared not a jot about the clashes between Whig and Tory, Jacobite or Orangeman, papist or dissenter. King William's painfully built-up coalition against France meant nothing to them—though their parents, with their Low Church connections, may have followed with interest the campaigns of the hero of Protestantism in Europe. The foundations of the national debt and of the Bank of England were of less importance to them than what was to be for to-morrow's dinner. What shall they know of England, who only Devon know?

Round about his sixth year Gay was sent to attend Barnstaple Grammar School, an establishment (as befitted a school in what claims to be the oldest borough in the kingdom) already hoary in tradition. It was like everything else in Barnstaple, a stone's throw from the Red Cross—a fact which doubtless suited Gay's lazy nature very well. There he struggled through "the long tyranny of Grammar schools," and was presumably "lashed into Latin," that necessary process for the supercharging of all pupils with the works of Ovid, Horace and Virgil. (His principal teacher was a Mr. Luck, a man who kept his own muse bottled up until after the death of his most illustrious pupil and who then allowed it to burst out into a volume of imitative verse.

B

In this he inferred that he was practically the onlie begetter of *The Beggar's Opera* since it was the little plays which the Barnstaple grammar schoolboys had performed so long before which had first aroused Gay's interest in the theatre.) It is on such scraps of information as this that we have to subsist concerning his youth. How hard he worked, what sort of a position he occupied at school can be deduced only from what we know of his later years. From these we may be fairly sure that he could not read the Bible right through at three, like Swift, copy it right through at ten, like Defoe—that he did not lisp in numbers because the numbers sprang inevitably into his head, like Pope, and that he was never borne to school on his schoolfellows' backs like Johnson, an act of homage, surprisingly unusual in schoolboys, to the most brilliant pupil in the class.

But if popularity in later life is anything to go by, then Gay was popular at school. Lazy, chubby, friendly, inventive, a butt on occasions who bore no malice, and a boy who could make butts of others without ruffling them beyond endurance—we are not far out if we build up something after this pattern. Two relics only of his schooldays survive. One is a tale vouched for by Barnstaple relations—that the first verses he ever wrote were "in consequence of one of his schoolmates shooting a swallow in Barnstaple churchyard." No copy of this is extant, a fact which, bearing in mind the poverty of other first poems, is probably no loss. The interest of the anecdote lies principally in its inkling of tender-heartedness. It is somehow apposite that one of Pope's first poems should have been a satire on his schoolmaster at Twyford and that Gay's should have been on the death of a bird—a thing commonly regarded as fair game by all schoolboys.

The other relic is more typical of schoolboy activities.

It came about that the ten-year-old John Gay and a school companion, one Phineas Flett, were kicking their heels idly during sermon in the parish church one day, and that they chose to occupy the time by cutting their names on the oak pew in front of them. Phineas, by virtue possibly of superior age and pushfulness, cut his first, in large bold characters—PHIN FLETT, 1695. Underneath, in a smaller and much neater hand, John Gay cut his. The particular piece of pew, so inscribed, may still be seen in the Barnstaple Atheneum. Though they were doubtless trounced for it at the time it is difficult to blame them much in retrospect—at least to blame Gay, for he and his brother and sisters had many melancholy opportunities to attend church just then. A year before the pew-cutting incident their mother had died—carried off as mysteriously as the first-born child, nine years before. A bare year later, before the memory of the funeral obsequies had had time to grow dim in the minds of her children, the father followed the mother. The four orphans were thereupon transferred to the care of Thomas Gay, an uncle whose profession has remained as obscure as that of Gay's father. . . . Perhaps this too-early acquaintance with death induced in the adolescent John the first seeds of that depression which afterwards pulled him down so often. In this he was not original; for the Gay family, despite their name and the brave boast brought over by them from France:—

>*Toujours Gai*
>*Qu'il fasse beau*
>*Qu'il fasse laid*

had an undisputed tendency to melancholia. Whether inherited or original, the circumstances in which Gay himself was placed did much to increase it. Joy Street with all its associations was now no more; and life with an uncle, already (if the usual contemporary family is anything to go by) provided with a family of from half a dozen to a dozen children of his own, can have been no joke after Joy Street. Katherine and Joanna, Jonathan and John, dressed in their decent blacks, come to mind very much as extras in a kindly but probably hard-up household. The nineteen-year-old Katherine soon married a Mr. Baller—and then there were three. The thirteen-year-old Joanna, being a girl and consequently the Wrong Sex, could always be made useful about the house. As for the boys, the various uncles, maternal and paternal, studied hard to think what to do with the boys.

CHAPTER TWO

Apprenticeship and Adolescence, 1700-1706.

> "*Genoa, Dutch and English velvets, Paduasoys of all colours, Tabbys watered and unwatered, Rich brocades, damasks and all sorts of flowered silks, Rich Florence and English sattins, figured and stript lutestrings, Ducapes, Mantuas, Sarsnets and Persians. Likewise all sorts of half silks as English and Turkey Burdets, Cherry-derrys figures and stript Donjars.*"
> TRADE CARD, 1735

IN the early eighteenth century, if there were two sons in a family and that family had any pretentions to gentility there was only one possible decision to take. The elder son went into the army and the younger one was apprenticed to a trade.

The uncertainties of the more established professions during the succeeding turmoils of Revolution, Restoration and Glorious Revolution probably accounted for this arrangement. Anxious fathers, deliberating over the choice of a career for their sons, may have felt that being a soldier and taking an oath to the king was well enough, but when the rightful king was as disputable as he had been lately there was as much possibility of a bright young officer carrying a robe of penance as a field-marshal's baton in his knapsack, and that he had as good a chance of meeting a rebel's degrading death on Tower Hill as a glorious promotion on the field of battle.

The Church was in a similar quandary: the occupation of the throne successively by kings whose established rule seemed to be to swim against the religious tide, whatever it happened to be at the moment, only bore out, to anxious parents, Paul's warning that here we have no continuing city. Low church and High church influences swayed the populace with the alternating movement of a pendulum. And always, whichever he was, a man's religious tenets were inextricably bound up in, and influenced by, politics which should have been beyond the function of a churchman. The Law came in the same category of uncertainty. Of what avail the pomp and majesty of justice if at any moment a king could declare himself superior to its rulings and play Old Harry with Bills and legal terms? Thus all the truly gentlemanly professions had their drawbacks; only Trade jogged on, so virile in its salad days, that even periodic wars at all quarters of the British Isles did nothing to impede its advance in growth and prestige throughout the century. Small wonder that at this period, as G. M. Trevelyan has recorded—"In the best shops of the city the apprentices were sons of country gentlemen, likely to die richer than their elder brothers, and dressing in full-bottomed wigs when off duty."

But it was, be it noticed, the younger brother who was usually so apprenticed, and so it was with Gay. Jonathan, after doing some desultory reading for the Church, had discovered no vocation for it and so, about the time that John was apprenticed to a silk-mercer in London, his elder brother entered the army as a trooper under Marlborough's command. His commission, with the signature of Queen Anne, followed in due course.

So it was that John Gay, probably riding pillion behind an uncle or servant to London Town, was articled to a silk-mercer in the city; thus giving grounds for the familiar first gibe of his biographers. It has never been disclosed why that particular trade was chosen. The association has, of course, prompted the thought that the young Gay had a mind fit for nothing better than silk-mercering and such vanities; a supposition which seems about as reasonable as to suppose that, because his brother was a soldier, his brother was a pugnacious and particularly dashing sort of person. The round peg in the square hole is, after Adam's profession, the oldest profession of all, and that, instead of silk-mercering, turns out to have been John Gay's first lot in life. It was not one to his taste, and Dr. Johnson, in a manner which suggests that if it had been he who had been apprenticed and who had not liked shopkeeping he would still have worked out his seven years if not made it fourteen, remarks: "He was soon weary of either the restraint or the servility of the occupation, and easily persuaded his master to discharge him . . ."

Servility is unlikely, as it was not a state of mind which arose concerning apprentices, any more than with pupils at school, but the restraint to a country boy, and in all likelihood a boy who had been spoiled as the baby of the family—at least in the early years—may well have proved intolerable.

There was one thing at which Gay, in due time, was to prove pre-eminent, and that was reporting. He was to do in verse what the contemporaneous Hogarth did with his pencil and Defoe with his prose. "Few poets," says Southey, "seem to have possessed so quick and observing an eye." With these quick powers of observation lying ready to hand and with a wit which badly needed the sharpening contact of other wits to come to itself and outgrow its rusticity, a shop must have seemed a poor place to be immured in for seven precious years. And youth, which can best afford to be generous with its wasted time, is ever the most impatient of time misspent. *Youth's the season made for Joy; O how shall summer's honey and breath hold out against the wreckful siege of battering days: Gather ye rosebuds while ye may; Love and life are for to-day; Had we but world enough, and time; O, Year, grow slowly; What is this life if full of care we have no time to stand and stare? The life of man is but a span, it flourisheth like a flower. We are here to-day and gone to-morrow, and are dead in an hour; How can the bird that is born for joy sit in his cage and sing?; But ever and anon I hear Life's winged chariot hurrying by; Youth's a stuff will not endure* . . . These were the sentiments which unsettled apprentices, which coursed half-formulated through their heads when they should have been engaged on other things, suggesting continually that they, poor wretches, had chosen the worser half and that all that was lovely and worthwhile was going on outside, without them. There is a flush of rapture in each line, a hint that they belong to that earlier golden age when it was not *démodé* to wear your heart upon your sleeve, so long as both heart and sleeve were beautiful. And for Gay, whose mouth had been brushed at birth by the wing-tips of those earlier singers and whose heart was not yet tamed to the sedateness of a poet approved by Horace and Boileau, such suggestions were too much. *Youth's the season made for Joy* was the song that he was born to sing, not the dreary litany from the indentures of apprenticeship which ran: "*Taverns and alehouses he shall not haunt, at cards, dice tables and other unlawful game he shall not play, matrimony he shall not contract nor from the service of his said master day nor night shall he absent himself.*"

Such terms were harsh under a bad master, but good master or bad, Gay was determined not to submit to them, a decision which was probably of advantage to the silk-mercering business. Dr. Johnson denounced the whole affair as one thoroughly discreditable: he could not see that to a young man bounding with life, planted down for the first time in the very hub of England and yet compelled by his apprenticeship to see nothing of it, the situation was difficult, if not impossible. If Gay had stayed to give customers short measures of Paduasoy, and to mislay the bales of lutestring (as he assuredly would have done); if he had spent seven years making up wrong accounts for his master concerning cherry-derry and stript donjar, all he would have been would be a bad apprentice and perhaps never a poet. *Trivia* and the *Fables* and *The Beggar's Opera* would never have been, and Dr. Johnson would have been one short for his *Lives of the Poets* . . .

Gay was admittedly lazy, if laziness is refusing to do, all your life, so much as a hand's turn of what you don't want to do. He could be energetic and hard-working enough when the spirit moved him. That was his nature. It was the only way, with him, in which his small muse could feel free to sing. In a cage, whether it was of unhappiness or restraint, the mood left him, and the notes were strangled. It may therefore be regarded as a Good Thing for all concerned, that the indentures of that particular Idle Apprentice were cancelled. In the lofty strain of a commentator compelled to put the best face possible on the situation: "This station not suiting his liberal spirit he began to show his disgust to a shop, almost from his first entrance therein, and giving little attendance and less attention to the business, he in a few months procured a release on easy terms and took a final leave of his master."

Nothing would have suited the Idle Apprentice better at this juncture than to stay in London and explore its delights at his leisure: to saunter under the swinging shop-signs and ogle the girls at the windows as they threw out the slops. To snatch an apple from a fruit-wagon as its steaming horses slipped on the cobbles and dragged the unwieldy burden past him, bound for Covent Garden: to snuff up the different odours of Smithfield and Billingsgate and watch, ever at a safe distance, the brawls and quarrels which enlivened the existence of the overworked and drunken carriers and fishwives: to squat on the river bank above the forest of masts which filled the river below Tower Bridge and study at leisure those ant-like labourers who spent life in unloading spices and nutmeg and coffee and mahogany from New Guinea, coal from Newcastle and Wales, fish from Grimsby, cotton goods from Manchester, lace from Nottingham, brandy and gin and rum from Holland, claret from France, Port from Portugal, tea and snuff and the eternal cherry-derries from India, hemp and pitch from the Baltic, tin and iron from Cornwall, charcoal from the Forest of Dean, corn and cheese, beef and woollen goods from East Anglia, pottery, leather and woollen goods from his own native county, and labour from all quarters of the world.

When this palled (as some time it would to a boy already acquainted with the activities of a seaport) what other interminable delights lay waiting! To thumb the books outside booksellers until warned off; to linger in warm evenings at the tavern doors in St. Giles' Fields, and let the ballad music that issued out of them together with the smoke and din soak into an already musical apprehension: better still, to lie abed late in a soft bed in the mornings, and let the cries of London, succeeding each other down the street like a chime of bells, seduce the listening ears and fill the closed eyes with tears of inexplicable joy. O the houses, shops and churches (making up the losses of the Great Fire) which were still in course of building, the brick-dust and cheerful clamour which surrounded them! farther afield the great houses of the nobles, standing like so many palaces in the tree-shaded gardens of Chelsea and Kensington, Greenwich, Blackheath and Marylebone, and modelled so admirably upon that Hellenic principle which should be, Gay knew, the *modus exempli* of poets as well as of architects. The lavender-gardens at Mitcham called out to all idle apprentices—come, smell me. The snipe in the Battersea bogs drummed—come, shoot me or net me. The bear-gardens and cock-pits of Hockley and Marylebone, the leopards in the Tower of London, the lunatics at Bedlam, the prisoners in Newgate, the condemned-to-death at Tyburn, the fairs of St. Bartholomew and May Day—where else in the four quarters of the world could so many entrancing spectacles be gathered together within so convenient a compass, and viewed so cheaply? And when *these* palled, there were the theatres in Lincoln's Inn Fields and Drury Lane—entertainments which made too great a strain upon the purse of an apprentice, especially an absconded one, but which, nevertheless, an ingenious young man might manage to come at by bribing officials and footmen and by other such hole-and-corner methods. Earth had not anything to show more fair to a sixteen-year-old country boy. All he asked was to be allowed to stay in London and, free at last of stifling proscriptions, to rifle its delights at his own sweet will.

It is hardly surprising that his request was not granted. Whatever money had been left by his father, most of his share had in all likelihood been swallowed up in the fees of apprenticeship, and his elder brother Jonathan would have accounted for the lion's share of the rest. He had secured a release from the silk-mercer upon 'easy terms'; a vague statement which certainly means that his master was so glad to be rid of a bad bargain that he had no scruples about letting him go, but which does not disclose whether the desirable principle of money-back-if-not-satisfied was in force. At any rate the reaction in Devon was the one to be expected: the long arm of an enraged uncle reached out and snatched him back to Barnstaple. No bells rang at the parish church on the return of the prodigal nephew, and no fatted calves were killed at the residence of Mr. Thomas Gay. That particular uncle no doubt felt, as with reason he might, that he had done quite enough for his nephew. He had brought him up, together with his brother and sisters, had seen him through his schooldays and arranged for his apprenticeship. Now that the silk-mercer and all that he stood for had been as it were flung back in his face, he washed his hands of the whole business. Another uncle could shoulder the responsibility.

Only a few months after his first excursion to London therefore, John Gay was received into the house of his maternal uncle at Barnstaple, the Reverend Jonathan Hanmer, and from that inauspicious homecoming until he reached his majority some six years later all trace of how he lived, and what he did, is lost.

It would have been convenient to have filled the gap with the evidence from *Gay's Chair*—but this slim volume (slim especially in the slang or Boer sense of the word) issued 88 years after Gay's death, has always been suspect and has now been authoritatively disposed of as fake by Mr. George Faber in the most scholarly of all the editions of Gay's works—the one from the Oxford University Press. Like most successful fakes the book has its foundation in just as much fact as will serve its purpose. The chair itself is undoubtedly Gay's chair. It has in its time been vouched for by several trustworthy residents of Barnstaple and contemporaries of the poet as having belonged undeniably to him—even as being his 'favourite' chair; and it is hardly likely that having seen such a chair once any of them would have forgotten it or bestowed it upon an unimportant relative of the Rev. Hanmer's unless it really belonged to him; for it reverses all the usual principles of chair-sitting and combines with its qualities of being a new kind of chair, several labour-saving devices such as a shelf for writing on and candle-sticks for illumination. Since therefore the chair was certainly Gay's, and his favourite chair, and since it remained in Barnstaple until long after his death—it seems that we may be sure of one thing at least: that he used it at this time—during his stay with the second uncle and after his return from London. But the business of the chair's secret drawer, and the subsequent publication of the verses attributed to John Gay which were found in it, is where fact leaves off and fantasy begins. Readers interested in literary forgeries are referred for the full story to the Oxford University Press edition of Gay's collected works, where Mr. Faber's ingenious and admirable detective-work has unravelled the whole secret. . . . Farewell, therefore, to those hints of romance which the Editor of *Gay's Chair* was so thoughtful as to find for posterity, in the secret drawer. Farewell to Miss Jane Scott and the invocation to the chair itself, to the Epistle from the maids of Exeter and all the other *ben trovata.*

Reduced to bare fact all we know of those six years is that Gay had the chair and that if he sat in it at all he sat humped forward, leaning his elbows across its back, and astride it. Nothing that he afterwards wrote can be ascribed to this period, of which he never spoke, so far as we know, and in the atmosphere of which he found no inspiration. *How can the bird that is born for joy, sit in his cage and sing?* How could a Gay, especially one so volatile, be *toujours Gai*, when his circumstances separated him from all that seemed to him desirable and lovely? Life in the house of a Dissenting Minister can hardly have been the atmosphere in which an idle, inquisitive and intelligent young man would thrive best. Not for nothing was Gay born in the seventeenth century; he was destined to carry the memory of its lyrical qualities along with him, and to mingle it later with the more sophisticated and disillusioned cadences of the century in which he died. But neither romance nor sophistication was at home in the Rev. Hanmer's house in Barnstaple. If he sought romance then he sought it outside, kicking his heels along the green banks of the Taw or in the fields and woods outside the town—"alike indulgent to the muse and love." If he sought sophistication then he must turn to his favourite Horace, and find it in Rome in the century before Christ rather than in his acquaintances or the scene about him. The ingredients of good poetry—sound judgment, succinct precepts, elegance, morality, polish, wit—all lay conveniently to hand in the same volume. . . . We may safely guess that he went on trying his hand at verse (though not the fake specimens quoted in *Gay's Chair*) possibly encouraged by his late schoolmaster, Mr. Luck. And since he could also play on the flute and sing, it seems likely that during these years he did as much of both as was fitting to the character of the nephew of a Nonconformist divine. Of one thing we may be certain—that he did not sulk and complain intolerably about his condition.

"The sweetness and simplicity of Gay's temper and manners," writes Joseph Warton of Gay at a later period, "much endeared him to all acquaintances, and made them always speak of him with particular fondness and attachment." The sweetness and simplicity, and the notes of a flute are the only echoes which come down to us from these early years. His feet marked time while the feet of others strode on. Two other 'old boys' from Barnstaple school, school-fellows of his, were both admirably occupied; the first, his friend and relative-to-be, William Fortescue, in all the rural cares and activities of a large estate—the second, Aaron Hill, in finishing off in Constantinople an education begun at Barnstaple and Westminster. These were the playmates and companions, the old familiar faces of childhood. Of those other far greater names, the lightning and the thunder of the eighteenth century, Gay can as yet have had no notion, nor even realised that the friendships and acquaintances he had already found were only to be so much practice material—the general rubbing-up that a pebble on the shingle receives from the tides, till round and smooth and shining at last it may compete with the best of its associates as a finished article. It may have been an apprenticeship every whit as hard as the one already relinquished, but it was one which fitted him well for the place he was later to occupy in the friendships of two of the greatest men of his time.

History meanwhile passed on, leaving him behind. The death of James the Pretender at St. Germains, the death of King William at Hampton Court, and the accession of Queen Anne, had less effect on the lives of the inhabitants of Barnstaple than the Great Storm of 1703 which, gathering itself together in some dim region beyond the calculations of Augustan seismographists, fell with a fury unequalled before or since on the south and west of England. The smoky splendour of Blenheim (unless Jonathan Gay, and his brother officers, writing home from the campaigns told them something of it) affected Devon men and women of the time far less than the loss of half the fleet and merchant vessels in the Irish Sea and the Channel, during the tempest, and the destruction of half the houses in nearby Bristol and distant London, so that both, we are told, had the appearance of bombarded towns. Uprooted avenues of elms and oaks lay with the regularity of ladder-rungs, across the length and breadth of England. But the sheltered woods of Windsor in the Thames valley were spared, and riding through their Corot-like shades came young Alexander Pope and his admirer Sir William Trumbull, talking on all sorts of classical subjects and discussing that lost memory of Wycherley's which made him, poor old thing, repeat himself and other people in his works, not once but a dozen times. . . . While in Ireland, in the living of Laracor, the forty-year-old Dr. Swift laid out his gardens as much as possible after the style of the Moor Park where he had spent so many years. . . . The forked lightning of little Mr. Pope was not flickering yet even with the gentle tongue of a snake. The thunder of the Doctor in Dublin was still unreleased; still to reverberate down upon the thieves and harpies, fools and coxcombs who were to cross his path. But the sky, so far, was clear. The century itself was a mere infant. Barnstaple, Binfield, Laracor—three places with one focal point towards which the thoughts of three inhabitants tended, with the inevitability of the needle pointing to the true North—the focal point of London.

CHAPTER THREE

1707-1711. Early Years in London. 'Wine.'
'The Present State of Wit.'

> *So the young Squire, when first he comes*
> *From country school to Wills' or Tom's,*
> *And equally, in truth, is fit*
> *To be a statesman or a wit;*
> *Without one notion of his own*
> *He saunters wildly up and down*
> *Till some acquaintance good or bad*
> *Takes notice of the staring lad. . . .*
> PRIOR: 'THE CHAMELEON'

IT has been stated in the previous chapter that in the early years of Queen Anne's reign Swift was back in Ireland, a newly-appointed rector of an unimportant parish, while Pope's precocious verses had still attained no further than to be passed about from one admiring acquaintance to another. True, both had friends of some influence: the aged Wycherley found that the sparks from young Mr. Pope's wit often lay smouldering in the ashes of his own brain afterwards, and sometimes enabled him to keep the home-fires of poetry burning; and the compliments which passed between the old man and the young one were so heavy and laborious that it is marvellous that the letters which contained them should ever have managed to make the journey. And for Swift, though marooned like Prospero on what was to him never better than a desert island—Swift whose mind was a conjured spirit which like Ariel "would do mischief" if he "did not give it employment"—the stars for the future were equally auspicious. His *Battle of the*

Books had attracted much attention. His *Tale of a Tub* had titillated the curiosity of London, and thrown the church into an intellectual ferment which was bound to gratify a man greedy for power. Indeed, as he stood on his desert island, his face for ever towards that El Dorado, London—the very waves at his feet must have seemed to him to rock uneasily with the wash created by his hurled thunderbolt. Although his work was anonymous, the authorities had more than a shrewd suspicion whose hand it had come from, which was, of course, no more and no less than Swift had intended. . . . Laracor he might well think at this stage was only a step in his career. Ministers already recognised his potential abilities in State affairs, and in the literary world he had Addison for a friend—Addison who had called him the greatest genius of his age. Where might not a man end, who had such a testimonial from the author of *The Campaign* up his sleeve? But London as a whole knew little so far of Swift; and still less of Pope. There were others just then whose names made news.

The curtain goes up on the London scene with an illustrious cast assembled. At the top of the pyramid sits Queen Anne, offering up prayers of gratitude for the continued victories of her forces both on land and sea, and keeping up an obstinate resistance against those palace influences which try to drag her perpetually into one political camp or another. Behind her chair stands the Duchess of Marlborough, and her kinsman Godolphin the Lord Chancellor. Numerous other noblemen in tufted wigs, and blazing with orders, decorate the outskirts—with every man's left hand in the pocket of the man in front of him and every man's right hand on the hilt of his sword so that he may defend his honour against the faintest whisper of corruption. The bishops in their lawn sleeves stand in a phalanx to the left and preach sermons which might be creditable to a contemporary Fabian Society—so thoroughly intellectual and bereft are they of any mention of divinity unless it concerns that still-deservedly debatable topic the divine right of the Stuarts. In a phalanx to the right stand the Sir Roger de Coverleys—the country squires who have come up to see London, dispose of their daughters for as much as they can get for them and vote in the House against a standing army and against Marlborough (because he is an army man, and they know what redcoats are—remembering Cromwell and King James's army upon Hounslow Heath). Robert Harley, Speaker of the House of Commons, stands behind an arras, button-holing Daniel Defoe and promising all things to that most useful of all his spies and propagandists. Behind another arras stands his rival, Henry St. John, Secretary of War, the man described later by Augustine Birrell as "the most accomplished of all our political rascals." *His* beautiful hands button-hole a Jacobite gentleman—any Jacobite gentleman because, after all, a statesman never knows which way the wind will blow—and if one day it blows the Pretender at St. Germains back to the throne, Henry St. John means to be ready to receive him. Variously grouped about the stage are other *tableaux vivants*. Captain Steele, for instance, come breathless from his Prue, and his creditors; that admirable character, Mr. Addison, come to pay his respects to the Queen, before he departs on that so tactful visit to Hanover; Mr. Prior (on his way, as it were, from Log Cabin to White House) come to see whether there is yet any chance of that embassy-ship which, if merit were anything to go by (which of course in that year of Grace it is not) he certainly deserves. Here is Christopher Wren, back to report further progress on the building of St. Paul's, talking to Isaac Newton, his friend from the

Mint. Here is Dr. Arbuthnot, just appointed Physician-Extraordinary to the Queen owing to that lucky accident of happening to be at Newmarket when poor Prince George of Denmark had his fit there; Arbuthnot the kindliest of wits, and wittiest of kind men, who could yet probe with an irony more biting than his own steel scalpel—"that treasury of vileness and corruption which I find to be the heart of man." Next to him let that other cynic stand: Robert Walpole's shadow does not yet loom large but later it is to overwhelm all the rest of his contemporaries, as Gulliver overwhelmed the Lilliputians. . . . Let the supers crowd the corners dressed variously as sycophants and place-hunters, as diseased children come to be 'touched' by the Queen, as poor relations who want money, as bankrupt young men who want heiresses, as country patrons who want fame, beauties who want notoriety, as down-trodden who want justice, as spies who want information, as informers who want masters, as poets who want patrons.

"As poets who want patrons . . ." In 1706 John Gay came of age and presumably into what little had not already been advanced to him out of his patrimony. He did the expected thing, pocketed it and made a bee-line for London. There he lived some time "like a private gentleman," says one sympathetic chronicler—a statement which various later biographers have fallen upon with glee, pointing out that his former circumstances had certainly not led them to expect any such conclusion and that in any case they don't believe it. Far more likely, they think, that he lived by his wits. Well, if a wit should not live by his wits, at the wits' end of the town, it is debatable who else should. Mr. Austin Dobson adds that "rumour assigns to him as his earliest employment, that of secretary to Aaron Hill." To refuse a rumour when facts are still so few and far between, would be ungracious. It is likely at least that Gay called on Hill when he arrived back in London, on the grounds that until other friendships have been established the bond of the old school tie is usually a fairly strong one.

Hill (as befitted his name) had already had his ups and downs in life; an uncle of his, Lord Paget, Ambassador at Constantinople, had carried him off to foreign courts like a young Bolingbroke or Chesterfield. But then the ups had ceased, and he had been swept as suddenly out of his uncle's favour as he had been swept in, and since then the young man had filled in the time as best he might trying his hand at verse and prose and drama, and acting as bear-leader to a young lording through the courts of Europe. Hill, in fact, may be taken as a very fair example of the man of the Augustan period. Trained up to no precise profession he was expert only in the art of dabbling. Assisted through his education by an uncle—like Prior—sent travelling over Europe and the East—like Addison—he returned home to England to bait hooks for catching rich patrons —like Young (and indeed, like every other young wit). He had a vast coffee-house acquaintance amongst people as unimportant as himself and a hearsay one with the Great Ones.

The first literary production he published was *A Full Account of the Ottoman Empire*, through which he had recently travelled. Addison had just published the history of *his* travels on the Continent, and Hill was not slow to follow his example. But he was a much more desultory worker than Addison, probably because various other extraneous schemes for lotteries or colonies or academical theatres would keep popping up, like King Charles's Head, and distracting him from the Ottoman Empire. Gay's secretarial work for his friend was presumably the neat transcription of these travels from the first 'foul papers' to another sheet. In between the strain of composition and the attacks of writer's cramp, author and secretary possibly made for whatever coffee-house suited them best. *Button's* if to see or listen to Addison and Steele was their fancy, *The Smyrna* where Swift and Prior talked in corners on State affairs, *Wills'* where the great Dryden had once presided, which Congreve still favoured, and where the young Mr. Pope took refreshment on his jaunts up to town, and where poets, critics and patrons moved freely together. Any one of these paradises was open to the general public and cost only a penny for admittance. Tired of straining their ears to catch the classical tags of Mr. Addison, or of watching Swift—that visitor from Ireland—stride silently up and down the sanded floor by the hour together; or of observing Congreve sit in state conjuring up visions of the fame he had long survived in the steam of his coffee-cup; or of hearing Prior, with his odd melancholy clown's face, troll out the ditties with which he had enlivened life at the Hague, young Mr. Hill and young Mr. Gay may well have made tracks for *The Chapter* —the coffee-house haunt of publishers, booksellers and their assistants. Poets and statesmen and wits were all very desirable acquaintances—but a friendly bookseller, like Mr. Tonson or Mr. Lintot, was even more desirable. Naturally, neither Hill nor Gay was as yet on anything but the fringe of his profession, and what they lived on (beyond a small patrimony each) is pure conjecture. Fortunately, a full life in London was cheap. Comfortable lodgings might be had for ten shillings a week— and the warmth and company of a coffee-house were any young man's on payment of the first penny—and subsequent tuppences for cups of coffee or tea. It was not living like a lord—but it was living like a

Londoner, and that was all, at the moment, that Gay wanted.

After the precarious session with Aaron Hill "he was presumably engaged," says Paston, "on hack-work for the booksellers." Hack-work may be interpreted as copying. Authors were not always dependable in the matter of providing fair copy, and a neat and accurate hand was therefore a most desirable acquisition, so that to be puzzled as to how Gay lived during these early years is to overlook the law of supply and demand. Gay was, in the opinion of his best editor, "a very laborious and careful writer." Furthermore, he was honest, tractable, sober and industrious enough when necessary —a treasure, in fact, amongst copyists. There is every reason to suppose that he was kept steadily employed and that he learned quite a deal from his employment —even if the income was not yet sufficient to provide him with the fine clothes he promised himself in his later address to Lord Bolingbroke in *The Shepherd's Week*.

In 1708, however, the secretary became an author, and a piece of blank verse, entitled *Wine*, was published. Its motto, from his favourite Horace, may be translated boldly: "Poems written by water-drinkers cannot live long, or have a long life"—an odd declaration from a young man who seldom had much cash to spare for claret or Bordeaux (sometimes as much as five shillings a bottle)—though beer at a penny and porter at threepence might come within reach of his purse.

Blank verse was a medium about as well suited to Gay's lyrical muse as Pope's couplets would have been to Wordsworth; and the wonder is that the Temperance movement has not long ago snatched this brand from the burning and printed it as a Horrid Example of what happens when spirituous liquors are invoked. Part of it, according to the custom of the time, is devoted to toasting *Great* Anna, Prince George of Denmark (compared infelicitously to a turtle), the *Hero* Marlborough, *Illustrious* Devonshire, *Prudent* Godolphin, *Faithful* Sunderland, and Halifax, *the Muses' darling son*. It was tactful of the young poet to describe Halifax in four words instead of the customary one—and tactful to draw attention further to Lord Halifax's position as a Mæcenas, seeing that the patronage that lord had already bestowed on Addison and Prior and other poets might still, with any luck, be bestowed on Gay. . . . But the whole thing is done with a jovial sort of carelessness —as if to say that, if they'll swallow this sort of stuff from other people let's see if they'll swallow it from me. The concluding lines, which describe the breaking-up of an evening party, are the best and disclose, as Mr. Austin Dobson puts it, something of "the minute touch of *Trivia*."

There is no record of the poem's reception beyond the fact that it received the honour of being pirated by the notorious printer R. H. Hills, which was something to boast of or complain of in the coffee-houses. Nevertheless, its publication gave Gay the status of an author and brought him a step nearer to the 'principal table' in the coffee-houses where the great men sat. His acquaintance with Aaron Hill had already introduced him to the lesser writers—and a greedy study of everything that came out from the press was enabling him to gather a very fair impression of contemporary English literature. No wonder that the coffee-house became Gay's spiritual home: it embraced under one roof, in a way that no other place has ever done since, the triple functions of Lyons' Corner House, a Public Library and a first-class Debating Society—and being thus too perfect a combination to last, disappeared soon after newspapers became general. But for the first quarter of the century the coffee-houses were at their zenith. The weekly gazettes which they took in were full of Marlborough's victories—Ramillies, Oudenarde, Malplaquet. Defoe was editing *The Review*—a pro-Government publication devoted to disseminating views rather than news, and Steele had just begun his *Tatler*—with occasional contributions from Swift, Addison and Bolingbroke.

Journalism was stirring for the first time in England: gossip, criticism and satire were being transferred from the impermanent atmosphere of conversation and hearsay to more permanent paper. The *Daily Courant* and the *Daily Gazetteer* came out every day and concerned themselves with births, marriages, deaths, the state of the weather, and health of the Queen, with the Court appointments and military and naval despatches—the last two printed just as soon as a kind wind allowed them to be blown over the Channel. They gave *news*—coloured to the particular shade the Government of the moment required—but nevertheless news. These dailies were as manna to the coffee-house highbrows, who could sit all day long with their legs on the table, dissecting the battles of Marlborough, Peterborough and Eugene, and finding, like Captain Fluellen, comparisons from the classics for every engagement or blockade. But men may not live by wars alone —and neither the wits in coffee-houses nor the ladies and squires in the country-houses found their appetites were completely satisfied by the gazettes. They wished for something more—though they knew not what— and the wish, in due course, was father to the *Tatler* and its many imitators. The sort of readers which the publishers of these periodicals found ready waiting for them might be described as the perfect readers. They were eager, intelligent, appreciative, and (since on occasion *The Spectator* reached a circulation of 20,000 copies) best of all, they formed so large a part of the London population that it might be safely said that three people out of every hundred bought *The Spectator*. (The wildest dreams of the circulation manager of any modern 'highbrow' publication never aspire to such figures. Nowadays 3 per thousand is much nearer the mark.) This brings us to the dismal but inevitable conclusion that the level of culture in London was immensely higher in the eighteenth century than it had ever been before or is ever likely to be again. As has been stated before, the population split up neatly into the three parts of gentlemen, merchants and mob. Of these the first two could read and did, and the last could not. And because the first two could read they were provided with the best and most entertaining material that the editors of weekly reviews could compass: they were, perforce 'highbrows,' whether they wanted to be or not.

The Tatler, say the enthusiasts, was started by Steele helped by Swift, Addison and Bolingbroke. A very slight acquaintance with the characters of these three easily suggests what part each played at the inception. Swift presented Steele with his own already successful pseudonym — *Isaac Bickerstaff* — a gift which would amount nowadays to Walt Disney presenting an editor of a new children's paper with *Mickey Mouse*. He probably supplied as well some of that stupendous common-sense which he had in such abundance and which Steele forever lacked; Addison contributed articles to his friend's paper, and so began those famous essays which, week after week, opened up before the delighted eyes of readers like those artificial flowers from Japan, dropped into a tumbler of water and spreading out their tiny petals with graceful *sang-froid*. . . . St. John, not yet Bolingbroke, who according to a friend combined in his own small way the wisdom of Socrates, the dignity and ease of Pliny and the wit of Horace, undoubtedly expressed as much of those commingled qualities on paper as Steele would let him. The fact that his contributions are sunk under the unutterable tediousness which was the genuine Bolingbroke was unfortunately not perceived by his contemporaries. All writers were not lords in the Augustan age—but all lords, automatically, were writers (if they chose to exercise their ability)—and Steele could not go against this unanimous opinion or disdain to make use of an influence as powerful as St. John's.

All things considered, however, the credit for this new journalism must go to Steele and Addison. Criticism varies, as the years go by, in the value placed upon their mutual contributions. Like the old man and woman in the house that tells the weather, when Addison is out and in full favour, then Steele is in, and *vice versa*. The subject was a pretty one for controversy even then, and received full attention, while scores of imitative journals were rushed from the press. A new way of treating the English language had been discovered and Dryden's thundering numbers were followed by the light fantastic toe of a couple who sought as they themselves expressed it, "to enliven morality with wit, and to temper wit with morality." The unusual ingredient in the recipe was of course not the wit but the morality, and the fact struck Gay, as greedy a reader of periodicals as the average bright young man who can succeed in getting a look at them for nothing. The result, in May 1711, was the publishing of a pamphlet of his, entitled *The Present State of Wit*, and addressed to "A friend in the country." The identity of the friend is not discoverable and the pamphlet itself was signed only by Gay's initials —so that for some time its authorship was a mystery. Swift, who by then had ceased to be the visitor from Ireland, and was indeed at the summit of his influence in English politics, though not of his ambition, read it with as much patience as he could spare to an author who cheerfully declaimed that he cared not one farthing either for Whig or Tory. "He seems to be a Whig," the Dean wrote to Stella, "yet he speaks very highly of a paper called *The Examiner* and says the supposed author of it is Dr. Swift. But above all things he praises *The Tatler* and *Spectator*; and I believe Steele and Addison were privy to the printing of it." This charitable opinion was probably held by others, who (true to the influence of the age) could never understand a pæan of praise which was not commissioned and paid for in advance. But there seems little foundation for it in fact. In the first place Swift was inaccurate, for the meed of praise was not bestowed equally upon Addison and Steele; nor was there, as would have seemed reasonable—a floral tribute of due proportions to lay on the grave of the now-defunct *Tatler*—and a very much larger bouquet for the still flourishing *Spectator*. This to eighteenth-century standards of morality would have seemed reasonable. For Steele, *The Tatler's* late editor, was an unknown quantity, and subject to the usual buffets of Fortune. A very uncertain help, in fact, in times of trouble. But Addison had been born with a silver spoon in his mouth—a spoon which, all his life, ladled out to him large helpings of everything desirable. How sensible it would have been, therefore, for Gay to 'plug' the name of Addison—and to give *that* the highest place of honour . . . Addison, who had been recommended by Dryden to old Tonson the bookseller—and by Tonson to Congreve, and by Congreve to Charles Montagu, Chancellor of the Exchequer—and by Montagu to the Lord Chancellor to whom (so tactfully) Addison had dedicated the first issue of *The Spectator*! It was truer to say of such a man, not that he knew on which side his bread was buttered, but on which side his cake was iced. . . . *The Tatler* is dead, should have been Gay's cry. Long live *The Spectator*! But instead, J. G. gives the chief part of his praise to *Mr. Bickerstaff* who, as everybody ' in the know ' knew, had been three-parts Steele and one part Addison. It is a charming if ungrammatical specimen of criticism:

"I shall in the first place observe," he writes, "that there is a noble difference between him (Bickerstaff) and the rest of our polite and gallant authors. The latter have endeavoured to please the age by falling in with them, and encouraging them in their fashionable vices and false notion of things. It would have been a jest, some time since, for a man to have asserted that anything witty would be said in praise of a married state, or that devotion and virtue were in anyway necessary to the character of a fine gentleman. Bickerstaff returned to tell the world that they were a parcel of fops, fools and vain coquettes—but in such a manner as pleased them, and made them more than half-ashamed to believe that he spoke truth.

"Instead of complying with the false sentiments or vicious tastes of the age, either in morality, criticism or good breeding, he then boldly assured them that they were altogether in the wrong; and commanded them, with an authority which perfectly well became him, to surrender themselves to his arguments for virtue and good sense. It is incredible to conceive the effects his writings have had on the town; How many thousand follies they have quite banished or given a great check to! How much countenance they have added to virtue and religion! how many people they have rendered happy by showing them it was their own fault if they were not so! And lastly, how entirely he has indeed rescued it out of the hands of pedants and fools, and discovered the true method of making it amiable and lovely to all mankind. . . . His writings have set all our wits and men of letters on a new way of thinking, of which they had little or no notion before; and although we cannot say that many of them have come up to the beauties of the original, I think we may venture to affirm that every one of them writes and thinks much more justly than they did some time since."

The pamphlet was a decided success—and those friends of his who had not already concluded that Gay wrote the whole thing for cash down from Steele, were probably not wrong in guessing that such appreciation led subsequently to a letter of thanks from the man who had inspired it—and then to a meeting. Once Gay had met Steele, the wind was set fair for the future. The ex-apprentice would no longer sit at the little tables by the door in the coffee-houses—he would join the Great Table—a wit among the wits!

Gay's muse could not be said to carry him along like a whirlwind. 1708 had seen the publication of *Wine*, and all that 1709 produced were fifteen lines from him "To the learned ingenious Author of *Licentia Poetica Discuss'd*"—a Dr. Coward whose niche in authorship is now as dim as his niche in medicine. Aaron Hill also produced verses on this occasion, of about much the same merit. But obviously, despite the slenderness of their output, the two young men were enjoying themselves. Only one shadow fell across Gay's path at this time, the news of the death of his brother Jonathan in the summer of 1711. It was not a glorious death in battle but according to the story "after a dispute with his Colonel" the young Captain shot himself.

If records are anything to go by, there is nothing to make us conclude that the death of his brother proved a shattering blow to Gay. He never spoke of his family that we know of and possibly he and Jonathan had never had much in common. But the tie of blood is a curiously enduring one, and this sudden refting-away of an only brother but a few years older than himself, and on the threshold of life just as he was, was enough to cast a shadow over happiness. It may have reminded him of that easily-induced depression from which he himself occasionally suffered. His reaction to death was, however, the reaction of a normal man. He never dwelt on the subject with the calm hopefulness of Pope, or with the barely concealed dread of Swift; he turned from it, always, as the normal man turns instinctively and hastily from the sight of anything distasteful. So he now turned from his brother's death in France to his own life, lived fully and freely in the London about him. Here at least he had no cause for repining. He was no longer the entirely unknown "young gentleman from Devonshire." The coffee-houses, always easily accessible to anybody who held the key of wit, had opened their doors wide to him, and he, the newcomer, the pamphleteer, was being welcomed in by the established writers.

In what order and through whose agency is not particularly material, but we know that by 1711 he had met Swift, and that during that year he met Addison, and Tickell and Budgell—Addison's friends—and Parnell, and Pope—the last through Swift, and very possibly all through Swift. He was hustled to Court in his best clothes to pay his respects to the Queen, and to meet the various lords who held the reins of political power and liked to make the acquaintance of poets who could fit them neatly into eulogistic rhyme. Swift, as always, was the propelling force. It was Swift who introduced him to St. John, the Secretary for War; to Harley, the Lord Treasurer; to Erasmus Lewis, the card-playing Welshman who was Harley's secretary; and to Dr. Arbuthnot, who was everybody's friend—and nobody's friend in the sense that fundamentally he was sufficient to himself alone.

In the midst of this charmed circle what W. H. Irving has called Gay's marvellous faculty for friendship first came into play. Its marvel lay less in its depth than in its disinterestedness—a quality by then almost extinct in the men amongst whom he moved. Wits is too short a word adequately to describe the pride of lions which any gathering of brilliant and ambitious Augustans was bound to be. The entry of Gay into such a company must have been like the entry of a gambolling kitten; and yet he too had claws and teeth and could rend and bite if he cared to. He seldom did care to, and this lack of malice is not to be put down to what Pope was once short-sighted enough to describe as "a fearfulness of offending" in him. Vices that we ourselves are liable to are apt to be transformed into virtues in the secret chambers of the heart—and Pope was no stranger to this kind of alchemy. Neither he nor Swift would ever have admitted that they enjoyed the sensation of being violently rude to other people; they doubtless described the process to themselves as a conveyance of a much-needed chastisement. But Gay was a simpler and directer person. Being rude, to him, was still being rude. Giving pain was still giving pain. Moral chastisement did not come into his scheme of things until a long course in its administration had been inculcated into him by the two men whose hatred of humanity (in the individual or in the mass) made up the major part of most of the hatred of the day. But hating never came naturally to Gay. He was to learn it painfully of his masters and adapt it slowly into his work. Meanwhile in the green days of his youth, when he was in Johnson's words "the general favourite of the whole association of wits," the events of these later years were still obscure.

A portrait of him, done at the age of twenty-four by John van der Banck, belongs to this period, and supplies a hint—though no more—of his popularity. In this canvas, as in whatever portrait was done of him in later life, the curious innocence of the man shines out. In days when goodness and honesty were at a premium, here goodness and honesty might be seen as large as life itself. Nowadays the duller virtues are as abundant as mass-production can make them, and brilliance is a rare jewel. But brilliance was the order of the day then, and even dull virtues few and far between. Gay had them, and in him they were not dull. He was alive, and eager and grateful, and young and honest, and extremely friendly amongst the suspicious, charming, disillusioned men who surrounded him. The bloom of the country had not yet been rubbed off him by constant contact with staler people. Thackeray, whose essays on the eighteenth-century humorists contain precisely the sort of blunders that one expects on occasion (and forgives) in brilliance, was not blundering when he remarked that, amongst the portraits of the literary worthies of that period, Gay's face was perhaps the pleasantest of all.

D

CHAPTER FOUR

1711-1714. 'The Mohocks.'
Employment with the Duchess of Monmouth

"*The world is wider to a poet than to any other man.*"
SWIFT IN A LETTER TO GAY, JANUARY, 1732

The Present State of Wit was naturally not the only piece of criticism which appeared in London in 1711. Other pebbles were dropped into the intellectual pool and produced ripples of greater circumference. One was Pope's *Essay on Criticism* in which, in one blameless rhymed couplet after another, the young author laid down essential rules of literary good taste. The poet, however, instead of remaining on this lofty impersonal level throughout, and scorning to mention personalities only to bestow praise (as Gay had done in his pamphlet) chose instead to indulge in a little knife-play. The victim was John Dennis, the veteran critic and, in Pope's view, a mere left-over from an earlier age and incompetent at the best of times.

Autres temps, autres moeurs; few young authors nowadays would assume that the quickest way to fame was over the body of the most important member of the selection committee of the Book Society. That, in effect, is what Pope's action amounted to. The attacker may have reasoned that one cannot very well discuss criticism without discussing critics, and that in any case it would be fun to have a stab at Dennis. So he had a stab at Dennis, and Dennis rose at him, and the Pope-Dennis affair became an engrossing topic in the coffee-houses—the first of many such topics which would come to gladden the tables there and a good proportion of them attributable to Pope.

But both criticisms, though interesting enough as coming from such youthful assessors, were less than nothing when compared with a third. The times were stirring ones. Politics, national and international, occupied a greater stage than letters, and politically speaking, what both Pope and Gay seemed to forget was that there was a war on. What the Ministry wanted was *another* kind of criticism—criticism pungent enough and public enough to pull Marlborough off his war-horse for good and all, and to stop the ceaseless pouring-out of public monies which, they considered, had been occasioned by his activities and which benefited English allies against France, but never England.

Thus argued the Tories. There was only one man in England big enough to undertake such a task—so Swift wrote for them *The Conduct of the Allies*. It was a magnificent but wildly exaggerated indictment of a war begun by William III and continued, from glory to glory, and with only occasional defeats, by Marlborough. But the centre of operations had shifted from France to Spain, and English politicians who (when they were not in league with St. Germains) had much to fear from France and very little to fear from Spain, chose at this juncture to turn strongly pacifist. Apart from this major point—to convey an accurate impression of English politics at the time is almost impossible. To say that the Ministry was divided against itself would be putting it mildly. Personalities, not principles, directed the scene. When Queen Anne was friends with the Duchess of Marlborough, then the Whigs were in the ascendancy and Mrs. Masham was nothing—and Marlborough and Godolphin and Addison and Steele and Prior and Tickell, were in high favour. When the see-saw tipped the other way, then Mrs. Masham rose to the heights (with her friend and kinsman, Tory Harley, and St. John and Dr. Swift and *his* friends, Pope and Parnell) and the Whigs and the Duke and Duchess of Marlborough fell off. When Queen Anne was friends with the Bishops and Upper House, then the Commons and the general body of the Churchmen were against her. When she attempted to please the general body of Churchmen and the Commons—then the Bishops in the Upper House and the country Tories abused her and renewed their correspondence with her brother at St. Germains. No wonder the poor lady wrung her plump hands and cried a plague on both your houses.

Her Ministry therefore was not only divided, but crucially divided. But the moment for dissolution was not yet to come. At the moment the star of the Tories was in the ascendant. Swift's *Conduct of the Allies* was one triumph swaying the opinion of the country, the dismissal of Marlborough from supreme military command was another, and the negotiations for peace with Louis XIV was the third. The Lords, Commons and country at large were naturally not informed of the negotiations. Rightly or wrongly the Ministry by now were so used to doing things secretly that it was impossible for them to come out into the open about anything at all. They quarrelled even amongst themselves, and Swift, called in to lend his brain to momentous matters of government, found himself compelled also to act as a liaison officer between Harley, now Lord Oxford, and his second-in-command St. John, now Lord Bolingbroke.

The quarrel between two comparatively dull Ministers of Queen Anne's reign has long ceased to interest posterity, but it is to Swift's credit that when he had eventually to make a choice between them, he chose the better man. Until that painful moment came, however, the unrewarded Doctor Swift wrestled with State affairs, with one hand on Mr. Secretary's arm to keep him from the bottle, and one on Mr. Treasurer's coat to hold him back from a pretty woman glimpsed on the Mall—and walking always between them, to keep the two gentlemen who controlled the Ministry which governed England from each other's throats. . . .

In such circumstances it is understandable that the pebbles which young Pope and young Gay had dropped into London's waters should have seemed small. Nevertheless they made some sort of a stir and Gay's few kind words on *The Tatler* were obviously warmly welcomed by Steele. (It is not stretching a point to guess that his eyes filled with tears when he read them: Steele was an emotional man.) The suave brilliance of Pope had even more effect upon the world of letters. Mr. Addison, temporarily off the exalted end of the political see-saw, but an intelligent critic at all times, was much taken with it—though his public school spirit regretted the attack on Dennis. The news filtered through to Pope and a Smithfield bargain was struck with the intermediary Mr. Steele, by which in return for some discreet modifications an introduction to Mr. Addison was to be forthcoming.

It was this introduction which had helped Pope to meet Swift—between whom and Addison the almost inevitable rupture had not yet taken place. Apparently no marvels were discovered in the sky on the day when Pope and Swift met. They themselves were probably not aware of anything unusual in the circumstances beyond an interest and respect for the intellectual abilities of another which for once in a way each could admire without dissimulation.

John Gay had come by the same circuitous route

into the acquaintance of Dr. Swift—probably through Captain Steele, and then Mr. Addison, and so to the Doctor himself. Swift, who had appreciated the cheekiness (as he considered it) of the young man's pamphlet set out to do good for him, as he did for all his friends. It was a kind of reflex action of which he was not completely aware. He set Gay in high places where he might meet the nobility just as he had set Harrison and Ford and Parnell. Better still, he introduced him to Pope. Two needy wits were unlikely to be able to furnish other than intellectual company for each other—but that to Swift (bereft of it himself in his youth) was not to be despised. They were both, in his opinion, deplorably luke-warm in politics, but even the most tepid Tory was welcome to the Ministry, if he showed signs of being able to write. Meanwhile—long live good company. *Vive la Bagatelle!*

The introduction of Pope to Gay proved to have been one of Swift's happiest actions. They "took to" each other immediately. Pope, still living with his parents at Binfield and able to visit London only occasionally, was doubtless delighted to receive Town and Court gossip in the letters of the ingenuous Mr. Gay—not to mention Parnell, the other Irish Divine, and Jervas the painter, and Cromwell, and Steele and Tickell. Gay had a gift for writing coffee-house letters, the kind of letters which whetted the appetite for more by their very volatility—their air of being straight-from-the-press and the centre of things. He also had a gift for enlivening quite ordinary statements by a species of ingenious inversion which, had he been Irish, would certainly have come under the heading of an Irish bull. Reading such letters brought Pope a vicarious smell of the coffee and tobacco-fumes in which his new friend wrote without any of the headaches which real participation in these pleasures always gave him. He loved Gay for keeping him so well-informed—as a semi-invalid invariably appreciates attention more keenly than a healthy person can do; and Gay loved him for writing back so kindly to some one as comparatively unimportant as himself. "If I know you aright," Pope wrote to him in the springtime of their acquaintance, "you are of a temper to cement friendships, and not to divide them." It was a happy guess.

Meanwhile, if Swift had any hopes of the friendship producing a rush of Tory propaganda from either of the two, he was doomed to disappointment. On April 17th, a play called *The Mohocks* by Mr. Gay was advertised to be performed "outside the watch-house at Covent Garden." But it dealt not with a wasteful Continental war but with a disgraceful situation in the London streets, where bands of unruly youths joined together to be a terror to the populace, and to mock the completely inadequate Watch supposed to keep order. It was light-hearted, topical, and amusing, and began with a dedication to the same Mr. Dennis who had already been treated with such disrespect by Pope. The subject, the author assured Mr. Dennis, was both *Horrid* and *Tremendous*, and founded on the same classical lines as Mr. Dennis's own *Appius and Virginia*. After this tongue-in-the-cheek opening it is hardly surprising to notice that the date at the bottom is April 1st. The piece, despite its advertisement, was never performed—probably for want of money to put it on. The noble lords who were pleased on occasion to patronise the drama by backing it were most of them in the Ministry, and being in the Ministry their attention was on larger problems. While they were busy with troubles abroad they would hardly care to give publicity to a play which drew attention so amusingly to a local trouble. So the stage *Mohock* was never put on to make mock of the real ones—though Mr. Lintot was good enough to publish it in pamphlet form (and probably to make something out of it as well).

A month later Lintot published something much more important—a miscellany of new poems edited by Steele, which contained as its *chef d'œuvre* Pope's *Rape of the Lock*. Gay contributed to the same volume some translations from Ovid which succeeded in demonstrating by comparison how good *The Rape of the Lock* was, and an *Epistle to Mr. Lintot* in which the poet, addressing the publisher familiarly as Bernard, sets out the desirable ingredients of a miscellany of poetry:

> Let all the Muses in the piece conspire;
> The lyrick bard must strike the harmonious lyre!
> Heroic strains must here and there be found,
> And nervous sense be sung in lofty sound:
> Let elegy in moving numbers flow,
> And fill some pages with melodious woe:
> Let not your amorous songs too numerous prove,
> Nor glut thy reader with abundant love:
> Satire must intervene, whose pointed rage
> May lash the madness of a vicious age;
> Satire, the Muse that never fails to hit,
> For if there's scandal, to be sure there's wit.
> Tire not our patience with Pindaric lays,
> Those swell the piece, but very rarely please:
> Let short-breathed Epigram its force confine,
> And strike at follies in a single line:
> Translations should throughout the work be sown,
> And *Homer's* god-like Muse be made our own:
> *Horace* in useful numbers should be sung,
> And *Virgil's* thoughts adorn the British tongue;
> Let *Ovid* tell *Corinna's* hard disdain,
> And at her door in melting tones complain:
> His tender accents pitying virgins move,
> And charm the listening ear with tales of love. . . .

Bust of Pope by Roubilliac.

Perhaps no better comment on the difference between the taste of Queen Anne's day and our own can be provided; for Gay was quite right in concluding that such a list as he had compiled had every chance of being a best-seller then, just as it would have less than none now. Satire, it will be seen, is honoured with a four-line description, instead of the couplet which disposes of each of the other ingredients. The "usefulness" of Horace is also done full credit to, a quality which has since curiously evaporated from that poet. But after this, Gay passes from the general to the particular, and with a proper sense of the order of priority, lists the geniuses of the day.

On the whole, tribute should be paid to his excellent taste. It must have been a tricky business for him to steer a clear course between the good friends who wrote bad poetry, and the bad or indifferent friends who wrote good poetry,—and not offend either. Fortunately several of Gay's good friends were also good poets—but if they had not been it is unlikely that Gay would have let friendship affect his verdict. Possibly it seems natural to posterity that the names he listed were Buckingham (one of the few lords who were also natural poets), Prior, Addison and Pope. But it should be remembered that at the time he was writing there were hundreds of other applicants to the title of poet—people with names like Popple and Cotton, Dodsley and Duck, Hurdlis and Needler, Dyer and Huddersford, Monk and Logan, Bedingfield and Brerewood, Smart and Straight, Whaley and Sprat, Wilkins and Jones. Gay in this, one of the first of his critical epistles, deserves credit for his perspicacity in not having added a mute inglorious Jones to the elect.

The *Epistle* itself is chiefly remembered for its appreciation of that poet who was later to become, and rightly, the undisputed master of eighteenth-century verse. In his enthusiasm for Pope, Gay's muse expands and he uses the triplet instead of the couplet form:—

> His various numbers charm our ravished ears,
> His steady judgment far outshoots his years,
> And early in the youth the god appears.

It was a compliment *in excelsis*. Pope is reported to have been charmed by it. No wonder he felt that Gay's temper was of a kind to cement friendship. It would certainly cement *his* with Mr. Lintot. The volume sold well, going into four editions—the last as late as 1722.

But mutual appreciation between poets, though gratifying, is not productive of bread-and-butter. If Addison had been in power just then, that friendly reference to his muse which "alike on every subject charms" might have produced an under-secretaryship for Gay. But Addison was not in power—and his rival Swift was. And Swift, when he could spare the time from mediating between his two quarrelling Ministers, and from drinking coffee with Vanessa at Kensington, and from writing his *Examiner*, and after that (when he got into bed) his letters to Stella, may have felt that he had already done his bit for his new friends and that, if they could not profit by his introductions, it was their fault, not his. What he would have liked from them, and what the Ministry would have liked, would have been some political contributions in the gazettes to push the peace negotiations forward and make them palatable to the public. But Pope, whose religion in any case debarred him from any chance of a State appointment and whose tastes were never at any time political, did not respond. Gay was just as disappointing; he still did not care a farthing for Whig or Tory, and consequently was worth about the same price to either party. So Pope went on living at Binfield and being the brilliant young author of *The Rape of the Lock*, and Gay continued to live on air, or a patrimony as invisible as air, with a return visit to Devonshire somehow sandwiched in between. He may have applied to his old schoolfellow for assistance from time to time. Aaron Hill had just made a rich marriage and had taken a share in the Drury Lane theatre, and the title of Master of the Stage there. From that time forward he was so busy writing blank verse tragedies with Anglo-Saxon settings that it is not likely he could spare much time for Gay. But another schoolfellow of Gay's was now in town. William Fortescue had come to London to study law at the Middle Temple. Gay's sister Joanna had married Fortescue's brother so the bond between them was now a stronger one. Gay was proud enough of this friend to introduce him to Pope, and Pope later was glad enough of the acquaintance to take hints from Fortescue about legal business. Meanwhile Fortescue, as a student of law and a stranger to London, was not likely to be able to give much practical help to a struggling poet.

At this point Pope came to the rescue. He had, through his friend Jervas, become acquainted with the old Duchess of Monmouth and, on the strength of this acquaintance, somehow procured the post of Secretary in her household for Gay. The Duchess was not in any sense literary. In an age of casual spelling she spelt even more at random than anybody else. But she was a 'character,' and Mr. Pope was a character—and with any luck, from her point of view, Mr. Pope's friend might turn out to be a character, too. Besides, it was good for a Duchess's reputation to be able to boast of a tame poet as secretary instead of the customary chaplain or niece: "Mr. Gay, you know—the author of *The Mohocks*. He takes my letters down." A poet cost no more to keep than a footman and was so *much* more house-trained. And Mr. Pope had written such a *delightful* testimonial. Some such reasoning as this may well have inspired the old lady to take the risk.

The relationship between poet and patron at the time of which we are treating has never been properly understood. It is usually treated as a lop-sided relationship in which the poet grows fat, lapped in luxury, and the patron provides all the benefits. Some sort of readjustment seems necessary. The arrangement—in the eighteenth century at least—was a matter-of-fact contract between two persons who knew the value of each to each and assessed each other accordingly. "You have money which I want," said Aristippes to Dionysus, "and I have wit and knowledge that you want." Never was a better bargain driven, and nothing better typifies the poet-patron relationship. What has obscured the picture for posterity is the almost Oriental ceremonial common to the time and the exaggeration of language of condescension on the part of the patron, and of gratitude and flattery on the part of the poet: language which nowadays too many of us are inclined to interpret at its face-value, but which was accepted on the part of both giver and receiver as formula. Each age has its own exaggerations. The puffing of the old is no more hypocritical and exaggerated than the puffing of the new. It remains a formula to benefit the writer, nothing more. *You have money which I want; I have wit and knowledge which you want.* Or, as Gay may have paraphrased it, *You have a spare bedroom and three square meals a day which I want, and I have a sense of grammar and the ability to spell which you want.* The consequence was that he joined the household of the Duchess of Monmouth at Chelsea.

Pope seems to have written his testimonial with no

more than a half-hearted conviction that what he said would do any good. He was apt to get out of touch with things at Binfield and by the time the Duchess received his letter the vacancy might well have been filled. But it was not filled, and on receipt of a letter from Gay apparently informing him of this and thanking him profusely for his good offices, Pope wrote to him:

> "It has been my good fortune within this month to hear more things that pleased me, I think, than in all my time besides, but nothing, upon my soul, has been so homefelt a satisfaction as the news you tell me of yourself: and you are not in the least mistaken when you congratulate me upon your own good success, for I have more people out of whom to be happy, than any ill-natured man can boast of!"

Aha—the cynic will say—one of the first of those letters which Mr. Pope wrote to Posterity—merely allowing John Gay (or whosoever his contemporary correspondent might be) to read it *en route*. It is true that in most of his correspondence Pope chose to represent himself as a kind of perpetually-dying Roman senator with all sorts of good wishes to confer on those about him before he dies, one eye on the limelight and the other on the rough draft of his speech. But in this case he happened to mean what he said, even though he was saying it beautifully. "I have more people out of whom to be happy, than any ill-natured man can boast of." Difficult perhaps to recognise, in such a sentiment, the man whom Lady Mary Wortley Montagu was later to describe as the "wicked wasp of Twickenham."

CHAPTER FIVE

1712-1714. Employment with the Duchess of Monmouth and the Earl of Clarendon. 'Rural Sports.' 'The Wife of Bath.'

> *Farewell—Now Business calls me from the Plains,*
> *Confines my Fancy, and my Song Restrains.*
> GAY: RURAL SPORTS (FIRST VERSION)

BY the time John Gay joined her household the Duchess of Monmouth was a back number. Less as regards her age—she was only fifty-one—than as regards the violent romanticism of her past life, which accorded ill with the times and policies of Queen Anne. There was really very little for such a lady to do except turn into a 'character' and sit down and write her reminiscences (especially now that she had a secretary to hand). She had been plentifully provided with material for them.

Before she was twelve Lady Anne Scott had been the Duchess of Buccleuch in her own right, and the richest heiress in the kingdom. Charles II, casting his eye round for a suitable partner for one of his illegitimate sons, selected Lady Anne Scott for the honour—and she and the young Duke of Monmouth had been married with suitable pomp and splendour in 1663. Unfortunately Charles II—like so many kings—lived to regret his generosity. Yet possibly it was easier to bear, from the Duchess of Monmouth's point of view, the father's displeasure than the son's indifference. James Monmouth may have been a bastard, but he was not his father's son for nothing, and he early deserted the Duchess for another favourite. She survived this, as she survived later his execution on Tower Hill after the Rebellion of '85, with the dignity becoming a lady who had almost been queen. She survived, too, the imprisonment of her children in the Tower, and the death of her eldest child there from confinement and homesickness. Dignity was the thing; dignity alone could not be taken from her. She conducted an acid and abominably spelt controversy with the legitimate King James during this period of misery, in which all the right was on her side and all the might on his, and left that unfortunate monarch probably feeling that the further off any possible Union with Scotland was, the better he would be pleased.

The magnetism of "King Monmouth" did not evaporate with his death. His personality had exerted so strong a spell upon the common people of the counties through which he had marched that for a hundred years afterwards they still believed that, by hook or by crook, somehow he would come again. His widow was not so credulous. Three years after his execution she married Lord Cornwallis—and later surviving that husband as well, returned to her former title of the Duchess of Monmouth. "To the end of her life," declares one chronicler, "she preserved a regal state." She was also somewhat lame and, rumour says, would allow no one to sit in her presence. She had a vigorous tongue, and an Elizabethan scorn for weaklings—as well she might have, seeing what she herself had been through. Her relatives, like the relatives of all border families, were legion, and she kept up an active correspondence with the Burlingtons, Hydes and Clarendons who most attracted her amongst those relations. But the mere fact that she had readopted the style and title of the Pretender was enough to keep her at arms' length from the Court. John Gay was later to declare, when talk turned on people being out of favour, that his friends were "commonly of that persuasion." There was certainly no active friendship between the Duchess of Monmouth and himself, but this part of his life might accurately be described as his first acquaintance with those out of favour.

The Duchess had bought the Lawrence manor house in Chelsea and rechristened it Monmouth House. Nothing remains of it now but a small wing which may have been one of the entrances to the house itself. The house itself was long ago demolished, but it was, in its time, a spacious building with grounds that stretched down to the river, as did the grounds of Wren's recently-completed Chelsea Hospital.

But life in the Monmouth household at Chelsea (apart from the activities pertaining to the post of domestic secretary) was very quiet for a wit. True, Gay's position was much such a position as Swift had held in *his* youth, first at the house of Sir William Temple and later with Lord Berkeley. The only discernible difference is that Gay, not being a chaplain, did not have to say prayers. But he was far more dependent on contact with the outside world than Swift in his youth had ever been. And now that he found himself living outside the radius of the town with all its delights and in a village separated by a common and a pond from that other and royal village of Kensington he cannot have been altogether happy. Yet he had the satisfaction of ' work in hand.' His entry into the household of the Duchess of Monmouth took place in December, 1712, and a month later his first pastoral poem, *Rural Sports*, was published by Lintot. Here was an opportunity for him to establish himself firmly in his new position by prefacing the poem with one of those epistles dedicatory in which the poet lies flat on his belly, inviting his patron to walk over him and admire the view. If he would not dedicate it to the Queen, then at least he might have dedicated it to the Duchess of Monmouth (on the principle that a bird in the hand is worth two in the bush). Dedications were still in full fashion and the art of writing them had as many steps and positions to it as a gavotte. In the first place, if the poet were young and unknown, he began by dedicating his work to an established lion in the literary world—preferably an aged and toothless lion who would be flattered by this sudden and unexpected revival of publicity, and whose curiosity would be sufficiently tickled for him to wish to make the acquaintance of so discerning a disciple.

Step Two would be a meeting between lion and disciple, with a great deal of trepidation and gratitude on the part of the disciple and a great deal of useful advice on the part of the lion, pencilled heavily on top of the original script. If the disciple were short-sighted, he went home and rubbed out the pencil-marks, but if he was sensible he revised the poem as suggested and sent it off once more to the lion, with a fresh outburst of gratitude. If after this Step Three was not an introduction to the lion's publisher (on the grounds that here, my dear sir, was a young man to watch, a *coming* man . . .) then something might be considered to have gone wrong *en route*. Step Three was the critical step. The publisher might just conceivably be putty in the young man's hands; similarly he might be of the opinion that the lion was in his dotage and that the poems were not worth the paper they were written on. In which case all was to do again. If however all went well, Step Four might be described as a *pas de deux* in that it could be done two ways. Either the young poet clung to his lion desperately at the coffee-house, stood in his walks and gambolled in his eyes, on the chance of being introduced

E

to a doddering ex-patron of the lion's and so be able to appropriate *him*, or to a possible new patron as yet unfledged (much the better kind); or else he hung about the shop where his poem was to be sold and which was run by his publisher-bookseller. Lords, after all, frequently came to bookshops. "Who," they might say, "my dear Tonson—or Lintot, is that interesting-looking young man in the corner?" It was simple after that, for then the poet might say to the publisher, "Lord Poldoodle is interested in me, you know perfectly well, my dear Tonson—or Lintot, that you should bring out a second edition" and Lord Poldoodle could brag at Whites or at Wills that evening that he had met young S—— or young X—— in whom old B—— was so interested, that the young man gave every sign of being a second Shakespeare; Poldoodle could do more, he could invite the poet to join his household for the next six months or so, so that genius might flourish in a congenial atmosphere. In taking such a course the patron benefited not only the poet but himself. In an age when letters were so closely allied to politics nothing went down better with the Government than the reputation of being a Macænas to a promising young writer.

The young poet naturally rushed out a new poem after this, with a handsome dedication to Lord Poldoodle on the title page. An introduction to Court circles was then practically inevitable, if only that Poldoodle might give proof of how well he was thought of by the wits —and subsequently all was plain-sailing. Everything that happened in a Court was automatically important, and *something* could be produced by a clever poet on almost any subject, of course with a dedication. . . . Thus Mr. Steele, who had mourned (along with dozens of other impecunious poets) the death of Queen Mary, had dedicated it to Lord Cutts of the Coldstream Guards

—and curiously enough shortly afterwards had received a commission in that very regiment. Mr. Tickell had won *his* under-secretaryship by writing in praise of Mr. Addison's *Rosamond*, and Mr. Addison had received *his* secretaryship by writing in praise of Marlborough. (As proof of how blameless and above suspicion such appointments were the address to Great Britain in Addison's poem *The Campaign* can testify:

> Thy favourites grow not up by fortune's sport
> Or from the crimes and follies of a court
> On the firm basis of desert they rise
> From long-tried faith and friendship's holy ties.)

All this, however, was tame compared with Mr. Edward Young's efforts to gain distinction. Nobody ever worked so hard at dedications before. The Duke of Wharton (who rewarded him to the tune of £2,000), Queen Anne, the Duke of Newcastle, the Duke of Dorset, Mr. Spencer Compton, Mr. Bubb Dodington and lastly Mr. Robert Walpole were all recipients of tributes from that persevering clergyman. How effectively he worked may be judged by the gratitude visible in his tribute to the last-named:

> My breast, O Walpole, glows with grateful fire.
> The streams of royal bounty, turned by thee,
> Refresh the dry domains of poetry . . .

All of which goes to prove that there was some method in the madness of dedications and that the rules of the game naturally decreed that Gay, at this stage, should have dedicated *Rural Sports* to either his patron or his queen. But Gay was always a little out of step, in such matters. He owed his present position to Pope;

he loved Pope, and consequently the poem itself was written to Pope, and had no kind of dedication at all. This was unfortunate but, as it happened, not fatal.

Rural Sports did not reveal itself as a classic any more than Pope's *Windsor Forest* (dedicated to Lord Lansdowne) had done the previous year. Both writers were a prey to that polite strained euphemism of the times which demanded that a spade should never be called a spade so long as it could be described as th' implement of toil. And although euphemisms went harmoniously enough with Louis XIV furniture and smart town tattle the employment of them on country subjects was doomed to disaster.

Windsor Forest remains an interesting specimen of Pope's earlier writing in which a young poet, confined to the country, amuses himself with fitting words into rhymed couplets around the subject which lay closest to hand. The result is a description of a forest whose tints would seem to be perpetually autumnal ones, and whose only natural denizens would be Watteau nymphs and swains. But as far as execution went the difference between it and *Rural Sports* was the difference between a full orchestra of harmonious instruments and a shepherd piping "on an oaten reed." Pope's execution was almost perfect—but the subject (if he could have admitted it to himself) bored him; with the result that it is boring to the reader. Gay's execution was accurate rather than perfect, and there is no more of the divine quality of imagination in *Rural Sports* than there was in the work of the superior poet; but for all that it is one of the few pastorals of the period which remains really readable, by virtue of that observing eye of the author's which pinned down facts as naturalists pin down butterflies in a case, and formed just as valuable a collection.

If Steele was the Tatler, Addison the Spectator, then

Gay was the Observer of his time *par excellence*. In this poem he recalls, ostensibly for Pope's interest, the various amusements which went to make up life in the country. They come down to us with the static clarity of a Japanese print, in which every delicate hair-line is visible; in which no detail of itself is significant but in which all the details, taken together, make up a complete and satisfying picture.

It is obvious that poets, being perceptive and sensitive creatures, are the prophets who have made plain the way for such reforms as the N.S.P.C.C. and the R.S.P.C.A. Pope, an expert in human vivisection, shuddered at the thought of cutting up dogs. So Gay in *Rural Sports* betrays a similar sensitiveness about fishing:—

> I never wander where the bordering reeds
> O'erlook the muddy stream, whose tangling weeds
> Perplex the fisher, I, nor choose to bear
> The thievish nightly net, nor barbèd spear;
> Nor drain I ponds the golden carp to take,
> Nor trowle for pikes, dispeoplers of the lake.
> Around no steel no tortur'd worm shall twine,
> No blood of living insect stain my line;
> Let me, less cruel, cast the feather'd hook
> With pliant rod athwart the pebbled brook,
> Silent along the mazy margin stray
> And with the fur-wrought fly delude the prey.

To be concerned with the blood of insects at a time when human blood itself was held of so little account that women were flogged to death for petty theft, and execution scenes at Tyburn were described as "diverting" was going to extremes indeed.

Despite its lack of dedication *Rural Sports* was a mild success. Other pastoralists welcomed the newcomer with condescension (after all, here was one of the first country poems which concerned country things in real detail) and the publication of it probably gave a fillip to conversation at the Monmouth dinner-table. It is safe to say that no poem afterwards suffered such alteration at the hands of the author. The earlier version is studded profusely over with capital letters, and contains the first iteration of that later too-familiar complaint that Court life is very wearing when no rewards are forthcoming. Here was another offence against *les manières belles et le je ne sais quoi qui plait*. But Gay was incredibly obtuse about this: he never could see that if people all around one with no greater claims to preferment were being rewarded all the time, that it was not etiquette to draw attention to the fact—except of course behind locked doors or in cipher letters. Thus in *Rural Sports* he drops a heavy brick by saying exaggeratedly that "in attendance" he had "wasted years in vain." He follows this brickbat up gaily with the usual formal bouquet to the Queen, who appears, in this Pets' Corner of perch, carp, hares, otters and partridges, rather as if she has been dragged in through a hedge backwards:—

> Let *Anna* then adorn your Rural Lays (he advises Pope)
> And ev'ry Wood resound with grateful Praise
> *Anna* who binds the tyrant War in chains
> And Peace diffuses O'er the cheerful plains;

The complaint side by side with the compliment made an ill-assorted pair; it was as if Gay had shouted from the housetops *Dear Madam you have treated me abominably but you are wonderful all the same*. There are many tactful approaches to royalty but this assuredly is not one of them. It is hardly to be wondered at, therefore, that in the 1721 version, when Great Anna no longer belonged to the sphere of influence, she and the capital letters and the complaints were all removed.

While Gay and Pope were busy on pastorals another poet had collaborated with statesmen in bringing off a piece of work of a very different kind. This was the Treaty of Utrecht. Though Mr. Secretary Bolingbroke and the various ambassadors concerned had all played their parts in its inception the man really responsible for carrying the treaty through was Matthew Prior. He was a poet and of "mean birth" as Queen Anne never forgot—but he had spent far more time on the Continent and in the conference-rooms of the Hague than the various noble lords who were created ambassadors and switched abruptly from Paris to Stockholm, and Hanover to Dublin as their most influential friends rose or fell from power. But precisely because he was a poet he was often overlooked when these general posts took place, and went on steadily living abroad as a mere secretary and working at the fabric of whatever piece of diplomacy was decreed from London. He was a good linguist, a cheerful friend and almost the best epigrammist in the English language. The high-light of his life had been when King William, to whom ability was ability whatever rank its owner held, took notice of him and made him a Commissioner of Trade and a Gentleman of his Bedchamber. But it was too good to be true, or lasting. When the horse Sorrel stumbled and threw his royal master at Hampton Court, Prior's hopes were dashed to the ground as well. After that, it had taken years of political sail-trimming, toil and dogged persistence for Matthew Prior to rise again into the confidence of the Government. His work was crowned with the Treaty of Utrecht. Europe had peace at last.

Pastorals like Pope's and Gay's were forgotten on so

momentous an occasion; something more solid was required, and Addison's play *Cato* was hurriedly taken out of the drawer where it had lain for some years, and put on at Drury Lane with a prologue written by Pope. Nowadays it reads like the dullest play ever put together in blank verse, but times and tastes change; a state of mind which could make Bishop Atterbury suggest that Pope could improve upon Milton's *Paradise Lost* by turning it into rhymed couplets was a state of mind which might very well appreciate the platitudes perambulating in togas which were Addison's men and women. And they *were* so appreciated. The politically-minded of both parties took all the phrases about liberty to typify their own side, and applauding loudly to show this and to drown the other side, succeeded in giving *Cato* a run—though not consecutively—of the breathless number of 35 nights.

A year that could produce two such marvels as a successful peace and a successful play was an *annus mirabilis* indeed. The spirit of faction seemed temporarily to have died down and both Whigs and Tories joined in the general rejoicing. Addison was at the zenith of his reputation, and the darling of the Government. Steele was still busy with *The Guardian*, but had been made Superintendent of the Stage at Drury Lane as well, doubtless in reward for his work in the theatre. Prior was receiving as many congratulations as Addison, and the Embassy to Turin—a carrot which had for long lured on this hardworking donkey—seemed at last almost within reach. Pope was up in town, courted by the publishers, sharing rooms and painting lessons with his friend Jervas, toying with the scheme of translating Homer and seeing much of all his other friends, including Gay. Swift, who had been disappointed countless times of hopes of preferment, was rewarded now with the Deanship of St. Patrick's in Dublin. It was a niggardly kind of preferment but Swift may have seen it, in his cheerfuller moments, as a mere step in the ladder. Things were not so bad, even for a gloomy dean, and Ireland would only be temporary.

As to Gay, whatever his duties in Chelsea, he seemed to find a good deal of time for his own writing. He still saw all his coffee-house acquaintances, talked with them, drank with them and wrote with them. He contributed a couple of articles on dress to Steele's *Guardian* about this time, and either tidied up or composed a number of poems which were to be published later. Soon after *Cato* was withdrawn, a play by him—*The Wife of Bath*, was put on (probably through Steele's influence) at Drury Lane. Steele had offered to "pack the house" for his friend's *Cato*, a precaution which proved to be quite unnecessary. *The Wife of Bath* needed all the packing it could get but it did not receive that attention. It did not succeed, and it is doubtful whether it really deserved to. The best that can be said in its favour is that it was another proof that Gay refused to abide by one model in his play-writing. *The Mohocks* had been lively prose. *The Wife of Bath* was rhymed couplets based on a Chaucer character and laced with Restoration morals. The only really interesting feature of it, the feature which survives, is its attitude of mind. It is as if Gay had set out for the first time in his work to advertise to all the world how extremely urbane and up-to-date he was, how exceedingly witty and smutty and knowledgeable and satirical concerning the humour of the town.

The particular angle from which artists tackle their subjects is often partly attributable to some friend's influence or to environment; what friendly influence or environment was it that led Gay off on this unsatisfactory adventure? Pope can have had little to do with it. He had not as yet resolved to tear the follies of the world to tatters himself and was, when not taking painting-lessons from Jervas, concerned chiefly with his scheme for translating Homer. Steele, who had helped to present *The Wife of Bath*, could never have given hints for a subject treated in a manner so alien to his own tender temperament. Swift was occupied with affairs of State just then more than ever before, and what time he could spare from them he gave to "selling" the idea of Pope's translation at Court, rightly preferring a still embryonic Homer to an aborted Chaucer.

A reasonable conclusion would seem to be that the atmosphere most conducive to the writing of *The Wife of Bath*, a play which, as Professor Allardyce Nicoll points out, "owes more to the dramas of the time of Charles II than to any other" was the atmosphere in Lawrence Street, Chelsea. Even the clumsy *doubles entendres* may have gone with a swing in that doubtless broadminded household. After all, a mere Restoration play, after the experience of having had a Restoration King for a father-in-law, must have seemed harmless enough.

To this period belongs an amusing reference to Gay in a letter from Pope to Swift, written in answer to the famous letter in which Swift had offered Pope half-a-crown to change his religion. Pope replied with the utmost good humour that although he might be able to save his own soul for that price, he could not answer for the souls of some of their mutual friends, which were in just as parlous case,

> "especially one Mr. Gay, an unhappy Youth who writes Pastorals in Divine Service—whose case is the more deplorable, as he hath miserably lavished

away all that silver he should have reserved for his soul's health, on buttons and loops for his coat . . ."

The Pastorals were presumably *Rural Sports*: the silver, as presumably, was his wages from the Duchess of Monmouth. Pope's reference may be slightly malicious but it is affectionately malicious. It is nice to recall that he ended another letter, of the same period, and also to Swift, with "I cannot name Mr. Gay without all the acknowledgments I shall ever owe you on his account."

CHAPTER SIX

1713. The Scriblerus Club.

"But then I must be a little easy in my mind before I can think of Scriblerus."
A LETTER FROM SWIFT TO POPE, JUNE 28, 1715

THE closing years of Queen Anne's reign had about them (except for the still hard-working backstairs politicians) a kind of sunset glow. Crops were good, trade was improving, employment was good. Her Majesty's forces abroad had just concluded a war whose triumphs had been inaugurated by King William and continued by the Duke of Marlborough. Scotland was united to England, to the benefit of both countries. The Pretender James was dead, the Jacobite scare had died down and a Protestant succession to the throne of England, based on the House of Hanover, had been assured. In such a happy atmosphere the men of the time met and conversed together, and from their congenial association rose many literary clubs and societies. Of them the most important was the Kitkat. The Kitkat was run by old Jacob Tonson the publisher. If the Whigs were representative then of 'right-wing' opinion (which is arguable, since they stood for Church and King more strongly than the Tories, who often preferred another Church and another King) then the Club might reasonably be described as a contemporary Right Book Club. Its political object, from 1700 onwards, was "the Protestant succession of the House of Hanover." It met sometimes at Barn Elms, near Putney, sometimes at the

Upper Flask Inn at Hampstead Heath. Practically every personage of the time had taken his seat, on some occasion, at the Kitkat table, though the atmosphere was better suited on the whole, to going than to coming men. It was, for instance, extremely suitable that men like Congreve and Sir John Vanbrugh and old Dr. Garth should be members. Retired wits, architects and doctors, all with comfortable incomes, could find no more comfortable association and could well afford the club excursions and entertainments. Others, like Swift and Steele and Addison and Arbuthnot, would have found these both a strain upon their time and their purse. The Kitkat, in the eyes of the 'coming' men, had these disadvantages, added to the fact that it was a strictly Whig association. When the split between the two parties became extreme, Bolingbroke had formed his Left Book Club—the Brothers' Club. This was a much more exclusive affair than the Kitkat and as Tory as the other was Whig. But little more of it has come down to posterity than the use of the word Brother as a term of formal address. There was no member of it who could (as Kneller had done for his fellow-members at the Kitkat) preserve on canvas the features of Swift and St. John, Parnell and Prior, Bathurst, Orrery and Lansdowne, as the band who had assembled under the name. Beyond a general benevolence exuded towards art and letters it is difficult to distinguish what the Brothers did when they met together, except to drink to the downfall of whatever damnable trick the Whig opposition might then be compounding.

With the Kitkat so Whig and so expensive and splendacious, and the Brothers so Tory, so exclusive and so nebulous, it is not surprising that Augustan men of letters must have felt that there was a gap somewhere, and that something was needed to fill that gap. So the

Scriblerus Club—that happy half-way house—came into being.

The formation of the Scriblerus Club has been mainly attributed to Swift. Certainly Swift found the Scriblerus far more to his taste than he had found either the Kitkat or the Brothers. He could never have been wholly at home in the sleek purring good-fellowship of the Kitkat, with its perpetual toasts to fine ladies who (as Swift in particular was always ready to aver) owed all their beauties to false eyebrows and padded stays. Many of its members indeed must have been anathema to Swift who, of all men, liked to pick and choose his company. Yet the feast of reason and flow of soul at the Brothers' Club, while much more intimate, still gave little play to Swift's peculiar wit and passion for trifles and *bagatelles*. Those meetings at Ozinda's chocolate-house in the Strand may have savoured a little too much of a convocation for the reading of serious literary exercises to please a man as perpetually impatient as the Dean.

Bearing this in mind, it is natural that Swift should have done all in his power to help forward the formation of a club more in line with his own desires. The Club itself, however, was certainly owing chiefly to Dr. Arbuthnot.

Posterity's opinion of that particular doctor, if he could have any inkling of it, would very much surprise him. He had so little opinion apparently of his own abilities. The incident chiefly recalled of him and his literary work is that he thought so little of it that he let his children make kites of his papers, and fly them on Hampstead Heath. Such behaviour in a less level-headed person might seem quixotic, yet if ever a man saw life steadily and saw it whole that man was Arbuthnot. From the correspondence between Swift and the Doctor at this time it is obvious that Swift was mentally closer to Arbuthnot—more of one mind with him—than with any other of his contemporaries. There was a robust dignity and common-sense about Arbuthnot which matched well with the robust spirit and common-sense of the Dean. But Dr. Arbuthnot had as well an overflowing invention ; he bubbled over with ideas at a rate which awed the more jogtrot Swift. He wasted a wealth of words and images—abusive, descriptive, philosophic, scientific—what you will, on a casual caller, and seemed to draw up further ideas from an inexhaustible source, the faster he spilled them out. This astonishing fecundity, this delicious carelessness for his wit and what became of it, together with a continual obligingness and kindness to all his friends, are good and sufficient reasons why Swift sought and clung to his company. He remarked of this friend " the Doctor has more wit than we all have, and his humanity is equal to his wit." As to his position with regard to the creation of the character Martinus Scriblerus and the Club built up about that legendary personality, it is made abundantly clear in this letter from Swift, dated July 3, 1714:

> "To talk of Martin [Scriblerus] in any hands but Yours is folly. You every day give better hints than all of us together could do in a Twelvemonth. And to say the Truth, Pope who first thought of the Hint has no genius at all to it, to my mind: Gay is too young: Parnell has some Ideas of it but is idle: I could putt together, and lard, and strike out well enough, but all that relates to the Sciences must be from you."

How pat Swift's friends come when they are called! Pope, who willingly supplied "the hint"—the motive of ridicule which was to expose the pedantic Martin as Cervantes had exposed the chivalrous Don; Gay, who though Pope's senior by a year, was "too young" (too young, Swift meant, in the matter of the world's wickedness); Parnell, the literary parson who like Swift spent so much time chasing across the Irish seas between his duties in Dublin and his pleasures in London, and who was probably only too willing to be "idle" once he had reached that El Dorado; and the Dean himself, magnificently capable as he knew of editing the series but aware for all that that in swift invention and fancy Arbuthnot was his master. The letter is a generous tribute from the man that Addison judged to be the greatest genius of his age to the man whom Johnson later judged "the greatest of them all."

The Scriblerus Club was even more exclusive than the Brothers. It had only one member of the peerage amongst its cronies and there is a suspicion that, in strong contrast to the Brothers, the motto the Scriblerus acted upon at their meetings was something very like Verlaine's *Et surtout nous parlons pas littérature*. Its members were Dr. Arbuthnot, the Dean, Pope, Parnell, Gay, Congreve, Fortescue, Bishop Atterbury and Lord Oxford. Presumably Swift as a foundation member had proposed Harley (now Lord Oxford), and his presence adequately explains Bolingbroke's absence.

The charm of Harley, like the charm of St. John and so many of their more ephemeral contemporaries, has evaporated with time passing. There must have been *something* about them, we urge ourselves, some special quality which enabled them to make other men, of far greater distinction, admire them and work for them devotedly. Perhaps it was Harley's humanity which enabled him to collect men as successfully and persistently as he collected that manuscript library

Bust of Swift by Roubilliac.

which subsequently he had no time to sit down and appreciate. He was not like the cold brilliant Bolingbroke, who could drink any man under the table and still remain sober; Harley could be warm and fuddled with the rest of good company, and laugh at small jokes with the rest of good company, and yawn his head off, and confide innocuous State secrets to his neighbour in the most flattering manner in the world. It must have been this quality of humanity which won Swift's heart and made him over-estimate his employer, later, as "the mildest, wisest and best Minister that ever served a Prince . . ."

But even Swift would have admitted that the only prestige Lord Oxford ever conferred on the Scriblerus Club was the prestige of allowing that Club to count the Chief Minister as one of its members. He was the most sleeping of all sleeping partners. Congreve was another member whose name was of immense prestige but whose genius had been suddenly snuffed out at the age of thirty and who now preferred to live (as he informed Voltaire) "as a private gentleman." If the Scriblerus Club had wanted private gentlemen it could have had them ten a penny—but the presence of Congreve was still valuable, as a reminder. He might be compared to a slender candle of the purest tallow which has only been lit for a quarter of an hour and then snuffed out; but a candle in the most ornate of candlesticks and still a magnificent centrepiece for any table, even if the wick of wit no longer blazed and sparkled at the top of it. Congreve could still talk, and if he could no longer write witty plays he could still appreciate wit in others, though he was too much of a private gentleman to go to the rude labour of manufacturing it for himself.

If Lord Oxford was Swift's nominee, Bishop Atterbury was as certainly Pope's. He was, says Professor Churton

Collins, "the most finished product" of the Universities, with his "refined taste . . . and polished and luminous eloquence." He was also a confirmed Tory—a sign of great grace—and a secret Jacobite. Probably he formed, together with Congreve and Fortescue (Gay's friend) and Lord Oxford, the appreciative audience for the creations of the rest.

The "hint" from Pope, on which the Club was founded, was:

> "to have ridiculed all the false tastes in learning, under the character of a man of capacity enough, that had dipped into every art and science but injudiciously in each."

With this in mind, the function of the Scriblerus Club, and the general direction of the Club's products become a little clearer in outline. The members were the highbrows of their generation. Because superstition, science, mathematics and pedantry were still clumsily entangled they made these their sport. The same Club, if it were contemporary, would join with contemporary highbrows in mocking new madnesses in the same old world—bookblurbs, armament-shares, the burning of necessary products to keep up prices, the doctrines of Totalitarian States. Low's Colonel Blimp has arisen as a commentator on contemporary vices: Martin Scriblerus filled much the same function in 1713.

Goldsmith in his life of Thomas Parnell has some interesting details about the Club. Swift and Arbuthnot, he wrote,

> "had taken up the rising young poets Parnell, Gay and Pope. All five met Saturday evenings at Arbuthnot's rooms in St. James's Palace, where the

Scriblerus Club, as they called themselves, plotted a burlesque biography."

He adds:

"It is past a doubt that they wrote many things in conjunction and that Gay usually held the pen."

Goldsmith presumably went on good evidence in making such a statement, and there is no reason to doubt it. If Gay was "too young" to enlarge on the hint of Martin himself, he was quite old enough—and quite obliging enough—to do the donkey-work for the others.

The Club's products, however, were by no means confined entirely to chapters in the life of Martinus Scriblerus. That was their *chef d'œuvre* but there were many other extraneous fragments of prose and verse, apparently spontaneously combusted from the coruscation of so many exquisitely bright wits. Pope parodied the low Church Bishop Burnet's *History of my own Times;* Arbuthnot wrote the mock scientific *Annus Mirabilis;* the *Treatise on Bathos* came equally from Pope, Gay and Swift. Epigrams, puns, lampoons poured out on to the table every Saturday evening—sometimes from one, sometimes from the other, sometimes from all together. Years afterwards some volumes of miscellaneous poems, edited by Pope, contained all that was mortal of the Scriblerians, and all that was left of those hours at St. James's.

The chief requirement, it will be noted, was a not-too-gentle mockery of some social or intellectual topic. Gay justified *his* position as a Scriblerian by his take-off of contemporary newspapers, filled, as they were just then, with news of naval and military campaigns and with political gossip. This parody was entitled *The*

Country Post, and some of its more quotable extracts run:

>*From the Great Pond, August the 1st.*
>
>Yesterday a great sail of ducks passed by here, after a small resistance from two little boys, who flung stones at them: they landed near the barn door, where they foraged with great success. This afternoon being rainy they set sail again and took several frogs. Just now arrived the parson's wife, and twenty ducks were brought before her, but for what sin we know not; however, two of them were condemned.
>
>*From the Great Yard, August the 2nd.*
>
>It is credibly reported, that there is a treaty of marriage on foot between the old red cock and the pied hen, they having of late appeared very much in public together: he yesterday made her a present of three barley-corns, so that we look upon the affair as concluded. This is the same cock that fought a duel for her about a month ago.
>
>*From the Hen Roost, August the 4th.*
>
>The black hen was last night safely delivered of seven young ducks.
>
>*From the Church, August the 8th.*
>
>Divine Service is continued in our parish as usual, though we have seldom the company of any of the neighbouring gentry: by whose manner of living it may be conjectured, that the advices from this place are not credited by them; or else regarded as matters of little consequence.

Although the meeting-place was nearly always the

Doctor's rooms, it appears that the products of the Club by no means always remained in his charge. Thus we get Arbuthnot, after the break-up of the Club and the public disgrace of Oxford, lamenting humorously to Swift that the Scriblerus papers had not been found on the Minister's premises by the Committee of Enquiry —as, he suggested, they would certainly have been interpreted as some dangerous plan in cipher, to overturn the State.

But that was still to come: meanwhile the members, met together to laugh at folly, found plenty of folly to laugh at in the week just past. Over the door they might have written, if they wished, *Purveyors of wit to Her Majesty the Queen*. Were they not Tories, and had not the Tories the royal approbation, and was there any reason why such a pleasant state of affairs should not last for a very long time indeed? History—and recent history—showed that a pleasant state of affairs never *did* last a long time—but the Scriblerus Club, at this period, gave no signs of being aware of this. Unimportant in itself the Club, because it came at this particular period in the lives of its members, was of special significance. This, each member may have thought in his heart of hearts, is the pleasant way in which we occupy ourselves while waiting for *real* recognition. Does not the sun shine down on each one of us? The Doctor is Physician-Extraordinary and the Queen will certainly confer special honours upon him before she dies. The Dean is Dean of St. Patrick's—but with Lord Oxford for his friend and patron why should he not be Archbishop of York eventually? Parnell is worth a deanery or the poet laureateship at least, or shall Gay be the Poet Laureate—seeing that Pope cannot be nominated for a State appointment? Which shall Fortescue be, Lord Chief Justice or Master of the Rolls?

Where shall Bishop Atterbury end, except as the Primate of all England? And Congreve, who already has so much of everything he wants—why should not he not have that final respectability—a title? If these, or something like them, were the expectations of Scriblerus members—what were Pope's expectations? Only to be the first poet of his age. Long after the Club was broken up—and the friends of the immortal Scriblerus scattered, as Pope said, "over the face of the earth," he alone may be said to have achieved his ambition.

Except for Gay's friend Fortescue—who in any case is unimportant, but who became Master of the Rolls.

Nothing particularly momentous was ever achieved during the eighteen months of close companionship which made up the Club's short existence. But its members were happy together. The awful uncertainty of life lived round them made such an association doubly precious. A study of the social history of the times, and of its correspondence, suggests innumerable dark wastes, bogs and impenetrable heaths, on all sides of which little men in vast periwigs sat in solitude by the light of a single candle and cried to each other on paper: *Are you still in the world of the living? Are you still of my way of thinking? Are you still assured that I love you, and that I have not changed?* Much might intervene before one correspondent saw the other. Health was precarious, weather was precarious, the post was precarious, royal favour was precarious, party feeling was precarious—and friendships dependent on such will-o'-the-wisps as these were more precarious than all the rest. Conscious of the wilderness of uncertainty about them, the Augustans clung together like shipwrecked men whenever they could and formed what frail ties they could to enable them to survive the barren stretches of solitude between.

Again and again, in studying the correspondence between these men and their contemporaries, one comes across the poignant insistence on the durability of their friendship one for another. Pope, writing to Jervas, says: "I fancy no friendship is so like to prove lasting as ours, because, I am pretty sure, there never was a friendship of so easy a nature." Swift writes to Lord Oxford: "I believe, in the mass of souls, ours were placed near each other." Arbuthnot, writing to Swift, expresses himself in similar fashion: "That hearty sincere Friendship, that plain and open ingenuity in all your Commerce, is what I am very sure I shall never find in another man." Swift to Pope, much later, adds, "to be remembered for ever on account of our friendship is what would exceedingly please me."

It seems odd that in the age of Reason, an age which thought of love between man and woman as little better than the foundation of a smutty joke, should yet have succeeded in producing such exalted types of friendship between men and men. And yet—is it really odd? Does not it rather indicate that the friendship has been sublimated at the expense of the love—and so has developed a curious patina of tenderness and devotion previously associated chiefly with sexual affection? In any case this sublimation of friendship into love's place is a definite feature of masculine association in the reign of Queen Anne.

The chief claim of the Scriblerus Club might well be that in an age when men were so strangely dependent on each other, and so often deserted by each other; so independent of women and so un-helped by them in consequence—every friendship cemented within the rooms of Dr. Arbuthnot at St. James's Palace endured. Various members of the Scriblerus Club might afterwards be impeached for treason, exiled or disgraced; they never wavered in their obligations to each other, no matter what revenges Time's whirligig might bring in. Each man must have subscribed a part of himself in that remarkable pooling of affections; a sort of virtue went out of him which was not called forth by any other of his daily associations. The strength of that affection naturally varied. It was strongest perhaps between three of the Club's bachelors—Pope, Swift and Gay. The relevance of whether they were married or single is more than would at first appear, when it is remembered that most of the leading wits of the time were single men. (Steele leaps to the mind as an exception but Addison is remembered principally as the urbanest of bachelors, and Congreve, Prior, Atterbury, Savage and the three already mentioned were all unmarried.) These men were, in flower language, self-fertile. Their propagation was conducted in a whirlpool of intellect which, if it was not always pure, was at least always sparkling and vibrant. The atmosphere which suited such men best was the warm friendly coffee-house one of conversation, anecdote and debate. Still more noticeable —though they were unmarried, yet they kept no mistresses. In an amoral age this abstinence had no particular morality about it. It was simply that they discovered in each other's company a delight and comfort which other, duller men discovered in brothels. True, one of the Editors of Gay's works remarks superciliously that his vulgarer poems show that he was "intimately acquainted with the *bagnios* of the time." He might as well have said that since Swift showed unusual nautical knowledge in *Gulliver's Travels* he was intimately acquainted with Admiral Rooke. No doubt Gay had, on occasion, visited brothels, as had Pope—but to imagine that either did so habitually is to misinterpret their characters. It may be difficult, these days, to recapture the kind of intoxicating delight which these men felt when they met together with other intelligent men and could exchange ideas with them. Culture has disseminated itself since then. It now grows thinly and widely where before it left great patches bare—or else filled corners profusely. In these green oases were congregated the wits. Where they met there was, inevitably, a well of sparkling fancy which overflowed and irrigated every subject which came up for discussion.

Small wonder that in such circumstances, such men could afford to dispense with marriage or with mistresses. Small wonder that they liked to grow drunk upon words and ideas as well as upon claret or champagne. In these surroundings the embryonic Gulliver and Martinus and Macheath first found life. These were the only children of the wits, but more enduring than mortal ones. Bacon in his Essay on *Parents and Children* has a relevant passage here. "The perpetuity by generation," he says, "is common to beasts; but memory, merit and noble works are proper to man; and surely a man shall see the noblest works and foundations have proceeded from Childless men, which have sought to express the images of their minds when those of their bodies have failed." The literary products of the eighteenth century were not often noble, but such as they were, they came principally from childless men.

Dr. Arbuthnot was the man who made up the fourth of the chief Scriblerus quartet; and of the four he was the only one married, and with domestic ties. But even if he had not had them, that strange effervescent bubbling-over of ideas kept him preoccupied and independent—always a little apart from the rest. "The Doctor," complained Swift, "is the King of Inattention." So Arbuthnot might love his friends—but he never needed them, while Pope and Swift and Gay, unconscious as yet that they were ever to need each other desperately, only knew that they were friends, and that such a friendship as theirs was one of the best things the world had ever seen.

One meeting between three of its members must be recorded again in detail, as it has been preserved in detail in *Spence's Anecdotes*. It is Pope's own account of a visit made by him and Gay to Swift:

> On our coming in: "Hey-day, gentlemen," says the Doctor, "what's the meaning of this visit? How came you to leave all the great lords that you are so fond of, to come hither to see a poor Dean?" "Because we would rather see you than any of them." "Ay, ay, one that did not know you so well as I do might believe you. But since you are come, I must get some supper for you, I suppose?" "No, doctor, we have supped already." "Supped already? that's impossible: why, 'tis not eight o'clock yet." "Indeed we have." "That's very strange. But if you had not supped, I must have got something for you. Let me see, what should I have had! A couple of lobsters? Ay, that would have done very well: two shillings: tarts, a shilling. But you will drink a glass of wine with me, though you supped so much before your usual time, only to spare my pocket?" "No, we had rather talk with you than drink with you." "But if you had supped with me, as in all reason you ought to have done, you must have drunk with me—a bottle of wine, two shillings—two and two in fact; and one is five; just two and sixpence a piece. Here, Pope, there's half a crown for you; and there's another for you, sir; for I won't save

anything from you, I'm determined." This was all said and done with his usual seriousness on such occasions, and in spite of everything we could say to the contrary, he actually obliged us to take the money.

The activities of the Scriblerus members were not all indoors ones. Goldsmith states that "they often made excursions together to the country, and generally on foot." If Swift had anything to do with the excursions they would certainly be on foot—but the interesting thing is that Swift, that terror of the drawing-room in London—the same man who had made Lady Burlington burst into tears by swearing that she *should* sing, or he would make her, was the butt of the companions amongst whom he walked. If a trick was played he was always the victim. The temerity of daring to play a trick on Swift is a striking indication of how well the men who played it stood in the Dean's affections—and how little they cared for his objurgations and scoldings. It is a pity that a country excursion now suggests nothing more exciting than a Greenline bus to an urbanised Chalfont St. Giles; but in the days when London measured only eight miles from east to west and three from north to south a man's boots might be white with country dust before he had reached Hampstead, walking past the duckponds and between the hedges, "redolent of hawthorn," of Tottenham Court Road. . . . Little enough is known of the places which the Scriblerus members honoured with their irreverent attentions, but a tale is told of a visit to a certain Lord B——'s seat (probably either Bathurst or Bolingbroke) 12 miles from London. The idea, apparently, was to walk down there, spend a couple of days and walk back again. Whether the company was expected or not is not divulged—but the story is that Swift, as usual, walked fastest, in order to be first and so get the best bed. Parnell, to outwit him, procured a horse and rode hell-for-leather to Lord B——'s by another route. On arrival he stated that his friends would be following him—and how many of them there would be. He also had time to bribe the servants into the statement that the house had recently been infected with smallpox; knowing that Swift (who had an unusual dread of this disease) would in that case never set his foot across the threshold. The joke worked neatly. Swift turned up later with the rest, was so informed, and spent a very angry uncomfortable night in a disused and draughty summerhouse. . . . The only moral of the tale would seem to be that it takes one Irish Dean to get the better of another.

CHAPTER SEVEN

1715. 'The Fan.' 'The Shepherd's Week.'
The Hanover Adventure.

"*Courts are, unquestionably, the seats of politeness and good breeding.*"
LORD CHESTERFIELD: LETTERS TO HIS SON

EARLY in December 1713 Richard Steele brought out a poetical Miscellany which contained, among other things, several pieces by his friend Gay. Of these the longest and most ambitious was *The Fan*, the subject of which was supposed to have been suggested to the author by Pope. It is a pity that Pope did not keep the suggestion to himself. The fan was the pre-eminent social emblem of the age; it might have been amusing if depicted pithily in a few short stanzas—but to stretch it out to the extent of filling thirty-two pages as Gay did, to embellish it with the inevitable classical images and dissect the subject as painstakingly as he had dissected flora and fauna in *Rural Sports*, made the finished production tedious beyond words. And tediousness, as Dr. Johnson later declared, is the most fatal of all faults. It may be claimed that this was the only time that Gay ever committed it.

Nothing brings home to us better the paucity of entertainment in the early eighteenth century than the fact that poetry as laborious and intrinsically trivial as *The Fan* was not only printed but read, and not only read but discussed, as if it really mattered. Its verses were in the best of taste but that was all that could be said of them. True, *The Rape of the Lock* had recently set the fashion for discoursing at length upon trifles, but there was a technical grace and dexterity about that piece which raised it immeasurably above its rivals. The matter was less than nothing; the manner everything. But Gay was never happy in a boudoir setting. He was too large, too clumsy, too healthy (at this stage) to be seen at advantage in an indoor atmosphere. Which is not to say that *The Fan* is entirely devoid of wit; it contains several neat lines and happy images which, if the reader cares to seek them out, he may feel have justified his search.

Other poems of the same triviality but mercifully shorter were *Araminta* and *Penthesilea*, two eclogues which would have point only if they had been artistically shocking, like Prior's work, or maliciously satirical, like Pope's. As it was the young ladies of the title-piece fell between several stools, and the eclogues ended up as the sort of poems any minor poet of the time might—and did—turn out twice a day.

In both *The Fan* and the eclogues Gay had gone abroad for his idea or his treatment, and the result was unsatisfactory; but in the other two poems which he contributed to Steele's Miscellany he was very much more himself. These were *A Contemplation on Night* and *A Thought on Eternity*. A man born in any other age than the age of Reason would of course have reversed the titles—considering a thought long enough to devote to a night and the larger-sounding contemplation more suited to eternity. But the titles were the least part; what matters is that Gay allowed a little of that natural melancholy—a melancholy which others have found it so difficult to credit in any one of his name—to infuse his work. He was also showing further signs of originality in trespassing—for his subject-matter—on the forbidden ground of metaphysics and religion.

Grappling with spiritual matters in verse had gone out of fashion since the days of Milton and Crashaw and Herbert and Donne. After them, if a man desired to cultivate the inward eye he confined himself to hymns as Addison and Watts had done. Young's *Night Thoughts* were not yet in being. Newton's fall of an apple was temporarily more important than the fall of one of God's sparrows, and mental problems were considered to be more properly adjusted in the prose of Berkeley and Locke, than in the lines of ' occasional ' poets. A place for everything, and everything in its place—it is the perfect motto for the Augustans.

Bearing this in mind, there is a kind of bravery in Gay's preoccupation, in these two poems, with matters larger than that of fans and the ladies who wielded them. After all, he was a young and healthy poet, as yet unaffected by any of those hammer-blows of fortune which sometimes forced the victim, even though he were an Augustan, to stop and ask himself, for once in a way, precisely what everything meant, and why. So Gay could write, in the midst of what for him was a period of youthful happiness:

> O may some nobler thought my soul employ
> Than empty, transient, sublunary joy . . .

He could, whilst his contemporaries chose as the *summum bonum* of existence a rural retreat in old age with a quiet wife, a tidy garden and a bottle of wine a day, look beyond this prospect to something further. In *A Thought on Eternity* he writes:

> Who then would wish to stretch this narrow span
> To suffer life beyond the date of man?
> The virtuous soul pursues a nobler aim,
> And life regards but as a fleeting dream.

a dream in fact for which it was hardly worth catering, or providing even the rural retreat, the quiet wife, the garden and the bottle of wine a day. These two poems of Gay's suggest a stage of development beyond the 'prentice stage and an impression that when he went to Divine Service he sometimes gave his thoughts to other things than writing pastorals.

But this morbid preoccupation, as his friends would certainly have termed it, did not last for long. Gay seems to have made hay while the sun shone with the Duchess of Monmouth—and his own hay at that. She was either a woman of little correspondence or else he successfully managed to be out of the way when required. Early in 1714 *The Shepherd's Week*, the first of his better-known poems, appeared. The too-innocent young man had by this time learnt wisdom of a sort, and so he prefaced it, if not with a dedication, at least with a prologue containing the prettiest compliments to the man of the moment, Lord Bolingbroke:

>   There saw I St. John sweet of mien
>   Full steadfast both to Church and Queen
>   With whose fair name I'll deck my strain,
>   St. John, right courteous to the swain;
>   For thus he told me on a day
>   'Trim are thy sonnets, gentle Gay,
>   And, certes, mirth it were to see
>   Thy joyous madrigals twice three
>   With preface meet and notes profound
>   Imprinted fair and well y-bound.'
>   All suddenly then home I sped
>   And did ev'n as my Lord has said.

"The Preface meet" before this acknowledgment to Bolingbroke is addressed to the Courteous Reader. In it Gay, burlesquing the language of Spenser, that "Bard of sweetest memorial," informs the world that in this unusual pastoral the poet's object will be "to set before thee, as it were a picture, or lively landscape of thine own country, just as thou mightest see it, didst thou take a walk into the fields at the proper season." That is to say, he was out to de-bunk pastoral poetry as it was then known and celebrated in the writing of Ambrose Phillips—to strip it of all the urban appurtenances it had picked up since the time of Theocritus and return to the simplicity best suited to such a subject.

Gay's editor Underhill has suggested that in spite of the innocent statement in the preface Gay's principal object in writing *The Shepherd's Week* was to make mock of Ambrose Phillips—much as Pope had done in a recent issue of *The Guardian*. Phillips had breathed such hot thoughts of revenge for this treatment that, according to Underhill, Pope "prevailed upon his friend Gay to continue the warfare and burlesque Phillips' performances in a series of realistic representations of country life." Whether there is any truth in this or not, the fact remains that while the few who believed it read *The Shepherd's Week* with additional relish on that account, the general public remained unaware of any such intention and the poem had a good sale on its own merits and not on the demerits of Mr. Ambrose Phillips; a distinction which would have pleased the gentle Gay more than the ungentle—and even ungentlemanly—Pope.

The Shepherd's Week was published in April. How Gay amused himself during the month of May is not known, for half his friends were out of town. Pope with Parnell was down at Binfield, working on his Homer and writing the most affectionate letters and invitations to the secretary-poet in Chelsea. Swift, in a mood of the bitterest disillusion after a trying year, was in Berkshire, living at board wages with another clergyman to whom he did not speak more than six words a day. Deafness and giddiness were beginning to assert their rights over him, and that dreadful sense of isolation from the rest of the world, which came on him spasmodically and enveloped him like a shroud. He was indeed a conjured spirit, and a spirit which had not been able, despite its astounding powers of alchemy, to distil into one harmonious political essence the mercury which was Bolingbroke and the lead which was Oxford. But even from a distance he could still wield an influence.

There is strong evidence at this stage that he was invited to wield that influence on behalf of two members of the Scriblerus Club—Gay and Parnell. Lord Clarendon had recently been appointed Envoy-Extraordinary to the Court of Hanover; several small places in his retinue were, in the Scriblerians' opinion, suitable places for them to fill. Parnell had hopes of landing the post of chaplain to my Lord Clarendon; Gay, as far as can be discovered, did not specify his preference. But there is reason to believe that all had not been running too smoothly in the Monmouth household, that Gay had confided this to Pope, and that Pope had passed it on to Swift when he and Parnell visited the Dean in his hideaway. They may even have suggested, to drag him out of his black abstraction, that he might be able to facilitate negotiations.

An appeal to Swift's powers of influence was always a safe card to play. He must have stirred himself in that Berkshire vicarage to some purpose after they had ridden away, for early in June Gay was appointed secretary to Lord Clarendon. How much Gay's step up the ladder was owing to Swift may be guessed from the following letter, written by the successful applicant two days after the appointment:

> "Since you went out of town, my Lord Clarendon was appointed Envoy-Extraordinary to Hanover in the room of Mr. Paget, and by making use of those friends, which I absolutely owe to you he has accepted me as his secretary . . . I am quite off from the Duchess of Monmouth . . . I am every day attending my Lord Treasurer for his bounty, in order to set me out, which he has promised me upon the following petition which I sent him by Dr. Arbuthnot:
>
> > I'm no more to converse with the swains
> >   But to go where fine people resort;
> > One can live without money on plains
> >   But never without it at court.
> >
> > If when with the swains I did gambol
> >   I arrayed me in silver and blue
> > When abroad, and in court, I shall ramble
> >   Pray, my Lord, how much money will do?
>
> We had the honour of the Treasurer's company last Saturday, when we sat down upon Scriblerus. Pope is in town and has brought with him the first book of Homer . . .
> It is thought my Lord Clarendon will make but a short stay at Hanover. If it was possible that any recommendation could be to make us more distinguished than ordinary, during my stay at Court, I should think myself very happy if you could contrive any method to procure it, for I am told that their civilities very seldom descend as

low as the secretary. I have all the reason in the world to acknowledge this is wholly owing to you. And the many favours I have received from you, purely out of your love of doing good, assures me you will not forget me during my absence. As for myself, whether I am at home or abroad, gratitude will always put me in mind of the man to whom I owe so many benefits."

There is something very humble about that "I am told their civilities very seldom descend as low as the secretary," but such a tender complaint was, as Gay well knew, the shortest of short cuts to the Dean's sympathy. He was acting the kitten here and curling up with pretty confidence within the shelter of the lion's paw; it was the best course he could have taken. Four days later he received an acknowledgment from the Dean, which begins with characteristic grumbling and concludes with as characteristic good advice:

"I wonder how you could have the impudence to know where I am; I have this post writ to Mr. Harley [the Lord Treasurer's nephew] who is just come from Hanover, to desire he would give you a Letter; I have described you to him, and told him I would write to you to wait on him. . . . You begin to be an able Courtier, which I know from two Instances: first for giving me thanks for your Preferment, to which I only contributed by saying to Dr. Arbuthnot and Mr. Lewis that I wished it. [*Only!* Observe the royal nonchalance of the Dean. He cannot help rubbing it in . . .] Secondly, for wheedling my Lord Treasr. with an Epigram which I like very well, and so I am sure will he, and I reckon you will succeed;

but pray learn to be a Manager, and pick up Languages as fast as you can, and get Aristotle upon Politics and read other Books upon Government; . . . and be a perfect Master of the Latin, and be able to learn everything of the Court where you go; and keep correspondence with Mr. Lewis, who if you write letters worth showing will make them serviceable to you with Ld. Tresr. and take Mr. Lewis's advice in all Things, and do not despise mine, and so God bless you, and make you able to make my Fortunes. I am glad Mr. Pope has made so much despatch; my service to him and the Parnelian."

Never was a letter so full of such soft-heartedness and such hard good sense. Yet, though Swift could be cheerful enough to Gay after hearing the good news, as soon as he had sent off the letter his shroud of gloom descended again. A man could be certain of nothing in this world. Suppose he had led Gay on to be unduly optimistic about getting that money out of my Lord Treasurer? Suppose that even the spell of a rhymed petition should fail to win over that problematical Minister? . . . The Dean could not bother to speak more than six words a day to his Berkshire host, but he could bother to get pen and pencil to reassure himself on this tiresome point. He wrote to Arbuthnot, with a return of that morbid humour which Arbuthnot knew so well how to rally—and no one else: "I thank you for your kindness to poor Gay. Was the money paid or put off till the day after he went?"

To which Arbuthnot returned the reply which would give him most satisfaction: "Gay had a hundred pounds in due time and went away a happy man."

Parnell had no such reasons for being happy. His

hopes of the chaplaincy soon vanished into thin air. Swift had pulled the string of Lord Oxford to get Gay his job; he would have to pull Bolingbroke's string for Parnell, and at that juncture Oxford and Bolingbroke could be trusted to adopt completely different courses of action, even over so trifling a matter as a small appointment. The only man who does not seem to have been consulted over the whole affair is Lord Clarendon.

The Envoy-Extraordinary remains a cipher, and may be concluded to have been that kind of amiable nonentity which best filled a post where little more would be required than that prestige should be upheld in as inconspicuous and English a manner as possible. The fact that the Earl was nearly related to the Duchess of Monmouth was probably conveniently overlooked. The Electress Sophia of Hanover had died on June 6th, and the Earl's mission was to convey Queen Anne's condolences to her son, the Elector George Augustus, who would one day inherit the crown of England. . . . Yes, the Earl would certainly be a nonentity. Queen Anne, who could never hear of her lawful successors without intense irritation, was certainly unlikely to have wasted a good envoy on him. Pope later described him as "honest"—a word which covered a multitude of sins and was seldom employed in the strict dictionary meaning of the word—*that* had perished from disuse in the Court of Queen Anne—but where we should say *so-so, all right, nothing wrong with him*. It is not known how he received his secretary (though one seems to hear, echoing through the years, a malicious cackle from the old Duchess of Monmouth that cousin Clarendon should be landed with one of her cast-offs).

But because the Duchess of Monmouth might have found Gay unsatisfactory is no reason to consider that it was therefore a bungle on the part of Authority to appoint him political secretary to some one else. Swift would go a certain way to favour his friends, but his practical common sense would never have dreamed of allowing him to put forward Gay as a suitable person for advancement if Gay were really as incompetent as some of his biographers have made out. It was not mere chance that influential Ministers picked their men for political posts from amongst those who could express themselves with the greatest clarity and fluency. The English language had not yet been freed from those coils of hyperbole and euphuism which the Elizabethans had hung about it. Anybody who will trouble to look up the reports of Lord Oxford's speeches at that time will immediately sympathise with that gentleman's desire to surround himself with people capable of explaining his own language to him, or making it persuasive to others. And to be persuaded the ear of the contemporary Augustan had perforce to be wooed, tickled by the easy wit of Prior or Gay or Pope, soothed by the melodious, astonishingly easy periods of Addison, touched by the happy man-to-man tone of Steele, awed by the hammer-stroke simplicity of Swift.

But Time, with its usual irony, has reversed these matters: it has suggested that the wits and poets were hangers-on to an indulgent Ministry—mere parasites on Whitehall—whereas the real situation was that the Ministry, entirely sensible of the extreme usefulness of writers who could set the populace on fire with loyal excitement, like the author of *Cato*, or ' sell ' the idea of a hero-king to a stodgy public, as Prior had done for William III, or make that politically-important body the Dissenters look small, as Defoe had done, were the men to be cultivated with the utmost assiduity. So the Whig Ministry (when it was in) cultivated the Whig wits and poets, and the Tory Ministry, succeeding the Whigs, cultivated its own band of wits and poets, and so made certain, in *its* turn, of 'favourable mention.'

That Gay should be appointed as diplomatic secretary at this stage is therefore not so surprising. A Tory Ministry was in, and his position as member of a Tory club (the Scriblerus), showed him to be of the right political colour. True, he had still to live down his early reputation for caring neither for Whig nor Tory and for refusing, as Pope put it, to be "dipt in the dirt of party writing." But he had a pretty wit, and a conscience, and several passages in his recent work referring to such things as standing armies, trade or religion were admirable. He might, according to the authorities, require some careful nursing before he began to be fruitful—but one has to take chances and certainly Gay was amongst the more promising of many applicants for preferment.

There is nothing illogical in such reasoning, nor need it be supposed that since he had not got on with the Duchess of Monmouth he would therefore make a bad secretary to the Earl of Clarendon. That lady was notoriously eccentric, and 'difficult'—and apparently mean also about money matters, since he left her in so threadbare a condition. (Arbuthnot told Swift that much of the advance Gay succeeded in getting out of the Treasury he had spent on "shoes, stockings and linen, of which . . . he was much in need.") Whether he bought as well the expensive library on political law and languages which Swift had advised is not divulged; but in any case the men who had appointed him knew his limitations in that line. They counted not on his bad Latin but on his good English to keep them informed of events—not on his knowledge of law, but on that general air of charm and friendliness which people found it so difficult to resist and which would exert, they might well suppose, a mollifying influence on whoever he met and talked to in the court at Hanover.

Meanwhile, at that same Court, the dreariness of palace existence waited to swallow up both Envoy and secretary. The Elector George had modelled his Court —as did most other European rulers—on the Court of Louis XIV at Versailles. But of all the adaptations of French ideals, that of Hanover was probably the most unhappy. The correctness and rigidity of Versailles might be articles suitable for export, but the redeeming gracefulness was not. So the gardens at Herrenhausen with their avenues of orange-trees where the Elector loved to walk were vistas only of intense boredom to his English visitors, and the assemblies like nothing so much as waxwork shows, with dummies curiously perambulating. It says much for the fortitude of various Englishmen and women that they were prepared to go and bury themselves there, in hopes of a more glorious resurrection (at a later date and under the sun of the royal favour) at Kensington Palace.

Some time in the dog-days of July the Earl of Clarendon and Mr. John Gay arrived to present their credentials at Hanover, and there, wrote Gay afterwards, he was first initiated into the arts of "bowing profoundly, speaking deliberately, and wearing both sides of the long periwig before." The dullness of existence at Hanover is something of which he seems to have been only half-aware, yet it is exemplified extremely well in a letter of his, written jointly to Swift and Arbuthnot soon after his arrival in foreign parts:

"You remember I suppose that I was to write to you abundance of letters from Hanover, but as one of the distinguishing qualities of a politician is Secrecy, you must not expect from me any arcanas of State; there is another thing which is necessary to establish the character of a politician, which is to seem always to be full of affairs of State, to know the consultations of the Cabinet Council, when at the same time all his politicks are collected from Newspapers. Which of these two causes my Secrecy is owing to I leave you to determine. . . .

"My Lord Clarendon is very much approved of at Court, and I believe is not dissatisfied with his reception. We have not much variety of diversions, what we did yesterday and to-day we shall do to-morrow, which is going to Court and walking in the gardens at Herrenhausen. If I write any more my letters will be just like my Diversions, the same thing over and over again, so

"Sir,

"Your most obliged humble servt.,

"J. GAY."

Amongst the brave body of adventurers which had left England to pay their respects to the King-Elect at Hanover was a certain Henrietta Howard, wife of the Honourable Charles Howard—a discontented young gentleman of good family who had succeeded in making a Rake's Progress through his wife's dowry and had repaired abroad, like so many, to improve his fortunes. According to rumour, one of the first improvements was effected by allowing his wife to cut off her hair and sell it to pay for a dinner-party in honour of the Hanoverian Ministers. Whether true or not the story has about it all the rapaciousness which Mr. Howard later showed himself as possessing and all the complaisance of his wife.

Mrs. Howard made the best of Court life at Hanover

and let her mild gaze rest on the orange-trees at Herrenhausen, and the high hedges of hornbeam which, mile by mile, shaded the decorous walks. She was never beautiful, but in that city of Dutch dolls ("all the women have literally rosy cheeks, snowy foreheads and bosoms, jet eyebrows and scarlet lips, to which they generally add coal-black hair," wrote Lady Wortley Montagu in 1716) her fairness of colouring and gentleness of disposition were conspicuous as they never would have been at home. Her fortunes were still extremely precarious. Though the electoral Princess was friendly to her, and had promised a future post as Woman of the Bedchamber when Queen Anne should die and King George succeed her—all this was still conjecture. Living, it was true, was cheap at Hanover and creditors could not reach one there so easily, but still it was a strain to keep up the appearance of a fine Court lady on borrowed money. Her husband, on whom in her extremity she might have leant, was worse than useless. He was not as popular at the German Court as she was—and he cost, sad to say, just as much to feed and clothe. In circumstances which demanded that the two of them should live by their wits, Charles Howard had little or no wits to live by. His wife must have them all. His chief ability had been in spending the dowry of six thousand pounds which she had brought him, seven years earlier, and, that exhausted, there was little left. At such a time the appearance of a compatriot as simple, unassuming and understanding as Gay was a God-send. The kind, open face of the Ambassador's secretary could look into the kind, gracious face of Mrs. Howard and recognise a fellow-feeling there. It was an experience, safe to say, new to them both.

They were attracted to one another from the first, and Mrs. Howard was important to Gay because she was the first woman he ever looked upon as a friend. It is odd that this attribute of his has never been commented on before, for it is certainly important. He could be flippant and cynical enough on the subject of women in his poems or plays—such things were the seasoning that flavoured the dish—but he could also be as sincere and serious with a woman as with a man. He could meet her as another human being with the same intelligence, hopes, fears, capable of feeling the same pains and pleasures as himself. From a thorough examination of letters and MSS. of the times only one other man emerges with this curiously civilised outlook—Richard Steele. To Steele is owing a sentiment concerning a woman friend which no other man of the time could have begun to compass: "To love her is a liberal education." Only Gay, after Steele, could have come near echoing that sentiment. He remained, all his life, gracious and reasonable in his behaviour to women and curiously unbiased by the insidious bias of his age.

Women, said Chesterfield, *are much more like each other than men; they have, in truth, but two passions, vanity and love; these are their universal characteristics.* As the American slang has it, he should know . . . But the thing which must be taken into account is that Chesterfield was not speaking merely for himself, but voicing the convictions of the vast majority of his fellow-men. Addison, that model of intelligence and common-sense, echoes the same sentiments. Compare any one of his *Spectator* essays with Steele's, especially where he is addressing himself to what he would call the Polite Sex, and observe the damnable condescension, the intolerable toying with trifles, the complete consciousness that when he speaks to "the ladies" he must adapt himself to a world as circumscribed in interest as a squirrel's cage. No wonder the wiser Swift said: "I'll have nothing to do with his *Spectator*, let him fair-sex it to the world's end." If ever a man was born to edit a woman's page that man was Addison. He was a lucid and persuasive essayist, but he emasculated journalism to such an extent—for "the ladies"—that the whole tone of the press has subsequently accepted his standards.

Other men, greater than Addison and Chesterfield, were just as much at fault. The least likeable part of Pope's character is his odious gallantry towards women. How the Blount sisters ever survived it is a tribute more to their long-suffering than their good sense. Presumably in private conversation he was capable of dropping that mixture of small obscenity and adulation which he held to be the proper stuff for females. But that he believed it to be the thing there is no doubt. He found it almost impossible to address a woman naturally or speak of one without attributing to her the parts either of an angel or a devil. Even so, perhaps he was happier than Swift. His religion taught him that women were depositories of iniquity and he never quarrelled with its teaching. No doubts crossed his mind, and he slept freely at nights without troubling himself about such matters. But Swift was in more parlous case; his mind tore him two ways. His good sense forced him to admit, time after time, that he found as much intellectual stimulation in the company of Vanessa and Stella as he did in that of much male company; his natural misanthropy, combined with the training of the times, urged that if man were by nature foul and vicious, then woman must be much more so.

This being so, neither Pope nor Swift could ever look upon women as companions. Pope's "crazy carcase" may have inhibited him, as Edith Sitwell suggests, so badly that he was apt to interpret women's interest in him as either curiosity or pity—neither of which his too sensitive spirit could endure. Swift, with depths of grossness within him which would have boiled over a cauldron even in hell, shuddered with nausea at the simplest female physiological functions and expended his disgust on paper. At their worst the one was all oily adulation to women, the other the vilest, most cold-blooded reduction of them to the level of the Yahoo. It would be exaggerating to suggest that the average man of the time could or did follow either Pope or Swift in their estimate of women. He could not be quite so arch as Pope without being self-conscious; he could not be quite so dirty as Swift without feeling that this was really carrying the thing too far. He kept on the whole to a sort of middle path between the two, less extreme but no more estimable. On this male opinion, both from the extremists and the not-so-extreme, the mild and gracious features of Mrs. Howard look down from Heath's engraving. The exception, and practically the only exception of her acquaintance, was John Gay.

Another compatriot of Gay's at Hanover was James Craggs, who has descended to posterity as Craggs the Younger. This young man arrived only at the end of Gay's stay in the country, but he had a way with him and appears subsequently in Gay's verse as "Bold, gen'-rous Craggs, whose heart was ne'er disguised." He was a friend of Addison's, so that it is a great tribute to him if his heart was sufficiently undisguised for his doubtless Whig sympathies to embrace an apathetic like Gay. M.P. for a Cornish borough, he was sent over to Hanover during Queen Anne's last illness—"to inform George the First of measures taken to secure his succession to the throne"—a message which afterwards achieved the position of cofferer to the Prince of Wales' household for James Craggs. Before Craggs' arrival, however, Gay's thoughts and conversation were chiefly at the disposal of Mrs. Howard. Did they pace sedately together in the orangery at Herrenhausen those hot August days, followed by their obsequious shadows as they too followed the shadows of their superiors? Did the fifty antique busts of the Roman Emperors which the Elector had imported (of course from Paris) look down on the extremely innocent confidences of these two English courtiers, as impartially as they looked down on the scufflings and whisperings of royal love-affairs, or listened to the dullness of Hanoverian Court conversations? Certainly it was Mrs. Howard who rescued the secretary from comparative oblivion and introduced him to the Princess-elect.

Caroline was, to all intents and purposes, as graciously interested in Mr. Gay as she had been in General Marlborough, Lord Halifax, Mr. Joseph Addison and the other London celebrities who had come to Hanover from time to time to pay their respects. She was a lady born to do the right thing in every circumstance: history indeed only fails to record of her that she had the usual royal memory for faces—but she knew how to deal with an English poet. She might have no more pretensions to judge of poetry than Pope later declared that Mrs. Howard had—but she asked Gay for a copy of his poems all the same. Alas! this was one of the few things that the secretary had neglected to pack in his hurry when he left. He could only apologise profusely and promise to have one sent out. Such an omission must have upset Swift when he heard of it. Tut! Tut! He had told Gay to take out volumes of *Grotius* and *de Jure;* why had it not also struck him to remind that transparently honest man to take copies of his own works as well, just in case? It was just possible they might be asked for. And now they *had* been asked for and what had happened? It was incidents like these which made the Dean and Pope shake their heads together over Gay, as anxious parents over a careless and forgetful child. Such continually recurring anxiety lent a pleasantly domestic note to the correspondence between two of the least domestic men of the time. Dr. Arbuthnot, caring less about such remissness, could comment quite cheerfully on the incident: "Is he not a true Poet, who had not one of his own books to give to the Princess, that asked for one?" The man who could make kites of his own verses saw nothing but humour in the incident of the man who had left his verses at home. But Pope and Swift viewed the matter in a graver light. Occasions like this prejudiced Gay's chances of preferment, as they knew. They worried a little about their protégé. He was safe of course, as long as Lord Clarendon was still Envoy, but what would happen afterwards?

Fate was to take the problem of Gay's future, as of their own futures, right out of their hands.

CHAPTER EIGHT

August 1714-1715. The Death of Queen Anne.
Gay's Return to London. "A Letter to a Lady."

> "*The Earl of Oxford was removed on Tuesday; the Queen died on Friday. What a world is this, and how does Fortune banter us!*"
> LETTER FROM BOLINGBROKE TO SWIFT, AUGUST 3, 1714

QUEEN ANNE died on August 1st. If at the gates of Heaven that poor tired heart was given any choice of accommodation one thing is certain; it would have asked to be directed to a place where there were neither Whigs nor Tories, but where instead men were as the angels. She had lived quietly and unassumingly, yet in her death she managed to bring toppling down with her the careers of half the best Englishmen of the time. Time had brought in his revenges once again and the fair wind which carried His Majesty George the First to his adopted country blew nobody any good there except the Whigs, the friendly Whigs who had been faithful, through everything, to the Protestant Religion and who might be depended upon in that respect as the Tories could hardly be depended on in anything. Scratch a Tory and find a Jacobite, was George's supposition. He made a clean sweep therefore with his Hanoverian broom and the Tories were brushed unceremoniously out into the roadway.

Oxford had been "removed," as Bolingbroke wrote to Swift, three days before the Queen's death. It was the last cabal in which Anne had been prevailed upon to concern herself, and his dismissal was a triumph for the extremist Tory faction and a blow to the moderates. It was a short-lived triumph, and fortunately so for the rest of the world. Oxford retired to his country seat in Dorset to fuddle himself even more completely with drink, and Bolingbroke stepped eagerly into the position of his rival. Then the Queen died.

It must be admitted that Bolingbroke took the blow with the gracefulness one would have expected from a combination of Socrates, Pliny and Horace. As he himself put it, he "lost all, except spirit" by the death of the Queen. Nor was he the only one. Lord Harcourt, who had recently succeeded Godolphin as Lord Chancellor, was forced to resign his seals. Lord Peterborough, summarily recalled from taking up his new position as Governor of Majorca, was snubbed at the new Court on arrival. Prior was "sent to Coventry" in Paris and called home later to face imprisonment and possible death. The great Duke of Marlborough was insulted by the omission of his name from the list of new Lords Justices. Swift's and Gay's friend, Duke Disney, lost his regiment; whilst the various members of the Scriblerus Club fell like a pack of cards. Their most illustrious member, Lord Oxford, was about to be impeached for high treason. Swift, whost last hopes of a bishopric had expired with the last breath of the Queen, returned to Ireland, "a beaten man" in politics. Arbuthnot lost his post as Physician-Extraordinary, Atterbury, like Oxford and Prior, saw impeachment ahead of him, Gay with his master Clarendon had been recalled post-haste from Hanover—and Pope alone of the better-known Club members escaped punishment altogether. Meanwhile Addison, the favourite returned to power, raised his voice to give three sedate cheers for the new King, in a poem addressed obliquely to Kneller. Hosts of lesser Whig scribes rushed into print on the same theme. But the Tories found voice for neither song nor sonnet. Pope, a Tory more by virtue of his friendships than his convictions, wrote to Arbuthnot about the old days of the Scriblerus Club as if the days of the Club were in a book and that book closed and locked and the key lost for ever. Those were the days!

"Then it was," he wrote, "that the immortal Scriblerus [meaning Arbuthnot] smil'd upon our endeavours, who now hangs his head in an obscure corner, pining for his friends that are scattered over the face of the earth."

But this elegiac tone did not suit the practical doctor at all. He replied with some spirit that, though he no longer resided at St. James's,

"*Martin's* office is now the second door on the left hand in Dover Street, where he will be glad to see Dr. Parnell, Mr. Pope and his old friends, to whom he can still afford a half-pint of claret."

Pope was enchanted:

"I rejoice," said he, "at the prospect of my Amusements in winter-quarters with you in London. Our friend Gay will still continue secretary, to Martin at least, tho' I could be more glad he had a better Master for his Profit, for his Glory he can have none better."

These tender thoughts of his friend Gay are one more example of how kind Pope could be to those he really cared for. In all his multitudinous collection of letters, no kinder one exists than his letter to Gay on that despondent secretary's return to England:

"Dear Mr. Gay, Welcome to your native soil! Welcome to your friends! thrice welcome to me!

Whether returned in glory, blessed with Court interest, the love and familiarity of the great, or melancholy with dejection, contemplative of the changes of fortune, and doubtful for the future, —whether returned a triumphant Whig, or a desponding Tory, equally all hail! equally beloved and welcome to me! If happy, I am to share in your elevation; if unhappy, you have still a warm corner in my heart, and a retreat at Binfield in the worst of times is at your service. . . . If you are a Tory, or thought so by any man, I know it can only proceed from nothing but your gratitude to a few people who endeavoured to serve you, and whose politics were never your concern. If you are a Whig, as I rather hope, and as I think your principles and mine, as brother poets, had ever a bias to the side of liberty, I know you will be an honest man and an inoffensive one. . . . Therefore, once more, whatever you are, or in whatever state you are, all hail!

. . . During your journey I knew not whither to aim a letter after you; that was a sort of shooting flying. Add to this the demand Homer had upon me, to write fifty verses a day, besides learned notes, all which are at a conclusion for this year. Rejoice with me, O my friend! that my labour is over. Come and make merry with me in much feasting, for I to thee and thou to me. We will feed among the lilies. By the lilies I mean the ladies, with whom I hope you have fed to satiety. Hast thou passed through many countries and not tasted the delights thereof? Hast thou not left thy issue in divers lands, that German Gays and Dutch Gays may arise to write pastorals and sing their songs in strange countries? . . . We are now at the Bath—where—if you are not, as I heartily hope better engaged—your coming would be the greatest pleasure to me in the world. Talk not of expenses; Homer shall support his children."

Homer concludes, with unusual practicableness: "Pardon me, if I add a word of advice in the poetical way. Write something on the King, or prince, or princess. This can do no harm."

The death of the Queen, Pope may well have thought, was an Act of God. It was nothing to do with the way Gay had or had not performed his secretarial duties. And surely, since he had got on so well at Hanover, it would be tactful of him to do as Addison and Tickell and Young had already done and to greet the new Royal Family with three times three. Parnell probably added his urgings to Pope's; certainly Dr. Arbuthnot did, and Gay's new friend Mrs. Howard. It is easy to guess on what lines their reasoning ran. Who was it who asked for your poems? The Princess? Well then, obviously a pæan of praise on the Princess is obligatory. . . . Insincere? What everybody does? Not in your line? My dear sir, it's the merest good manners. It's the bread-and-butter letter that you owed to them all at Hanover, you admit, and which you were too lazy to write. . . . Besides you know, there is that unfortunate dedication to Bolingbroke. . . . What, it isn't a dedication? You don't go in for dedications? You won't "spatter a minister with fulsome praise"? Well, what's in a word, my dear sir? You addressed that very admirable *Shepherd's Week* of yours to him—and now, well, if he doesn't lose his head he'll be lucky. . . . It is really essential that, bearing that dedication—that "address"—

in mind, you should bring out something else quickly. As things stand, it is bound to leave a nasty taste in the mouth—not *our* mouths of course, but these wretched Whigs are bound to recall it and use it as evidence against you. Besides you've nothing *against* the Princess, have you? You and she got on very well together, didn't you? Well then, don't you see how nice it would be for her to have some sort of friendly acknowledgment from you, when she arrives here? . . . and so on, and so forth.

Some such reasoning as this must have prevailed upon Gay finally to abandon his old habits and to join the ranks of the poets who, in Congreve's phrase, weighed words, and sold praise for praise. He struggled before he gave in. The manly Arbuthnot reports to Swift that Gay was in such "a grovelling condition that his muse would not stoop to visit him." Perhaps the trouble was, that she could not readily stoop to such practices. Even so, the finished product shows, for those who care to look twice, that his tongue is very apparently in his cheek. Only Prior had ever tried the same tactics and by a similar kind of graceless grace and cheeky I-don't-care-if-I-get-it-or-not manner, had managed to pull it off. In his epistle to Lord Dorset he had remarked:

> The sum of all I have to say
> Is, that you'd put me in some way

of competency, or sinecure, or preferment. . . . Nothing could be franker than that. Even so Gay waited until the new Princess of Wales had landed at Margate, and then launched his *Epistle to a Lady*—as flagrant a piece of open-handed begging as had ever appeared in print. It is as if he had replied to his friends, "Well, you told me to write it and now I've done it, how d'you like it?" The Lady he addressed it to was, of course, his new-found friend the honourable Mrs. Howard. The poem is an odd mixture of confidences as to how difficult he has found it to suit his pen to the theme,

> Long open Panegyric drags at best
> And praise is only praise when well addressed

and bursts of panegyric as exaggerated as (but no more ridiculous than) Addison's or Tickell's. He was fulfilling only too thoroughly in these verses the functions of an Augustan poet: he was showing how well he could "sell" the idea of the rather dull Hanoverians to a rather apprehensive British Public. This is the kind of thing:

> From her [Caroline] form all your characters of life
> The tender mother and the faithful wife.
> Oft have I seen her little infant train
> The lovely promise of a future reign;
> Observ'd with pleasure ev'ry dawning grace,
> And all the mother opening in their face:
> The son shall add new honours to the line,
> And early with paternal virtues shine:
> When he the tale of Audenard repeats
> His little heart with emulation beats;
> With conquests yet to come his bosom glows,
> He dreams of triumphs and of vanquish'd foes.
> Each year with arts shall store his rip'ning brain,
> And from his Grandsire he shall learn to reign. . . .

The Prince of Wales when he read this might have exclaimed with the feelings of *MacDuff*—

> What all? O hell-hound, all?
> All my little chickens and their dam
> At one fell swoop?

For certainly Gay had done them all. Once embarked on the panegyric he was taking no chances—he meant to make a clean sweep of the lot.

The part of the *Epistle* that is sometimes quoted by self-righteous critics to Gay's disparagement are the lines where he describes his own behaviour:

> Since all my schemes were baulked, my last resort,
> I left the Muses to frequent the Court;
> Pensive each night, from room to room I walked
> To one I bowed, and with another talk'd.
> Enquir'd what news, or such a Lady's name,
> And did the next day, and the next, the same.
> [Exactly as at Hanover, he might have added.]
> Places, I found, were daily giv'n away,
> And yet no friendly Gazette mention'd *Gay*.

How disgusting! bellowed the critics. What appalling bad taste to put into so many words just what most panegyrists are really out for! I mean to say, one knows such a state of affairs *exists*—but really nice people never talk about it. And here is this chap giving the whole show away, in the sort of fashion one could depend upon Addison or Tickell or Young never to do. Obviously the fellow is the most miserable scrounger and scringer on the face of the earth—why, he admits it himself!

But the self-righteousness of critics never takes us very far. What would take us much further would be to know what effect *The Epistle* had on Mrs. Howard and on her royal mistress. There is unfortunately no record of their reception of it, but they were probably too busy, in those hectic pre-Coronation days, to do anything about it, in any case. It may be supposed that Mrs. Howard did her best for it in Court circles, that the Princess Caroline received it with the good-humoured suspicion which she very wisely directed on all offerings in this strange, new country—and that the Whigs, caballing amongst themselves, sniggered at the idea of Johnny Gay trying to creep back into favour—and after that Bolingbroke dedication too!

So the year drew to its close.

> Farewell old Year, for thou with broomsticks hard
> Hast drove poor Tories from St. James' Yard

as one chronicler wrote. The members of the Scriblerus Club were even more scattered over the face of the earth than they had been before. Dr. Arbuthnot had taken a long-deserved holiday and gone (rather tactlessly—considering the Pretender was there) to France; Swift was still marooned in Dublin, a savage Gulliver nursing his disappointed rage amidst a troop of Lilliputians falling over themselves to attract his notice. Parnell was here, there and everywhere as he had always been—his favourite resting-place seemed to be Chester. Atterbury was in discreet retreat; Oxford, that fallen Colossus, drinking himself to death at Wimpole. Fortescue was immersed in his final studies for the bar—and Pope and Gay alone of all the tribe were left.

As for Pope, he had seen as much of the excitements as he had wanted to see, and now he was ready to get back to Binfield and to Homer. But not without finally persuading Gay, whom he had urged to the step at different periods of the same seismic year, to come with him. And just so that everybody should know how entirely unmoved he himself remained by the unimportant activities of the Court and country he rededicated himself to the task of rendering Homer into English, in verses which bid good-bye to all the dear delights of London—delights which at their highest and most exquisite, Pope's supersensitive wits could realise were, for him and his comrades, over for ever. Yet he could part from them all—and from all his cronies but one, without a backward glance:

> Adieu to all but Gay alone
> Whose soul, sincere and free,
> Loves all mankind, but flatters none,
> And so may starve with me.

CHAPTER NINE

1715. 'The What D'Ye Call It.' 'The Journey to Exeter.' 'Mr. Pope's Welcome from Greece.' The writing of 'Trivia.'

"*Gay works hard.*"
A LETTER FROM JERVAS TO POPE, 1715

THE year 1714 had seen more than the death of the Queen; it had seen the death in this country of government by a crowned head. Henceforth His Majesty's Ministry, aided immensely by His Majesty's lack of the King's English, was to take the reins into its own hands. Robert Walpole had not yet come into his own as supreme dictator. The Government was still no more than a junto of Whigs laboriously explaining the Constitution to a foreign king—a government in which Sunderland and Stanhope, Walpole and Townshend all marched forward with a briskness and unanimity inspired not so much by their own convictions as by the weight of enthusiastic Whig feeling behind them, pushing them on. The king was in their favour; Parliament was in their favour; Trade was in their favour; the Church was in their favour—everything, so far, was in their favour. The beginning of the Whig *régime*, indeed, was a very different spectacle from the miserable one of hole-and-corner bickering with which the Tory ministry had ended.

Marlborough, who had been his country's saviour and evil spirit alternately during the last two reigns, was once more reinstated in the position of Commander-in-Chief. If there were any panegyrics written to welcome the reinstatement they have not come down to us, but in truth the town was getting just the least bit tired of *Catos* and *Campaigns*. Besides, the need for such puffs had vanished with a Government which felt itself, as the new Whig Government felt itself, really secure. The day of the politically-minded wit was as dead and gone as Queen Anne.

It was to such unpropitious surroundings that Gay returned early in February. He had not been altogether idle on his country holiday, however, for soon after his return a new play of his, *The What D'Ye Call It*, was put on at Drury Lane. This piece he described compendiously as a tragi-comi-pastoral farce. He did not add, as he might have, that it was a parody as well. Its author was well acquainted with the theatrical literature of the past; he had made himself familiar with the works of Shakespeare, Dryden, Otway, Rowe and others of lesser calibre and all these may be found gaily parodied in *The What D'Ye Call It*—especially the witches in Macbeth.

The preface is a masterpiece of its kind:

> "As I am the first to have introduced this kind of Dramatick entertainment on the stage, I think it absolutely necessary to say something by way of Preface, not only to show the nature of it, but to answer some objections that have been raised against it by the graver sort of Wits and other interested People."

There is a suspicion in "the graver sort of Wits" that he is having a dig at Sir Richard Steele, who was supposed to have been offended by the fun poked at Addison in this most inoffensive of plays.

> "The whole art of the Tragi-Comi-Pastoral Farce lies in interweaving several kinds of the

Drama with each other, so that they cannot be distinguished or separated. The objections that are made against it as a Tragedy are as follows:—
... As to the characters; that those of a Justice of the Peace, a Parish-Clerk and an embryo's ghost, are very improper to the dignity of Tragedy, and were never introduced by the ancients. ... Yet whoever will look into Sophocles, Euripides, or Seneca will find that they greatly affected to introduce Nurses into all their pieces, which every one must grant to be an inferior character to a Justice of the Peace: in imitation of which, also, I have introduced a Grandmother and an Aunt."

The delicious mock-seriousness of this nonsense, directed as it was against the prevailing French talk about 'unities' in the theatre, would be hard to beat. Gay then proceeds to answer another so-called 'objection'—that "the sentiments are not Tragical, because they are those of the lowest country people." In reply to this he answers boldly:

"... The sentiments of princes and clowns have not in reality that difference which they seem to have: their thoughts are almost the same, and they only differ as the same thought is attended with a meanness or pomp of diction, or receives a different light from the circumstances each character is conversant with."

This is tame and obvious enough stuff nowadays, but how almost revolutionary in those days in which Bolingbroke could complain, after his knighthood, that he had been placed in rank beneath men that he was not "born to follow"; and in which Swift, stung into irritability by being addressed as Dear Swift in a letter from a comparative stranger, could still reply, after *Pish* and *Psha!* "But he is a lord, and so let it pass. . . ."

The best part of the Preface is that in which Gay, forestalling any possible criticisms, gleefully outlines his own purpose:

> "After all I have said, I would have these critics only consider, when they object against it as a Tragedy, that I designed it something of a Comedy; when they cavil at it as a Comedy, that I had partly a view to a Pastoral; when they attack it as a Pastoral, that my endeavours were in some degree to write a Farce. . . . The Judicious Reader will easily perceive that the unities are kept as in the most perfect pieces; that the Scenes are unbroken, and Poetical Justice strictly observ'd."

He adds proudly (or is it only mock-proudly?):

> "The Ghosts of the Embryo and the Parish-Girl are entire new characters. . . ."

However light-hearted the play (and despite the prefix Tragi there was little real tragedy about *The What D'Ye Call It*) the opening night struck a somewhat dismal note. It was a gathering of the ghosts, come to see an hallucination by one of their own kindred. Most of the Tories who had fallen from high places and who had not yet retired to a proud rusticity were there—Bolingbroke, with the rumours of impeachment and execution hanging over his head, Bathurst, close friend of both Pope and Gay, Harcourt, the ex-Lord Chancellor, Erasmus Lewis, Oxford's ex-secretary—they were all there, the old familiar faces, all Gay's friends except Swift (still biding his time in Ireland) and Oxford.

It was an occasion appropriate to the burying of a Cæsar at least, or the last sad speeches of a Cato. Instead, however, the audience found itself faced with a mischievous hotch-potch of which at first it could make nothing at all. We are told that Pope's deaf friend Cromwell, sitting in the stalls and comparing the tragic expressions of the actors with the hilarious reception around him, could make neither head nor tail of it. The pit also grew more and more restive the more their amazement grew . . . until it was obvious, from the expressions of the nobility in the side-boxes, that the play was comical. The pit concurred and a general good humour was restored, ending in unfeigned delight.

After the first night *The What D'Ye Call It* ' took.' It did more, it became a craze, and after a craze, a piece of slang which passed into the English language and remained current until the days of Horace Walpole—a long stretch for slang. In it Gay had again covered fresh ground, both in manner and matter. He was rewarded by making the—to him—munificent sum of a hundred pounds.

Nobody reads *The What D'Ye Call It* nowadays, though in its neat economy of dialogue it comes near to reaching the technical level of *The Beggar's Opera*, and though Gay's best-known ballad, " T'was when the seas were roaring," lies embedded in its midst. (The tender melancholy of this ballad made it an instant best-seller—a fact which was very gratifying to Mr. Lintot, the publisher, and to all the pirate publishers and broadsheet sellers, but not of much use to Gay.) The real point of interest of the play, however, as in so many of Gay's things, is the light it throws on contemporary social laws and customs, especially those which needed revision. Pope might sometimes be sensitive about the treatment of animals, Swift might show *his* sensitiveness to the condition of the Irish poor by his pamphlet the *Modest Proposal*, but the man who observed cruelty and injustice as steadily as he observed other and more cheerful things, was Gay. He may not have commented on them with either the grace of Pope or the force of Swift, but that did not prevent him from giving them the place they deserved in his work. In *The What D'Ye Call It* he first indicts the outrageously cruel press-gang laws and game laws, putting the words into the mouth of that 'comic' character, the Aunt:

> O tyrant Justices! have you forgot
> How my poor brother was in Flanders shot?
> You pressed my brother—he shall walk in white,
> He shall—and shake your curtains every night.
> What though a paultry hare he rashly killed
> That crossed the furrows while he ploughed the field;
> You sent him O'er the hills and far away,
> Left his old mother to the parish pay. . . .
> *Wat* killed a bird, was from his farm turn'd out;
> You took the law of *Thomas* for a trout. . . .
> Now will you press my harmless nephew too?
> Oh, what has conscience with the rich to do?

The game laws were however game for anybody to jeer at. What was doubtless not quite so acceptable to the authorities were Gay's indictments of the Press Act, which had provided soldiers for Marlborough in the late wars. In a perfect orgy of ghosts, including the celebrated Ghost of an Embryo, he lets himself loose on this somewhat delicate topic:

> 1*st Ghost:*   I'm Jeffry Cackle—You my death shall rue

	For I was pressed by you, by you, by you. (*Pointing to the Justices.*)
2nd Ghost:	I'm Smut the Farrier. You my death shall rue
	For I was pressed by you, by you, by you.
A Woman's Ghost:	I'm Bess that hanged myself for Smut so true
	So owe my death to you, to you, to you.
Ghost of an Embryo:	I was begot before my mother married
	Who, whipt by you, of me poor child miscarried.
Another Woman's Ghost:	It's mother I, who you whipt black and blue,
	Both owe our deaths to you, to you, to you!

This sympathy for the downtrodden, especially for downtrodden women, is a feature of all Gay's work. He could pity and have mercy on the afflicted, as Hogarth could and did in his engravings. He could outline a thumbnail sketch as vivid as any of Hogarth's, as in:

> Thus have I seen a pregnant wench
> All flush'd with guilt before the Bench,
> The judges (wak'd by wanton thought)
> Peer to the bottom of her fault;
> They leer, they simper at her shame,
> And make her call all things by name.

These slight but lively fragments are very different stuff from the flabby couplets of *The Fan;* in them Gay is on the subject of the underdog, a subject on which he is always effective and to which he was to return later with increased success.

Parodies usually offend somebody, and Steele found cause of offence in *The What D'Ye Call It*. He did not fancy his own dramatic style parodied—nothing as simple as that—but he *did* smell out a most irreverent mockery of Addison's *Cato*. Possibly because there is no trace of Addison himself having resented this, Steele resented it all the more. At any rate, he cooled off distinctly towards his former friend Gay, and went so far as to say that, had he been in town (in his capacity of Master of the Stage at Drury Lane) he would have forbidden the piece to be performed.

Two letters belong to this period. The first is written to an absent Scriblerian, Parnell, in a spirit which seems to suggest that Gay's position as successful playwright was not an entirely happy one. It is written, as so often, from a coffee-house:

> "Mr. Pope is reading a letter, and in the meantime I make use of the pen to testify my uneasiness in not hearing from you. I find success, even in the most trivial things, raises the indignation of scribblers; for I, for my *What D'Ye Call It* could neither escape the fury of Dr. Burnet, or the German Doctor; then when will rage end, when Homer is to be translated? . . . I am in hopes that we may order our affairs so as to meet this summer at the Bath; for Mr. Pope and I have thoughts of taking a trip thither. You shall preach, and we will write lampoons . . . I have no place at Court, therefore, that I may not entirely be without one anywhere, shew that I have a place in your remembrance."

The next letter is more cheerful. The pin-pricks inflicted by the German Doctor and Dr. Burnet have vanished and all that remains now is the successful playwright, rather short of money again perhaps, but still light-hearted. It is written to a close Catholic friend of Pope's, Mr. Caryll of Sussex:

"Mr. Pope is going to Mr. Jervas's where Mr. Addison is sitting for his Picture, in the meantime amidst Clouds of Tobacco at William's Coffeehouse I write this letter. We have agreed to spend the day in visiting. He is to introduce me to a Lord and two Ladys. And on my part which I think will balance his visits, I am to present him to a Dutchess. . . Mr. Pope's Homer is retarded by the Great Rains which have fallen of late, which causes the sheets to be long drying, this gives Mr. Lintot great uneasiness, who is now endeavouring to corrupt the curate of this Parish to pray for fine weather. . . . Mr. Pope and I have thoughts of doing ourselves the honour of making you a visit in Sussex, as soon as he hath ended the year's Labour with the Book-seller; where I promise myself the greatest pleasure and satisfaction; may the gout be favourable to you that we may walk together in your Park; Mr. Pope will make his condition before he will venture into your Company that you shall not allow him any of your Conversation in the mornings; he is obliged to pay this self-denial in complaisance to his subscribers; for my part who does not deal in Heroes or ravish'd Ladys, I may perhaps celebrate a Milkmaid, describe the amours of your Parson's daughter, or write an Elegy upon the Death of a Hare; but my articles are quite the reverse of his, that you will interrupt me every morning or ten to one I shall be just as troublesome and interrupt you."

The identity of the "Lord and two Ladys" remains undiscoverable but since Pope introduced his friend Gay about this time to Lord and Lady Burlington, and the dowager Lady Burlington, possibly the reference is to them. As patrons of the arts, they certainly took him up with the eagerness with which they had taken up Pope. There was a further link than literature, too, between Lord Burlington and Gay, for Burlington had an estate in Devon, for which county and "native land" Gay still retained the greatest affection.

Lord Burlington was ten years younger than his new friends Pope and Gay. Horace Walpole, summing him up fifty years later, remarked that he had "every quality of genius and art except envy." Horace Walpole was nearly always generous in his estimate of a Lord's capacities, but Lord Burlington seems to have deserved this fulsomeness more than most. He was a young æsthete whose head was full of the architectural beauties glimpsed in his recent Italian tour, and whose wife's head was full of the music of the day, including her favourite Handel's. Somehow, between these two prevailing passions, the passion for literature was also accommodated: the Burlington family was nothing if not erudite. In their visits to Burlington House, which was still unfinished, Pope and Gay had perforce to pick their way gingerly between the trestle-tables and foot-rules of the Duke, and the musical manuscripts and artistic paper-work of the Duchess. At least they were seeing life.

The summer was a full one for both poets. Their circle of friends had increased steadily, despite the new political circumstances, and in non-Whig circles they were made welcome wherever they went. Besides visiting the Burlingtons at Piccadilly they also visited them at their country house at Chiswick, at the house which was (remarked Lord Hervey with his usual malice) too small to live in and too large to hang on a watch chain. From Chiswick it was only a walk across the fields to Richmond, where the Scriblerian Fortescue lived, and where the Maids of Honour had their lodgings.

Further along the Thames at Hampton Court the Prince and Princess of Wales welcomed those courtiers who preferred the more amusing life and prospects of his Royal Highness's household to the duller ones of His Majesty's. There, in the green days of summer, with the chestnut trees alight with their huge bloomy candles of pink or white a pretty fair imitation of Fontainebleau or Versailles was set up—with Maids of Honour all in a row to lend the youth and the merriment which had been so sadly lacking at Hanover. Add to this that there was the "good sense, good breeding and good nature" of Mrs. Howard to preside over all, and make welcome, regardless of their politics, the John Gay she had known at Hanover and his friend Pope. A Mrs. Howard as near to being a single woman again as was possible in those days of pre-divorce—since her husband had deserted her on their return to England and obtained some small appointment at the King's Court, thus making their estrangement a political as well as marital one.

One inevitable conclusion may be drawn from a close study of the relationships of this period. It is that we are far better acquainted with the turbulent disputes which were prevalent than with the placid good-feeling which occasionally existed between one human being and another. Such feeling, either later or earlier in English history, might be accepted as common stuff, barely deserving of mention—but place it in relief against the constant bickering and quarrels of the early eighteenth century, and it takes on a light almost unique. The prevailing note, in fact, is one of disillusion and dislike. The rarities are affection and esteem. Because it was a rarity it is worth recording that Mrs. Howard was a woman capable both of inspiring and returning affection. Few people have ever been aware of the extremely beautiful friendship which existed between that lady and Gay until the end of his life. The stuff of which her friendship was made was not always so enduring, but that she was good-hearted and honest and charming is past doubt. Lord Peterborough honoured her with his song "I said to my heart between sleeping and waking" and apostrophized her in the last four lines:

> O, wonderful creature! a woman of reason
> Never grave out of pride, never gay out of season,
> When so easy to guess who this creature could be
> Would one think Mrs. Howard ne'er dreamt it was she?

This is pleasant enough, but Pope was to honour her still more by his better-known address, the sixth line of which is a deliberate plagiarism of Lord Peterborough's second line. Presumably Peterborough was as honoured by this as Mrs. Howard. Possibly he was already aware that Pope was a literary kleptomaniac and could no more keep his mind from picking and stealing than he could stop breathing. At least we learn of no complaint and the lines are graceful enough to be forgiven any theft:

> I know a thing that's most uncommon
> (Envy—be silent and attend!)
> I know a reasonable woman
> Handsome and witty—yet a friend.
> Not warp'd by passion, aw'd by rumour
> Nor grave through pride or gay thro' folly,
> An equal mixture of good humour
> And sensible soft melancholy.
> "Has she no faults then" (Envy says) "sir?"
> Yes, she has one, I must aver,
> When all the world conspires to praise her
> The woman's deaf and does not hear.

It was true that, all her days, Mrs. Howard suffered from a slight deafness. Whether it was this which gave her the calm detachment and impartiality that enabled her to avoid taking sides in any dispute or whether, sharp-eared or not, her nature put her above passionate interest in such things, can never be discovered. She did however remain outside intrigues and cabals to such an extent that her neutrality won her the nickname of "The Swiss" and her apartments the name of the Swiss Cantons. Such impartiality naturally won the respect of Pope, the least impartial of men. It is not always true that like attracts like.

But the joys of Court and country, while they took precedence in May, faded into the background in June. Momentous things were happening. Pope's *Iliad* was being born. And simultaneously with Pope's version came the first volume of Tickell's version—an event which succeeded in ending for ever the feast of reason and flow of soul between Pope and Addison. It had long been a suspicion of the younger poet that Addison was growing jealous of his (Pope's) genius. Addison had told him not to add to *The Rape of the Lock* when he had read the MSS., when Pope knew perfectly well that it could only benefit from addition. Such advice obviously meant that Addison did not wish that his genius should be allowed to pour into the world unchecked. . . . And now here he was, first of all refusing to read and advise on the first draft of Pope's *Iliad* on the grounds that he had read a similar first draft from Tickell, and that therefore it would not be fair! After much brooding over his strategical cups of tea Pope decided that Tickell was nothing more than a blind. *He* had never translated any Homer! It was Addison again, Addison jealous of the praises of his rival, who had done the translation in Tickell's name and now, aided and abetted by Tonson, was out to spoil the market for Lintot and Pope.

The more Pope thought about it, the more furious he grew about such criminal double-dealings. (Why, is a little difficult to say. It is so exactly the sort of thing he would have done himself.) And needless to say there was no truth in it at all. Tickell *had* done the translation, and news went round that Addison thought his translation better than Pope's— the public differed and Tickell very honourably and sensibly withdrew from the unequal encounter. . . . But the damage to friendship had been done. Pope and Addison never met again willingly, and Pope, in an epistle to Arbuthnot (published much later), flayed the guiltless Addison as Atticus for all the world to see.

Part at least of Gay's early *Epistle to Lintot* had come true; over Homer, Tonson yielded "to Lintot's lofty name." *The Iliad* in English was not only a best-seller, it was a riot. All in all, the exultant poet made by it over five thousand pounds—enough in those days of cheaper living to make him independent for life and much more

Alexander Pope
   his safe return from
      T R O Y
a Congratulatory Poem on
the compleating his Translation of Homer's Ilias.
   in the manner of the beginning
   of the last Canto of
         Ariosto.

1.

Long hast thou, Friend been absent from thy soil
Like patient Ithacus at siege of Troy
I have been witness of thy Six years toil
Thy daily Labours and thy night's annoy,
Lost to thy native land; with great turmoil
on the wide Sea, oft threatning to destroy.
Methinks with thee, I've trod Sygaean ground,
And heard hoarse Hellespontic shores resound.

2.

Did I not see thee when thou first setst Sail
To seek Adventures fair in Grecian Land
Did I not see thy sinking Spirits fail
And wish thy Bark had never left the Strand?
Ev'n in mid Ocean often didst thou quail
And oft lift up thy holy eye & hand
Praying thy Virgin dear, and Saintly Choir
Back to the Port to speed thy Bark entire.

The first page of the MS. of Mr. Gay's "Mr. Pope's Welcome from Greece."

than any poet has ever made subsequently. All this was very gratifying—and very gratifying too was a warm tribute from that best of friends, Gay, which, entitled *Mr. Pope's Welcome from Greece* was, soon after *The Iliad* came out, in private circulation. "It is curious," says Professor Faber, "that this 'pretty poem' which was thought well of by Gay's circle of friends, was not printed . . . until 1776"—that is until long after Gay's death. It is not only curious, it is another proof that Gay was not inspired, as some writers seem to suppose, solely with the intention of bestowing "praise for praise" and getting a place at Court. If so he would certainly have had the *Welcome from Greece* printed and seen that it received a much larger circulation. Some other critic speaks of its particular interest because it shows the poet's extremely wide circle of acquaintance at Court, even in the evil days of Whiggism. The *Welcome* is a long one, and in it Gay speaks first of Pope's tenacity and industry:

> Long has thou, friend! been absent from thy soil
> Like patient *Ithacus* at siege of *Troy*
> I have been witness of thy six years' toil,
> Thy daily labour and thy nights' annoy . . .

(Others, of course, had also been witness, principally Parnell and the assistant translators who, if they were not such good poets as Pope, were infinitely better Greek scholars.) Gay continues his pæan of joy as Pope's ship comes home:

> O what a concourse swarms on yonder key
> The sky re-echoes with new shouts of joy:
> By all this show, I wean, 'tis Lord Mayor's day;
> I hear the voice of trumpet and hautboy;

> Lo—now! I see them near—oh, these are they
> Who come in crowds to welcome thee from *Troy*.
> Hail to the bard whom long as lost we mourn'd
> From siege, from battle and from storm return'd!

The ship once in harbour, Gay proceeds to jot down, with appropriate adjectives, all the anxious subscribers waiting to receive the poet. Lady Mary Wortley Montagu takes pride of place in the final edition—the four lines previously devoted to Mrs. Howard probably being taken from her, with her generous consent—and bestowed instead on so influential a piece of goods as Lady Mary:

> For she distinguishes the good and wise.

To make up for this rape of a compliment Gay adds ingenuously:

> Now to my heart the glance of *Howard* flies.

One hopes he was forgiven. He has a not-too tactful reference next to Lord (Fanny) Hervey, notorious for paint and powder:

> Now *Hervey*, fair of face, I mark full well
> With thee, youth's youngest daughter, sweet *Lepell*.

(Mary Lepell was a Maid of Honour and a particular protegé of Mrs. Howard's. She afterwards married Lord Hervey.) A compliment to Pope's two woman friends comes next:

> I see two lovely sisters, hand in hand
> The fair-haired Martha and Teresa brown.

Then two more Maids of Honour are listed, and the mysterious "Dutchess" again appears on the scene:

> Yonder I see the cheerful Dutchess stand
> For friendship, zeal, and blithsome humours known.

Lady Scudamore and the Countess of Winchelsea follow, with Miss Howe—another scatter-brained Maid of Honour:

> Nor knows with whom, nor why she comes along,

and two others. After that it is the men's turn. *Fam'd Buckingham,* and *Bathurst impetuous.*

> Whom you and I strive who shall love the most.

And now the subscribers hurry up, like the oysters in Carroll's poem—and thick and fast they came at last, and more and more and more. Generous Burlington (a host already, to Pope and Gay), goodly Bruce (a mystery which never materialises), Dan Prior next, "belov'd by every muse"—(but not by Walpole's ministry), "friendly Congreve, unreproachful man." (Congreve might well be friendly: *The Iliad* had been dedicated to him, and he had had nothing to reproach himself or others with since Lord Halifax, twenty-two years earlier, had rewarded his genius with half a dozen fruitful Government Commissions.)

> Earl *Warwick* comes, of free and honest mind;
> Bold gen'rous *Craggs,* whose heart was ne'er disguised.
> Oh why sweet St. John, cannot I thee find?
> *St. John* for ev'ry social virtue priz'd.

> Alas, to foreign climates he's confin'd,
> Or else to see thee here I well surmiz'd:
> Thou too, my *Swift*, dost breathe Bœotian air
> When wilt thou bring back wit and humour here?

Harcourt, Lansdown, Rochester, Carlton, Chandos, Hanmer, Ned Blount and the Carylls "by dozens," Arbuthnot, "whose company drives sorrow from the heart," Kneller, Jervas, Dartneuf, Ford, Maine, Dennis, Gildon, Cromwell, Wanley, young Lord Harley, Evans, Young, Booth, Mawbert, Frowd, Digby, Southern,

> Yea, *Steele* and *Tickell* mingle in the throng
> Tickell whose skiff (in partnership they say)
> Set forth for Greece, and foundered by the way.

A sly dig which must have pleased Pope immensely—and all the anti-Addison school. The poem closes, after a few further references to other friends, with the lines:

> How lov'd and honour'd thou! yet be not vain;
> And sure thou art not, for I hear thee say
> All this, my friends, I owe to *Homer's* strain,
> On whose strong pinions I exalt my lay;
> What from contending cities did he gain,
> And what rewards his grateful country pay?
> None, none were paid—then why all this for me?
> These honours, *Homer*, had been just to thee.

June, the month *The Iliad* appeared, was the year's climax. Parliament closed at the end of June, so that the country squires who sat there could return home to gather in their harvests, and their wives and daughters either went with them, or with richer friends and acquaintances to Tunbridge Wells or the Bath. Wherever the fashionable world went, and whatever they did, the great thing was to get out of London—for with all one's friends and acquaintances out of London, London was no longer endurable. . . . Pope and Gay had had plans, as Gay's letter to Parnell indicated, of meeting him in the summer at Bath, but there is some mystery on this score because they were certainly not all there together. The plans for a holiday in Sussex with John Caryll also fell through. Both Pope and Gay had caught the prevailing fever—a contagion from which a quarter of London's whole population of seven hundred thousand seemed to be perpetually suffering, and afterwards they decided to convalesce—Pope at Bath as earlier arranged for, and Gay in Devon. Lord Burlington seems to have given Gay the horse and/or the funds to get there, for he was rewarded later with the bread-and-butter poem which was customary on such occasions from poet to patron.

Judging from the natural history notes in the poem, *The Journey to Exeter*, Gay set out to make his horse-back journey some time in August. As a piece of topographical information it does not equal Defoe's *Journey through the whole Isle of Great Britain*, or, later, Cobbett's *Rural Rides*, but it has advantages over these in that it can be read through at a sitting, and that it describes pithily and accurately every town through which Gay and his two companions passed on their way from London to Exeter. Such detail has immense charm for those who like to dig down to that buried England in which Gay and his companions lived and moved and breathed. Reading it is like seeing turned up in the track of a modern plough, the curved and iridescent lip of a piece of Roman ware—buried for centuries, now come to the surface again:

> While you, my Lord, bid stately piles ascend
> Or in your *Chiswick* bow'rs enjoy your friend;
> Where *Pope* unloads the boughs within his reach
> Of purple vine, blue plums and blushing peach
> I journey far—you knew fat bards might tire,
> And, mounted, sent me forth your trusty Squire.

Gay continues to describe their exit out of London. "No carts the road infest," for it is Sunday, and "still on Sundays country horses rest." After leaving Turnham Green they jog on, three dusty miles to Brentford:

> Thence o'er wide shrubby heaths and furrowed lanes
> We come where *Thames* divides the meads of Stanes.
> We ferry'd o'er; for late the water's flood
> Shook her frail bridge and tore her piles of wood.

Next they faced the danger of Jonathan Wild and other highwaymen across the dangerous Bagshot Heath, then Hartley-Row, Sutton, and Stockbridge where the three cavaliers paused for dinner and the night. There they partook of a perfect dinner after a dusty ride on a hot August afternoon:

> O'er our parched tongue the rich metheglin glides
> And the red, dainty trout our knife divides.

Next day the sun rises early and burns strong and clear, a pure summer day, while they jog across twelve miles of plain, until they see Salisbury's spire pointing up into the shimmering sky:

> Our horses faintly trot beneath the heat
> And our keen stomachs know the hour to eat.

After Salisbury, Blanford, and then Dorchester, where an incident of the ride is recalled for Lord Burlington's amusement:

> Here sleep my two companions' eyes supprest
> And propt in elbow chairs they snoring rest;
> I wakeful sit, and with my pencil trace
> Their painful postures and their eyeless face,

"eyeless face", as Polonius would say, is good—very good—a literary adventure rather beyond Gay's usual attempts. There are two more pleasant lines in *The Journey to Exeter*. One is where he describes a lunch at Marcombe, where they:

> Strip the lobster of his scarlet mail,

and the other, where they fall into foul weather west of Honiton:

> Now swelling clouds rolled on; the rainy load
> Stream'd down our hats, and smoak'd along the road.

The symbol "smoking" is again extremely good and above Gay's usual level of symbolism. It shows he could do it when he tried; but he did not try, very often. He knew that the usual pedestrian stanzas which he wrote might look deceptively easy, but that to turn them out with the simplicity and ease with which he did it, was real art.

Throughout, his two companions remain a mystery. They are mentioned under pseudonyms, which, however, get us nowhere. There is a possibility that they were Arbuthnot and Cheyne; in which case whoever else enjoyed the journey to Exeter, certainly the horses did not, for a month later we find Pope writing to Gay from Bath:

"Pray consult with Dr. Arbuthnot and Mr. Cheyne, to what exact pitch your belly may be supposed to swell, not to outgrow theirs, who are yet your betters."

Gay by now was certainly getting fat, ridiculously fat for a man of thirty. Swift put it down to his 'shilling habit' of taking a sedan chair or a coach for even the shortest distance. Congreve put it down to his hearty appetite. He once said that the proper Latin text for Gay would be, not *cogito, ergo sum*, but *edo, ergo sum*. The cause, however, is usually supposed to have been indolence. Well, he had little time to be indolent in 1715. He had written a play and two long poems and was working throughout the year on *Trivia*, his verses on the London streets. Jervas, reporting to Pope on Gay at about this time, wrote: "He works hard" . . . The epistle is ended with a pleasantly patriotic couplet at the sight of Devon:

Hail, happy native land!—but I forbear
What other counties must with envy hear.

Whether it was Arbuthnot and Cheyne who accompanied him on the trip to Exeter we shall never know; nor who was the 'flame' whose name Gay scratched with a diamond on the window-pane at Dorchester. The hold she had on his heart was certainly as frail as the window-pane later proved to be. If Swift had happened to be looking over his shoulder as he wrote it, he would have told him:

> The glass by lovers' nonsense blurred
> Dims and obscures our sight!
> So, when our Passions Love has stirr'd
> It darkens Reason's light.

but Gay never needed to be told. He was never terrified of love, and of what it would do to him, as was Swift. His diamond-scratch was a gesture, nothing more, a piece of romance which, like the 'lasses' kisses' at Salisbury, he thought would spice the poetical dish agreeably for his patron Burlington.

This is the point at which the truthful biographer must brace his shoulders back and break the news—to those who have not already guessed it—that Gay never was in passionate love with a woman in his life. The deepest emotions he ever felt—and they *were* love, though not sexual love—were for Pope and Swift, his friends. If he was in love with anything else at all it was with life. And he had every excuse. He was living in perhaps the most beautiful age his country had ever known. His *Journey to Exeter* was also a journey to Heaven, along a primrose path, in an England unchanged since Chaucer and Shakespeare—a still perfect inheritance for her children. The crabbed fashion of the age curbed his natural enthusiasm and bade him speak of these glories only in the metrical couplets laid down by Boileau—but he had not been so bound in his preface to *The Shepherd's Week*, in which, he said he knew of "no age so justly to be enstiled Golden, as this of our Sovreign Lady Queen Anne."

Another way in which Gay occupied himself during this year was in translating and annotating a new edition of the works of Horace just published by Tonson and Watts and edited by the Frenchman Mattaire. This volume, which is preserved in the Forster Collection in the Victoria and Albert Museum, is notable not only for the extreme neatness and legibility of the written notes by Gay but for the glimpses that they give us of Gay's interest in and knowledge of other lands. Again and again he adds to Horace's abrupt statements such classifications as: "Assyrio-pardo: a plant growing in India called spikenard. Assyrio, because the Roman merchants bought it in Syria"; "He chuses the South wind before any others, because it is most tempestuous, and particularly so upon the Adriatick and Sicilian sea"; "Upon the sea-coast, 17 or 18 miles from Formiæ. There are now left only the ruines of it under the Rock of Mount Dragon"; "6 miles from the present Capua"; "6 or 8 miles from Beneventum"; "Baruiae, a pretty large town upon the borders of the Adriatick sea." Such statements are not casual gleanings. They represent an enthusiastic and arduous search into the histories and geographies of the time, and are born of that earlier-stated desire of Gay's, derided by Pope, "to see foreign lands."

After this interest in tracing Mediterranean towns Gay's other interest in wine comes into its own. Chian, he reminds himself in the narrow margin of Mattaire, was a sweet Greek wine; Falernian was rough. On yet another margin, he repents about Falernian and describes it as a small, pleasant wine. He adds the historical details that *interiore nota* means the innermost *marked* hogshead—that is—the oldest wine, and that "for want of ice, the ancients cooled their wine in running water." It is difficult to classify his other Horatian annotations, copious though they are. All that can be said is that it looks from them as if he were playing with the idea of translating into English yet more of the works of that already over-translated poet. Later he must have given up any such scheme, but the notes remained. Some of them, being concerned with comfortable and friendly things, are typically Gay. In Ode XIII, for instance, he translates a passage: "Whose love being never interrupted by quarrells and complaints, shall not be dissolv'd sooner than their death." And of Satire III he remarks with appreciation, "The design of this satyr is to show that we ought not to censure others for follys which we are guilty of ourselves; that we ought to palliate the foibles of a friend"; still further on he adds repetitively, "We ought not to loathe the frailtys of our friend"; for the rest, he remarks of a God whom he never had the pleasure of meeting: "Faunus is the protector of Poets, as he is a sylvan God, and Poets are fond of the country." He translates *parasitae* deftly as Poor Cousins, says of Crispinus that he was "a clear-ey'd Stoick Philosopher and a very bad Poet"; harks back (possibly a little wistfully) to the experience of his strict Biblical upbringing by saying obliquely of Ode 38: "The two first chapters of the book of Esther give a very good image of the magnificence of the Persian feasts." But all is disconnected and apparently casual and for the student the chief value lies in his extraordinarily neat calligraphy and the beautiful ' balance ' of the type on the page.

Meanwhile, Queen Anne was dead, but summer still returned, and autumn and all her autumnal beauties. Walpole had been consolidating his position and when Parliament met again he reappeared as Chancellor of the Exchequer, with Pulteney as Secretary of War. Here was the first hint of what was later to be ministerial Dictatorship—though possibly nobody was aware of it as yet. Practically coincident with the new Parliament came the Great Frost—as severe as the Great Storm of 1703. It froze the Thames over the whole of the winter, so that booths and stalls were erected on the ice and fairs arranged for the duration of the frost.

An equally great frost was the abortive invasion of Scotland by the Young Pretender—whose plans were mismanaged for him in London by Sir William Wyndham and in Paris by Lord Bolingbroke. That unfortunate Lord was to muff every job he undertook whether it was for rightful King or the King over the water. When the tumult and the shouting died away—and a handful of insurgent leaders had been arrested and executed, Bolingbroke retired with what dignity he could muster and began to cultivate his garden at St. Cloud. Horticulture can be a very present help in time of trouble.

The Tories in England who were not Jacobite rejoiced at the collapse of the invasion of '15 as heartily as did the Whigs; but in the other Great Frost they read signs and portents. Here was the wrath of Heaven making itself felt very emphatically concerning the maladministration of the Whigs. In this portent, however, they were partly unlucky, for although the ice over the Thames would only last till the warm weather came again, the Walpole administration was to go on interminably.

But that, luckily, was a thing that Gay and his Tory friends could not possibly foresee.

CHAPTER TEN

1716. 'Trivia.' 'God's Revenge upon Punning.' 'The Espousal.' The Visit to Bath and Burlington House.

> *There Handel strikes the strings, the melting strain*
> *Transports the soul, and thrills through every vein.*
> GAY: TRIVIA

"THE world, I believe, will take so little notice of me that I need not take much of it. The criticks may see by this poem, that I walk on foot, which probably may save me from envy. I should be sorry to raise that passion in men whom I am so much obliged to, since they allow'd me an honour hitherto only shown to better writers: That of denying me to be the author of my own works.

"Gentlemen, if there be anything in this poem good enough to displease you, and if it be any advantage to you to ascribe it to some person of greater merit, I shall acquaint you, for your comfort, that among many other obligations I owe several hints of it to Dr. Swift. And if you will so far continue your favour as to write against it, I beg you to oblige me in accepting the following motto:

> *Non tu, in Triviis, indocte, solebas*
> *Stridenti miserum stipula disperdere carmen?"*

Prefaced by this brave 'advertisement' John Gay produced, in January 1715, the poem which after *The*

Beggar's Opera and the *Fables* is the best-known of all his works. This was *Trivia, or the Art of Walking the Streets of London*. Since its first publication it has been reprinted more frequently than any other of his poems except the *Fables*, and it deserves this position of honour. If it is granted that Gay's chiefest gift was a kind of photographic accuracy in reproducing the contemporary scene, and this may well be maintained, then it must also be granted that in *Trivia* that gift is seen at its best. The London of the early part of the eighteenth century may have irretrievably vanished, but in *Trivia*, like insects preserved in amber, many of its scenes have been preserved intact. It is superb reporting—free from the bitterness which jaundiced Swift's *City Shower*, that earlier precursor, or of the tendency to burst into irrelevant philosophy which sometimes marred even the best prose pieces in *The Spectator* or *Guardian*. There were of course occasional classical references—the times demanded them—and these later called down the wrath of Dr. Johnson, who could not endure his styles to be mixed; but they are very unobtrusive classics and do not mar the general effect.

Gay seems to have set out on his walk through London with his eyes washed clear of any prejudice, determined to paint what he saw in the neatest and aptest English available. The poetry of *Trivia* remains pedestrian, which after all suits a walking theme very well; though it is one of the longest of his occasional pieces it is not proposed to quote from it here, as those familiar with it already will not need reminders and the rest are advised to read it in its entirety.

Trivia did not enjoy a tremendous success in its first edition, though Gay made £43 from it, and it worked up slowly but surely to a tenth edition. It is doubtful, however, if his contemporaries ever fully realised the implicit virtues of the poem. They lived too close to the London described in it to find it more than entertaining. One interesting point, however, is that Gay seemed to know about those implicit virtues. As his 'advertisement' showed, he was not a man given to over-estimating any of his productions (*The Beggar's Opera* when it came was prefaced with the motto *Non hæc novimus esse nihil*) and yet he ended *Trivia* in a manner almost bombastic. As he inscribed the words he may even have intended them for a joke—but with the lingering hope that after all it was just barely possible that there might be *some* truth in what he wrote, that *Trivia*, despite its name, was not entirely trivial:

> And now complete my generous labours lie,
> Finish'd, and ripe for immortality.
> Death shall entomb in dust this mould'ring frame,
> But never reach th' eternal part, my fame . . .
> When critics crazy bandboxes repair
> And Tragedies, turn'd rockets, bounce in air
> High-rais'd on *Fleet Street* posts, consign'd to fame
> This work shall shine and walkers bless my name.

At least the poem started the year well for its always penurious author. If it was not a *succès fou* it was still a distinct *succès d'estime*, except in the opinion of those crabbed critics who had refused from the first to believe that Gay could ever write anything at all—only that he was allowed, on occasion, to print Swift's and Pope's cast-offs under his own name to earn a little money. Even an inoffensive person may have enemies, as witness the enemy Mr. Sedley who, precursing Pope's *Dunciad* by several years, can write on the favourite topic of Dullness:

> See, how his awful Godhead does dispense
> At *Childs* and *Wills* his solid influence!
> How willy-whisps P(ope's) senses quite away
> And sheds his whole collected force on G(ay)!

It is sometimes forgotten, when nice-minded people deplore the way Pope employed the more vicious side of his genius that, in school language, the other boys started it first. Long before *The Dunciad* Pope and his friends were subjected to abuse very like the example just quoted and often in far more execrable verse (which was insult added to injury). Pope's exalted position made him especially vulnerable. It would have been praiseworthy if a healthy and insensitive character had ignored such slanders; for a sick and sensitive man to do so was well-nigh impossible. But these points are often overlooked and the world as a whole has preferred to take its impressions of Pope from men like Broome who could write of him: "I often resemble him to a hedgehog; he wraps himself up in his down, lies snug and warm, and sets his bristles out against all mankind. Sure he is fond of being hated."

He was *not* fond of being hated—though he enjoyed being the hater himself. Nevertheless he was hated, and with an intensity which came near rivalling his own, though far below it in effectiveness.

But Pope, had he known it, had after his *Iliad* soared far beyond the reach of envy, calumny and hate and blame. Meanwhile he was delighted to see his friend, his *elève*, as people called Gay, receiving congratulations on *Trivia* from the clustered Maids of Honour at Court, and gracious compliments from Mrs. Howard and the nameless Duchess, and Lady this and Lord that. One only of the notabilities listed in *Mr. Pope's Welcome from Greece* failed to observe a similar good-nature—and the

Countess of Winchelsea, mentioned in that poem as "still meditating song," is reported to have remarked that Mr. Gay's *Trivia* showed he was more proper to walk before a chair than to ride in one. Nobody knows what inspired her to make such a statement, but a very possible explanation is that she, who was herself a genuine poet, deplored so much enthusiasm over something which was not top-rank poetry. Mr. Gay, she may have felt, had the advantage of her simply by reason of his sex. He could 'get away with' the pedestrian *Trivia*, and silly little ballads and mock-pastorals to amuse Court ladies, while anything serious which *she* wrote was received with the maddening gallantry which was all that polite wits extended to ladies who (in their jargon) fancied themselves as Sapphos. She could never be sure of receiving criticism uninfluenced by the fact of her sex. Poor woman, she had been born out of her time even more thoroughly than Gay—who forsook, when necessary, his natural sentiment for his just as natural but far more acceptable gift for reporting. But whilst he was complimented on all sides she had to endure either shallow flattery from her followers or only too sincere sneers from the wits. Something of the same nature which had induced Lady Winchelsea's attack on Gay may later have made Lady Mary Wortley Montagu declare that Pope and Swift were "no better than link-boys"—another piece of bad temper because men of little birth and breeding, and not much better educated than herself, could command a respect which she could never compass.

The early months of the year were happy ones for both poets. Gay, said Arbuthnot, "had made so much money by his art of walking the streets that he was ready to set up his equipage." Pope had made a fortune from *The Iliad*. The success they had both won showed that even poets who had been friends of Bolingbroke's were not necessarily damned for ever. Besides, though Bolingbroke had discreetly fled abroad, Arbuthnot was back in London, and Fortescue had succeeded in obtaining work in the enemy's citadel itself—a private secretaryship under Robert Walpole. Swift it was true was still in Ireland, defending, as he contemptuously put it, his small dominions against the Archbishop, but if the joint letters of Pope and Gay would not serve to call him back to London then nothing would. Parnell too was due for another visit. After all perhaps the Scriblerus members were not scattered for ever beyond recall.

Meanwhile, as Pope and Gay waited for that day of happy reunion, the two of them led their usual busy life. The Prince of Wales's houses at Leicester Fields and Hampton Court grew more and more familiar ground to them: they became the established favourites of the Maids of Honour, and the courted cronies of Mrs. Howard, Lady Mary Wortley Montagu and other fine ladies, as well as welcome visitors to the town houses of my lords Lansdowne, Bathurst, Harcourt, Peterborough, Chesterfield, Pulteney, Hervey and Burlington. Now that their pockets were lined they could better afford the continual drain of *pourboires* which went, as a matter of course, to the noblemen's flunkeys and which made a 'free' dinner at a gentleman's table more expensive for poets than supper at a coffee-house. Life became a perpetual masquerade—a glorious Clubland in which a man met every one who mattered, talked to everybody about everybody else, kept off politics (which were fundamentally boring in any case) composed fresh scandals or passed on old ones, fenced with bright practised wits against redoubtable conversational opponents and went home to lodgings at the end of the day tired out but happy, convinced that the most enjoyable purpose of life was to mingle with fine ladies and gentlemen capable of appreciating one—and to feed perpetually upon strawberries and cream.

A small record of this almost too-good-to-be-true period of the joint lives of Pope and Gay, entitled *Court Poems*, is preserved in a volume published by Roberts in March of the same year and advertised as being printed "faithfully as they were found in a Pocket-book taken up in Westminster-Hall." The Poems were Pope's *Basset-Table*, Lady Mary Wortley Montagu's *Drawing-Room* and Gay's *Toilette*, all published anonymously. There is no discernible difference of level in any of them: each is as good as the other and none of them amounts to more than a skilful exercise—but they probably sold well in the circle which knew the authors. Another and more amusing work is a pamphlet issued anonymously about the same time and entitled *God's Revenge Against Punning*: a prevalent vice just then, especially at Court. This has been attributed to both Gay and Swift but it is certainly more in Gay's *genre*; especially the lines which concern

> "a shoemaker at Turnstile in Holborn, who was so given to the custom and did it with so much success, that his Neighbours gave out he was a Wit. Which report coming among his creditors, nobody would Trust him; so that he is now a Bankrupt and his family in a miserable condition."

Belonging to the same period is a letter from Gay to Addison concerning one or other volume of his verses:

> "SIR—I have sent you only two copys of my Poems though by your Subscription you are entitled to ten, whatever Books you want more

Tonson or Lintot upon your sending will deliver.

"I cannot neglect this Occasion of returning you my thanks for the Benefits you have done me and I beg you to believe that I have such a just sense of them, if you ever could think of doing more for me you could not engage me further, for 'tis impossible to owe you more Love and Gratitude than I do already.

"I am, sir, etc.,
"JOHN GAY."

A short letter but important, because it shows that however complete the rift between Pope and Addison now was, Gay and Addison could still remain friends—and Pope could forgive Gay for remaining friendly. As to facts, it is difficult to discern which were the benefits which Gay declared Addison had bestowed on him, beyond taking out a handsome number of subscriptions for his poems, which after all scores of others had done—so difficult indeed that the ingenuous sentence, "if you could ever think of doing more for me you could not engage me further," looks almost like irony. If any man *could* do anything to help necessitous friends that man was Addison, a secretary to Lord Wharton at £2,400 a year, and a Lord of Trade and Plantations at still more: a Whig man of letters moreover of such repute that even Walpole could respect his publicity-value and desire to keep him in good-humour. But Addison was perhaps too gentlemanly to take advantage of his position to benefit a poet who, however lukewarm in politics, had still prefaced a poem to that arch-traitor Bolingbroke and been hand-in-glove with the apostate Swift. . . .

Some of the time in that spring Pope spent airing

Jervas's house for him while he was out of town, and Gay lived in lodgings: some of the time they both spent in Burlington House. "Beauty within, without Proportion reigns," wrote Gay. If he meant by beauty Lady Burlington it is to be hoped she was mollified by the compliment but rumour declares that she sometimes grew a little impatient of these stray geniuses her husband picked up. Perhaps Handel, who was staying with the Burlingtons at the same time as Pope and Gay, was some solace to her. That guttural genius could sit and play to her in one beautifully-proportioned room while in another Pope and Gay read extracts from their latest piece to the Duke. And over their heads and behind their backs all the time Burlington House was still a-building: the Palladian pillars went up and the ladders came down and workmen tramped across the draughty hall and dust and grit blew all over the Louis Quatorze furniture and the Italian marbles.

The more one contemplates the figures which scurry across the two-hundred-years'-old screen the more one is struck by the incredible richness of the company— not richness reckoned in terms of money but in character. It would have been enough honour for Burlington House to have had George Frederick Handel as inhabitant—but three-quarters of the great names of England were made welcome there, at one time or another, by the Burlingtons. The elegant new building became a kind of Whipsnade in which social, literary, musical and artistic lions might roam, feed, or lie down and sleep at will. Handel had qualified as a lion by his *Rinaldo* in 1711—a production which (taken in conjunction with the failure of Mr. Addison's own opera *Rosamund*, in the same year) had drawn from Mr. Addison the following remarks in *The Spectator*:

"At present our notions of music are so very uncertain that we do not know what we like, only in general we are transported with anything that is not English. So it be of foreign growth—let it be Italian, French or High Dutch it is the same thing. In short English music is quite rooted out, and nothing yet planted in its stead."

But 1711 was not 1716: by 1716 it was quite clear that something *had* been planted in the stead of English music, and that was Italian music. "There's nobody allowed to say, *I sing*, but an eunuch or an Italian woman," Gay was to write to Swift seven years later. But it was true at this period as later. Italian opera had become the rage, and men and women who could not tell B sharp from a bull's foot still went enthusiastically to the opera, night after night, and debated hotly the rival merits of singers whose technique they had never begun to be able to appreciate. And Handel, with his Italian training behind him, and the success of *Rinaldo* to encourage him, set out to give the London public what it wanted: *Paster Fedo*, *Teseo*, *Silla*, *Amadigi*—they poured forth from him, driven ever on by his tireless German industry. Real public esteem was not yet his—royal patronage was not yet his (indeed, by absenting himself so continuously from Hanover in those early days, he might almost consider himself as under the Royal Displeasure) and the days of the great cantatas were still in the distant future when three young men, just over thirty, lived for a while together in Burlington House.

It is to be regretted that no records were kept of that distinguished menage, or of how its component parts fitted together—but from the fact that there are no records a grotesque picture may be conjured up in the imagination of Burlington House with all its rooms exposed to full view at once, like a doll's house, with Lady Burlington cutting out paper most artistically in one room, Lord Burlington etching in, with his thumbnail, his emendations on Kent's architectural plans in another, Handel rapt over his harpsichord in a third, Pope stopping his ears at the din in another and Gay mocking the repetitive cadenzas of *Amadigi* on the flute he had played in his school-days and never quite grown out of, in the last. Whether the picture is true or not, certainly Pope's suggested reaction is not out of keeping. It is hardly necessary to read his poetry to realise that he had—like so many other literary men of his day—no ear for music. And Handel, whose grasp of English prose was still elementary, was hardly likely to be interested in English poetry—except of course as libretto. Pope and Handel had, in fact, no mutual interests at all—except in so far as they were both Lord Burlington's guests. Gay and Handel had a common bond of conversation in that Aaron Hill, in his Drury Lane capacity, had originally commissioned *Rinaldo* and had talked long and earnestly to Handel (and probably written too) concerning the possibility of using an English libretto for his music. Handel had remained unconvinced. Apart from his ignorance of the language, English obviously lacked the mellifluousness and tunability of Italian. . . . But he was a man ready to experiment when opportunity offered, and here opportunity had thrown him a couple of poets. If he ever approached Pope with the idea (as surely he would have approached the first poet of his age) then Pope was Not Interested. (The only song of Handel's of which the libretto is definitely attributable to Pope is the enchanting ' Where'er you walk, cool gales shall fan the glade' from *Esther*. But Handel may well have set this long after it was written.) Gay with that musical sense and those flute-trained fingers of his was a different proposition. Imagination again suggests an irreverent Conversation Piece, in which all three guests are gathered together with their host and hostess and in which Handel in that slow abominable English of his repeats Aaron Hill's enthusings on the subject of English libretto. Imagine the Burlingtons' enthusiasm —Lady Burlington with the scissors of her latest occupation still dangling from her hand, Burlington delighted with a vision of Burlington House as the great house which had germinated and cultivated this Magnificently Co-operative scheme—but . . . He fixes Mr. Pope with his forefinger—Pope, what a scheme, eh? But Pope's eyes, just visible through the steam of the best Bohea which he has raised to his lips, are glassy and unmoved as a codfish. He swivels his eyes round to Gay. Try *him*, he indicates to Lord Burlington. Does Handel observe? It is to be hoped not. His broad back is probably to the company, his stubby fingers calling out of the harpsichord those skilful combinations of sound which, to Mr. Pope, resemble nothing more than the howling of tomcats. This is not such a Good Idea from Lord Burlington's point of view. He sees himself as a compère, compelled to engage a second-best artist just when he has been on the verge of being able to announce the most distinguished Double Turn in England. Mr. Gay by all means—but he had envisaged Mr. Gay more in his familiar rôle as helpmeet and assistant than as composer—Mr. Gay possibly to write down Mr. Pope's libretto and explain it to Mr. Handel. . . . Something congenial in *that* way. . . . But the author of *Trivia* is delighted at the idea. He has a theatrical sense (which Mr. Pope has not) and a musical sense (which Mr. Pope has not) and an itch to try something new (which Mr. Pope never had). By all means, he would try to think of something for the purpose. He would rack his brains. Here Handel swings round again on his stool. He upstairs in his *schlafstimmer* a little piece has on a theme of which he is very fond—*Acis and Galatea*. Do play it, Mr. Handel. O fetch it, do, Mr. Handel, and let us hear it. But that is not the point. The point is the charm of the story of *Acis and Galatea* and its entire suitability as theme for an English libretto. He had already composed music on the theme to an Italian libretto—as long ago as 1708. . . . Is Mr. Gay so keen now? Mr. Pope's eyes, more glazed and cod-like than ever, say to Mr. Gay over his still raised tea-cup: "There you are. That's the worst of these musical people. He'll be dictating the words to you next, as well as the subject. . . ." But Mr. Gay is not to be called off. He remembers the story of *Acis and Galatea*. Of course he does: they all do. Ovid's metamorphoses are, next to Horace, the things they know best and like best in the world. . . . He will see what he can do with the idea. "When you have time," says Handel, waving his hand magnificently, "I have plenty to occupy myself at the moment."

This, at least, is a permissible exaggeration of how *Acis and Galatea* came to be created. It would have been delightful for Lord Burlington to feel that the operetta was really being composed in that home of the muses in Piccadilly, and doubtless Gay roughed out some part of it there and gave it to Handel to work on. But he would not have had time for much more before the beloved disturbing presence of Swift was again in London—a Dean tempted over less by promises of introductions to the Prince's Court (though there were these) than fleeing from the terrifying image of a Stella fallen sick and wasting away before his eyes. It is sad

L

to admit but in 1715 it was truly less love for his friends than loathing of his Irish circumstances which brought him to England.

Whatever the reason, his presence was enough to send Pope and Gay nearly off their heads with joy. Pope himself had been negotiating for a new home in a place called Mawsons' Buildings, Chiswick, near enough to be "under the wing of my Lord Burlington" there—and to this new home he now took the visiting Dean. Chiswick from Pope's point of view had enormous advantages over London in its proximity to the heart of things. A short ride or trip up-river took one to Hampton Court with all its excitements: and the houses of the nobility and gentry—the intelligentsia, that is, were planted as thickly as willows on both banks of the river. It is safe also to whisper that just then the nymph of the river was Lady Mary Wortley Montagu, the irresistible Sabrina whose syren-song could lure wise little poets on into a destruction of which they, as yet, had no inkling.

From the artistic viewpoint, Mawsons' Buildings was about as lovely as its name, but with Pope, Gay and Swift together once more it could count three supremely happy men beneath its roof—and happiness, like cleanliness, is next to Godliness. A trio of wits, with Mrs. Pope as a sort of benign influence in the background.

But Mrs. Pope did not occupy the background of Mawsons' Buildings alone; metaphorically speaking the dark eyes of the Blount sisters peeped over her shawled shoulders at Pope—and the shades of Stella and Vanessa hovered like contending ghosts over the head of Swift. Especially that summer was the shade of Stella a presence that might be felt. She was something in the air, an indefinable something sensed by the ultra-sensitive Pope as disturbing the perfect happiness. What was she to Swift then? Swift who had fled to England to escape from the sight of her suffering? Not so much Stella as death and corruption made manifest. In such circumstances, it was not to be expected that the reunion between the three friends was a perfect one. There were moods which shattered the harmony of the occasion—Pope's headaches, Swift's preoccupation with Stella, Gay's preoccupation with his own hopes and fears, and Mrs. Pope continually pouring out the tea and rocking herself in the shadows while her dear boy talked and his friends listened—and the Thames rolled on.

At about the same time that Pope moved to his new address at Chiswick, Addison moved to Holland House in Kensington. But his move was a little more momentous in that it involved a marriage as well as a house. The Countess of Warwick was the bride; and we cannot help feeling that it must have been some satisfaction to Mr. Addison (chief bachelor-wit of all the bachelor-wits that ever frequented a coffee-house) that, since he had to succumb eventually to marriage, he should be able to do the thing so discreetly. For it is elementary mathematics that the greater cannot be absorbed within the lesser, and consequently the Countess of Warwick could never become merely Mrs. Addison. Their association, therefore, would always have a pleasantly irregular sound about it—almost like the association of Voltaire and Madame de Chatenay—and yet fundamentally it was so thoroughly correct, just as one would expect anything in which Addison was concerned to be correct. So the Countess of Warwick and Mr. Addison returned to live in Holland House, and the coffee-houses Wills' and Button's and Don Saltero's knew Mr. Addison no more (for a time at least). The man of letters had been merged into the statesman and the statesman, however imperceptibly, into the husband.

The honeymoon in Holland House was set fair for the rest of the year—but the reunion at Chiswick was destined to come to a sudden end. The Dean, that most secretive of all secretive persons except his host, said nothing, but a day came when his friends divined by the signs that he had had worse news of Stella. Torn between a horror of re-encountering her suffering and a like horror of the possibility that if he did not hurry he might not see her alive again, Swift fled back to Ireland as peremptorily as he had left it. His going left a gap. He did his best to fill it by writing back to Pope in England as soon as he had returned to Ireland and by characteristically throwing off a hint which was to bear, later, most satisfactory fruit for the weakest member of the three:

> "There is a young ingenious Quaker in the town, who writes verses to his mistress, not very correct, but in a strain purely what a poetical Quaker would do, commending her Looks and Habit, etc. It gave me a hint that a set of Quaker Pastorals might succeed if our friend *Gay* could fancy it, and I think it is a fruitful subject; pray hear what he says. I believe, further, the Pastoral Ridicule is not exhausted; and that a Porter, Footman or Chairman's Pastoral might do well. Or what think you of a Newgate Pastoral, among the Whores and thieves there?"

It would be pleasant if all the good seed sown in this world fell on such fruitful ground. Gay was a delightful person to make suggestions to, at this period of his life. He was intelligent enough to realise Swift's genius and to pounce with joy on most of the suggestions which came from that august quarter. Did Swift love him partly because of that pounceableness, that instant happy falling-in with his suggestions? Perhaps so; in a world where, latterly, all his statesmanlike suggestions had passed unheeded it was comforting for an exiled Dean to feel that in the literary world at least he had a sympathetic and obedient audience.

The suggestion led ultimately to much more than Swift could ever have foreseen. Soon after the letter arrived Gay wrote *The Espousal*, an Eclogue between two Quakers, which either needed a nastier mind than his to give it any point at all, or a more savage sense of satire. Gay could never be savage—especially against a sect not unlike, after all, the Dissenters' sect in which he had been brought up. *The Espousal* may have made the sophisticated ladies and gentlemen of the Prince of Wales's court titter with mirth—but much of the point has departed from it these days. However, if the verses pleased Swift they may be claimed to have served their purpose.

It has been suggested that Gay followed straight on here with the beginnings of his *Beggar's Opera*—based, as was the *Eclogue*, on the idea of a ' Newgate Pastoral.' It is likely that he toyed with the scheme but doubtful that he had time to do more with it—for we know that during this year he was also busy with Pope and Arbuthnot on the comedy *Three Hours after Marriage*. No sooner did he finish that than he was off again to Devon, this time accompanied by Lord Burlington, and on the way back he ' took in ' Bath, which lay convenient for the purpose.

If good Americans go to Paris when they die, then as assuredly good eighteenth-century Englishmen went to Bath. And both good and bad went to Bath during life, just as soon as the London season ended. In this way that bane of existence for the intelligentsia—the house in the country—might be avoided. A house in the country was, to the eighteenth-century mind, the *summum bonum* of existence on paper and in verse—but the actual thing was desolation, an island separated by alternate seas of mud in winter or clouds of dust in summer from everything which made life worth living. In Bath, after all, one lived exactly as one did in London, but at a deliciously accelerated pace. (The smaller the wheel, the faster it revolves.) One enjoyed oneself tremendously—and if one took the waters, then all the time there was the pleasant consciousness of duty done and a possibility of better health as a result. . . . One always, in an imperfect world, suffered from *something*.

John Gay's excuse for Bath at this stage of his life would have been more the congenial company than the need for the waters. The internal troubles from which he was to suffer came upon him later. Besides, as well as the congenial company he had money in his pocket; a third edition of *The What D'Ye Call It* was being brought out and so far it may be supposed he had not had time to spend the income from *Trivia*. Bath at least would give him the opportunity for that. It is the first record we have of his visiting that delectable city— though far from the last. The soft west-country air was native air to him, and he found nothing relaxing in it. The town's small compass with everybody within a stone's throw of everybody else (and naturally plenty of stones were thrown) matched his indolent spirit exactly. At Bath, too, he could exercise his inimitable gift for making friends with everybody he met; and, while the rest of the town like Gaul was divided into two parts —Tory and Whig, Jacobite or Hanoverian, Pro-Walpole or Anti-Walpole—he could still be on happy terms with them all.

The length of time he spent in the city was probably determined by the movement of his companions the

Burlingtons, or else by the news from London. He seems to have kept in touch with Pope throughout the autumn, and we get a laconic statement in a letter from Pope that "Mr. Gay has had a fall from his horse and broken his fine snuff-box"—a fate which looks remarkably like a punishment for vanity since we have his own word for it that he never took snuff.

Once in London again, he seems to have taken lodgings of his own, presumably for the sake of keeping close to the centre of things. Pope records of him proudly to Martha Blount, as of a favourite child: "Gay dines daily with the Maids of Honour." But though he might dine with the vivacious Bellenden, the prettily-mannered Lepell and the dashing Miss Howe, he did not spend all his time at Court. That he speedily renewed contact with all his old cronies is evidenced by a letter to that still-absent Scriblerian, Parnell—addressed "from a chop-house near the Exchange," where he was sitting, as so often, in company with Jervas, Arbuthnot and Pope:

"Dear Sir,—I was last summer in Devonshire, and am this winter at Mrs. Bonyer's. In the summer I wrote a poem, and in the winter I have published it; which I have sent to you by Dr. Elwood. In the summer I eat two dishes of Toadstools of my own gathering, and in the winter I have been sick with wine, as I am at this time, blessed be God for it, as I must bless God for all things. In the summer I spoke truth to Damsels, in the winter I told Lyes to ladies. Now you know where I have been and what I have done. I shall tell you what I intend to do the ensuing summer; I propose to do the same thing I did last, which was to meet you in any part of England you would appoint; don't let me have two disappointments. I have longed to hear from you, and to that intent teased you with three or four letters, but having no answer, I feared both yours and my letters might have miscarried. I hope my performance will please the Dean, whom I often wish for, and to whom I could have often wrote, but for the same reasons I neglected writing to you. I hope I need not tell you how I love you, and how glad I shall be to hear from you; which next to seeing you, would be the greatest satisfaction to

"Your most affectionate friend and
Honourable Servant,

"JOHN GAY."

Put letters like this against Pope's masterpieces of carefully-edited correspondence—or against Swift's mingled strength and sweetness in *his* letters, and they fade back into the obscurity in which they have lain hidden for so long. For they contain nothing startling, or admirable, or beautifully said. . . . But they have a place here, because the spirit of Gay himself breathes out of them (even when, like the above, they were obviously written under the influence of the chop-house's good wine)—something simple, friendly, anxiously beguiling . . .—and always full of plans and eager for life. *Toujours gai, qu'il fasse beau, qu'il fasse laid.* Yes, so far we might almost say *Toujours gai.*

CHAPTER ELEVEN

1717. 'Three Hours after Marriage.' 'Ovid's Metamorphoses.' 'Epistle to William Pulteney' and to 'William Lowndes.' Visits to Aix-les-Bains and Paris.

> "*Gay is well at Court, and more in the way of being served than ever. However, not to trust too much to hope, he will have a play acted in four or six weeks, which we have drawn a bargain for.*"
> POPE IN A LETTER TO MARTHA BLOUNT, DEC., 1716

THE month of January, which had hitherto proved so auspicious for *Rural Sports* and *Trivia*, let Gay down badly in 1717. On the 16th of the month a play called *Three Hours After Marriage*, accredited to him, was put on at Drury Lane. Considering that the play itself seems to have been built round private prejudices—a subject always uncongenial to so genial a man—it comes as no surprise to learn that the piece was not his alone but the joint production with him of Arbuthnot and Pope. The idea was to take a thoroughly Restoration plot, and decorate it with vicious caricatures of those persons whom the authors deemed to be deserving either of punishment (for having been rude to them) or else ridicule, because fundamentally they were so ridiculous. The chief character was *Fossile*, based obviously on a contemporary geologist of some repute named Woodward—a man who had recently earned Arbuthnot's hearty contempt for the nonsense he had been writing about earthquakes and the Flood. Pope, not to be outdone, contributed *Sir Tremendous*, "the greatest critic of our age"—another hit at the unfortunate John Dennis,

—and Gay may be taken as having contributed (doubtless under the urgings of his friends) a caricature of his late employer the Duchess of Monmouth, under the title of the *Countess of Hippokokeana*. . . . As if this were not enough Colley Cibber, well known to Drury Lane audiences, was held up to scorn as *Plotwell*. Then the Countess of Winchelsea was not overlooked, for having made that sneering reference about being fitter to walk in front of a chair than to ride in one. She is introduced as *Mrs. Phoebe Clinket*, eternally composing plays and poems on the Universal Deluge. After mangling the poor lady in the play the authors killed her off neatly in the epilogue with:

>Whom can our well-bred Poetess displease?
>She writ like Quality—with wonderous Ease.
>All her offence was harmless want of Wit;
>Is that a crime?—Ye Powers, preserve the Pit!

It may not seem incredible that Pope (who after all never cared for the theatre), or that Arbuthnot (who had multitudinous other interests) should have been so short-sighted as to imagine that such words would not harm their authors; but it does seem incredible that Gay, who had had from his 'prentice days a keen interest in and knowledge of the stage, should have allowed himself to be so influenced. The three of them seem to have been content to fly in the face of Providence with complete light-heartedness. In so doing they managed to offend everybody that mattered. Poor Steele, recently let down as he fancied by Addison's marked preference for Tickell and still sore with Gay because of the *What D'Ye Call It*, had not been consulted at all over the new piece; in other words Gay as well as Addison had deserted him, and he was still that influential being, 'Master of the Stage' at

Drury Lane. His feelings towards *Three Hours After Marriage* may be imagined.

Now it may be excusable to ignore the Master of the Stage or theatre where one's play is being produced—especially if he is in high dudgeon—but to mock Colley Cibber as well—the great Colley, actor-manager and playwright and most important of the three licensees and patentees of the same theatre, was the last straw. The stage superintendent ignored, the patentees ridiculed, potential patrons insulted—what further blunder remained but to accuse members of the audience (in the epilogue) with want of wit? That blunder, as has been seen, was duly committed. In view of all this it would have been remarkable if even a good play could have succeeded. But *Three Hours After Marriage* was far from being a good play. It was an invention to which Arbuthnot had brought his familiar ridicule of pedantic fools, Pope his barbed malice and Gay—it seems inevitable—the schoolboy smuttiness of the plot. After all he had to bring *something* besides the actual labour of writing it, —and the other features are so obviously from the hands of Arbuthnot and Pope. The play we are told "ran feebly for seven nights" and then deservedly collapsed. The *pièce de résistance* had been the introduction of a mummy and a crocodile, whose bodies were employed to convey the inevitable lovers into the house of the inevitably to-be-cuckolded professor. . . . The audience stood the rest of the play fairly stolidly, but the mummy and the crocodile were too much for even *their* broadmindedness. These surprising objects were greeted by boos, cat-calls and that angry knocking of cane-tips on the floor which always heralded disaster.

Such a flop coming from the hands of such distinguished authors naturally gave the greatest pleasure to the town tattlers and the staunch Whig wits. A

Complete Key to the Three Hours After Marriage was immediately issued by one E. Parker, philomath, together with a full account of the authors. It was about as witty as the play it mocked (which is not saying much) and about as malicious (which is saying a lot). The frontispiece was a crude woodcut representing the three authors with Pope particularly shrunken, Arbuthnot in a resplendently curly wig, and Gay in a fool's cap. Mr. Parker was generous enough to give anecdotes as well as verse, and had much pleasure in telling the world that on January 21st Gay, Pope and Arbuthnot all called in at Mr. Lintot's, the bookseller's, to see how the piece sold, "but they did not find a single customer in the shop."

When it first became apparent which way the wind was blowing—and that it was an ill wind that was going to blow nobody any good, Gay wrote to Pope in the following terms:

> "Too late I see, and confess myself mistaken in relation to the comedy; yet I do not think, had I followed your advice and only introduced the mummy, that the absence of the crocodile had saved it. I cannot help laughing myself . . . to think how the poor monster and mummy were dashed at their reception. . . . As to your apprehension that this may do us future injury, do not think of it; the Doctor has a more valuable name than can be hurt by anything of this nature, and yours is doubly safe. I will, if any shame there be, take it all to myself, as indeed I ought, the notion being first mine, and never heartily approved by you."

The failed playwright thereupon left London and spent a week with the quality at Hampton Court. His letter is both a generous acceptance of blame, and acquittal of Pope. But however stoutly Gay might insist that the play had been entirely his, and however discreetly Pope remained in the background, public opinion was difficult to convince. Gossip still went about the town that Pope was using Gay as a stalking-horse, and evading his responsibilities. Everybody who had a grievance against Pope—and all the friends of Mr. Ambrose Phillips that celebrated pastoral-writer had, and all the friends of that celebrated critic Mr. John Dennis had—and all the friends of Mr. "damn-with-faint-praise,-assent-with-civil-leer" Addison *certainly* had, delighted to accuse Pope of ill-treating Gay. The onslaught was so violent that Pope believed genuinely that he might be waylaid by hired bullies on some dark night and put out of the way. At all events he wrote to the Blount sisters: "I have lately been told my person is in danger and (in any such case) the sum of £1,121 will be left for you in Mr. Gay's hands. I have made this matter secure against all accidents." But his opponents preferred to meet him on his own literary ground, even though they carried inferior weapons. Here is a typical attack from the pen of Mr. Leonard Welsted and Mr. James Moore-Smyth. After predicting the Nemesis which was to attend Pope for all his misdoings the authors add:

> "Midst this vain tribe, that—and thy setting ray
> The Muse shall view but spare ill-fated *Gay*;
> Poor *Gay* who loses most when most he wins
> And gives his foes his fame, and bears their sins;
> Who more by fortune than by nature cursed
> Yields his best pieces and must own thy worst."

whilst another and anonymous gentleman rushed in about *Three Hours After Marriage* with:

"Thou once clubs't Nonsense for dramatick stuff
And there thy Folly met a just Rebuff;
Th' indignant town could easily divine
The grain of wit was Gay's, the mass of scandal
 thine."

Even Pope's worst enemies found it impossible to hate Gay.

While these comparatively trivial literary incidents were happening, the political world was also in a state of upheaval. It has been truly said that nothing is as dead as dead politics—and attempting artificial respiration on the particularly defunct body politic of the mid-eighteenth century would be a waste of time. The infection of bribery and corruption had spread slowly but steadily ever since the Restoration—through every man connected (no matter in how remote a way) with statesmanship. Members of Parliament who delighted to cap each other's quotations from Horace in both Houses adopted the morals of Rome with as much faithfulness as its literature. Not all, indeed, could quote Horace with glibness—but even the most insignificant mealworm of a back-bencher could stab his friend (metaphorically speaking) in the back, poison the minds of his enemies—plot against the King, bribe others to plot against the King, deny the bribe when discovered, pay another bribe to have the remembrance of the first bribe effaced, blackmail whenever opportunity offered and preserve, above all, a marble façade of the Perfect Statesman, whose toga protected him from all corruptions and whose patriotism conveniently excused all his faults. Almost inevitably, however, as events have receded from us, attention has been centred on the most prominent figure of the times—Robert Walpole—and as a magnet attracts steel shavings so all the bribery, corruptions, baseness, and vileness of the period have been subsequently swept up together and attributed to him. Names make news, and the news that Walpole made is eternally misquoted as "All men have their price." What he actually said was "All *these* men have their price "—meaning, as he spoke it, the latest half-dozen or so who were endeavouring to shake him, in some way or other, from the seat of power. But if he had included all the Opposition in that statement, history has proved abundantly that it would have been no exaggeration. That he also made full use of the political system which he inherited he would have been the last to deny. Walpole, at least, despised the marble façade and the unsullied toga. All these men had their price, and so long as he controlled the Treasury and the Civil List they should *have* their price—when they were worth it.

Robert Walpole, indeed, stands out as a supreme example of one type of Politician in the reign of George I, and Pulteney, Chesterfield, Sunderland and Bolingbroke may be bunched together as examples of the other type. If, as Dr. Johnson said, Chesterfield's *Letters* showed the morals of a whore and the manners of a dancing-master, it is equally true that the whole of the Walpole Opposition showed the morals of Nero and the manners of Petronius Arbiter. Is there any one these days who can prefer the windy Pecksniffianisms of *The Patriot King* (written to curry favour with one of the few members of the Royal family that Bolingbroke had not yet had the opportunity to betray) to the straight reply of Walpole to a cringing applicant for preferment: "I know you have a great interest with the Prince and Princess, but that shan't do, for no interest in England shall hinder my giving this [place] to Horace Walpole, who I can deny nothing he has a mind to have". . . ?

As the lesser of two evils, certainly the manner of Robert Walpole has its points.

But in 1717 Bolingbroke was still discreetly abroad and Robert Walpole still turned his attention more to home than to foreign affairs. Stanhope and Townshend were in charge of the latter, and between them had recently sent out diplomatic feelers all over Europe, seeking to renew the old alliances and trade agreements which the Tory isolationist policy had recently snapped off. But to expect two Ministers to act together in harmony over foreign affairs is to expect the millennium. Though a Triple Alliance between Holland, France and Great Britain was achieved under their joint management there was far from being any sort of Triple Alliance between Stanhope, Townshend and Walpole themselves. Stanhope's views on foreign policy were backed up by the Earl of Sunderland, a man politically negligible but extremely cunning. Long before Queen Anne's death he had been in close and sympathetic touch with Hanover and now, with the King's ear as attendant to him as it seldom was to an English subject, he made the most of that early acquaintance. He blew hot when George blew hot on foreign policy or the outrageous behaviour of the Prince of Wales; he blew cold when George blew cold. Outside the royal precincts, however, Stanhope remained at the temperature necessary for the transaction of international business and with supreme tact managed to conduct foreign affairs in such a way that George (influenced by Sunderland) felt that that was how he had wished them to happen all along.

All, therefore, would have gone merrily as wedding bells if it had not been for the Dual Control system, consequent upon employing Ministers both for the Southern and Northern departments of Great Britain.

Stanhope as Southern Minister had to work not only against Tory factions at the coffee-houses and at Leicester House, but also against his own colleague Townshend. The split at last became so apparent that the only possible way out was to get rid of Townshend. Just as Mussolini nowadays always appoints dangerous rivals to nice hot governorships in Libya, so in the eighteenth century an English statesman who was endangering the *status quo* was always sent to Ireland. So Townshend, much to his chagrin, found himself packed off one fine day to be Lord-Lieutenant in Dublin. If he had not had Walpole for a father-in-law, that would have been the end of him as it had often been the end of much better men. Doubtless at Walpole's instigation he made himself so difficult in Ireland that his dismissal followed,—and was in turn followed by the resignation of Walpole and of half-a-dozen lesser politicians. This might not affect foreign affairs adversely, but one of its results was that Walpole, the only man in the Ministry who knew anything about national finance, went out of it, and the Earl of Sunderland took his place, with disastrous consequences. But in 1717 the huge uncontrollable bubble of the South Sea Company was not yet blown; the interesting point is that one of the lesser politicians who followed his leader on this occasion out into the wilderness was Mr. William Pulteney, Secretary of War. Pulteney was a rich young Whig with occasional Tory sympathies, a gift for writing extremely neat verse and the reputation for having succeeded Bolingbroke as chief orator in the Lower House.

Two unfavourable opinions of Pulteney are preserved in Dr. Johnson's "Pulteney was as paltry a fellow as could be; he was a Whig that pretended to be honest," and Chesterfield's more graceful periods in "The only judgment I can form of him is that he will get as much money and as much power as he can, and upon any terms." It is Pulteney's misfortune that more pleasant opinions have not survived. Obviously the man had charm; his verse indicates wit and scholarship, and the fact that he could have friends amongst the Tories redounds more to his credit than discredit. He had married the daughter of a wealthy glass manufacturer. After the amiable fashion of the times she too is preserved in acid—first in Lord Harvey's denial that she had "any one good agreeable or amiable quality except beauty" and again in Pope's portrait of her as "Fantastic, vain and insolently fair." These various verdicts, however, belong to a later period of two long lives. At the time of Walpole's resignation the Pulteneys were a couple of rich young people with plenty of friends—who had taken a political step backwards, merely *pour mieux sauter* later on.

As Oxford had once represented the moderate Tories, so Walpole and Pulteney had later represented the moderate Whigs. Their influence had resulted in the breakdown of the case against Oxford, and his subsequent release from the Tower. Their departure led to a much stricter treatment of Prior by the Sunderland-Stanhope Government, and the keeping of this poet in 'protective custody,'—a blunder which cost them much. . . .

One of the friends of the Pulteneys amongst the Tory side of their acquaintance was John Gay. Though Pulteney had been busy lately with affairs of State, and Gay with getting himself and his friends out of the slough of despond resulting from *Three Hours After Marriage*, both had found time to meet with others, on the mutual ground of St. James's or at Richmond. Perhaps the hostess of the Swiss Canyons, Mrs. Howard, made them both welcome in her apartments; there, to the stimulating raillery and laughter of the Misses Bellenden and Lepell, it was easy enough to forget the present discontent,—for a time. But habit was too strongly ingrained in Pulteney to allow him to stay in England after his withdrawal from active political life. The next step of a statesman out-of-office was inevitably to go abroad. In June, therefore, William Pulteney and his wife, accompanied by their friend Mr. Gay, set out on a little tour of France, beginning with a visit to Aix-les-Bains and ending up in Paris.

It says something for Pulteney's probity—at this stage of his career at least—that he could actually set foot in France without immediately being termed a Jacobite. After all, the rebellion of '15 was only two years old—and its arch-inceptor, Bolingbroke, was still in Paris. It is likely that the two men met there and touched antlers like a couple of graceful suspicious deer whose delicate, full-blown nostrils take in every whiff of the other's being but who have no intention of doing more than observe the necessary courtesies to a stranger.

Indeed, the more one considers it, the more the periwigged elegant men of the time resemble deer: they move stepping softly in droves like deer. They are all graceful, all distinguished, like deer. Their soft, brilliant eyes look at you out of their portraits by Kneller or Van Loo or Jervas or Richardson with the proud, animal assurance of deer. And what a hard spirit they have— what a discernment of the moment when the leader of the drove is sick or aged or somehow incapacitated! Then they can rub the bloom off their beautiful antlers with a will, and with their branched horns gash and gash again the sides of the fallen leader. And the chief perpetrator cannot be caught, or indeed singled out from amongst the members of the herd who have been most forward. He is away like the wind, his small feet leaving prints on the snow, discreetly, delicately indistinguishable from the prints of the rest.

But what first drew Pulteney to France was the waters of Aix, not the *beaux yeux* of Bolingbroke. Gay, it may be cheerfully admitted, went just for the ride. He wrote to Pope from Aix that he was taking the waters and excused himself from literary composition on the grounds that "writing is not good with the waters." In other words he was on holiday and meant to stay so. He had no particular 'scheme' in hand just then. Money had been short and Parnell had very kindly made him a present of the 'copy-money' due for his own just-published *Battle of the Frogs*; but sixteen pounds two and sixpence would not take him very far, nor yet the forty-three pounds odd that Lintot had just paid him for the copyright in the despised *Three Hours after Marriage*. This was June and he had been paid that in January. From every point of view the trip abroad with the Pulteneys was ideal.

It was Swift who, on being asked once to a dinner-party, demanded to be shown the bill of company rather than the bill of fare. Pulteney was going one better and, in taking Gay as a travelling companion, making sure that one member of his company at least would be to his taste. There is, alas, no prose record of the excursions the party took; these must have been various, since they stayed abroad until November. When it was all over Gay (as was to be expected) repaid his host with a bread-and-butter poem about the trip.

This particular *Epistle* is negligible except in so far as it shows the trends of Gay's thought. It contains exactly the sort of bright hard tittle-tattling which, strung together on one topic, sparkle like so many sequins, and may be supposed to have amused and pleased people like Maids of Honour in much the same way. If nobody could accuse Pulteney of being a Jacobite, still less could Gay be accused. He was a true Augustan in that France still represented to him the centre of everything unpleasant and insincere. But he writes his *Epistle* with a sneer which sits very uncomfortably on that round face and those pleasantly-curved lips. . . . The simple "Loving Countryman" who had written *The Shepherd's Week* is no more: he is become a man of the world. He knows Lady Mary Wortley Montagu now, who can wield the bitterest and most poisoned pen in the world (next to Pope), he is acquainted with Swift's ever-increasing misanthropy, he has observed family affection at its strangest in the notoriously bad relations between King and Prince of Wales; and has heard the tinkling sophisticated laughter of the Maids of Honour and observed the unruffled complacency of Mrs. Howard at the whole thing; they and people like them are the potential audiences for whatever new work he or Pope or Swift may write. So sophistication and cynicism are the notes to be struck now. Queen Anne and the good old days are dead. Long live King George (or the Prince of Wales, if you belong to His Royal Highness's Party).

It is easy to trace in the *Epistle* how very closely Gay's mind has by now been tuned to Pope's. The resemblance comes out first in a bad imitation of Pope's advice to a poet. But if he could not equal Pope's onomatopœias he could, on occasion, be just as successful in delineating ' characters ':

> *In Paris there's a race of animals*
> (*I've seen them at their Opera and balls*)
> *They stand erect, they dance when'er they walk,*
> *Monkeys in action, paroquets in talk ;*

There is something rather distressing in seeing the man who has been so often described as the most artless and undesigning and good-tempered of poets, so thoroughly converted to the thought of the day. How Pulteney must have enjoyed hearing his jester rail so—seeing that so much of the *Epistle* is given up to it! Some of it is superficial, but in this description of manners it is possible there may be a hint of bitter experience:

> How happy lives the man, how sure to charm,
> Whose knot embroider'd flutters on his arm!
> On him the Ladies cast the yielding glance,
> Sigh in his songs, and languish in his dance,
> While wretched is the Wit, condemn'd forlorn,
> Whose gummy hat no scarlet plumes adorn;
> No lady's favour on his sword is hung
> What though Apollo dictate from his tongue
> His wit is spiritless and void of grace
> Who wants th' assurance of brocade and lace.
> While the gay fop genteely talks of weather,
> The fair in raptures doat upon his feather.

In a later ballad, *The Despairing Shepherd*, Gay again depicts the difficulties of the man hampered, in his love-affairs, by lack of funds:

> How wretched is the faithful youth
> Since woman's hearts are bought and sold;
> They ask not Vows of sacred Truth,
> When'er they sigh, they sigh for gold.
> Gold can the powers of scorn remove
> But I, alas! am nought but Love.

Possibly the bitterness of that repeated cry was inspired

by the treatment meted out to Gay on some occasion or other. If they had come from another man one might regard such sentiments as a mere bowing of the knee to convention, for in all the plays and poetry of the time there was but one chief convention: if the swain was faithful then the shepherdess was not so—and vice versa. But in these pieces, belonging to what one may describe as the middle period of Gay's life, there is a certain consistency about their recurrence which suggests that, even though such sentiments *were* fashionable, still the fact that Gay chose to represent women as faithless and avaricious does suggest that he had frequently found them so, all except Mrs. Howard.

> Yet let us not their loose coquett'ry blame;
> Women of ev'ry nation are the same.

Thus the *Epistle*. A meeting with a French fop leads to an amusing travesty of national pride:

> *Well, now you've Paris seen, you'll frankly own*
> *Your boasted London seems a country town;*
> *Has Christianity yet reach'd your nation?*
> *Are churches built? Are masquerades in fashion?*
> *Do daily soups your dinners introduce?*
> *Are music, snuff and coaches yet in use?*

Gay's reply to the fop is quite as bitter as anything Pope could achieve. The *elève* has learnt well of his master:

> Pardon me, Sir: we know the *Paris* mode,
> And gather *politesse* from courts abroad,
> Like you, our courtiers keep a num'rous train
> To load their coach; and tradesmen dun in vain.

> Nor has Religion left us in the lurch,
> And, as in France, our vulgar crowd the church:
> Our Ladys too support the Masquerade,
> The sex by nature love th' intriguing trade.

True to the laws of verse, he turns from the general to the particular and in some especially nasty lines (calculated, no doubt, to set Pulteney's table on a roar) fills in every detail of woman's inconstancy:

> *That frozen bosom native fire must want*
> *That boasts of constancy to one Gallant!*

It is the voice of Alceste in the last act of Molière's *Misanthrope*—sardonic, laughing at his own stupidity that he cannot really see anything to laugh at in such a state of affairs:

> *The next, the spoils of fifty lovers wears*
> *Rich* Dandin's *brilliant favours grace her ears*
> *The necklace* Florio's *generous flame bestow'd*
> Clitander's *sparkling gems her fingers load;*
> *But now, her charms grown cheap by constant use,*
> *She sins for scarfs, clock'd stockings, knots and shoes.*

Exquisitely diverting, is it not? and turned as deftly as a goldsmith's work. One sees the poor whores doubled up by such pleasantries—as amused as Pope was when he read attacks on him like Phillips's and Dennis's . . . The poet concludes with the strictly insular statement:

> All *Frenchmen* are of *petit-maître* kind.

These extracts may suggest that Gay's first foreign tour was just one damned disappointment after another

—but allowance should be made for the convention of the times. Gay, after all, was writing in his established character of a Wit. And a wit was willy-nilly a cynic. So we have the spectacle of the Loving Countryman turned cynic. Like Dr. Johnson's remark about dogs walking on their hind legs, it is not done well, but the surprising thing is that it is done at all. Any examination of Gay's early works will prove abundantly that he did not easily wear even so much as a corner of the mantle of Molière and Voltaire, of Pope and Swift. The misanthropy of the age sat as unhappily on him, to begin with, as did the restraint of the rhymed couplet on his natural ebullience. He constrained himself later to the misanthropy as he constrained himself to the rhymed couplet. Both were necessary to complete public appreciation. But the manner of writing, after a time, will influence the manner of thinking (even supposing that most of the experiences quoted were not based on fact) ... It was not so much a case of the iron entering into Gay's soul as of the warm pulsing heart's-blood being let out of it.

The only other traceable work from Gay, during this year, was another *Epistle*, this time "to my worthy and ingenious friend W—— L—— Esq., author of that celebrated treatise in folio, the Land-Tax Bill." W—— L—— has been deciphered as William Lowndes, secretary to the Chancellor of the Exchequer. Here again we have a proof of Gay's capacity for attaining and retaining friendship. Surely with friend Pulteney out of the ministry—and the ministry a Whig ministry at that, Gay should have known better than to keep friends with Mr. Lowndes. But the man was incorrigible—he liked Lowndes and was amused to work out a short poem comparing that under-secretary to Homer and the classics because the Land-Tax Bill had naturally a large

circulation and was bound to raise a lot of money. . . .
Unimportant again as the *Epistle* is, Gay betrays himself
at the end of it as a staunch opposer to a standing army.
He might be uninterested in more detailed politics,
but he remained a convinced Tory on this point. He
exhorts Lowndes:

> Truce with thy dreaded pen; thy annals cease;
> Why need we armies when the land's in peace?
> Soldiers are perfect devils in their way,
> When once they're raised, they're cursed hard to lay.

It is a little sad to think that the most interesting part of the poem is now, not that Gay was against a standing army—but that Tories in general could ever have been against a standing army. *How does Fortune banter us!—* as Bolingbroke had already observed.

CHAPTER TWELVE

At Cockthorpe, Oxfordshire, with Lord Harcourt;
In Dijon, "rambling from place to place." 1718-1720.

"Let the mind be joyful of the present good, nor be sollicitous of what is to come."
MSS. TRANSLATION OF A LINE FROM HORACE,
ODE XVI, IN THE FORSTER COLLECTION

THE next two years of Gay's life are singularly bare ones as far as literary productions are concerned. But if he was not writing himself, he was doing everything that he could (together with Pope, Swift, Parnell and other of Prior's friends) to help collect subscriptions towards a new edition of Prior's collected poems. That unfortunate poet had been made the scapegoat of the previous Administration, and had escaped with his life from a badly-bungled "enquiry" into his affairs by the Whig Government, but without much else. And after the great ones had finished with him, it was obvious that he could expect little or no aid from the smaller fry, especially under a *règime* so particularly discouraging to poets of the wrong political colour. His original patron was dead; his late patron, Lord Oxford, lay under the shadow of the King's displeasure as much as he did himself. In such circumstances, his brother-poets rallied round Prior. There, each one of them might well think, but for the grace of God, go I.

How else did Gay fill in the early months of 1718? Where was he staying? Pope's Chiswick home was always open to him, Burlington House could spare him a room at any time, and my Lords Peterborough and Bathurst, together with Mr. William Pulteney and other out-of-office statesmen, were always delighted to welcome him in. When these hosts of his spoke of going to Court, they meant of course to the Court of the Prince of Wales at Richmond or at Leicester Fields. No self-respecting wit or Tory went near St. James's Palace, where a dull German king kept Court together with an ugly German mistress—the Duchess of Kendal—who sold His Majesty's assorted favours at a thousand pounds a time. In a (Tory) nutshell, age and its attendant vices of dullness, greed and gluttony were rampant at St. James's; youth, beauty and wit shone round the figures of the Prince and Princess of Wales—and of that company of wit was Gay.

Probably it was to amuse the Maids of Honour and their chaperon Mrs. Howard that he wrote those light, slight things, *Damon and Cupid*, and *Daphnis and Chloe*. Pope, though a less frequent attendant at Court, composed similar bagatelles to divert the same public. Those who care for such trifles may find them in the collected works of the period, but Gay and Pope did not monopolise the trade. Numerous lords could wield as pretty a pen as they on such subjects as my lady's fan or lap-dog, and frequently did. Much more important than the Court poems is the eclogue called *The Birth of the Squire*, which, while it cannot be ascribed to any one year, may certainly be accepted as belonging to this period of Gay's life. The lines are not good poetry (how often, alas, must the same thing be said of Gay's verse!) but if they had done no more than inspire Dr. Johnson's later lines beginning "Long-expected one-and-twenty," which it is quite arguable that they did, they would have been more than justified.

The Birth of the Squire is not so much a rake's progress as a country booby's progress, from the cradle to the grave. The country boobies, of course, had already been held up to gentle scorn in Addison's *Spectators;* they were indeed the favourite sport of the most urban-minded literary public since the Roman public of Horace. But there was even more sport to be got out of them at this juncture. Since the days of *The Spectator*, the country booby had enlarged his sphere. He was no longer confined to the country where, each succeeding week, he could let loose impotent abuse on Mr. Addison's word-pictures. The country squire (according to Gay and Pope and Swift and the Maids of Honour at least) had not only come up to town, but was now exerting his muddy influence in Parliament, and stifling the arts and killing all initiative at the Court of St. James's. He was ignorance and pomposity and shoddiness rolled into one. He was that worst of all things to a wit—Dullness personified.

In such circumstances the attack on country boobies in *The Birth of the Squire* was read with a double pleasure. Gay was always topical; he had, as Mr. Courthope has left on record, "a unique gift for discerning the drift of the public taste." His picture of the Squire, learning in youth "to lisp the names of all the hounds"; listening to the hunting boasts of his father, evading even elementary school lessons ("Why should he wiser prove than all his race?") seducing the milkmaid, breaking his collar-bone hunting, infringing those monstrous game laws which are the only laws he has the wit to understand, and eventually drinking himself to death, is again comparable to any picture of Hogarth's:

> Methinks I see him in his hall appear,
> Where the long table floats in clammy beer,
> 'Midst mugs and glasses scatter'd o'er the floor,
> Dead-drunk his servile crew supinely snore;

> Triumphant, o'er the prostrate brutes he stands,
> The mighty bumper trembles in his hands;
> Boldly he drinks, and like his glorious sires
> In copious gulps of potent ale expires.

Another *Epistle* belonging to this period was the one written to Paul Methuen. Little is known of Methuen beyond the fact that he came of a family which had served the country well in diplomacy and that he held a minor position in the Ministry. Obviously he had been generous to Gay and the *Epistle*, as usual, is Gay's way of saying thank you. But although he paid the prettiest compliments to Methuen, he was not so tactful concerning greater persons. Indeed, he seems to have set out on this occasion to make clear how art and culture were neglected in the reign of George the First:

> Why flourish'd verse in great Augustus' reign?
> He and Macænas lov'd the Muse's strain.
> But now that wight in poverty must mourn
> Who was (O cruel stars!) a poet born.

He continues with some of the bitterest and most-quoted lines that he ever wrote:

> Yet there are ways for authors to be great;
> Write rancorous libels to reform the State;
> Or if you choose more sure and ready ways
> Spatter a minister with fulsome praise;
> Launch out with freedom, flatter him enough;
> Fear not, all men are dedication-proof.

But it is not in him to end on a savage or angry note. He hastens to add:

> Yet let not me of grievances complain
> Who (though the meanest of the Muse's train)
> Can boast subscriptions to my humble lays
> And mingle profit with my little praise.

With June, the peak of the year was reached and London by then had grown too hot to hold the quality. The noblemen's houses, scattered like imposing doll's houses at various intervals through the brick village that was London, and sheltered from their neighbours by spreading trees, presented a blind face to the world. The leaves of the trees were thick with white dust cast up by the passing wagons and chariots; dust-sheets were spread over the Louis XIV furniture and half the servants left, on board wages, to get even more drunk than they did during the Season. . . . Bath was calling, Tonbridge was calling, the various spas of France were whispering their attractions—and those that could afford it were *en route* to them. But Pope was busy on another volume of his *Iliad* in June and had no time for the strenuous— and expensive delights of watering-places. He therefore gratefully accepted an offer of the late Tory Lord Chancellor, Lord Harcourt, to occupy his country seat at Stanton Harcourt, and incidentally honour that place by writing an epic there. At the same time Lord Harcourt invited Gay to join him at Cockthorpe, another estate of his which lay a few miles distant from Stanton Harcourt.

Lord Harcourt's life had fallen distinctly into two halves. During the reign of Queen Anne he had advanced slowly but steadily from Solicitor-General to Attorney-General, to a peerage—and finally to the Lord Chancellorship. After the Queen's death he had promptly retired to his country home, and never after endeavoured to take up a court or ministerial existence. Apart from this bare record the character of Lord Harcourt has faded into the nebulous outline which overtakes the characters of most human beings. It remains to his credit that he did not waste his time after 1714—first in parliamentary intrigues and then in denying those intrigues, as did his brother peers Bathurst and Bolingbroke, Pulteney and (on occasion) Chesterfield. Pope describes him as "The mouth of justice, oracle of law"—but the phrase remains a mere line to fill out a verse. He was three times married, unusual in a singularly un-uxorious age—and Pope arrived in Oxfordshire in time to contribute a graceful epitaph on his lately dead son and heir. (For that only the loan of the house at Stanton Harcourt might be considered worth while.) Gay presumably was to divert his host from dismal thoughts by cheerful prattle, while his friend Pope—together with Parnell—continued to grapple with Homer a few miles distant. Sometimes, we are told, they rode over to see each other. But singularly little remains of that Oxfordshire visit, except a well-known letter on the subject of two lovers struck to death by lightning while sheltering behind one of Lord Harcourt's hay-cocks. This letter has been variously described as being originally (a) from Gay to Fortescue and (b) from Pope to Lady Mary Wortley Montagu, and is only one example of the confusion which has sometimes resulted from the fact that the difference in the handwriting of Pope and of Gay was so slight as to be practically undetectable—as any one who has studied their original letters in the manuscript room of the British Museum may see for himself. Apart from the problem of authorship, however, the letter is unimportant.

Not content with epitaphs and translations, and a highly literary flirtation with Lady Mary, Pope also found time to amuse himself at Stanton Harcourt with redecorating the Scriblerian burlesque on Bishop Burnet's

History of my own Times. Gay, on the contrary, did nothing. And how well these methods compare with that earlier summer holiday propounded to John Caryll in which, Gay declared, Pope would not allow himself to be interrupted in his morning studies but he (Gay) might be interrupted just as much as Caryll pleased! In the same way it may be supposed he interrupted Harcourt, or Harcourt interrupted him, all that summer at Cockthorpe—and nothing at all was written but much amusing gossip and tittle-tattle of the Hanoverian Courts was relayed to Queen Anne's late Minister.

What else remains to relate of this time? That Swift, from Dublin, still worked wonders in obtaining subscriptions for Prior's works; that Lady Mary Wortley Montagu and her husband, returned ingloriously from Constantinople had settled themselves into a new house at Twickenham to be near the famous Mr. Pope; that Mr. Handel had left the wing of my Lord Burlington for an appointment under the Duke of Chandos at Canons; that the war with Spain—renewed the moment that Walpole had taken himself outside the sphere of influence—was conducting itself, after a first dashing naval victory—in the desultory and unsatisfactory fashion of wars and adding more to the National Debt than to the national prestige; that money was cheap; and that the South Sea Company was introducing itself, more and more, as a great national self-help scheme and a topic of conversation amongst all the educated people of the day. His Majesty the King (induced to it no doubt by large presents of South Sea stock to the Duchess of Kendal) was himself the Governor. Only Walpole, in retirement, still saw flaws in the scheme, but his captiousness was, naturally enough, attributed to spite because he had not been consulted.

The close of the summer brought the Quality back

to town again—just in time to buy and read the new volume of Prior's collected works. If Homer in English had been a success, then so was Prior's master, Martial. Prior's best-seller rewarded him to the tune of four thousand pounds. This munificent sum was promptly doubled by his still faithful patron, Lord Oxford, and the grateful poet was enabled to buy a small estate in Essex in which to enjoy that *ruris honoribus* which was every Englishman's avowed ambition. . . . Virtue rewarded so amply must have been a gratifying sight to other penurious poets: they rejoiced at Prior's success as heartily as they hoped one day to achieve it themselves.

Doubtless the Scriblerus members would have rejoiced just as whole-heartedly, if their merriment had not been shattered, in October, by the sudden death of Thomas Parnell. He was not yet forty—but death in those days took small account of age. It is certain that the suddenness of this news shocked the other members of the Scriblerus Club. Swift had tried hard to make Bolingbroke as much the patron of Parnell (in the palmy days before 1714) as Oxford was the patron of Prior; but as often with his good intentions, they had failed. Parnell was never more than a minor Augustan writer with one good poem to his credit—and a personal charm which endeared him much to other poets, especially to Pope and Gay. But even in the midst of their despondence the two poets remembered the unexpected success of Prior's collected works. They began to collect together and edit what it is inevitable to describe as the slender remains of poor Parnell; and when that was done Gay began to consider a collected works edition of his own poetry. He, too, had suffered like Prior from the downfall of the Tories; might not he, too, like Prior, reap the reward now of virtue and of patience?

There were several excellent reasons why he could

not do so. In the first place Prior was an experienced Minister—deprived it is true by his "mean birth" from holding the full title—but nevertheless perfectly acquainted over a long period of apprenticeship with the work of a plenipotentiary. It was for his work in connection with the Treaty of Utrecht that he had been displaced and subsequently imprisoned—not for his work as a poet. Besides, he was Gay's senior by nineteen years . . . He had, as it were, nineteen years' start in notoriety. Perhaps it was foolish, after all, to think of being able to make a success of a ' Collected Works.'

The idea, however, lingered in Gay's mind after the manner of pleasant ideas, and seems to have precluded him from more active composition. Then another and more important death than Parnell's held up the living traffic and forced men to think for one moment, like their Elizabethan ancestors, of corruption, and the grave. Addison had always said he would like to die in the summer, because then, surrounded with natural beauties, his mind was filled most with thoughts of God. That wish was granted—as so many of his wishes were granted, but before he died that June, in the forty-seventh year of his life, an incident occurred which deserves attention. Joseph Warton and Macaulay have both described it and Macaulay, whose account is the more grammatical, puts it in these words:

> "Addison sent to beg Gay, who was then living by his wits about town, to come to Holland House. Gay went, and was received with great kindness. To his amazement his forgiveness was implored by the dying man. Poor Gay, the most good-natured and simple of mankind, could not imagine what he had to forgive. . . . There was, however, something wrong, the remembrance of which

weighed on Addison's mind and which he declared himself anxious to repair. He was in a state of extreme exhaustion, and the parting was doubtless a friendly one on both sides."

Warton goes further and suggests that the damage Addison had done was "in respect to his (Gay's) gaining some appointment from the Court."

If this were so, the contrition on Addison's part was both noble and necessary. He had doubtless hurt many people in the course of his career—what statesman can avoid it?—but never one so innocent and inoffensive as Gay. Perhaps Gay's name, after his *Letter to a Lady*, had been put forward by some well-wisher as deserving of a place: did Addison, influential, State-Secretary Addison, damn with faint praise *then*? And if so, was it because he knew Gay to be a close friend of his old enemy Pope? Certainly if the King had had anything to do with the appointment it would not have been difficult to dissuade him from helping somebody who had written in praise of "*cette diablesse, Madame La Princesse*"—and perhaps some word to him from Addison tipped the verdict the wrong way. Some such affair must have occurred to have aroused Addison later to such an enthusiasm of contrition. He was showing the world how a Christian could die—and since Gay was a necessary adjunct to the picture, Gay was called in. Praiseworthy though such behaviour may be the best part of the story is that which demonstrates Gay's absolute ignorance of any offence done him by Addison. Ignorant of offence—and yet nursed upon the self-same hill as Pope—ignorant of offence, and yet a disciple of the great Dr. Swift! Here is a triumph of character indeed.

As soon as June was ended Gay fled, as usual, from

town. Though he might, as a kindly person, regret Addison's death, the change in the secretaryship of State augured well, for James Craggs—his old Hanover acquaintance—was appointed to it. And here we come to an adventure which has given some trouble to earlier biographers—for he went abroad, and apparently he went alone. Now that of itself is so momentous that many of the biographers have preferred to doubt the whole proceeding. What—Gay the sycophant, the impoverished wit, the haunter of levees, the place-man—go jaunting abroad and apparently unaccompanied? It is manifestly impossible. Letters, however, exist to prove that the impossible sometimes happens. There is the one from Pope remarking with some surprise that Gay always had "a strange desire to see foreign lands," —and there is one from Gay, headed Dijon, written to his much-admired Mrs. Howard, and dated September 8th, 1719:

> "If it be absolutely necessary that I make an apology for not writing, I must give you an account of very bad physicians, and a fever which I had at Spa, which confined me a month, but I do not see that I need make the least excuse, or that I can find any reason for writing to you at all— for can you believe that I would wish to converse with you if it were not for the pleasure to hear you talk again? Then why should I write to you when there is no possibility of receiving an answer? I have been looking everywhere since I came into France to find out some objects that might take you from my thoughts, that my journey might seem less tedious; but since nothing could ever do it in England, I can much less expect it in France.

"I am rambling from place to place. In about a month I hope to be at Paris, and in the next month to be in England, and the next minute to see you. I am now at Dijon at Burgundy where, last night at an Ordinary, I was surprised by a question from an English gentleman, whom I had never seen before; hearing my name, he asked me if I had any relation or acquaintance with myself and when I told him I knew of no such person, he assured me that he was an intimate acquaintance of Mr. Gay's at London. There was a Scotch gentleman, who at supper-time was teaching some French gentlemen the force and propriety of the French language, and, which is seen very commonly, a young English gentleman with a Jacobite governor. A French marquis drove an Abbé from the table by railing against the vast riches of the church, and another marquis, who squinted, endeavoured to explain transubstantiation: 'that a thing might not be what it really appeared to be, my eyes,' said he 'may convince you: I seem at present to be looking at you but, on the contrary, I see quite on the other side of the table.' I do not believe that the argument converted one of the heretics present; for all that I learned from him was, that to believe transubstantiation it is necessary not to see the thing you look at.

"So much I have observed in the conversation and manners of the *people*. As for the *animals* of the country, it abounds with bugs, which are exceedingly familiar with strangers; and as for *plants*, garlick seems to be the favourite production of the country, though for my part, I think the vine preferable to it; when I publish my travels at large I shall be more particular; in order to which, to-morrow I set out for Lyons, from there to Montpelier and so to Paris; and soon after I shall pray that the winds may be favourable, I mean, to bring you from Richmond to London, or me from London to Richmond. . . ."

Years later, Lord Orrery was to remark to Pope, " Mr. Gay's letters do him no honour as a wit, but they are, as they must be, the letters of an honest man" . . . Here at least it may be declared that Lord Orrery was partly wrong. If this is not a witty letter, then no other letter published in the same year could lay claim to any wit either. In it Gay is displaying, like a peacock, himself at his most decorative. He is wooing Mrs. Howard here with the best part of him—his wit, and simply out of a very human desire to display himself to the best advantage. . . . The peacock unfurled his tail with a dry rustle like a lady opening the sticks of her fan; and the peahen? She took it as complacently and quietly as peahens always do. Mrs. Howard was not born in the eighteenth century without knowing how to conceal, to perfection, any signs of irregular enthusiasm.

CHAPTER THIRTEEN

1720. 'Poems on Several Occasions.' 'Acis and Galatea.' The South Sea Bubble.

"*To tell you the truth I am almost South Sea mad.*"
A LETTER FROM MRS. E. MOLESWORTH
TO MRS. HOWARD, MARCH, 1720

GAY did not have long to wait to imitate Prior with his collected works. After his return from his solo tour of France, and at a time which cannot be estimated more closely than that it was "some time in the first quarter" of 1720, the celebrated publishers and booksellers, Mr. Jacob Tonson and Mr. Bernard Lintot, co-operated in producing *Poems on Several Occasions*, a collection in two volumes of the works of Mr. Gay. Here was an excellent example of what Pope had called Gay's gift for 'cementing' friendships, for it must have required something quite as tough and as adhesive as cement to bring together the two rivals.

As to the actual date—if Gay had had any say in the matter he would have chosen January. *Rural Sports* had appeared in January; and *Trivia*. Whatever month it was, the publication was a success. (Not so great a success as Prior's perhaps—but then Prior was a good deal older than Gay, had written more and had had a *cause célèbre* to give him advantages in the way of publicity.) Altogether he made about a thousand pounds from *Poems on Several Occasions*—only a quarter of what Prior had made but still a staggering sum for poetry. Lord Burlington and the Duke of Leeds both took 50 copies; Mr. Pulteney took 25; Lord Bathurst, Lord

Warwick, Mr. Pelham and Mr. Craggs each took 10 copies and the Earl of Essex, Lord Hervey, the Hon. Simon Harcourt, Lord Lonsdale, Lady Masham, the Duke of Queensberry and the Earl of Stair took five or more. Mr. Robert Walpole put himself down for a couple and others in the list were the more-to-be-expected Arbuthnot, Congreve, Bolingbroke, Pope, Kneller, the two Miss Blounts, Lady Mary Wortley Montagu and Handel.

It was thoughtful of Handel to show, by buying one of Gay's books, that he remembered that author's earlier collaboration with him in *Acis and Galatea*, for he was fully occupied just then with plans for the foundation of a Royal Academy of Music, built up on a capital of £50,000 with the King as chief patron. Interest in Italian opera had temporarily slumped in 1720, but interest in new financial ventures was very strong indeed. What better, the promoters of the Academy thought, than to harness these two things together and by means of money pull up Italian opera again to the place of honour it had occupied for so long? If companies in that year of grace could be formed successfully for casting sawdust again into plain planks, for making perpetual motion a marketable commodity and (best of all) "for carrying on an undertaking of great advantage, but nobody to know what it is," then surely a Company for the promotion of Grand Opera was a comparatively safe bet. There was, at least, no difficulty in obtaining subscribers for it.

Who, after a lapse of two hundred years, can begin to solve the mysteries of the South Sea Bubble? And who, in an age which still produces its Hatrys, Staviskys and Krugers can afford to smile superciliously at the simple Georgians, who believed that making money had suddenly become as simple as taking pennies out of a blind man's tin? The speculative frenzy was not confined to England. John Law and his Mississippi shares threw France in 1719 into the same greedy ferment that Sir John Blount threw his compatriots into, in the early months of 1720. And both men, without a doubt, facilitated their financial 'business' by every means of bribery and corruption that occurred to them. The gross, cloudy bubble of the South Sea Company, swaying insecurely above the cunning pipe that had blown it, could afford to have expended upon its behalf more than a million pounds in bribes to men in public office.

But though it gave rise to the biggest financial scandal in the country's history, the Company was by no means entirely conceived in sin. In 1711 Robert Harley had seen the advantages of making over the floating debt to some other concern than the Government and, after some bidding from such respectable institutions as the Bank of England, had disposed of it to the South Sea Company and steered the Bill for the formation of this Company of Merchants safely through both Houses. The South Sea merchants were to be paid six per cent interest on as much of the National Debt as they had taken over until the debt was finally paid off and to be given a monopoly of trade in the South Seas. True, when all the Bill's fine paragraphs were finally boiled down all that this monopoly amounted to was an extremely limited permission to trade with Spanish (Central and South) America. But the Treaty of Utrecht had later enlarged the Company's scope by adding to this permission the Assiento, a far more valuable monopoly of the traffic in negroes from Africa to America. So far, so good. The Company remained in existence, doing neither very ill nor very well, but on the whole justified of its inceptors. It conducted a mediocre trade in mahogany, potatoes, tobacco and other American goods, a very much better trade in the Assiento, and took in annual interest from the Government amounting to six hundred thousand pounds.

And there the matter might have rested; certainly if Walpole had never left the Ministry the South Sea Company would have remained a Company and not a Bubble. Walpole was no extremist, and if Sir John Blount's proposal that he should take over the whole of the National Debt of fifty-one millions, instead of merely part of it, was not extreme, then nothing was. With Walpole away, however, there was nobody left in the Stanhope-Sunderland Government to oppose Sir John Blount, or even to know what he was talking about. Sir John was determined at all costs to get Parliamentary assent to his plans and oiled the way with the utmost assiduity, with discreet gifts of a hundred South Sea shares here and a thousand shares there, and bonuses to 122 noble Lords and 462 faithful Commons —who all supposed that their own pockets would benefit enormously by being stockholders in a Company whose liabilities were suddenly bumped up from a debt of ten to a debt of fifty-one millions. No wonder that later the word most frequently applied to the South Sea Company was madness!

At the beginning of the year the affair was still of small proportions. But soon the news of Sir John Blount's proposal to the Government was common property and the publicity thus achieved resulted in a hopeful run on the shares. There was talk after that of a third subscription being issued. If Sir John had proposed then (as well as taking over the rest of the National Debt) that he should also take over exclusive rights to the opals which lay on the mountains of the moon, still more money would have been forthcoming for so enchanting a scheme. This, however, did not occur to him. But what *had* occurred to him stood him in good stead. It was known that he was well in with the members of both Houses; that the King (and the Duchess of Kendal, who held a huge slice of shares), both approved of the scheme; that the Prince of Wales (whose palm also had been oiled) went so far on this occasion as to agree with his father. If Court and country and royal family so harmonised in opinion what was a weak-minded, heavily over-bribed Government to do?

It is not suggested of course that sophisticated persons such as the Prince of Wales, Mrs. Howard and the Maids of Honour, and distinguished lords such as Hervey, Bathurst and Chesterfield really *believed* all that the South Sea prospectus said. But they and their prototypes were shrewd enough to know that the more the shares were cried up, the higher the price at which they would be able to sell out. Robert Walpole himself, from his country retreat, bought low and sold ultimately at a thousand per cent profit, "fully satisfied." He had never believed that the Company could carry the additional debt it now proposed to undertake, but he knew that a fool was born every minute—none better—and that there were hundreds of fools ready to purchase his intrinsically worthless stock. He was right. They rushed, frenziedly falling over themselves in the effort to become shareholders in the most glorious money-for-jam scheme England had ever known. When they could not buy South Sea stock, they bought anything else that happened to be going. The *London Journal* described the situation:

> "The hurry of stock-jobbing bubbles has been so great this week as to exceed all ever known. Nothing but running about from coffee-house to coffee-house and subscribing without knowing

what the proposals were. The constant cry was
' for God's sake let us subscribe to something; we
don't care what it is.'"

In such a furious commotion, when princes, lords,
ladies, merchants, actresses, bishops, bankers, laundresses
and country doctors were all losing their heads; when
Threadneedle Street and 'Change alley were "turned
into counting-houses and blocked with chairs and
desks," it was small wonder that simple poets should
also be involved. Prior subscribed heavily, and wrote:
"I am lost in the South Sea; the roaring of the waves
and the madness of the people are justly put together.
It is all madder than St. Anthony's dream." What
happened to Prior eventually is very much what happened
to John Gay.

The *Poems on Several Occasions* brought Gay, as aforesaid, a profit of a thousand pounds. No sooner had the news of this been circulated than a host of advisers flew upon him and besought him to follow their directions. Erasmus Lewis, cautious Welshman, advised an investment in the Funds; Arbuthnot, still more cautious Scotsman, advised keeping tight hold of it—a box under the mattress and trust in Providence. The majority of his acquaintance, however, begged him to buy a nice safe annuity with it so that, however events might develop in the future, he would be provided for for the rest of his days.

First and foremost of these advisers of course was Swift. 1720 happened to be the year in which Swift, torn between Stella and Vanessa, and embarrassed beyond words by the latter's arrival in Ireland, might well have been excused from other matters. But deeply involved though he was in this new complication, he could still find time to write to his poor innocent friend Gay, and work out a budget for him in which, by means of a carefully-applied annuity, he could make himself sure, as the Dean put it, of a clean shirt and a shoulder of mutton a day.

Had it been any other year Swift's advice might possibly have prevailed—but to ask Gay to think of anything as dull as clean shirts and mutton at a time when every one else was thinking of gold and diamonds and slaves and ivory was asking too much. The "simple, good-natured" man rebelled. He had, on occasion, the obstinacy of all simple good-natured people and now he showed just how obstinate he could be. James Craggs the Younger had recently presented both him and Pope with a large slice of South Sea stock: now Gay augmented this by putting the whole of his thousand pounds profit from the poems into the South Sea Company as well. It is somehow typical that we should know this, and that Pope should never have disclosed what he did with *his* shares from Craggs. He afterwards circulated a kind of senatorial rumour that he neither lost nor gained over the whole business, but unless he threw his shares into the Thames it is difficult to see how he could have compassed this ethical but highly unusual end. But whatever he did with his own shares it is known that he added his entreaties to Swift's over the affair of Gay's money. But Gay would not budge. He would have nothing to do with the preposterous idea of an annuity. He was no longer a Coming Poet, he was a poet who had arrived and who, now he was there, meant to *stay* there. A clean shirt and a leg of mutton a day, forsooth! What a way to talk to the author of *Poems on Several Occasions*, and to the holder of stocks which were daily increasing in value; the close friend of Mrs. Howard, and the new friend of the Duke and Duchess of Queensberry!

Years afterwards, if Gay cared to look back on the black year of 1720, he might have remembered that though he lost much in that year he also gained the warmest friend of his life in Catherine Hyde, Duchess of Queensberry. Presumably it was at the Prince's Court that he and Pope had first met this blazing, amazing young beauty. She was twenty years old and still in the first year of her marriage. Her husband was a Scot whose family had done useful work for Queen Anne in the troubled times before the Union with Scotland, but from all accounts he was a slow talker and thinker and nothing of a wit. He provided a title for his bride but little intellectual companionship—and the duchess was an intellectual *manquée*; she had had the usual scrappy education and could never have coped with the classical prattle of Lady Mary Wortley Montagu but she had, for all that, more of what Dr. Johnson would have called "a bottom of good sense" than Lady Mary. Not for nothing was she descended from the lineage of Clarendons and Rochesters. If her mind had ever received more than the mere surface cultivation that it did receive, much of her unbounded energy might have gone exploring into those regions which all her life she saw from a distance but could never reach. As it was, the energy (and the ability) were forced to run in more domestic channels. Her extreme fastidiousness concerning table linen and table manners at that time were so noticeable as to gain her a reputation for eccentricity, especially since she enforced the observation of her own rules whenever she entertained. It was a small way in which to enforce her authority but it was a way, and so she used it. To her indigenous intelligence was also added extreme beauty of person; but just as the intelligence had never been really cultivated so the beauty also was left to run wild. In youth, as in age, the Duchess was remarkable for her almost sacrilegious disregard of fashion. If her beauty triumphed above that of her contemporaries, as it certainly did, then this was because it evolved from an inward core—opening petal after petal like a flower, instead of being plastered on and built up from the outside. Her figure was apparently as lovely as her face, and Pope, writing of her with that odd mixture of coarseness and compliment which was the mode, complained:

> If Queensberry to strip there's no compelling,
> Then from a handmaid we must take a Helen . . .

—a rhyme to make others wince beside the Duchess. Pope's friend Jervas has painted her in the costume of a milkmaid—an affectation which was about the only concession to popular taste that she ever made. If he was sensible he did not waste compliments on her while he worked. There are just occasionally women who are bored by praises of their person, and the Duchess had found her own beauty a tedious subject ever since Prior, with the best intentions for every one, had written her up when she was still a sub-dèbutante in *The Female Phæton*:

> "Thus Kitty, beautiful and young
>   And wild as colt untam'd
> Bespoke the Fair from whence she sprung
>   With little rage inflam'd:
>
> 'Must Lady Jenny frisk about,
>   And visit with her cousins?
> At balls must she make all the rout
>   And bring home hearts by dozens?

Portrait of Catherine Hyde, Duchess of Queensberry, attributed to Jervas.

What has she better, pray, than I,
  What hidden charms to boast,
That all mankind for her should die
  Whilst I am scarce a toast?

Dearest Mama! For once let me
  Unchain'd my fortune try;
I'll have my earl as well as she,
  Or know the reason why.'

Fondness prevail'd, Mama gave way;
  Kitty, at heart's desire
Obtain'd the chariot for a day
  And set the world on fire."

The year of the Bubble was a year of important events for a great many of the persons concerned in the final catastrophe, and in those early months, after Parliament had given its gracious consent to the handing over of the National Debt to the Company, and when South Sea stock was rising by fifties and hundreds into the regions of a thousand pounds for a hundred pounds' worth of stock . . . and when the Third Subscription was selling like the legendary hot cakes (and burning, like the hot cakes, the fingers which held it) it may be worth while to try to pick out some of the individual reasons for remembrance. The Queensberrys might remember the year as the first year of their marriage, and of their introduction to London society. Pope could remember it as the year in which he flitted with his mother from Chiswick, to the pleasant white house lying almost on the lip of the river at Twickenham, the year in which he was "busy laying out his pleasaunce," with the company of the convalescent Maid of Honour Molly Lepell to cheer him while he worked, and Lady Mary

Wortley Montagu back from Turkey and exchanging the gallantest *billets-doux* with him. Prior might remember it as the year when he first settled down as country squire in his Essex home and enjoyed there all the happiness left to him after the collapse of the South Sea. Mrs. Howard might remember it as the year when the Prince of Wales first conferred upon her the honour of making her his mistress, even while the Princess of Wales was *her* mistress; and a year which—although she had done very well in the South Sea—her husband contrived to make miserable by his frequent threats and abuse from the Palace of St. James's. The Burlingtons might remember it as the year in which one of their dearest projects, the Royal Academy of Music, was founded—and the year in which they transferred their musical affections from Handel to Handel's own rival, Bononcini. Handel himself might remember it as the year in which he was released from the gilded cage of the Duke of Chandos' Canons, and enabled to take part in the exciting task of choosing the singers for the next season of Italian opera. . . . Did he, with so absorbing an occupation and with more majestic music in his ears than he had ever yet put down on paper, notice the roaring of the waves of the South Sea? He was free: and comfortably pensioned—and before he left Canons he had been able to give, amongst other things, a select audition of that enchanting cantata *Acis and Galatea*, to which Gay had contributed the libretto five years earlier.

Meanwhile other people with less distracting occupations were able to devote all their energies to the new game of making money with stocks and shares. "The whole world," it has been said, "was engaged in a conspiracy to run up the prices of shares." Within a few months over a hundred 'bubbles' with a capital of about three hundred million pounds between them were put on the market. Besides the chimerical implausibilities of these, the largest Company of all, the South Sea one, may well have looked as sound and rock-like as St. Paul's. And so it might have remained if Sir John Blount had been content to let well alone. But he did not like the look of the other Companies on the market. Their very existence cast a shadow over the tremulous glories of his own pet bubble. Their manifest absurdities might make ignorant people consider that the South Sea Company was also based on illusions and absurdities. In reasoning thus he reasoned rightly, but he took the very worst psychological course possible. By dint of his influence and the influence of other well-to-do financiers the King was persuaded, soon after a return from his beloved Hanover in June, to knit the royal brows and express royal disapproval at the general trend of events. The result was "a bill for suppressing unlawful bubbles," on June 11th, which succeeded in pricking the majority of the smaller bubbles and bankrupting a great many ignominious semptresses, whores, footmen, parsons, farmers, shopkeepers, and sea-captains, that nobody had ever heard of. For the moment all went as Sir John had expected. The rival companies were wiped out, but the South Sea Company, the Bubble of Bubbles, the Bubble Royal, went on swelling gently all the while.

When John Gay's humble profits, invested in the self-same Company, were enlarged some time in June to the respectable proportions of twenty thousand pounds, his anxious friends renewed their urgings. It was all, they felt, too good to last. If he sold out now, he would have enough to live on in splendour for the rest of his days. Would the silly man kick against what was so manifestly to his own advantage? The silly man would and did. In the tremendous exhilaration of being rich he apparently forgot his favourite Horace—or he might have remembered a very apposite piece of advice from that author to one Licinius:

> "In adverse hours show ye a man of mind
> And mettle; yet not less thou'lt wisely know
> To reef the prosperous sails, when comes the wind
> Too good to blow."

Here, without a doubt, was the wind too good to blow, —but Gay simply would not believe it. The explanation, nevertheless, is a comparatively simple one, and is best shown by quoting an extract from Sir Walter Besant on the same subject:

> "Nobody knew . . . what enabled people to believe in the Mississippi and South Sea schemes. To the French company a vast country called Louisiana, was assigned. To the latter, nothing more than an exceedingly limited permission to trade. . . . It is wonderful that the people should believe in inexhaustible mines of wealth to be got at when the Spaniards during two hundred years had found no such mines. *Probably they did not think of it in this way but regarded the shares, like the shares of the smaller bubbles, just as a means of making money by buying cheap and selling dear.*"

The key sentence of that paragraph has been italicized. It exactly expresses what ninety per cent of the subscribers undoubtedly did think. They were sceptics, and many of them immoral sceptics. They bought cheap and sold dear—and some of them who bought too late were left to hold the baby. But Gay was not a sceptic—not even a moral one. He was an honest man who believed what he read on prospectuses, and if he had been asked why on earth he was holding on to his shares when he had made over a hundred and fifty per cent profit he would doubtless have replied that he was holding on because the South Sea Company was a good investment —because once trade really started going again (now this Spanish war was over) the Company would be an even better thing to hold shares in. In other words he honestly believed in the mines of wealth in the Indies, and the ivories, and the ruby-strewn coast, and hardly any one else did.

In July a hundred pounds worth of shares stood at a thousand pounds, and subscribers sold out, recognising the first breath of that wind "too prosperous to blow," but the Bubble belied its name in that it did not burst with the soap-in-the-eye suddenness of a real bubble. Rather it swelled and discoloured like a tumour which, when it finally bursts, disgusts the onlookers with sight and odour. Sir John Blount's plan was beginning to go wrong. Rumours began to spread that if the hundreds of other companies, recently killed by the new Bill, had been based on improbabilities and had ruined thousands of shareholders might not the South Sea Company also be fundamentally unsound? At first a mere whisper in the coffee-houses, the rumour grew and grew. Nervous shareholders began to unload blocks of shares on the market, communicating their fears to others the minute they had taken the profit. On September 2nd the shares which had stood at a thousand pounds had dropped to seven hundred and fifty, and rumbles of disapproval were heard. Less nervous shareholders still pooh-poohed any idea of unsoundness but knowing what a panic could do should it come on they prudently sold out. Then the rush began; far more were selling now than buying. A week later the same shares were £350 down on *that* price.

In the first two weeks of October they stood at £280 and £240 respectively. The world of the Georgians was crashing about their ears. They ran hither and thither with whatever they succeeded in rescuing out of the crash—like ants suddenly disturbed under a stone, rushing hither and thither with their cumbrous opaque white eggs. . . . By the end of October shares in the South Sea were unsaleable at any price.

After the tumult had died away it was possible to observe the absolute impartiality of whatever deity had presided. The just and the unjust were both shackled together in hideous losses (if they had held on too long) or in colossal gains; the actual financial situation of the country remained unaffected by this General Post, though individuals were alternately ruined or enriched. Sir Godfrey Kneller lost heavily. The King and the Duchesses of Schulenberg and Kendal, the Prince and Princess of Wales all had the luck associated with Royalty. The Duke of Wharton claimed to have dropped £120,000; Mr. Jacob Tonson made another fortune. Old Sarah, Duchess of Marlborough, made a £100,000 profit. Dr. Radcliffe lost everything and poor *Night Thoughts* Young lost heavily as well. Sir Isaac Newton, with a business perspicacity not usually associated with scientists, made a comfortable £4,000. But to make up for this the Duke of Chandos lost three hundred thousand and the Duke of Portland and Lords Lonsdale and Irwin were only saved from penury by being made colonial governors. None of these cases was an exception: each one could be multiplied a hundred times over. The Bubble had burst and it is safe to say that not one person in ten escaped from the drenching of cold reality that followed the bursting.

As for Gay—not only his thousand pounds of literary profit but his two thousand pounds worth of shares from James Craggs, and his extra seventeen thousand pounds profit were all vanished into thin air. A few weeks before this catastrophe completed itself, however—and while the poor subscribers must have been waiting for the price changes with bated breath—Mr. Tonson saw fit to ask Mr. Gay to settle a few financial details. Gay's answer is more in sorrow than in anger:

"*Friday morning.*
"I received your letter with accounts of the Books you had delivered. I have not seen Mr. Lintot's account, but shall take the first opportunity to call upon him. I cannot think your letter consists in the utmost civility, in five lines to press me twice to make up my account just at a time when it is impracticable to sell out of the stocks in which my fortune is engaged. Between Mr. Lintot and you the greater part of the money is received, and I imagine you have a sufficient number of books in your Hands for the security of the rest. To go to the strictness of the matter, I own that my note engages me to make the whole payment in the beginning of September; had it been in my power, I had not given you occasion to send to me, for I can assure you I am as impatient and uneasy to pay the money I owe, as some men are to receive it [a nasty one for Tonson] and 'tis no small mortification to me to refuse you so reasonable a request, which is that I may no longer be obliged to you.
"I am, sir,
"Your most humble servant,
"J. GAY.

On the whole a very dignified excuse, which hints but

does not divulge what Gay really thought of Mr. Tonson as a fellow-human.

The Tonson affair and similar worries added their weight to the intolerable worry of the South Sea shares. When it was too late to hope any more and obvious that all was irretrievably lost, Gay, we are told, fell "desperately ill"—of dejection and disappointment. It is at such a moment that one hears the stern verdict of Dr. Johnson reverberating down the years—"Such is not the character of a Hero." But Gay never pretended to be a hero. He was a little man who had never been really comfortably off—and whose dreams of being comfortably off had just been, he fancied, cruelly quenched for ever. Other biographers have recorded the event as if Gay had been in a minority to be so foolish as to be gulled by the Bubble—and certainly in a minority to be subsequently depressed. Whereas both happenings were really happenings in which at least fifty per cent of his fellow-countrymen were concerned. The minority were people like Dr. Radcliffe who, after losing his five thousand pounds, remarked that it only meant climbing five thousand pairs of stairs more.... Meanwhile the *débâcle* continued. The Stanhope-Sunderland Government collapsed. No Government so implicated could possibly have survived. The Postmaster-General committed suicide, the Chancellor of the Exchequer was expelled from the House and imprisoned, James Craggs died tactfully of smallpox, Lord Stanhope fell into an apoplectic fit whilst defending himself in a House full of members far more guilty than himself, and died of it—the estates of the Directors of the Company were confiscated, Sir John Blount and hundreds of others fled the country and the cashier—to provide an artistic finish—absconded with the register and till. All the King's horses and all the King's men could never put the greatest financial scheme in the world on to its feet again—though strangely enough the Company, a very much attenuated and shrunken ghost, continued to linger on. . . .

Through all these recriminations and reverberations Gay lay ill at Hampstead. Dr. Arbuthnot attended him and the Duchess of Queensberry immediately constituted herself his nurse. Pope, from the far-off haunts of Twickenham, wrote charming letters to him, and owned that if his mother had not been ill at the very same time nothing would have kept him from Gay's bedside. There is, unfortunately, every reason to believe that Pope was not above using his mother as a Bunbury when it suited his purpose; but at this time his mother actually *was* ill—and he meant every word he said.

Exactly where Gay lay at Hampstead is not discoverable. He had in the past frequently paid visits to Dick Steele there—at Steele's cottage opposite ' The Load of Hay,' which lay, he declared, "in a solitude between Hampstead and London." And F. E. Barnes, in his *Records of Hampstead*, states that Gay, "falling ill on one occasion, was carefully tended by his friend." But in 1720 he was certainly being nursed by Lady Queensberry, and Steele, who had been one of the few people to fulminate in print against the South Sea Company, was intensely occupied at this period with pamphlets and Fleet Street schemes, and so would hardly have been at Hampstead. It is possible his house was borrowed by Arbuthnot for Gay's convalescence on account of Hampstead's much purer air. There—if it was there—Gay came slowly, very slowly, back to life and hope. He ' worked off ' his despondency eventually in a *Panegyrical Epistle to Mr. Thomas Snow*—which was published early the next year. In this he seems to be apostrophising himself and other poets rather than Mr. Snow:

> "Why did 'Change Alley waste thy precious hours
> Amongst the fools who gaped for golden showers?
> No wonder if we found some poets there
> Who live on fancy, and can feed on air.
> No wonder they were caught by South Sea schemes
> Who ne'er enjoy'd a Guinea but in dreams;
> No wonder that their Third Subscriptions sold
> For millions of imaginary gold."

There is a touch of unusual bitterness here. Gay had lived and learnt—but he could not be easy under the learning. Swift once wrote to Vanessa, "The best maxim I know in life is to drink your coffee when you can, and when you cannot, be easy without it." It was a maxim he never applied himself; and Gay—a far smaller man—had had *his* cup of coffee dashed from his lips just as he had been about to drink; he might, in the circumstances, be allowed a touch of bitterness.

A less personal slant on events appears in this piece of satire, taken from a contemporary newspaper:

> "A rat of uncommon size having been taken alive in the South Sea House, the mob laid violent hands upon the poor creature, and without proceeding according to law, carried him to a pillory erected for that Purpose in Broad Street, where they nailed his ears, and over his head was written: 'A Director of the South Sea.' The inscription so exasperated the populace that the poor creature was first pelted and then blown up."

CHAPTER FOURTEEN

1721-1722. 'Panegyrical Epistle to Mr. Thomas Snow.' 'The Shepherd's Week' (third edition). Another Visit to Bath.

> "*It is a miserable thing to live in suspense;
> It is the life of a spider.*"
> SWIFT: 'THOUGHTS ON VARIOUS SUBJECTS'

THE illness from which Gay had been suffering in 1720 was later to be an old enemy of his—colitis. And part of the penalty attached to that unpleasant indisposition is intense depression both during it and during convalescence. It pulled Gay down to the deepest Slough of Despond he had ever known—and not all the brisk, well-meant attentions of the young Duchess, the compliments of the Duke, or the warm wishes of Pope could succeed in making him really happy. Besides, one of the drawbacks of convalescence was that, under Arbuthnot's orders, he had to knock off wine drinking—and all his life Gay had had an almost superstitious reverence for the inspiration to be derived from wine. Take wine from him—and he could no longer write, or so he believed.

It is possible to see how the superstition arose. For Gay, like his dead friend Parnell, was subject to recurrent fits of melancholy. It was part of the volatility of his nature—and no amount of invocations to the Goddess Reason, who reigned supreme over the eighteenth century, could ever cure him of it. He needed wine, occasionally, as more than a mere symbol of good company; he wanted to drink sufficient of it to produce the illusion that anything he said was supremely important, witty or entertaining—and the twin illusion that the great men about him were no more important, witty or entertaining than he was. All of which is perfectly understandable. There is no record of his drunkenness—any more than there is of the drunkenness of Swift or of Pope. Wine was necessary, further, because it was aseptic (all drinking water was suspect). . . . The fact that Arbuthnot had put a taboo on wine at this stage may have cured the colitis, but it rendered convalescence much more difficult for the patient—and there seems to have been some truth in Gay's suspicion that he drew inspiration from it, for during the next two years he wrote practically nothing.

His physical troubles gradually adjusted themselves: his mental ones were slow in going. One gets an impression of his sitting despondently about in grand houses and refusing to be roused. His friends continued to adjure him, as Mrs. Dombey had been adjured, to 'make an effort.' They also, it is quite clear, tried to cheer him up by holding all sorts of delicious prospects before his eyes. It may be supposed that Lord Burlington told him that, since he was so well in with the Queensberrys—and the Duke of Queensberry held a good Governmental position—certainly Gay would be in possession of a well-paid post in a few weeks; the Queensberrys, on the other hand, may have suggested that the Princess of Wales, although she had not yet signalised her pleasure concerning his poetical references, was just on the verge of doing so. Lord Chesterfield may have dropped a hint that Lord Bathurst who took such pleasure in the company of wits knew a man who knew a man who knew somebody who knew Walpole and could pull strings with *him*. Above all, all Gay's friends knew that he knew Mrs. Howard and assured him that if Mrs. Howard was not influential—and doing her best to get him something—then nobody was.

They did it all in the best of good faith, but the fact is that Gay trusted and believed them, time after time, and was disappointed, time after time, at a period when his physical condition was poor. A year of broken promises and unfulfilled hopes sapped his energies just at a time when he needed most to conserve them. Not even the beauty and proportion of Burlington House (when viewed in long stretches from the inside) could make him volatile and cheerful again. Not even the interest of watching the Queensberrys build *their* splendid new home in Burlington Gardens could keep him lively for long. As for Pope, he was still busy, as Lady Mary Wortley Montagu wrote to her sister: "continuing to embellish his house at Twickenham." He was also continuing to embellish a discreet love-poem to the same lady—and appreciated his friend Gay at this juncture more as a faithful Horatio to whom he could pour out his sentiments about dear Sappho, than as a personality valued for himself alone, which must have been a little dampening for a colitis convalescent.

Meanwhile the Burlingtons and the Queensberrys seem to have played battledore and shuttlecock with Gay: the wonder is what pleasure was to be found in his society just then, to keep both families so particularly friendly. Of course, there must have been flashes of the old Gay at times—and at other times no doubt he had a very appealing, beguiling manner which went to the hearts of Lady Burlington and the Duchess of Queensberry and made them long to mother him.

It is necessary to point out that Gay at this time was thirty-six and both ladies in their early twenties—and that, despite these close associations, there is nowhere any hint of a Hollywood situation. Which shows how conventions change. No doubt the convention which the Duchess of Queensberry was acting with Gay was the one of the lady-and-the-poet—which Swift had played with Vanessa—which Lady Mary Wortley Montagu was engaged in rather over-playing with Mr. Pope—which Prior had played with Lady Elizabeth Harley—which the young Duchess of Marlborough was playing admirably with Mr. Congreve. Sex seldom entered into the contract, no matter how closely the two parties associated. The poets acted as educators to the women, and the women practised on the poets during the day the wit and wisdom which they would let loose upon the world at night.

That the system worked admirably is proved by the fact that despite dozens of such associations hardly a breath of scandal—in a generation which adored scandal-mongering—blurs the images seen in the glass. . . . Kitty Queensberry is still beautiful and young—and exceedingly unorthodox—and Gay is still adaptable and susceptible and has an undoubted way with him—whether with men or women—but the picture is not blurred: the association does not spill over into something else: it remains the situation of Cadenus and Vanessa (as Swift preferred to picture it)—an immense friendliness of the mind.

In Government affairs, the havoc consequent on the bursting of the Bubble, and the death in June of the Duke of Marlborough, occupied the public mind. Swift's reaction to the Duke's death was an unparalleled piece of malevolent invective in verse which the Duke himself was beyond hearing (as he had always been beyond caring) but which must have succeeded in wounding the old Duchess and her children and grandchildren as Swift had intended it should. Gay's reaction was an unusually clumsy epistle, *To her Grace Henrietta Dutchess of Marl-*

borough, beginning as if with an apprehensive little cough *Excuse me, Madam, if amid your tears*, but ending with a splendid eulogy of the name that Swift was busy rolling in the mire. The attitude of the general public was more disinterested. After all, we must all die some time or other. What really concerned people was who or what was going to lift the country out of the financial tangle in which she had become enmeshed. There was only one answer—Robert Walpole. Walpole, recalled from his self-imposed exile as the only man who had seen all along what a fraud the South Sea Scheme was (though he had not disdained to profit from it) now settled down to forming a chastened and subservient Ministry—and offended his former friend William Pulteney mightily by leaving him out of it.

The Queensberrys like the rest of the Quality left town when the August heat came on. Gay went with them to Bath, partly to recover from another attack of his old distemper. He seems still to have found it difficult to join in the general light-heartedness, even though dear Dr. Arbuthnot and Mr. Congreve and the young Duchess of Marlborough were also there. A letter from Maid of Honour Lady Margaret Bradshaw to Mrs. Howard at the end of August gives us a glimpse of the convalescent:

"I would fain persuade Mr. Gay to draw his pen; but he is a lost thing, and the colic has reduced him to pass a humdrum hour with me very often. I desired him to club a little wit towards diverting you, but he said it was not in him."

Three weeks later the same writer adds:

"I met Mr. Gay by chance, and told him your message. He is always with the Duchess of Queensberry, for we are too many for him."

One wonders how Mrs. Howard took the news that her tame 'shepherd' was always with the Duchess of Queensberry. Presumably she brought her usual good sense to bear on the situation. The combined testimony of Swift, Pope, Lord Peterborough, Lord Hervey and Horace Walpole all goes to prove that Mrs. Howard simply could not be roused into a display of any strong emotions. How such a fundamentally respectable woman ever came to be the mistress of a King is beyond comprehension. The thing seems to be a contradiction in terms. To turn from Mrs. Howard to the Duchess of Queensberry was like exchanging the placid reaches of the Thames at Twickenham for the turbulent sparkling beauty of a Scots mountain stream, and Gay must have found it so. Until he had acclimatised himself to Scotland, it would all have been a little exhausting.

Death was determined to make a year of it. Another depressing occurrence for Gay at this time was the death of Prior. First Parnell, Addison, then young Craggs, and now Prior. Friends seemed to be falling as fast as autumn leaves. The circumstances could not affect a normally healthy person, but Gay was not yet normal, and no doubt Prior's death (so soon after his heavy losses in the South Sea) may have filled him with morbid comparisons. Besides, Pope, worn out by the new threat to the life of his friend Atterbury (who had been impeached for treason) and with constant attendance on his mother, was himself in unusually poor health. But this did not deter him from occupying whatever time was left him with work—the melancholy task of editing poor

Parnell's poems for the press—a desultory reading-over of Shakespeare in preparation for a new edition which, in his heart of hearts, he knew he had not enough scholarship to undertake.

What kept Gay and Pope apart this year would seem to have been bad health on both sides. But if they could not see each other, they could still write to each other. Gay's correspondence of this time has disappeared, but there is a short and comparatively cheerful letter from Pope in obvious reply to one of his:

"*September* 11*th* 1722.
"DEAR GAY,—I thank you for remembering me. ... I am sorry I could not have a glimpse either of you, or of the sun (your father) before you went to Bath; but now it pleases me to see him and hear of you. Pray put Mr. Congreve in mind that he has one on this side of the world that loves him; and that there are more men and women in the universe than Mr. Gay and my Lady Duchess of M[arlborough]. There are ladies in and about Richmond that pretend to value him and yourself; and one of them at least may be thought to do it without affectation, namely, Mrs. Howard."

The dispute with Tonson was apparently settled amicably as both the *Epistle to Mr. Thomas Snow* and a fourth edition of *The Shepherd's Week* (presumably without the introductory address to Bolingbroke) were both subsequently brought out by him. Perhaps he found it as convenient to forgive Mr. Gay his debts as Swift found it convenient to forgive Gay his unvarying tendency to tenderness and good-heartedness. ... In Burlington House in December, Gay wrote to Swift:

"Dear Sir,—After every post-day for these eight or nine years, I have been troubled with an uneasiness of spirit, and at last I have resolved to get rid of it and write to you. I do not deserve you should think so well of me as I really deserve, for I have not professed to you that I love you as much as ever I did, but you are the only person of my acquaintance almost that does not know it. . . . I think of you very often: nobody wishes you better or longs more to see you. Duke Disney, who knows more news than any man alive, told me I should certainly meet you at the Bath this season: but I had one comfort in being disappointed—that you did not want it for your health. I was there for near 11 weeks for a colic, that I have been troubled with of late; but have not found all the benefit I expected. I lodge at present at Burlington House and have received many civilities from many great men, but very few real benefits. They wonder at each other at not providing for me, and I wonder at them all. Experience has given me some knowledge of them, so that I can say it is not in their power to disappoint me. You find I talk to you of myself. I wish you would reply in the same manner. I hope, though you have not heard from me for so long, I have not lost my credit with you, but that you will think of me in the same manner as when you espoused my cause so warmly, which my gratitude never can forget. I am, my dear sir, your most obliged and sincere humble servant."

It is, undoubtedly, a grovelling letter—and one over which Swift must have pished and psha'd a great many times. The lines "They wonder at themselves at not providing for me, and I wonder at them all" are about the most quoted lines of all Gay's correspondence. But taking all the circumstances into consideration, one can see that he is ruefully half-laughing at himself for putting it like that. Not that there was anything fundamentally amusing in the situation. He was extremely hard-up: he had done quite satisfactory work as a political secretary and had a certain importance as a poet and dramatist; he had welcomed the Whig Princess of Wales in a manner which all his friends assured him would be an immediate passport to a 'place.' In Queen Anne's reign Lady Masham's child, aged 2, had been appointed Chief Ranger of St. James's Park at a salary of £1,000 a year. The Duke of Marlborough in the same reign had managed, with his wife, to make himself worth £62,000 a year. Handel had received a small pension from the same queen and this had lately been added to by King George, while his salary at the Royal Academy of Music was £1,000 a year. Robert Walpole entirely supported a political nonentity named Joseph Mitchell, and had promised Edward Young (who already drew an income as Chaplain to the Prince of Wales) a further £200 a year. Defoe drew a permanent salary for his work behind the scenes of Government. Charles Ford, friend of both Swift and Gay, had, through Swift's influence, been appointed as gazetteer at £200 a year and perquisites. Gay had been rewarded with nothing —indeed to his depressed eye even the door-porters at the houses of the big-wigs (Walpole's door-porter was soon to be in a position where he could levy a toll of a guinea a man on every caller) were in a superior position to a poor poet.

Concerning this, not nearly enough blame has attached itself to those friends of Gay's who, with the best of intentions, had been voluble in inviting him to expect all sorts of benefits. Naturally other persons, similarly promised these visionary benefits, subtracted ninety per cent of what was said to them. But Gay was ridiculously trustful. For five years, now, he had been assured by his friends that prosperity was round the corner. But it still remained round the corner; he never seemed to catch up with it. If he had never been promised so much, then he would never have suffered such suspense—and he might have been, at this stage, a stronger character and consequently a happier man.

It has been supposed that all the time he expected to receive some important political appointment; but this is not borne out either in the correspondence or the circumstances. What he really wanted was a small pension like Young, or a gazetteership like Ford—something to enable him to live, do a little work for his salary, to see his friends and go on writing in peace. Young may not have deserved a pension any more than Ford deserved his job as a gazetteer; but if such things were going, then certainly Gay deserved one at least as much as the others did. There is not much more to it than that—and certainly nothing particularly derogatory in Gay stating so plainly what other people preferred to put in more ambiguous language. Where he erred was in saying that it was in no one's power to disappoint him. He had, especially when suffering from colic, an almost infinite capacity for disappointment.

It appears he was not living happily at Burlington House. The interest of its master and mistress had now passed almost entirely from literature to music. In their excursions and discoveries and devotions to this art it is barely possible that, like other artists, they occasionally forgot the comforts of their guests and fellow-creatures. One gets the impression that in the Burlington household at this stage the rooms were never properly dusted, the hot water was never hot, fires were never tended, the wine was never decanted, the servants were never supervised—and that the guests drifted in and out of the grand, chilly rooms like autumn leaves blown in by accident—and that they received as much attention from the host and hostess as autumn leaves would have done. . . . Concerning Gay's own plight there, there is the appalling anecdote of the Poultice. Dr. Arbuthnot is reported to have remarked in conversation to a mutual friend: "D'ye see, I went to visit him [Gay] and ordered him a poultice to his swelled face. He said Lord and Lady Burlington were very good to him, but the poor creature eat his poultice for hunger."

It is pleasant to be able to record that soon after the despatch of his letter to Swift in December, Gay *did* receive a "real benefit"—in other words he was made a Commissioner of the State Lottery at a salary of £150 a year, with lodgings in Whitehall. This Christmas present of good will and good cheer seems to have been owing less to any direct friend than to the Earl of Lincoln of whom, apart from this incident, there is no mention whatever in any of Gay's affairs. . . . In such strange ways is virtue—or, if you like it better, lack of vice—rewarded.

CHAPTER FIFTEEN

1723. Living in Whitehall. Writing 'The Captives.' Correspondence with Mrs. Howard.

> "*The Ministry is like a Court; there's a little door to get in, and a great crowd withont, shoving and thrusting who shall be foremost; people who knock others with their elbows, ignore a little kick of the shins, and still thrust heartily forwards, are sure of a good place.*"
> LADY MARY WORTLEY MONTAGU TO EDWARD
> WORTLEY MONTAGU, 24TH SEPTEMBER, 1714

THE Commissionership in the State Lottery suited Gay exactly in one particular at least: it was a sinecure. But the lodgings in Whitehall were real enough and he removed to that address with all celerity, shaking off remembrance of the poultice incident with the dust that had doubtless accumulated on the front doorstep of Burlington House. While he was still busy arranging his own furniture a Burlington House footman brought round Swift's answer to his 'grovelling' letter:

"Coming home from a short Christmas ramble [it said] I found your letter upon my Table, and little expected when I opened it to read your Name at the Bottom; the best and greatest Part of my Life, until these last eight years, I spent in *England*. There I made my Friendships, and there I left my Desires; I am condemned for ever to another Country: what is in Prudence to be done? I think to be *oblitusque meorum, obliviciendum & illis.* What can be the Design of your Letter but Malice, to wake me out of a scurvy Sleep? . . . I am towards nine Years older since I left you, yet that is the least of my Alterations; my Business, my diversions, my Conversations are all entirely exchanged for the worse. . . . Yet after all, this humdrum way of life would be passable enough, if you could let me alone. I shall not be able to relish my Wine, my Parsons, my Horses nor my Garden these three Months, until the spirit you have raised shall be dispossessed. I have sometimes wondered why I have not visited you, but I have been stopped by too many reasons. Upon my Return, after half a Year spent amongst you, there would be to me *Desiderio nec pudor nec modus* . . . [no bounds to my longing after you]. . . . Yet I often threaten myself with the journey, and am every summer practising to get Health to bear it."

At this point one imagines Gay, his leg over the side of his chair, settling himself down more satisfactorily in the midst of the chaos of his still unfurnished room to finish so pleasant a letter. . . . But when Swift turns from talk of himself and half-promises of an English visit to Gay's own problems—the smile is perhaps extinguished. The Dean, after all, does not yet know of the Commissionership in the State Lottery—or of the lodgings in Whitehall. He is, as it were, strewing unnecessary rue in the path of a friend who has, temporarily at least, discarded rue in favour of the laurels of rewarded virtue. Still, whatever the Dean writes is worth reading, even on a mistaken premise:

"I have been considering [continues the Dean] why Poets have such ill Success in making their Court, since they are allowed to be the greatest and best of all flatterers. The Defect is, that they flatter only in Print or in writing, but not by Word of Mouth. They will give Things under their hand, which they make a conscience of speaking. Besides, they are too libertine to haunt ante-chambers, too poor to bribe Porters and Footmen, and too proud to cringe to second-hand Favourites in a Great Family. Tell me, are you not under Original Sin by the Dedication of your Eclogues to Lord Bolingbroke? . . .

"I am of opinion, if you will not be offended, that the surest Course would be to get your Friend who lodges in your House to recommend you to the next Civil Governor, who comes over here, for a good Civil Employment, or to be one of his secretaries, which your Parliament men are fond enough of, when there is no room at Home. The Wine is good and reasonable; you may dine twice a week at the Deanery House; there is a Set of Company in this town sufficient for one man; Folks will admire you because they have read you, and read of you; and a good Employment will make you live tolerably in London, or sumptuously here. . . ."

[It is a tempting plan: it is *Scriblerus Redivivimus*—even if only a mere shadow of his former self. One imagines that, however, even as Swift wrote it, he realised what an unlikely scheme it was. If he *himself* had still been in power—still able to come to Ministers with Whigs and Tories in his sleeves, as he had once so long ago—the whole thing would have been fixed in a moment. That there was now no possibility of such an arrangement must have brought home to him, with double bitterness, his own impotence as well as Gay's.

He changes the subject abruptly, but with a kind of rough tenderness.]

> "I wish I could do more than say I love you. I left you in a good Way both for the late Court, and the Succession, and by the Force of too much Honesty or too little sublunary wisdom, you fell between two stools. Take care of your Health and Money, be less modest and more active; or else turn Parson and get a Bishopric here. Would to God they would send us as good ones from your Side!"

An extremely friendly letter, even if it did close with so damning a conclusion. To advise a man to turn parson then was equivalent to advising a man to peddle vacuum-cleaners now—and Swift was not deceived any more in recommending than Gay in receiving such advice. . . . Cast wits and cast beaux have a sanctuary in the church, as the Dean told Pope later. . . . But Gay's immediate task was to disillusion the Dean of the fact that he *was* a cast wit: he hastened to elucidate his new position and added instinctively a picture of London life at the time of writing:

> "As for the amusement of the town, it is entirely music; real fiddles, bass-viols and hautboys; not poetical harps, lyres and reeds. There's nobody allowed to say, *I sing*, but an eunuch or an Italian woman. Everybody is grown now as great a judge of music as they were in your time of poetry, and folks that could not distinguish one tune from another, now daily dispute about the different styles of Handel, Bononcini and Attilio."

It was a true picture of the times—done, doubtless

from the best of intentions, to show the Dean how little he was missing. For the Dean had no more ear for music than Pope and he would have been extremely impatient of the latest enthusiasm. Perhaps from the distance of an Irish exile the Dean could not perceive that there was more to it than a real or implied love of the art. There was a political side as well. Handel, who had, since his *Water-Music*, been received back into the royal fold, was the King's favourite: Bononcini was the man for the Prince of Wales. When he in his turn came to the throne George II. 'took over' appreciation of Handel as inevitably as he took over the crown and sceptre.

Not that there was nothing but Italian music to listen to. At the theatres the Italian operas might usurp the whole position, but in the inns and taverns all over England—in the especially musical region of St. Giles, in London, the rough native music of the ballad still held sway. Gay, who loved to linger in taverns when other friends would accompany him there, had himself composed ballads which, put to music by popular ballad singers, had sung their way into people's hearts as steadily as Barbara Allen or Chevy Chase.

How else did the new Commissioner spend the spring? Court life doubtless kept him busy at Leicester Fields, and here it seems that he could be of use. The honourable Charles Howard, as Groom of the Bedchamber to His Majesty, was not sufficiently a loyal subject to be prepared to wink at his wife's association with the Prince of Wales. That being so, Mr. Howard continued to pester the life out of his wife by threats of abduction from the moment the news of her position as royal mistress was public property until the death of George I.

A study of the correspondence between them, like a study of much of the correspondence of the time, leaves one prejudiced on neither side. Mrs. Howard has forfeited her hold on posterity's sympathy in apparently ignoring the existence of her only child after the first year or so, as placidly as a cow ignores its calf after the suckling period. Nobody found anything unusual in such a state of affairs at the time—except Mr. Howard, who might be expected in any case to make use of ridiculous quibbles—and perhaps it was preferable to ignore the child from the first than to end, like Lady Mary Wortley Montagu and her husband, in hoping that their son would break his neck every time he stirred out of doors. But granted this initial weakness (which, after all, fits remarkably well into the tepid character ascribed to Mrs. Howard by Pope in his later verses) Mrs. Howard had a great many points in her favour. She saw little purpose in returning to a husband who had run through her dowry with great celerity and failed to support her in the position to which she had been accustomed ever since. He had, moreover, a violent temper. So had the Prince of Wales—but there are things which may be forgiven in a royal lover a great deal more easily than in a husband.

Was there any love lost between them? It seems doubtful: Mrs. Howard was faithful to the Prince of Wales because she was as tepid sexually as emotionally, and because she had, besides, a stricter sense of honour than most of her contemporaries. She accepted his attentions because they were royal attentions and because they conferred upon her a position of envied eminence which even a comparatively honest and sensible woman found it hard to resist. Why did George Frederick choose her? She was kindly and even-tempered and the very opposite of the German type he was accustomed to—and since it was incumbent upon him to take an English mistress to discountenance his father's German one, he doubtless chose the most inoffensive lady of his acquaintance.

John Gay was just as faithful to her, though in another way. He still reserved the chief place in his affections for the 'second-hand favourite,' Mrs. Howard. There must have been many times in that period of conversational fireworks, of endless glitter and pose, when it was restful to lower the lamps and sit in the twilight, without speaking, without posing, with a friend. The mask of indifference could come off then; the fan of concealment come down. On such twilit occasions in the Swiss Cantons at Richmond or at Leicester Fields, the subjects of Gay's prospects, Swift's suggestion of turning parson, and of Mrs. Howard's tiresome husband, always threatening to make scenes, could be quietly discussed. "In the arrangement of this disagreeable affair, Mrs. Howard was assisted by Gay and Arbuthnot," says Croker. In other words, Dr. Arbuthnot presumably lent the practical good sense, and Gay incorporated it for her in her letters to her husband. And always, through fair and foul weather, the deepest sympathy existed between the two friends. Mrs. Howard might belong principally to the Prince of Wales—as Gay belonged principally to the Duchess of Queensberry—but there was still ample room for other friendships and this was one by which both set great store.

In July, true to his habit, Gay forsook the town—this time not for Bath but for Tunbridge Wells. Here he might take the waters, walk on the parades, shop under the shelter of the Pantiles or visit the neat little tree-shaded theatre behind its fence of wooden palings. If he tired of the play he and his cronies might drink and talk the warm evening hours away at the Sussex Tavern next door. There were, indeed, endless pleasures, very like the Bath ones.

It is extraordinary how seldom he could persuade Pope to accompany him on these excursions, but besides the perennial excuse of his mother Pope could produce another excellent reason for staying at home this year. Bolingbroke was returning, like Ulysses, from years abroad. The King had pardoned him sufficiently for a home-coming to be allowed him, and Walpole permitted the pardon with his habitual generosity to beaten foes. Besides the prospect of having the admirable St. John close at hand again, Pope was also toying with the idea of embarking on another Homeric voyage—the Odyssey. He had, then as ever, a sufficiency of plans and occupations, and seems to have bidden Gay Godspeed to Tunbridge Wells quite cheerfully:

> "We shall remember you in our potations and wish you a fisher with us on my grass-plot. In the meantime we wish you success as a fisher of women at the Wells; a rejoicer of the comfortless and widows, an impregnator of the barren and a playfellow of the maids."

Mrs. Howard also wrote to Gay:

> "I dare say you are now with your friends, but not with one who more sincerely desires to see you easy and happy than I do: if my power was equal to theirs, the matter should soon be determined.
> "I am glad to hear you frequent the church; you cannot fail of being often put in mind of the great virtue of patience; and how necessary that may be for you to practise, I leave to your own experience. I applaud your prudence (for I hope it is entirely owing to it) that you have no money

at Tonbridge. It is easier to avoid the means of temptation, than to resist them when the power is in our own hands. . . .

"The place you are in has strangely filled your head with cures and physicians; but (take my word for it) many a fine lady has gone to drink the waters without being sick, and many a man has complained of the loss of his heart, who has had it in his own possession. I desire you will keep yours, for I shall not be very fond of a friend without one, and I have a great mind you should be in the number of mine."

A prudent, lady-like letter—with enough platitudes in it to show that the writer was not of tremendous intellect and enough pretty assumption of authority to show that a royal mistress knew how to rule, as well as her lover. The 'friends' she referred to were evidently the Burlingtons, who were also at Tunbridge, and Lord Chesterfield, who likewise wooed her with letters from there. There appears to have been a current Court joke about the word wheat-ear, for Chesterfield's letter to Mrs. Howard refers to a wheat-ear and Gay brings in the same allusion in his reply:

"The next pleasure to seeing you is hearing from you and when I hear you succeed in your wishes I succeed in mine—so I will not say a word more of the house."

[He refers to the plans of a house at Marble Hill in Twickenham, which he had found in her rooms at Richmond, and which she had begged him not to mention as—strangely enough!—"there is a necessity to keep the whole affair secret." His letter continues:]

"We have a young lady here that is very particular in her desires. I have known some ladies who, if ever they prayed and were sure their prayers would prevail, would ask an equipage, a husband or matadores; but this lady, who is but seventeen, and has but thirty thousand pounds, places all her wishes in a pot of good ale. When her friends, for the sake of her shape and complexion, would dissuade her from it, she answers with the truest sincerity by the loss of her shape and complexion she can only lose a husband, but that ale is her passion. I have not yet drank with her, though I must own I cannot help being fond of a lady who has so little disguise of her practice, either in her words or appearance. If, to show her you love her you must drink with her, she has chosen an ill place for followers, for she is forbid with the waters. Her shape is not very unlike a barrel; and I would describe her eyes, if I could look over the agreeable swellings of her cheeks, in which the rose predominates, nor can I perceive the least trace of the lily in her whole countenance. You see what £30,000 can do, for without that I would never have discovered all these agreeable particularities: in short she is the *ortolan,* or rather *wheat-ear* of the place, for she is entirely a lump of fat, and the form of the universe itself is scarce more beautiful, for her figure is almost circular. After I have said all this, I believe it will be vain for me to declare I am not in love, and I am afraid that I have showed some imprudence in talking on this subject, since you have declared that you like a friend that has a heart at his disposal. I assure you I am not mercenary, and that £30,000 have not half so much power with me as the woman I love."

A communication which, on her own evidence, Mrs. Howard was at a loss how to estimate. She probably knew from current gossip that there was a rich and stout young heiress named Mary Jennings—devoted to ale and now at Tunbridge Wells—and there would have been nothing odd or unexpected if Gay had been really 'fond' of the lady, laid siege to her and married her for the sake of the thirty thousand pounds. Smollett's and Fielding's novels show us just such a situation in almost every chapter. Would Mrs. Howard then have lost him? It is unlikely. Marriage interfered less then than any other indoor game with one's choice of friends. Still, there was a prejudice, even in such enlightened days, in favour of a single rather than a married suitor. Mrs. Howard resolved to find out how the land lay:

> "I have taken some days [she wrote] to consider of your *wheat-ear*, but I find I can no more approve of your having a passion for that, than I did of your turning parson. But if ever you will take the one I insist on your taking the other: they ought not to be parted; they were made from the beginning for each other. But I do not forbid you to get the best intelligence of the ways, manners and customs of this wonderful *phénomène*; how it supports the disappointment of bad ale, and what are the consequences to the full enjoyment of her luxury? I have some thoughts of taking a hint from the ladies of your acquaintance, who pray for matadores and turn devotees for luck at ombre; for I have already lost above £100 since I came to Richmond.

"I do not like to have you too passionately fond of everything that has no disguise. I (that am grown old in courts) can assure you, sincerity is so very unthriving that I can never give consent that you should practise it, excepting to three or four people that I think may deserve it, of whose number I am. I am resolved that you shall open a new scene of behaviour next winter, and begin to pay in coin your debts to fair promises. I have some thoughts of giving you a few loose hints for a satire, and if you manage it rightly, and not indulge that foolish good nature of yours, I do not question but I shall see you in good employment before Christmas. . . ."

In giving such good advice so light-heartedly Mrs. Howard can have had no idea of the impossibility of the principles she was trying to inculcate. She might just as well have written to a hen: "I have a few loose hints for enabling you to lay pheasants' eggs, and if you manage it rightly, and not indulge that foolish good nature of yours I do not question you will soon have pheasants for children. . . ." She had known Gay now for nearly ten years and yet she still had hopes of being able to make that 'natural man' who, as Spence said, "was wholly without art or design, and spoke just what he thought and as he thought it," into a courtier. The fact that she speaks of not indulging his good nature has led some historians to believe that what she really wanted from Gay was literary blackmail—unpleasant lampoons the victims of which would bribe him not to publish them and which would enable him, by fear if not by favour, to achieve something better than a Commissionership in a State Lottery. The thing was not unknown. What unpleasant vice *was* unknown in the days of the early Georges? A lampoon was a kind of Ingrowing Dedication which drew attention to all a great man's vices instead of his virtues but which produced, ultimately, the same results. As Lady Mary Wortley Montagu had written, it was the people who knocked "each other with their elbows . . . and still thrust heartily forwards" who were sure of a good place in the Ministry—not the squeamish, modest ones. And one way of giving a good hard knock was by writing lampoons. Rumour had been circulating that Pope had blackmailed the old Duchess of Marlborough in the same way by threatening to publish the 'Character' of her husband—and that she had bought him off with a present of a thousand pounds. It is extremely unlikely. Pope would have been as insulted by such an offer as Swift once was by Harley's well-intentioned bribe. But this did not prevent the story from circulating. If Pope and Swift were both above such practices it is difficult to believe that Mrs. Howard would have taken to them. Yet she had, on her own admission, "grown old in courts," and Courts were forcing-grounds of vice. If it *were* true, who was it she intended Gay to attack? Walpole? He was speedily becoming the only Minister who mattered—but then over the business of persuading the King to buy Marble Hill for her he had been extremely obliging. At such a delicate stage of the negotiations, and knowing his friendliness towards her, would she have urged an attack on Walpole? If not, then what does her sentence mean?

Whatever it meant, Gay never intended to oblige her. He could indeed throw off quips in his letters about the Government which, when Mrs. Howard passed them round the Prince of Wales's Court, made that Court break into delighted giggles. He sent such a quip in the very next letter: "I cannot indeed wonder that the talents for a good statesman are so scarce in the world, since so many of those who possess them are every month cut off in the prime of their life at the Old Baily." But what he would do in letters he disdained to do as a piece of serious work.

Not enough honour has been given Gay for this. The temptation must have been great; the ability was there; but for all that he would not prostitute his little muse to make a Tory holiday. Besides, he was busy on a serious blank verse drama—*The Captives*—which was neither loose nor satirical; he probably felt as Shakespeare would have felt if he had been asked to stop writing *Hamlet* to compose libellous limericks on the King of Spain. He ends his letter to Mrs. Howard with the helpless-puppy pose which is the only pose he has ever troubled to cultivate and which disarmed masterly women when they became just a little too managing:

"I fancy I shall not stay here much longer, though what will become of me I know not—for I have not, and fear never shall have, a will of my own."

Gay returned to London in the autumn to find Bolingbroke returned and arranging to settle at Dawley, not far from Twickenham, and Pope a happy man in consequence. He had lost Bishop Atterbury—gone to exile simultaneously as Bolingbroke returned from it—but since Atterbury had to be exchanged for some one else St. John was a good exchange. In such circumstances, while he was as always delighted to see Gay, he may not have been able to spare him much undivided attention. Certainly *The Captives* suggests nothing attributable to Pope. It does suggest much earnest burning of midnight oil in Whitehall—the Independent Author Doing His Stuff. Presumably it was owing to Mrs. Howard's good offices that the Princess of Wales consented to a reading of the play in her apartments: The story was that Gay was so upset by the importance of the occasion that on entering he stumbled against a large screen, which fell and threw all the ladies into confusion. The scene is painfully reminiscent of the lines in that earlier lampoon on Arbuthnot, Pope and Gay—*The Confederates*—in which Mrs. Oldfield was made to say:

"But hark! Who's entering here? I'll run away;
For by the clumsy tread it should be Gay."

Whether the reading ever recovered from this bad start is not discoverable; but one thing is certain: Princess Caroline would have been as gracious as she had always been to him. However much the rude Maids of Honour may have tittered at the screen incident Princess Caroline would have behaved like herself—the nearest approach to a lady, barring Mrs. Howard, that the Court contained.

The Captives was the first blank verse play that Gay attempted. It was also the last. What other author of his acquaintance could make the same boast? Of all his works it is the most negative, neither better nor worse than hundreds of others of the plumed tragedies of the time. There are, however, some nice little touches about loyalty which Gay must have read with one eye cocked on his audience to see how they went down—notably:

"Why is power given into the hands of Kings
But to distinguish virtue and protect it?"

and "The Queen is gracious and delights in mercy." There is also a prologue wherein, if his eye was cocked on anybody, it was cocked on Mrs. Howard, and in which he satirised that lady's "loose hints for satires":

> "Poets should ne'er be drones; mean, harmless
>   things;
> But guard, like bees, their labours by their stings.
> That mortal sure must all ambition smother
> Who dares not hurt one man to please another.
> What, sink a joke? That's but a mere pretence—
> He shows most wit who gives the most offence—
> But still our squeamish author satyr loaths
> As children, physick; or as women, oaths."

The year closed with a letter from Swift in reply to one from Pope in which Pope (as he so frequently did) must have been talking about his favourite topic, friendship. The Dean replied:

> "Your notion of friendship is new to me; I believe every man is born with his quantum, and he cannot give to one without robbing another. I very well know to whom I would give the first places in my affection, but they are not in the way. I am condemned to another scene and therefore I distribute it in pennyworths to those about me, who displease me least, and should do the same to my fellow-prisoners if I were condemned to jail. . . . I have often tried to establish a friendship among all men of genius, and would fain have it done. They are seldom above three or four contemporaries and, if they could be united, could drive the world before them. I think it was so among the poets in the time of Augustus; but envy and party and pride have hindered it among us."

It is a bitter outcry from one who was exiled from everything in the world (except Stella) that he loved. The years passed; the seasons came and went, but winter filled the heart of Swift. He could not bear Pope to chirrup of happiness and friendship so freely: it was tempting the gods. Remembering Vanessa, he wrote: "I am of opinion that there is not a greater folly than to contract too great and intimate a friendship, which must always leave the survivor miserable." Once, long ago, there had been a world in which poets were happy. "I think it was so . . . in the time of Augustus." But Augustus was dead long ago; even Queen Anne was dead. All was vanity and vexation of spirit and the English Government, when it thought of Ireland at all, thought only of measures to deride and gull it, like this damnable scheme of the new coinage. Everything, obviously, was for the worst in the worst of all possible worlds, and in such a spirit the Dean took epistolatory leave of his friend Pope—and tried to shut his mind to London and Twickenham and all their manifold delights.

CHAPTER SIXTEEN

1724-1725. 'The Captives' produced at Drury Lane. A Visit to Bath. The Howard-Peterborough Correspondence. 'The Newgate Garland.'

" *The Life of a Wit is a warfare upon Earth.*"
POPE: PREFACE TO HIS POEMS, 1716

ON January 13th of the new year Gay's tragedy *The Captives* was put on at Drury Lane, with the famous Mrs. Oldfield in one of the chief parts, and with their Royal Highnesses the Prince and Princess of Wales in the audience. Even this could not save it. It was not an instantaneous flop like *Three Hours After Marriage*, but it died gently, the breath ebbing out of it night after night. Here was one more proof to the author that Mrs. Howard was right—that the only thing to hold the stage in these degenerate days was satire. As long as he continued (as he admitted himself to be in the prologue) 'squeamish,' so long his plays would fail to take. That was the immoral moral of it.

Certainly of all ages that particular age was the very worst one in which to do things by half. Enthusiasm might be decried everywhere else, but on the stage some sort of exaggeration and gusto was still necessary, if only to make itself seen above the light of the four rings of candles which was all the illumination available—and heard above the cane-tapping of the young rowdies in the front of the houses, the chatter of the fine ladies, the cat-calls and groans of the pit and the Yahooism of the footmen monopolising the gallery. The theatre, as an English institution, was in a bad way. Some intermittent brilliance had redeemed it in the days of Vanbrugh and Wycherley and Congreve, but Wycherley was dead at last—gone after that memory which had so long preceded him—Vanbrugh had found the building of Blenheims likely to be more enduring than the building of plays, and Congreve had declined, long ago, into a 'private gentleman.' Who came after them? Mrs. Aphra Ben—more licentious than any of her contemporaries and with no redeeming wit; Colley Cibber, a fountain of good ideas but poor execution; Aaron Hill, as prolific as a barley-mouse and as inconsequent, and in between whiles, always in between whiles, Shakespeare 'improved,' with a happy ending for *Lear*, and his Elizabethan lushness lopped off to leave him as neat as a piece of topiary in a Versailles garden. . . . But whatever the play, the many-headed monster of the Pit domineered it. It was less an audience than a mob collected to bait human beings for once in a way, instead of cocks in Marylebone or bears in Hockley-in-the-Hole. The audience in the early eighteenth century had declined as steadily as the plays.

In such an atmosphere a so-so tragedy by a minor poet, even while the actors were helped by all the heroic plumed head-dresses in the world and the theatre favoured by the royal presences, could not succeed. Doubtless the productions of the Royal Academy of Music also helped to spoil the theatrical market this season. Italian opera, as Gay had observed to Swift, dominated the polite taste of the town. The theatre, poorly paid, therefore poorly recruited and attended, came in a bad second to the handsomely subsidised Academy. But the polite taste of the town could still support the printed word and *The Captives* when published went into a second edition, which must have been some small consolation to the author.

Truly, as Pope had said, the life of a wit is a warfare upon earth. Gay had just fought a losing battle with the stage, and both Pope and Swift this year were engaged in bitter warfare. It was the year in which Swift, turning his back in disgust upon the English situation, had let his eyes rest for the first time on the Irish situation around him. The state of the Irish coinage had been parlous for some time. Every kind of abuse from export to melting down and clipping had ruined the currency, just as the currency had been ruined earlier in England. And now here was one Wood, buying, from the King's mistress, the right to palm off his inferior brass in coins upon the Irish people. The contract was a 'job' through and through, albeit no better and no worse a job than most contemporary Government contracts. But Swift saw in Mr. Wood a useful cudgel with which he could up and beat the Whigs. He was admittedly inspired far less with love of Irishmen than with a loathing of English Ministers—particularly Walpole—but the result was the same. The old pamphleteering spirit, the spirit of *The Conduct of the Allies*, had returned to Swift; he became the anonymous *Drapier*, who in successive *Drapier's Letters* fell upon the ignominious Wood and the Walpole Ministry with all the old well-known knock-him-down-and-stamp-on-him style. It goes without saying that he became the idol of Dublin and—being the idol of Dublin —a subject of intense speculation in circles which were not informed (but would have liked to have been) in London.

If Pope or Gay had any idea who the anonymous *Drapier* was they kept it for the time being to themselves. Pope had other occupations; he too was busy with a private war—and with a much less savoury one. Any study of this episode in the lives of Pope and Lady

Mary Wortley Montagu inevitably suggests a slow stinging to death between two vipers. Or, to use their own epithets, it is Furious Sappho against the Wicked Wasp of Twickenham, with the advantage, finally, to the wasp. It is commonly supposed that the cause of the quarrel was Pope's overstepping the bounds between a purely literary flirtation and a real one, in that he made "a certain proposal" to the lady, and was rebuffed by laughter. There may be some grounds for truth in the story but certainly there were other grounds as well, and one of them was political.

At the period when Lady Wortley Montagu was still a divinity to Pope, that lady had amongst her friends Lord 'Fanny' Hervey, the Bristol family and Miss Molly Skerrit, the mistress of Walpole. She had been as well received by King George as a woman who was not fat could ever be, and she had been favourably looked upon by the Prince of Wales as well. Her wit and self-assurance made her extremely popular in Whig circles and in youth she had a certain *gamine* charm which passed for good looks. But her friends were almost entirely Whig—except for Pope. He alone had no strong political bias. Certainly the rest of Lady Mary's friends did not appeal to Pope. Whatever action first started the quarrel, remembrance of the notorious Lord Fanny, the vulgar Molly Skerrit, the tedious-beyond-words Edward Wortley Montagu, and the various empty-minded toadies who hung about Lady Mary's household must have lent depth to the accumulating anger in Pope's heart. Hell hath no fury like a poet scorned. Lady Mary fell, with a chiming tinkle as of smashed china, from her elevation as a divinity, to be trampled upon and smeared over in the neatest, filthiest line in all Pope.

The story of the split between the first poet of the

age and the first flirt filled every distinguished ear from Twickenham to Blackheath. No more delicious scandal came the way of the world that year. The whispers and sniggers about it are probably still sibilating in some distant corner of space. Naturally the enemies would never have been able to provide such good sport if they had not been in deadly earnest. The battle may have been protracted but the poison did its work. It drove Lady Mary eventually out of England; it all but killed Pope.

But these events still lay in the future; hostilities were only just beginning, and by the time the first blow was struck, Gay was already on his way to Bath. He appears to have changed his travelling-companions every time he made the journey, for this time there is no talk of the Pulteneys (whose marital disagreements would certainly have been the talk of the town if the more important Pope-Montagu affair had not usurped that position), nor of the Burlingtons, nor yet of the Queensberrys. And for once in a way Mr. Congreve and the young Duchess of Marlborough have vacated their seats in the Pump Room and their place in Gay's correspondence. This time a couple with the names of Lord and Lady Fitzwilliam burst into the picture with surprising abruptness. No good reason has ever emerged why Gay should have sought their society; and the feeling must have been mutual for after this season they disappear as abruptly from the picture as they entered it. On the way to the exit, however, they afford a line in one of Gay's letters to Mrs. Howard. It is written in one of his helpless-puppy moods:

"Dear Madam, [it said]
"Since I came to the Bath I have written three letters, the first to you, the second to Mr. Pope and

the third to Mr. Fortescue. Every Post gives me fresh mortification for I am forgot by everybody. . . . Lady Fitzwilliam wonders why she has not heard from you; and has so little resolution that she cannot resist buttered rolls at breakfast, though she knows they prejudice her health."

There is little more to it—but in any case Mrs. Howard was getting her money's worth that year in letters from Gay. He had confided to her that he hated writing letters. Yet in spite of this, somehow Mrs. Howard had coaxed and cajoled him into undertaking one of the most laborious tasks in the world—that of helping to compose, and editing, a gallant correspondence between herself and the seventy-year-old Lord Peterborough.

If every person in the eighteenth century with personality above the average were to get a paragraph to himself biographies of the period would be paragraphed at every sentence—but Lord Peterborough would deserve it if few others did. In person he must have resembled Don Quixote. In temperament he was as dashing and as sentimental as that ancient, but combined with those qualities an utter recklessness and tactlessness which made up altogether the oddest personality in the world. When a man was as reckless as Peterborough the obvious solution was to make him a soldier and give him an important command; if his recklessness 'came off,' then it was consummate military tactics and great bravery; if it failed, then it was only another blunder amongst many. Possibly some such reasoning as this had induced Marlborough, long ago, to advise Queen Anne to give Peterborough the command of the southern forces in Spain. By all the laws of common sense his command should have been an inglorious failure—but war does not abide by the rules of common sense, and only too often the fool gets away with it because the tide happened to rise at the right moment, or some other blunder as fortuitous as the first converts both blunders into a *coup* of the first importance. Military luck with Lord Peterborough had been fifty-fifty—fifty triumphs to fifty blunders—not a bad record for a soldier on the whole. And at least life under his command can never have been dull. "A hang-dog rascal but I love him," was Swift's comment, jerked out of him by the fact that once Lord Peterborough, hot from galloping across Europe, had marched across the room and embraced him warmly, Continental fashion, before a large company. That was Don Quixote all over. Whatever he did he preferred to do it before a large company. He kept Mrs. Anastasia Robinson the singer and her sister in his house at Parsons Green—and let everybody know it. He marched through Bath in his riding-boots, carrying home the chicken he had bought for his dinner for all the world to see, just as if Mr. Nash had never made any rules for polite society at all. He came publicly to blows with the Italian singer Senesino. Peterborough swore he had insulted Mrs. Robinson and would accept no denials. His motto, then as always, was thrash first and apologise afterwards.

As Lord Peterborough's career had come abruptly to an end with the accession of George I, he confined his attentions thereafter, like others in his position, to the Court of the Prince of Wales. There it was inevitable that he should encounter Mrs. Howard and inevitable after that that Don Quixote should be temporarily merged into Don Juan. And to do him justice he courted her, not as Chesterfield and Bathurst did, with his eyes on her supposedly influential position as the Prince's mistress, but out of sheer gusto and a desire to beat the younger lords at their own game. It was fun to pretend to be in love with Mrs. Howard (even while one really loved Mrs. Robinson). He prevailed upon Mrs. Howard to indulge in a Cadenus-Vanessa flirtation with him. And since Mrs. Howard had no pretensions to being able to play the sort of classical ping-pong which made up this particular correspondence course, she invited Gay to help her.

If ever a proof were needed of the man's good nature here is surely an excellent one. He disliked letter-writing of any sort—but to write love-letters for Mrs. Howard to a seventy-year-old suitor was surely of all letter-writing the most fatiguing. His heart was not in it, nor was Mrs. Howard's, nor certainly Lord Peterborough's. But their brains were all in it up to the brim, and that made it much harder work for the supernumerary. Between the three of them the correspondence ranged over the whole year.

Bearing this correspondence in mind it is not surprising that Gay's personal letters to Mrs. Howard tended to be short. Gay had also written to Pope, begging him to join him at Bath. One of the most touching features of the Pope-Swift-Gay relationship is that wherever each separate member of the triangle might be, he never stopped writing to both other members, offering to make all sorts of plans to get them transported to the same spot. For once in a way Pope weakened. His mother perhaps was temporarily in such good health that he could not decently use her as an excuse, and, much as he dreaded the effects of the dangerous three-day journey, he was prepared to risk it. He knew he would be shaken almost to bits in the coach, apart from the perpetual risk of a wheel coming adrift or of Jack Sheppard and his men on Hounslow Heath. But Twickenham for the time being was not large enough to hold both him and Lady Mary Wortley Montagu. He departed to join Gay at Bath, with Martha Blount as his companion. Dr. Arbuthnot went down too, possibly with that daughter of his of whom Pope wrote later to Swift, "I love her much: she is like Gay, very idle, very ingenuous and inflexibly honest." . . . In such propitious surroundings Gay may be supposed to have come to himself again. He was in his favourite watering-place surrounded by his oldest friends. The reputation of the Dean, besides, had swollen to almost its original proportions. When talk of the Drapier and his successful fulminations against the Government came up at Bath, no doubt it was extremely pleasant for Pope and Gay and Arbuthnot to be able to look down their noses complacently while they were pointed out as the friends of the great Dean—friends, moreover, who might just possibly be prevailed upon to supply the latest news about him. After all, nothing enhances a man so much in the eyes of company as the feeling that he possesses exclusive information. Doubtless Pope, Gay and Arbuthnot made the most of it. The only shadow to mar their happiness was the fact that Swift himself could not be with them—but that was a shadow to which by now they were well used.

It was just as well for Swift that Irish affairs took up his attention, for otherwise the death of Lord Oxford in midsummer might have affected him more than it did. But just then he was the Drapier more than the Dean whom Oxford had known; he took the happening in his stride and continued, from his Dublin stronghold, to hurl thunderbolts at the heads of Walpole and his Ministry. He happened to win that particular battle—Walpole recognised a country up in arms when he saw one—and the Wood contract for supplying the Irish coinage was cancelled. But one of the biggest things about Walpole was his ability to give way when necessary. He stands like a Gulliver smiling down, for twenty years, at the pinpricks inflicted by his Lilliputian adversaries. Swift was no Lilliputian but even his tremendous onslaughts could not affect Walpole in the long run. They might temporarily upset his plans; they never upset his equanimity.

Apart from the ever-increasing influence of Robert Walpole, the Pope-Montagu scandal and the Drapier's Letters, one other topic decorated general conversation at this time. After all, political and social scandals concerned chiefly London—but the exploits of Jack Sheppard, Joseph Blake and Jonathan Wild concerned the whole country. Joseph Blake was a highwayman whose only notorious act was the laudable one of trying to cut Jonathan Wild's throat in Court, after being arrested on that gentleman's evidence. Sheppard, the last word in escape-artists, and the wiliest thief who ever saw Newgate, had kept all England thrilled with his adventures in '24. But even the ablest artist meets his match in the end. The Government, stung at last by the fact that a single rascal was turning them into a laughing-stock, took account of the proverb and set a thief to catch a thief with great success. With Jonathan Wild's assistance they rounded up both Jack Sheppard and Joseph Blake and both died eventually as other thieves did—at the end of a halter. But a Government which had wits enough about it to set a thief to catch thieves was not above turning King's Evidence itself. No doubt Jonathan Wild considered it deplorably bad taste but the fact remains that shortly after Sheppard and Blake had been tried and condemned to death, Jonathan Wild was again called upon to face a jury, and this time he was the prisoner.

If Jack Sheppard had been a by-word in the land,

Jonathan Wild was even more of a by-word. Sheppard had been a romantic desperado. Jonathan Wild was a faithful forerunner of a Chicago gangster. His racket was anything which concerned making money by dubious means—filching stuffs out of shops, robbing coaches, stealing wigs and watches, cheating young heirs out of their estates. All these feats were achieved for Wild by a gang of lesser thieves—his 'boys,' in present-day slang. And when things got too hot for his boys, or his boys got too lukewarm for him, Wild was as prepared as a gangster is to turn them over to the police and put them out of harm's way. Consequently few tears were shed when Wild himself was caught and subsequently sentenced to death.

Naturally enough the capture and hanging of three well-known thieves was an occasion which fell like manna on the news-sheets and gazettes. They celebrated it as heartily as they knew how and innumerable ballads and broadsheets filled in the gaps which the ordinary journals had overlooked. Of these the best by far is *Newgate's Garland* by Gay. The full title of this work was imposingly set out in the original as

NEWGATE'S GARLAND
being
A New Ballad
showing
How Mr. Jonathan Wild's throat was cut from Ear to Ear with a penknife, by Mr. Blake, alias *Blueskin*, the bold highwayman, as he stood at his tryal in the *Old Bailey*, 1725
To the tune of *the Cut-purse*.

There are several interesting points about *Newgate's Garland*. One is that it shows that Swift's hint, nearly ten years earlier, of a "Newgate Pastoral" had not been forgotten. Gay had, with his acute journalist's sense, simply been waiting until Newgate was sufficiently 'hot' news to serve up for public diversion. Sheppard, Wild and Blueskin between them had brought the famous old prison on to the front page with a vengeance. Another interesting point is that an earlier form of the ballad, entitled simply *Blueskin's Ballad*, was published by Gay in '24. Obviously this was while Blueskin the highwayman was still at large, as much a danger on the wild stretches of heath which surrounded London as he was a subject of conversation at card-tables and Court. It was in his character as a romantic highwayman that Joseph Blake had captured Gay's imagination—even before his assault on Jonathan Wild. *Blueskin's Ballad*, in other words, is the first public appearance of Captain Macheath, as surely as Jonathan Wild in the later ballad is the first public appearance of Peachum.

As so often with verses of Gay's, there is a suspicion that a couple of verses of *Newgate's Garland* came from the hand of his betters—in this case from Swift. Nothing is more likely. Gay, knowing that Swift delighted to read satire on the Government, would have been quick to send him a 'rough' of the ballad. The Dean was good enough to respond by adding a couple of stanzas. The only difference between them and Gay's is that they do not run off the tongue with the nimble tripping ease of Gay's stanzas. Like most of the Dean's verses, they suggest rather a gang of arrested words, pressed forcibly into service and marching awkwardly before their captor at the point of the bayonet.

Ill-assorted or not, no ballad was ever so clearly a forerunner of something bigger than itself. It is usually accepted that *The Beggar's Opera* later burst upon London as a treatment entirely new. So it was—

in the theatre—but the gist of the thing is implicit in the ballad.

The first verse runs:

> Ye Gallants of Newgate, whose Fingers are nice
> In diving in pockets, or cogging of Dice.
> Ye Sharpers so rich, who can buy off the Noose
> Ye honester poor Rogues, who die in your shoes
> Attend and draw near
> Good news ye shall hear
> How *Jonathan's* throat was cut from Ear to Ear.
> Now *Blueskin's* sharp knife hath set you at Ease
> And every Man round me may rob as he please.

The tune of *The Cut-purse* to which it was sung has gone by now the way of the cut-purses themselves, but even without the assistance of a tune one can imagine the delighted apprehension of any listeners with a political sense—as to what was coming next:

> Some say there are Courtiers of highest renown
> Who steal the King's *Gold*, and leave him but a
>   *Crown*;
> Some say there are Peers, and some Parliament
>   Men,
> Who meet once a year to rob Courtiers agen;
> Let them all take their Swing
> To pillage the King,
> And get a Blue Ribbon instead of a String . . .

Is it all merely old and ' quaint,' now? Is it not possible to realise that once such lines were living and vibrant, and able to set the whole room roaring out the chorus with their very appositeness? It is difficult to believe that Walpole himself, after a good dinner, would not have turned for once from his favourite occupation of talking bawdy to laugh appreciatively at the neatness of:

> Some cheat in the Customs, some rob the Excise,
> But he who robs both is esteemèd most wise.
> Church-wardens, too prudent to hazard the Halter,
> As yet only venture to steal from the Alter.
> But now to get Gold
> They may be more Bold
> And rob on the highway since *Jonathan's* cold.

Co-operation even over so small a matter as a ballad must have been heartening to both Swift and Gay. It was a sign that though the years might pass and seas divide them, their sympathies were still attuned. But perfect sympathetic accord is not always sufficient in itself; it sometimes leaves a longing for the physical presence which used, of old, to accompany the mental one. Swift showed no signs of making this personal appearance. He had laid down his bludgeon as a Drapier to busy himself about *Gulliver*. He was still distributing his pennyworths of friendships among his Irish friends, making do with those when he could not enjoy his English ones. An important new addition to these was Lord Carteret, the latest lord to be put out of Walpole's way by being honoured with the dubious appointment of the Governor-Generalship in Ireland. In his position, Carteret was hardly likely to be over-fond of the man who had placed him there—and a dislike of Walpole was a fairly safe passport to Swift's affections.

In between his other activities (chief of which was *Gulliver*) Swift tantalised himself and his friends with half-promises to come over to London—promises no sooner given than retracted. But though he could not, or would not, come over, he was delighted to hear that Pope and Gay were together again at Twickenham; it always pleased him that they, at least, should be able to share each other's company; it showed that some friendships, after all, could endure in an unstable and unregenerate world. As for the world itself, he had done with it. He would show the world what he thought of it in *Gulliver*. He settled down to the task.

It was a task a great deal more congenial to him than was the task on which Pope was still engaged. This was the editing of a new edition of Shakespeare. He was never enthusiastic about the work; he knew nothing of the stage and cared less, and his study of the Elizabethans was too casual and full of condescension to be worth much. Indeed, if he had any inherent respect for the genius of Shakespeare he successfully concealed it. True, his master Dryden had known how to assess Shakespeare—and what Dryden said was always of importance to Pope. But their ideals, for all that, were singularly far apart. Dryden had declared that his chief endeavours were to delight the age in which he lived; Pope's chief endeavour was to deride and satirise it. A man with no sense of the theatre and a soured outlook on life is not the man to edit Shakespeare, however sound his scholarship may be; but even Pope's scholarship was questionable. The fact that Gay was called in to lend some assistance was doubtless comforting to Pope, but here again real scholarship was lacking. Gay endeavoured to fit himself for the task by reading hard for it, but even then two poets do not guarantee a successful edition of a third one. If they had been able to do it, it was clear that there was plenty of room for a new edition of Shakespeare. But whoever the man fit to produce this, certainly it was not Pope. From time to time, of course, inspirations descended upon him, and enabled him to illuminate a line hitherto obscure. But such strokes were few and far between. Furthermore, there was already available a real Shakespearean scholar —one Theobald who, as Pope knew, was only waiting for *his* edition to appear in order to fall upon it tooth and nail and point out all its errors of omission and commission. Pope, naturally, was not going to sit down under *that*. He worked in a state of angry apprehension and in the circumstances it is not surprising that his edition of Shakespeare is one of his minor achievements. (Not that he was not well paid for the task. Even Gay who was only assistant to the master was rewarded with the respectable sum of £25 7s. 6d.) But Pope had skimped and cribbed his way through it and Theobald, immediately after publication, fell upon it as expected.

Such behaviour shows that though he may have known his Shakespeare he certainly did not know Pope. That worthy, although still bitterly embroiled with the Montagu affair, was not averse to taking on another antagonist. He attacked both with redoubled venom—not yet in print, but in private papers which, on the principle that bad news travels fast, circulated just as effectively. Consequently the Pope-Theobald quarrel succeeded the Drapier-Wood quarrel, the Howard-Howard quarrel, the King-Prince of Wales quarrel, the Walpole-Pulteney and Walpole-Carteret quarrels, and all the other major quarrels of the past few months.

Quarrelsomeness is an infallible recipe for keeping one in the news, especially when it is perpetrated in forcible and incisive English. It now began to dawn upon people that two names were constantly to the fore when trouble was brewing, and that these were Swift and Pope. Counter-attacks upon the two great attackers were consequently continued from then almost until the times of their deaths. Sometimes Grub Street subsided a little, and a few months would pass without molestation, then some word or action of the victims would set them off again. A typical extract of the time comes from one Thomas Cooke, who published in 1725 his *Battle of the Poets*, an imaginary dialogue between Pope and Swift, in which they are supposed to be discussing their enemies:

Swift: Call them, without Reserve, Dog, Monkey, Owl
       and splutter out at once Fish, Flesh and Fowl
   To him thus, Pope.
Pope: Waste not thy breath again
   To give Advice to whom advice is vain.
   Who better knows than I his Dirt to throw?
   To wound in secret either Friend or Foe,
   Go preach to *Gay*, and such as are inclin'd
   Less to exert an enterprizing Mind,
   Who, slothful to pursue our glorious Ends,
   Lag, as if willing to make all their Friends.

No other extract better sums up current opinion upon Swift, Pope and Gay, and a study of other contemporary lampoons convinces one that some at least of the gibes were justified. Both Pope and Swift went after stupidity—what they called "Dulness"—with a ruthlessness and vigour which seem, to the more tolerant outlook of to-day, to have been out of all proportion to the crime. Other crimes there were and they too received their flaying, but they were always incidental to the main one. Stupidity stood for everything pompous and unimportant, prosy and mediocre. Mediocrity, to the wits, was the sign-manual of the Walpole regime, and that fact doubled its venality. Unsuccessful mediocrity was bad enough but mediocrity courted and listened to and finally pensioned, was beyond endurance. Gay's attitude was different. His natural kindliness and indolence would hardly have inspired him to join in attacks on other people's lack of brains or beauty or cleanliness. Privately he probably thought that we are all as God made us, and that we cannot help our faults. That he *did* "lag, as if willing to make all his friends" had already been noted by Thomas Cooke. At the same time the leaven was beginning to work; and with Pope and Swift never failing to point out to him, from now on, how dullness and vice were elevated to important positions and how brains and virtue were seldom rewarded it would have been strange if he did not finally see reason.

Still, it is relevant to turn to the other side of the medal. The one just exhibited is the one usually held up to the world; but there was a reverse side. At the same time that the crusaders were fighting their lone battles against dullness and Grub Street they were also engaged in gentle communications with each other on the subject, the eternal subject, of friendship. A serious illness of Arbuthnot's had once more brought the topic up. *O, the Dean had cried to Pope, if the world had a dozen Arbuthnots in it, I would burn my Travels!* So stupendous a compliment was almost more than Dr. Arbuthnot, in his weak state of health, could bear. He replied with an outburst of gratitude and affection such as Swift knew so supremely how to evoke, and he ended with the usual plea of Swift's friends, the plea that he would come over to England:

> "The hope of seeing once more the Dean of St. Patrick's," he wrote, "revives my spirits. I cannot help imagining some of your old club met together like mariners after a storm. For God's sake do not tantalise your friends any more. I can prove by

twenty unanswerable arguments, that it is absolutely necessary that you should come over to England."

It is the old cry, the one which Pope was to express best in his words to Swift at a later period of life: "Come and quicken me." There are some personalities which have this strange vitalising power; they are not necessarily attractive personalities, but in their presence a response is awakened in others, as if the last necessary link in an electrical connection had been made—and the current is suddenly switched on; the lamps which had been standing unillumined, are glowing. Swift had predominantly this vitalising, quickening effect. His friends longed for his presence for selfish as well as unselfish reasons. They knew that in that presence they themselves "came alive."

Pope followed up Arbuthnot's letter with something written a little more obviously for Posterity:

> "After so many Dispersions and so many Divisions, two or three of us may yet be gathered together; not to plot, not to contrive silly schemes of ambition, or to vex our own or each other's hearts with busy Vanities (such as perhaps at one time or another take their Tour in every man) but to divert ourselves, and the world too, if it pleases; or at worst, to laugh at others as innocently and unhurtfully as at ourselves."

C'est magnifique, mais ce n'est pas la Guerre. "Innocent" and "unhurtful" and Pope! But even in the midst of this unscrupulous watering-down of his own tactics Pope deserves his meed of praise. When he said "not to contrive silly schemes of ambition" he was not writing for posterity, he meant it. He alone remains without ambition, amongst all his fellows. As for Swift, he was quite able to read for himself between the lines addressed to posterity and the lines addressed to him. He was too polite—knowing Pope's sensitive spirit—to say so, but he knew all the business about innocence and unhurtfulness to be bunkum. He replied:

> "I like the scheme of our meeting after Distresses and Dispersions, but the chief End I propose to myself in all my Labours, is to Vex the world, rather than divert it; and if I could compass that Design without hurting my own Person or Fortune I would be the most indefatigable writer you have ever seen."

But Pope was not to be put off. He was in his dying-senator mood, and he resumed the topic in the same exalted manner in which he had initiated it:

> "I have often imagined to myself [he wrote] that if ever all of us met again, after so many vanities and changes, after so much of the old world and the old man in each of us has been altered, after there has been such a new heaven and new earth in our minds and bodies that scarce a single thought in the one, any more than a single atom of the other, remains just the same—I have fancied, I say, that we should meet like the righteous in the millennium, quite in peace, divested of all our former passions, smiling at all our own designs and content to enjoy the Kingdom of the just in tranquillity."

What sort of reply could an established pessimist

like Swift make to such optimism? Only that reiterated cry of despair from an earlier letter. . . . "I think it was so among the poets in the time of Augustus—but envy and party and pride have hindered it among us." He hastened to turn from the general to the particular; to enquire after Gay.

Granted that it is possible to have a fondness for a skeleton, then Gay was a perpetual skeleton in the cupboard to Swift—a person of whom, even though one had the best intentions, somehow one never expected to hear good news. Too often the prefix Poor slipped into the sentence; too often, it is safe to guess, the expression became commiserating on the spot. It did not seem to occur to either Pope or Swift—those self-constituted parents of a particularly refractory child—that the time for worrying about or commiserating over Gay was past and done with, since he had been rewarded for past services by a job which was a virtual sinecure, worth £150 a year. It was not much, but it would keep him out of the gutter and he had shown that he could easily supplement this by the profits from his writings. This obtuseness of theirs is the more to be deplored, since if they had been content with his salary and the position, almost certainly Gay would have been content too. But there never were three such oddly-assorted characters placed in such close conjunction together— Swift, who loathed and detested mankind in bulk, but would very willingly love Tom, Dick or Harry; Pope who could cheerfully put Tom, Dick or Harry on the rack and smile at his torments, but who preserved a vaguely benign outlook on mankind as a whole; Gay, who was fundamentally incapable of hating anybody, though he could love as deeply as Pope or Swift. Small wonder that between the two clashing misanthropies, Gay with his love for all men was nearly squeezed out of shape. The fact is that Pope, on occasion, and Swift, nearly always, found some sort of psychological release from their own passions and fears by attacking the world on behalf of Gay—and by ascribing to Gay and pitying Gay for, all the disappointments and snubs from which they too suffered, but which they were too proud to own directly. And if the cheerfulest man in the world is perpetually pitied for being ill-used, sooner or later such an attitude of mind must have its effect on him, and he will *become* ill-used. . . . And Gay was not the cheerfulest man in the world; indeed, when he was suffering from colic he could be one of the most miserable.

"I hear nothing of our friend Gay," writes Swift, "but I find the Court keeps him at hard meat." Pope replies in the same elegiac strain:

> "Our friend Gay is used as the friends of Tories are used by Whigs—and generally by Tories too. Because he had humour, he was supposed to have dealt with Doctor Swift, in like manner as when any one had learning formerly, he was thought to have dealt with the Devil. He puts his whole Trust at court in that Lady whom I described to you."

Tut, Tut! It was too bad that Gay, on the rare occasions when his friends were not either inciting him to false hopes or assuring him cynically that it was no use hoping because all men were blackguards anyway, should have fled to the more prosaic Mrs. Howard, with her doctrine of patience and words of soft but never-defined encouragement. He had not been wasting his time since the end of that uncongenial homework on Shakespeare. Once more he was out to try something new.

Ten years earlier Daniel Defoe, that literary jack-of-all-trades, had written *The Family Instructor*, a manual for bringing up and educating children. The book had sold well and in a recent edition had been much appreciated by the nobility, including the Prince and Princess of Wales. Possibly Defoe's success inspired Gay with his idea. He also would be a Family Instructor, but he would do it in verse. And, just so that there should be no mistake concerning his objects in writing, he would dedicate what he wrote to Prince William, the young Duke of Cumberland:

"Gay," wrote Pope to Swift in December, "is writing Fables for Prince William. I suppose Mr. Phillips [the old butt, Ambrose Phillips] will take this very ill, for two reasons, one that he thinks all childish things belong to him, and the other, because he will take it very ill to be taught that one may write things to a child without being childish."

A criticism which, if it is not fair to Phillips, is still an admirable commentary on Gay.

CHAPTER SEVENTEEN

1726. Swift comes to England, and stays at Twickenham with Pope and Gay. Gay writing his 'Fables.' Swift finishing 'Gulliver's Travels.' Pope busy on 'The Dunciad.'

> "*Pope and Gay and I use all our endeavours to make folks merry and wise, and profess to have no enemies except knaves and fools.*"
>
> SWIFT, IN A LETTER TO SIR WILLIAM WYNDHAM, JULY, 1732

WE come now to an Indian Summer in the lives of the three men with whom this book is most concerned—a period of reunion which lived ever afterwards in their memories as a time of great creative excitement and personal content. Perhaps there has never been another friendship quite so fruitful, so evocative of schemes and ideas, in those concerned. True, Tom, Dick and Harry have frequently got together and through sheer good-fellowship produced the illusion that what they were saying to each other was earth-shaking and important —and just as frequently the rest of the world, when informed of the subject under discussion, has not concurred in that opinion. But here we are confronted with a very different good-fellowship—one in which each member produced a work which, for good or bad, has come ever since under the heading of a classic. If one member of the group had produced a classic the friendship would have been important; if two, then unusual, but with all three it is unique. Which brings us back to the reflection that happiness has more of a say in creative matters than it is usually given credit for.

The association between Pope, Swift and Gay in the summer of 1726 produced ultimately *Gulliver's Travels*, *The Fables* and *The Dunciad*. It was able to do this because the three men concerned fitted into each other's different mentalities as neatly as the parts of a jigsaw puzzle. Out of their conjunction came inspiration, as certainly as a flower springs up from the conjunction of a seed and warm earth in spring. Again one should remember the vitalising presence of Swift. *Come and quicken me.* He had come, the greatest of them, with his all-but-finished *Gulliver* in his pocket, and immediately his presence had lit up inspiration in Pope and Gay. The connection was made, the current, from Swift's hand-clasp, flowed through them—and ordinary men turned again into poets. But just as Pope and Gay needed Swift's presence to become fully themselves so Swift in his own way needed them as badly. The active element is no greater than the passive; it is only another kind. No life of Swift or Pope can ever hope to be complete unless it lays stress on the tremendous personal importance both men held for each other, or unless it remembers Gay as the third element, a small but still a necessary one, in their feast of love. Of him it might be said, as Pliny said of another, *Amicos habuit, quia amicus fuit.* He had friends because he was a friend. Between the lightning which was Pope's genius and the thunder that was Swift's, Gay was the lightning-conductor and the refreshing rain which succeeded the storm. In the ensuing calm he could sometimes produce an effective kind of summer lightning of his own—brilliant but harmless; and even a reverberative roll of mock-thunder—but this was not his chief function. Primarily his position was the one which Pope had divined in him at the outset of their acquaintance—he had a temper "to cement friendships." He was the normal man between two abnormals, the connecting-link between two extremes of genius. Without such a link the natures of Swift and Pope would have clashed instead of fusing; with it, they were merged and enlarged.

This granted, Gay is seen in a somewhat different light from that of the "gentle parasite" which the Cambridge University Press edition of English literature is good enough to christen him, or from Thackeray's yapping lap-dog. To discerning persons the fact that Pope and Swift both loved him has always been sufficient to discredit such opinions—"Both," as Mr. G. C. Faber rightly remarks, "very great men, and not fond of fools."

In the spring of '26 Swift was a man just over sixty, with a political past as seemingly dead as the chief Minister he had once served, but with a new reputation as a mighty controversialist in Irish politics trailing clouds of glory behind him wherever he went. His English friends never ceased imploring him to come over into England, as into Macedonia, to help them. *Gulliver's Travels*, on which he had been working erratically for many years, was all but finished, but where in Ireland was the audience fit to try him out on? Doubtless Stella, when well, was employed in the capacity of tryer-out, rather as things are first tried out on the dog; but judging from the specimens of Stella's humour which the Dean has so affectionately preserved for posterity it can hardly have been an adequate test. His male friends in Ireland, with the exception of Sheridan and Lord Carteret (who both of them had their own affairs to attend to) were utterly unworthy of being allowed to receive *Gulliver* before he burst upon the rest of the world. The kindred spirits which would appreciate such a traveller were undeniably Arbuthnot, Pope and Gay. In such understanding company he would first receive the spirit of life, and leap off the written page. It was an inaugural ceremony impossible to resist. The Dean packed up his things in April and came over to London.

With his arrival, Pope's Twickenham household became itself again. The beloved presence acted on Pope with even greater force than usual, and sent him into a perfect frenzy of organisation. Swift later wrote to Tickell:

"I have lived these two months past for the most part in the country, either at Twickenham with Mr. Pope, or rambling with him and Mr. Gay a fortnight together. Mr. Pope ... prescribes all our visits without our knowledge, and Mr. Gay and I find ourselves often engaged for three or four days to come, and we neither of us dare dispute his pleasure."

The friends and companions, the old familiar faces, surged about the returned wanderer with a zest and enthusiasm unusual in so decorous an age. There was Bolingbroke at his Dawley estate to be embraced like the prodigal son he was. There was Bathurst in London and at his country place near Cirencester. There was young Lord Oxford at Wimpole, with his flattering appreciation of his father's old friend. There was Pulteney, Walpole's chief rival—and could any man, providing he was witty, ask for a better passport to the Dean's affections than that? Then Fortescue, that modest Scriblerian, was at Richmond and Arbuthnot at Dover Street and at the Court at Leicester Fields—where he had promised to introduce Swift, with all speed, to the

Prince and Princess of Wales. All these waited for him, apart from Pope and Gay. There was another woman besides the Princess of Wales whose acquaintance Swift desired to make, Mrs. Howard, that woman of reason eulogised by Pope and Peterborough. A reasonable woman, Swift knew, was as much a freak as his own houhynyms and yahoos. He longed to meet her.

As soon as the first salutations were over the reunion resolved itself into a triumphal progress; Swift, riding like a conqueror between his two hosts, visited Lord Cobham's private palace at Stowe, and Bathurst's estate at Cirencester, Bolingbroke among his haycocks and rural regalia at Dawley and Burlington in his pocket palace at Chiswick. For a fortnight the three of them rifled the south of England for all that it could yield them of noble sights and company. To Swift the gentle opulence of English fields, the well-cared-for farms and the shining healthy faces of the peasantry who ran out to watch the three cavaliers go by, must have been doubly precious. Contrasted with the starved savages which were Irish peasantry, and the hovels they lived in, the scene unrolling before him, mile after mile, was Paradise regained. . . .

The three cavaliers did not ride alone. *Gulliver* travelled along with them, and took his share of the conversation; Theobald, king of the dunces, was taken out of Pope's pocket, and dangled before the other riders to show them what *he* could do to a man who had dared to criticise him; Gay's *Fables*, whose ambling metre asked no better accompaniment than the sound of a trotting horse, joined *Gulliver* and *The Dunciad* on the excursion. And when these almost inexhaustible subjects of discussion flagged, they could occupy themselves with the prospect of a Miscellany consisting of the pieces dashed off, by one or other of them, in the early days of Martin Scriblerus—pieces until now in Pope's keeping. *That* miscellany, when it came out, would make Grub Street sit up a bit! Three cavaliers were riding, three knights against the dragons of folly and stupidity and vice. They were on top of the world.

At some point on this excursion they journeyed to the Rose Inn at Oakingham in Berkshire. There, in the course of a wet afternoon, and with the nonchalant gallantry proper to cavaliers they all three fell in love with the landlord's daughter, a young woman with the uneuphonious name of Molly Mogg. Molly Mogg was toasted by the fine gentlemen from London with the zest usually reserved—by other gentlemen—for the noble toasts of the Kitkat. It must have been extremely exhilarating for all concerned. The love was of suitably short duration—do not all cavaliers love and then ride away? but whilst it lasted it gave rise to the ballad of *Molly Mogg, or the fair maid of the Inn*. This was subsequently printed in Mist's journal as being "writ by two or three Men of wit (who have diverted the Publick both in Prose and Verse) upon the Occasion of their lying at a certain Inn in Ockingham, where the Daughter of the House was remarkably pretty" . . . and was an immediate success. Swift in later correspondence, however, described the ballad as being Gay's alone. At the best it is a slight thing, and the most that can be claimed for it is that it shows that two misanthropes and an occasional Groveller were not above being mollified, as much as ordinary human beings are—by beauty.

But Swift's visit to England was not entirely a pleasure trip; he had business to transact at Court and the question of the manufacture of Irish plaids to be brought before Mrs. Howard and the Princess. Whilst he was feeling his way on this momentous subject, Pope and Gay were "celebrating a birthday" at Mrs.

Howard's new house at Richmond—Marble Hill. A letter written to that lady concerning a visit there has always been put down to Pope, and frequently printed as his. This book for the first time prints the greater part of it as from its rightful composer, Gay. The confusion, as usual, has arisen from the extreme similarity between Pope's and Gay's handwriting, and their friendly habit of snatching the pen from each other and cutting into the correspondence without warning. The point is still open to controversy, unless a handwriting expert can settle it once for all but as it is one of the most readable letters ever addressed to Mrs. Howard, and, in my opinion, completely typical of Gay, it is right that for once it should go to its real author instead of to Pope. As to proofs, one can call forth no better arguments than intuition and deduction —intuition, because any student, after reading whatever of Gay's correspondence remains extant, and studying his poetry, begins to develop a super-sensitive ear to his style—so much more simple, so much less elegant, than Pope's; deduction, because the poets happened just then to be living together and because Pope's paragraph, read in this new light, fits in at the end with the proper lightness and not with (as it has done for so long) a laboured inconsequence.

Let the stage be set for the occasion; Mrs. Howard is in London. She has obviously invited Pope (who has helped her to lay out the gardens) and Gay (who has advised on the household arrangements) to make themselves free of her new house Marble Hill, in her absence. One imagines the two of them walking over from Twickenham to Richmond on a shimmering June day, with the river flowing sedately as watered silk beside them, and the willows half-hidden by waist-high foolsparsley and meadowsweet along the banks. Such a setting would recall vividly to Gay the bank of the Taw at Barnstaple—with its green swards and willows and shady elms. Were there dragonflies threading themselves like blue needles between the Thames reeds on that day?—or a kingfisher to stab the serene colour with his peacock hue? Every now and then in a life a day must be perfect, to make up for the many spoiled days in between. The tone of Gay's letter suggests that June 20th had been one of those perfect days. He writes to Mrs. Howard on his return from that highly-successful expedition:

"We cannot omit taking this occasion to congratulate you on the increase of your family, for your cow this morning was very happily delivered of the better sort, I mean a female calf; she is as like her mother as she can stare. . . . We have given her the name of Cæsar's wife Calpurnia, imagining that as Romulus and Remus were suckled by a wolf, that Roman lady was suckled by a cow, from which she took her name.

"In order to celebrate this birthday, we had a cold dinner at Marble Hill. Mrs. Susan offered us wine upon the occasion, and upon such an occasion we could not refuse it. Our entertainment consisted of flesh and fish and the lettuce of a Greek island called Cos. We have some thoughts of dining there to-morrow, to celebrate the day after the birthday, and on Friday, to celebrate the day after that, when we intend to entertain Dean Swift; because we think your hall the most delightful room in the world, except that where you are. If it was not for you we would forswear all Courts; and really it is the most mortifying thing in nature, that we can neither get into the Court to live with you, nor you get into the country to live with us. So we will take up with what we can get that belongs to you and make ourselves as happy as we can in your house."

This, I submit, is pure Gay. Note the trick of Biblical repetition, "offered us wine upon the occasion, *and upon such an occasion* we could not refuse it." It is the same as in his earlier "and in the winter I have been sick with wine, as I am not at this time, blessed be God for it, *as I must bless God for all things.*" It is not a trick Pope would have used, but it is one familiar in the rhetoric of the dissenting bodies of the Church, and one with which, therefore, Gay was quite familiar. The absorption in the present, too, is noticeable, in the actual comfortable delights which went to make up that day—the child-like preoccupation with food and drink. This part of the letter is like a Dutch picture, with the Cos lettuce painted beautifully in the middle, Mrs. Susan white-capped in the background bringing in a bottle of ruby-coloured Burgundy, and the black and white floor of the Hall at Marble Hill supplying the authentic touch. Then the naïveté of "we have some thoughts of dining here to-morrow—and the day after, and the day after that." It is not in the least in Pope's line. He could not blow such deliciously airy bubbles of absurdity; always, with him, they carried too heavy a ballast of gallantry. And would such a proud poet ever have made use of the word *mortified*? The man who was proud to see "men, not afraid of God, afraid of me?" Nobody with an eye on Posterity would ever have dreamed of confessing to even an artificial mortification, whilst Gay, who on everybody's evidence always spoke just what he thought, continually did it. Every post at Bath, he had told Mrs. Howard in another letter, had given him "fresh mortification." But detective work like this on single words is straining the point, when the whole tone of the first paragraph, its one-syllable words and utter simplicity of style and subject is so transparently Gay, and just as transparently not Pope. *Here* is Pope, in the second and much shorter paragraph of the same letter:

> "I hope we shall be brought into no worse company when you all come to Richmond; for whatever our friend Gay may wish as to getting into Court, I disclaim it, and desire to see nothing of the Court but yourself."

The tone is different at once. The toga is wrapped about the senator while he disclaims the desire to be at Court and hints, with inevitable malice, at the "worse company" of the life there. This new distinction clears up another point; it explains a reference which otherwise appears to have been dragged in with a ruthless inconsequence extremely unlike Pope. His reference to Gay's desire to get into Court, so long as we accept the idea that the letter is Pope's, must be taken to refer to the old, old story of Gay's *general* longing for and preoccupation with Court life—an inference as unfair to Gay as it would be clumsy in Pope. What he obviously refers to here is not that over-estimated general desire, but Gay's *particular* desire in the preceding paragraph—a small joke introduced for Mrs. Howard's benefit and because anyway as a joke it appealed to Gay, who liked on occasion to laugh at his own weaknesses.

So detailed a dissertation may appear out of proportion to the letter, which is after all extremely slight. But even thistledown has its value, and other bubbles besides the South Sea one may be allowed their place in the current scheme. These particular bubbles are very radiant and irridescent ones, floating in a sky without a cloud in it, because the weather is June weather, and friends are kind, and Swift is in England. They decorate a letter which immortalises one day in the life of Marble Hill. The ruby wine which was poured out by Mrs. Susan that day flows from an inexhaustible source, the fish and flesh are preserved in a still life for us, the Cos lettuce is as crisp and juicy and tenderly curved about itself as lettuces must be in Heaven, but seldom are on earth. And in the dark, milky-smelling cattlesheds outside is a calf, "as like her mother as she can stare."

There was more than one such happy occasion that year. There was an evening party at Pope's on July 6th at which Congreve and Bolingbroke and Swift were also guests, as well as Gay. Others have already lamented the fact that no record of that evening's conversation has come down to us. The candles tapered to an end and guttered out and the sentences spoken that night were extinguished in the darkness with them. The Thames flowed on at the foot of Pope's garden, but the conversation was gone for ever. Here, however, is Lord Bolingbroke at the end of the same month, exhibiting himself in the most amiable light in which it can be possible to catch that nobleman:

From Lord Bolingbroke to the three Yahoos at Twickenham.
"Jonathan, Alexander, John, most excellent Triumvirs of Parnassus. Though you are probably very indifferent where I am, and what I am doing, yet I resolve to believe the contrary. I persuade myself that you have sent at least fifteen times within this fortnight to Dawley farm, and that you are exceedingly mortified at my long silence.

To relieve you therefore from this great anxiety of mind, I can do no less than write a few lines to you; and I please myself beforehand with the vast pleasure which this epistle must needs give you. That I may add to this pleasure, and give you further proofs of my beneficent temper, I will likewise inform you, that I shall be in your neighbourhood again by the end of next week, by which time I hope that Jonathan's imagination of business will be succeeded by some imagination more becoming a professor of that divine science, *Vive La Bagatelle*. Adieu, Jonathan, Alexander, John! Mirth be with you."

From the Banks of the Severn. July 23rd, 1726.

Hard to believe that a man who could write like this would also sell his soul for a chance of power. Unfortunately the soul can only be sold once and Bolingbroke, together with the rest of his political cronies, had sold his long ago. The fact that a man has sold his soul however does not prevent his sometimes regretting it, and fits of melancholy from intervening between shouts of *Vive la Bagatelle*. Obviously that summer Bolingbroke was a despondent man. A constitution wrecked by youthful excesses and a career wrecked from other causes, were both liable to leave unpleasant after-effects. Pulteney wrote on his behalf to Swift:

> "Lord B. is so ill, and so much alone—the common fate of those who are out of power—that I have not left him one day since my return to London. Say something kind to Pope for me. Toss John Gay over the water to Richmond, if he is with you.
> "Adieu."

The ameliorative influence of Gay was apparently in

demand outside the home circle as well as in it. It appears that when the Triumvirate of Parnassus broke up temporarily and he went back to his lodgings in Whitehall, the friendship between Pope and Swift at Twickenham was not nearly so idyllic. Pope's small reedy voice could not penetrate the Dean's ever-increasing deafness; the Dean's endless stridings to and fro disturbed the painfully-achieved serenity of his host. It came to this: that they loved each other's minds as much as ever, but they could not long endure each other's physical presence without fatigue. Swift, summing up the situation as bluntly as usual, declared: "Two sick friends cannot live together." He did not add—though Pope divined—that the sickness of Stella occupied him more at this period than any other sickness. Making only the vaguest of excuses and guiltily conscious all the while that these were not really sufficient to give a host who had been as kind to him as Pope had been, he left Twickenham and came to stay for a while with Gay in his Whitehall lodgings. Here he was able to arrange the last details about the publication of *Gulliver* and to be introduced to the Court at Leicester Fields. Here, through Arbuthnot's influence, he met the Princess, and through Gay's, that paragon of all the virtues, Mrs. Howard. He was as successful with both as all his life he was successful with women. For a short time it may even have seemed to him that the Golden Age had returned and that in the flattering deference and attention that he could read in the eyes of the Princess and Mrs. Howard, Vanessa lived again, and Mrs. Masham, and Lady Bolingbroke, and all those earlier friends. There was something else to be flattered about, too: the arrival of the redoubtable *Drapier* had not gone unnoticed by Walpole. Using Peterborough as an intermediary, he asked Swift to dine with him at Chelsea.

Though there can be no doubt about Walpole's object, which was to try, by hook or by crook, to turn the sympathies of the Dean to the cause of the King instead of the Prince of Wales, Swift's is not so easily deducible. By meeting Walpole's flag of truce with one of his own it was possible that he might help Ireland—Irish trade, Irish industry, Irish pride; but there was another reason, too, and one closely associated with his friend Gay. A lampoon, somewhat worse than usual, had recently been widely circulated and report gave out that Walpole, usually the most imperturbable of men, not only resented it strongly, but declared he knew it to be the work of Gay. The curious thing is that, while Swift took this happening so intensely to heart, nothing exists of Gay's own attitude to the aspersion. Possibly he was so flattered by the fact that Walpole, at least, could believe him to be an author in his own right and not a mere signature to some one else's writings that he could not feel nearly as upset about it as Swift did. Possibly, too, he could not realise with Swift's mordant clear-sightedness that, if the story of his authorship were believed, any chances of Court preferment were irretrievably wrecked. Incapable of feeling great resentment himself as yet, and certainly incapable of believing that resentment could beget such bitter revenge, he undervalued the happening in all its aspects. This is the conclusion one draws from the fact that not one of his writings extant refers to it. He borrowed some sheets from Jervas to put Swift up, pooh-poohed Swift's fury at the base insinuation, probably advised him to sleep on it (on Jervas's pillow-case) and stubbornly refused to get worked up about the whole affair. Swift, who loved him for his innocence, could have smacked him for his stupidity. The most inoffensive of all poets had earned the wrath of the most powerful of all Ministers. It needed Swift to untangle such a coil of trouble. He put Gay's case to the Queen. Still more, he pocketed his pride and accepted Walpole's invitation to dinner.

His motives were excellent but his actions, alas, hardly came up to the same level. Instead of dealing with that frankness which would have endeared him to Walpole as it had already endeared him to hundreds of other men, he preferred to employ some of that tedious circumnavigation and mystery which, while it served to fill a dull afternoon in Dublin or at Richmond, just as certainly wasted Walpole's time. Consequently when Swift said that "when Great ministers heard ... things of a person who expected some favour, although they were afterwards convinced that the person was innocent, yet they would never be reconciled," Walpole chose to interpret this as meaning to apply to Swift and not to Gay. He is reported to have given this opinion in public and to have remarked that Swift had been along to see him and to apologise for past misdemeanours. Such behaviour was, in Swift's opinion, either knavery or crass stupidity. He loathed both, and never sought to see Walpole again. Instead, he let loose on his White-hall landlord (as he called Gay) the spleen and bad temper that he had been forced to keep in check in the nursing-home atmosphere at Twickenham, and the palace atmosphere at Leicester Fields.

Whatever other comforts he lacked at Gay's, he did not lack complete freedom of speech. And Gay, unlike Pope, never minded. He chattered on to Swift about his own private affairs and about Court affairs, and about Mrs. Howard and the Duchess of Queensberry, and Swift listened as long as he could and then cut the flood short with a *poof!* of impatience. But as long as the talk was endurable, he listened: he complained however that when *he* talked Gay did not always listen. He might *look* as if he were listening as they tramped along the cobbles of Whitehall or across the grass of the Mall or Leicester Fields—but when Swift, to test him, stopped short and asked him a question, only too often Gay answered with some irrelevance—some small personal point—while Swift had been busy with immensities! Nor was this the only objection. Swift also complained that Gay, whose lodgings looked down on the Whitehall traffic, would not even let his visitor have a window to himself. He *would* babble, and he would not listen, and he *would* come and lean over the Dean at the window when all the Dean wanted was to sit and glower down in solitude on the miserable Yahoos who polluted the walks of Whitehall. These were the leeches who battened upon the body politic; slaves in their turn of the arch-leech of Westminster, thief-in-chief of the public purse and persecutor-in-chief of all honest men. When Swift remembered such enormities Gay's faults faded into insignificance. Besides them, inattention and preoccupation in a host were unimportant—like the only fault he had ever been able to find in Arbuthnot—that he had "a sort of slouch in his walk." When treachery and corruption and hypocrisy stood in the high places of the world and mocked honest talent the Dean knew that he might thank God that the faults of his friends were such trifling ones.

But over all faults, trifling or serious, hung the menace of Stella's illness, which turned his heart to water and seemed to melt the very marrow of his bones with pity and terror. Torn with anxiety for her, a lesser anxiety for Gay, and a miserable consciousness that he had not dealt towards Pope quite as he ought, he departed as suddenly as usual—post-haste for Ireland. Pope accompanied him as far as Chester, and while Swift was still there waiting for a ship and a favourable wind he wrote to his late companion:

> "I am gathering up my luggage and preparing for my journey; I will endeavour to think of you as little as I can, and when I write to you, I will strive not to think of you; this I intend in return to your kindness; and further, I know nobody has dealt with me so cruelly as you, the consequences of which usage I fear will last as long as my life, for so long shall I be (in spite of my heart),
> "Entirely yours,
> "JON. SWIFT."

The cruelties inflicted on Swift by Pope are obscure, but no letter could be tenderer or more implicit of affection. Pope answered with the same fervour:

> "Many a short Sigh you cost me the day I left you, and many more will you cost me until the Day you return. . . . I wish I could think no more of it but lie down and sleep till we meet again, and let that Day (how far soever off it may be) be the Morrow. . . . Till then I will drink (or Gay shall drink) daily Healths to you."

However affairs may have been between the poets at the time of Augustus, there can have been few friendships equal to this one. But the air of Parnassus is a trifle too rarefied to keep human poets going long. A letter from Gay, following on these two testaments, brings things down to a more prosaic level. Swift, who used to advise Gay about household duties with the same seriousness with which he used to advise him about a life-work, must have been relieved to receive the following information:

"Mr. Jervas's sheets [wrote Gay] are sent home to him mended, finely washed, and neatly folded up. I intend to see Mr. Pope to-morrow or on Sunday. I have not seen Mrs. Howard a great while, which you know must be a great mortification and self-denial; but in my case it is particularly unhappy, that a man cannot contrive to be in two places at the same time; if I could, while you are there, one of them would always be Dublin. But after all, it is a silly thing to be a friend by halves, so that I will give up all thoughts of bringing this project to perfection, if you will contrive that we shall meet again soon."

Soon after this he was able to assure the Dean that his "opera" was all but finished and that he proposed to visit Newgate shortly, to fill in any necessary local colour, and no doubt he did. This is the first mention from him of *The Beggar's Opera*, and it is a long time before we, or Swift, hear of it again—and certainly long before it is finished. But as long as he felt the Dean's interest and encouragement wrapped protectively about him, Gay shook off his usual indolence . . . But by the time he sends the next letter a longer space has elapsed and a little of that tremendously heartening influence has begun to wear off. He writes:

"Let us hear from you as often as you can afford to write. I would say something to you of myself, if I had any good to say, but I am in much the same way in which you left me, eternally busy about trifles, disagreeable in themselves, but rendered insupportable by their end, which is to enable me to bury myself from the world, who cannot be more tired of me than I am of it, in an agreeable sepulchre, I hope to bring this about next, and shall be glad to see you at my funeral.

"Adieu."

In Dublin, Swift rejoiced to find Stella not so desperately ill as he had been led to suppose. His arrival had hastened her recovery, and consequently he was able to spare time for a lively correspondence with all the friends he had been forced to leave so abruptly behind him—especially with his new friend, Mrs. Howard.

Why a man as disillusioned as Swift should ever have hung his political hopes on so frail a prop as Mrs. Howard remains a mystery. She had no official position: she never made use of her function as royal mistress (as the Duchess of Kendal did) to sell Court favours to the highest bidder. She never gave promises of any sort, and when clumsy and ambitious courtiers sought to bribe her as they bribed other influential persons, the equanimity of Mrs. Howard's temper came nearer to being upset than at any other time. The most that can be said against her is that, though she never sold favours she never specifically denied that she was in a position where this might be done. Why should she deny it? As long as she held her tongue about it she was the goose that laid the golden eggs to the Opposition lords, and to all needy poets. For Mrs. Howard to declare unequivocally that she was not that goose, and that never at any time did she propose to benefit any one of her admirers by even a halfpennyworth of Court favour would have killed her popularity. The mystery and glamour surrounding her would have dispersed and the truth become painfully obvious to all beholders—that, outside the bedchamber, Mrs. Howard had no influence whatever upon the Prince of Wales. She kept that secret from most of her admirers with surprising success

The hon^{ble} Mrs Howard,
afterwards
Countess of Suffolk

throughout her long life. But Walpole, who could sum up his fellow-humans with the accurate and unforgiving eye of a stockbreeder watching cattle in a ring, knew very well that in the Court of the Prince of Wales there was only one person who mattered—and that was the Princess.

Pope was another who was not deceived by Mrs. Howard's position. He had, after several years' acquaintance, veered considerably from his original verdict. The story is that on one occasion when Martha Blount was ill, Mrs. Howard had turned (in Pope's presence) to one of her footmen and asked him to remind her to pay some little attention to the invalid. Martha Blount, from what has come down to us, was perfectly capable of fancying herself ill-used and insulted without any assistance from Pope—and Lady Mary Wortley Montagu was a good deal more accurate than usual when she described Miss Blount once as a thorn in the flesh. None of this really matters to posterity: if Pope was fond of Martha Blount she might be a perfect gorse-bush for all it concerned the rest of the world. But Mrs. Howard's ill-timed request to the footman damned her for ever with Pope. He derived some satisfaction from privately drawing up a new 'Character' of her, very different from that earlier one:

> With every pleasing, every prudent part
> What more can *Chloe* want? She wants a Heart,
> She speaks, behaves and acts just as she ought
> But never, never reach'd one generous Thought.
> Virtue she finds too painful an endeavour
> Content to dwell in Decencies for ever. . . .

In the same year the Duke and Duchess of Queensberry inherited from the Duchess's uncle, Douglas House

T

at Petersham, near Ham Common. This suited Gay's purposes extremely well, for it ensured him a choice of residences in the Richmond neighbourhood. He wrote that he was staying with the Queensberrys "in Oxfordshire and at Petersham, and wheresoever they would carry me." Legend further declared that Gay made use of the small summer-house at the river's edge in the Petersham garden; and that he sat there that autumn, while the spiders spun their gossamer across the tops of the Michaelmas daisies, and polished his *Fables* for Prince William. Perhaps this was the "agreeable sepulchre" he had pictured in his last letter to Swift. Forty years later—when the spiders were still spinning their gossamer in autumn, but when Gay had long been dead—the son of Robert Walpole was to sit in *his* little house across the river and write to a friend: "Ham walks bound my prospects, but thank God the Thames is between me and the Duchess of Queensberry."

It could not be expected that Horace Walpole should feel about the aged Duchess as Prior had felt about the young débutante. By that time she was more of an old war-horse than a colt untam'd. But when the house at Petersham was still a new acquisition, and Gay still available as a friend and companion, the Duchess was neither of these extremes. If we are to believe contemporary opinion, she was, instead, *Laura*, in Gay's verses "To a Lady on her Passion for Old China." The verses themselves are as brittle, well-shaped and glossy as the china they celebrate. No sooner did they appear than Lady Mary Wortley Montagu immediately flew into a pseudo-passion on the Duchess's behalf—and wondered how she could ever have allowed Johnny Gay to presume on her good nature so far as to address her, even poetically, as *Laura*. No doubt the lady did her best for her case by stating in all the drawing-rooms that you can't trust these poets and describing eternally how she had been forced to rebuff Pope in similar circumstances; and no doubt she liked to think that because she herself had never seen any wit in Johnny Gay, the Duchess of Queensberry preferred him in the capacity of a lover. She had, for a woman who aspired to wider feminine education, almost the smallest mind on record.

There are a great many possible variations about the *Laura* poem—that *Laura* was not the Duchess but somebody else; that *Laura* was the Duchess, but that the lines were a mere tribute to her beauty—the only coin in which poets could repay kindness and one which they delighted to employ; or that she was *Laura* and that Lady Mary Wortley Montagu concluded rightly that there was a Guilty Passion involved. The second alternative is the reasonable one. The Duchess had with the rest of the world just then a passion for collecting China pieces and Gay seized on this characteristic of hers and put it into a poem—linking it to a passion as artificial as the one that Daphnis felt for Chloe in all the pastorals of the period. That is to say the sentiment was artificial, but occasionally the lines were not. Indeed, in the midst of the constrained elegance of a typically eighteenth-century address to a lady, Gay's own natural lyrical qualities suddenly burst forth, and he inserts four lines as simple and lovely as raindrops. They come after a satirical account of the various fads of the period:

> Some gems collect; some medals prize
> And view the rust with Lovers' eyes.
> Some court the stars at midnight hours;
> Some dote on nature's charms in flowers.

All this is cracker-motto stuff. *Crack!* goes the cracker

—and out falls the paper cap or the string of pink beads. But the poetry is coming:

> But every beauty I can trace
> In Laura's mind, in Laura's face;
> My stars are in this brighter sphere
> My lilly and my rose is here.

The order of the beauties is significant. Laura's *mind* is celebrated—her mind, when all contemporary opinion argued that women *had* no minds! (Poor Lady Mary Wortley Montagu, though she received many complimentary verses from Pope, never received one containing so stupendous a compliment as that.) Naturally so sublime a level could not be sustained. From the Elizabethan simplicity of this avowal Gay descends to an ingenious comparison of the merits of China and of human beings. He follows this with the characteristic lines:

> Husbands more covetous than sage
> Condemn the china-buying rage;
> They count that woman's prudence little
> Who sets her heart on things so brittle.
> But are those wise men's inclinations
> Fix'd on more strong, more sure foundations?
> If all that's frail we must despise
> No human view or scheme is wise.
> Are not Ambition's hopes as weak?
> They swell like bubbles, shine and break.
> A courtier's promise is so slight
> 'Tis made at noon, and broke at night.

After more of this moralising the poem is rounded off neatly with one of the few sentiments which Gay and his contemporaries had been prepared to take over from the Elizabethans, lock, stock and barrel—the sentiment concerning the intransience of beauty:

> Love, *Laura*, love while youth is warm,
> For each new winter breaks a charm;
> And woman's not like *China* sold
> But cheaper grows in growing old;
> Then quickly choose the prudent part
> Or else you break a faithful heart.

These doubtless were the lines on which Sappho based her suspicions, but to the reader in possession of the whole story they have no more significance than the cracker-motto afore-mentioned; and almost certainly the Duchess accepted them at their true valuation—a prettily-expressed sentiment as unreal as the scenes painted upon her favourite Porcelain or Delft.

In the interval before the coming-out of *Gulliver* Gay sent a rhymed recipe for stewed Veal in a letter to Swift. But recipes were soon put out of both his and Swift's minds by an accident to Pope. A coach in which he was travelling overturned in crossing a stream and Pope was trapped in it as badly as Gulliver in the cage which Glumdalclitch had made for him, tossing on the sea. He was rescued only by being hauled ignominiously through the window by a footman and one of his hands was badly cut in the process. Swift was horrified to hear of it— at least as horrified as a man could be whose principal horror—Stella's sickness—had been allayed. He wrote anxiously to England, enquiring of all his friends about Pope; and all his friends sent back enthusiastically conflicting accounts. Unfortunately it was Pope's right hand which had been damaged—and while it was recovering it was inevitable that the right-hand man should be recalled. So Gay returned to Twickenham. No doubt he was delighted to be of use to Pope, and he sustained the position with as much dignity as he could muster. After describing in detail to Swift the progress of Pope's recovery he added:

> "I believe you will expect that I should give you some account of how I have spent my time since you left me. I have attended my distressed friend at Twickenham, and been his amanuensis, which you know is no idle charge. I have read about half Virgil, and half Spenser's Faerie Queene. I still despise Court preferments, so that I lose no time in attendance upon great men."

This noble renunciation must have come somewhat as a surprise to Swift—but it may not have been as thorough as it sounded. Robert Walpole's nickname was "The Great Man," and Gay may only have been referring to a decision not to go and put a guinea into the pocket of Robert Walpole's porter—that necessary preliminary to an interview with greatness. Otherwise, how could he say that he despised Court preferments when he was busy composing Fables with the avowed intention of winning a place at Court? He never wrote a sillier sentence in any letter. Only a month earlier a letter from Pope to Swift suggested a much more familiar state of affairs. Erasmus Lewis, their mutual friend, and Oxford's old secretary, had recently betaken himself and his social activities off to a fastness in Wales. Pope commented on such withdrawals:

> "I can't help thinking (when I consider the whole short list of our friends) that none of them except you or I are qualified for the mountains of

Wales. The Doctor goes to cards, Gay to court; one loses his money, one loses his time."

Another letter, which would seem to bear out that Gay had only renounced the idea of a personal appeal to Walpole and not his general hopes of Court preferments, comes from him to Swift at the end of October:

"I have of late been very much out of order with a slight fever, which I am not yet quite free from; it was occasion'd by a cold, which my attendance at the Guildhall improved."

He adds, obviously in response to some enquiry from Swift, a sentence which remains completely baffling:

"I have not a friend who hath got anything under my Administration, but the Duchess of Queensberry who hath had a benefit of a thousand pounds. . . ."

And then, just to show how thoroughly he is losing no time in attendance at Court, he adds:

"Next week I shall have a new coat and new Buttons for the [King's] Birthday, though I don't know but a turn-coat might have been more for my advantage. Yours most sincerely and affectionately."

At the same time as Swift received that letter, *Gulliver's Travels* was published in London. The warmth of the book's reception may be gauged from another letter to Swift from Arbuthnot, less than a week after publication:

> "Gay has had a little fever, but is pretty well recovered; so is Mr. Pope. We shall meet at Lord Bolingbroke's on Thursday in town, at dinner and remember you. Gulliver is in everybody's hands."

Gulliver was indeed in everybody's hands. Even the Princess of Wales read it, and Mrs. Howard wrote a long and enthusiastic letter to the author assuring him of the book's overwhelming success. . . . Gay, too, wrote to him endorsing this opinion, but justifying his title to "speaking just what he thought" by repeating to Swift some of the few adverse criticisms as well as the favourable ones. Lady Mary Wortley Montagu, who loathed Swift as much as she feared Pope and Arbuthnot and despised Gay, wrote to her sister, the Countess of Mar:

> "Here is a book come out, that all our people of taste run mad about; 'tis no less than the work of a dignified clergyman, an eminent physician and the first poet of the age; and very wonderful it is, God knows!"

She continued the sneer by bringing in the current dirty story about Quakers and horses and tying Swift and Arbuthnot and Pope on to it with malicious appositeness. But as long as Swift kept up the pretence of anonymity —a practice from which, in common with many other writers, he seemed to derive intense pleasure—he could not be annoyed if the usual erroneous conclusions concerning authorship were drawn. Actually, Lemuel Gulliver was as much his child as Martinus Scriblerus had been Arbuthnot's, as the King of the Dunciad was later Pope's, and as Captain Macheath was Gay's. . . .

The publication of the *Travels* inspired, as it was bound to do, many imitative pieces—and many tributes.

Gulliver, indeed, became so much the man of the moment that anything about him was bought up and read with avidity. Several pieces of verse from the hands of Swift's friends at Twickenham belong to this time. It is all but impossible to say, at this stage, who was responsible for what—but it is generally accepted that Pope wrote the cleverest and most indecent: *Mary Gulliver to Captain Lemuel Gulliver*, "a tenderly complaining epistle." (It is certainly like Pope's verbal ingenuity to be able to paraphrase the sound of neighing with "to hymn harmonious Houyhnhym through the nose.") Of the others, two are generally accepted as Gay's—a Lilliputian ode to *Quinbus Flestin the man-mountain*, and *The man-mountain's answer to the Lilliputian verses*. These in their way are as ingenious as Pope's effort—and must be the only poems extant whose lines are confined to the length of three syllables apiece. Accepted merely as flattering tribute to Swift (to whom most of these verses were posted by Pope) Gay's two verses are, apart from their form, insignificant. But it is permissible to wonder whether something more was not intended. Swift, after all, was at the height of his literary prestige with *Gulliver*. Gay had, as yet, achieved no more than small successes. It is possible that in these verses he was putting into the mouth of a Lilliputian poet—albeit humorously—his own feelings towards a friend who had soared, he felt, almost out of his reach:

> In amaze
> Lost, I gaze,
> Can our eyes
> Reach thy size? . . .
>
> Nigh thy ear
> In mid air

> On Thy hand
> Let me stand,
> So shall I
> (Lofty Poet!) Touch the sky.

If anything reinforces the deduction that in these verses Gay was addressing Swift in the guise of the Lilliputian addressing Gulliver, it is the sudden and unexpected use of the word Poet in the last line. Gulliver was many things in the course of his travels—but never a poet. Swift *was*, to many of his contemporaries. Unless there was some underlying meaning, why should the invocation "Lofty Poet" have been used? It was Swift who had risen up on to the heights. It was Swift whose presence invigorated and sustained his friends (On thy hand, let me stand)....

The reply of the Man-Mountain is couched in language both tender and common-sensical:

> On my hand
> Should you stand,
> If those that soar
> Fall the lower
> All Lilliput would yours deplore.
> Humbly then,
> With little men,
> Take your stand
> On firm land,
> Lest your place
> Bring disgrace:
> High in air,
> Great the care,
> To be free
> From jeopardy,

Careless found,
You might bound,
(Little Poet!) To the ground.

Any inner meaning is, however, supposition. It may well have been that there was nothing more in the verses than verbal ingenuity, compressed and compact as a Victorian nosegay and sent off to amuse Swift, who delighted in verbal exercises as much as later Deans delight in cross-word puzzles. They would have pleased him, had they pleased none else. As it was, they amused a good many other people. London was Gulliver-minded by this time and anything about him went with a bang.

The success of *Gulliver* made of Swift a very bouncing Dean indeed. He was full of virility and strength and pride in his achievement. He pooh-poohed Gay, sitting away in his little gossamer-strewn summer-house at Petersham, and toying with fables. "How comes Friend Gay to be so tedious?" he teased Pope. "Another man can publish 50,000 Lies sooner than he can publish 50 Fables." He also talked again of coming to England. (It would be his third visit since the *débâcle* of 1714—did he remember the superstition about third time lucky?) His friends were as enchanted as usual at the prospect—none more than Gay. He deplored the fact that the time of year made travelling so much more difficult and punned affectionately on his friend's name.

"But to us your Friends, the coming of such a Black Swallow as you are, will make a Summer in the worst of Seasons. . . . You fancy we envy you, but you are mistaken; we envy those you are with for we cannot envy the man we love."

The times indeed were auspicious. Gulliver had hoisted the Dean up on to the heights of his broad shoulders. The *Fables* were all but finished and Mrs. Howard seemed sure of their popularity. Pope was slowly recovering from his injury and delighted with the idea of the Dean's return. The Whig Government, so long in power, was as unpopular as anything ever is that exceeds the average allowance of time. The papers, wrote a French visitor to the country, "were universally composed of satires against the Government." Pulteney and Bolingbroke were taking over the newspaper *The Craftsman* and the Tories were convinced that such combined brilliance would be able to bring down Walpole where onslaughts from the general press had failed; the Prince of Wales's dislike of Walpole was notorious. The sympathies of what may be described as the Youth Movement in society and politics were nearly solid behind the heir-apparent—and not the King. In view of all these facts it might well have seemed to some Tories that only Swift's presence was necessary to set the stage for a real Tory come-back. Much correspondence crossed the Irish Sea just then between Swift and his friends, luring him on to yet another visit. But he was as coy as a girl about committing himself, and had a way of veering from the main subject to talk of something less important (to them). On one such occasion he wrote to Pope of Gay:

> "I hope my Whitehall landlord is nearer to a place than when I left him; as the preacher said, 'the day of judgment was nearer than it had ever been before.'"

The day of judgment was indeed near at hand; also the wailing and gnashing of teeth which formed its orchestral accompaniments.

CHAPTER EIGHTEEN

1727. The 'Fables.' Continuing 'The Beggar's Opera.' Turning down the appointment of Gentleman-Usher.

"*Amidst our hopes, Fate strikes the sudden wound.*"
GAY: 'A THOUGHT ON ETERNITY'

EARLY in the new year, Swift began to put into action his plans for coming to England. He had Irish plaids to discuss with Mrs. Howard, and medals to discuss with the Queen, the Miscellany of poems to discuss with the other Scriblerians—and all sorts of delicious prospects. He was sensible enough to know by now that plaids and medals were about as far as he could reasonably hope to go in Court favour. *The Tale of a Tub* had done its work too effectively for him to think that there was any longer a chance of his being transferred to an English Deanery. Even *Gulliver's* success could not atone for that. He knew, also, that Walpole had summed him up, after that unhappy dinner, and had decided not to bother with him further. Not only were his personal political hopes sunk, but his aspirations for Ireland were, it is all too clear, utterly baseless.

Even so, there was still plenty to attract the Dean in England. He wrote to Mrs. Howard:

"I hope you will get your house and wine ready; to which Mr. Gay and I are to have free access, when you are safe at court. As to Mr. Pope, he is not worth mentioning on such occasions."

And Gay and Pope wrote one of their joint letters back to him. One can only suppose that the dying-senator attitude was a catching one, for certainly in the part of the letter which was Gay's, Gay has it to perfection:

> "I believe 'tis my turn to write to you, though Mr. Pope hath taken all I had to say, and put it in a long letter. . . . I refused supping at Burlington House to-night in regard to my health and this morning I walked two hours in the Park. . . . The contempt of the world grows upon me, and I now begin to be richer and richer, for I could every morning I wake be content with less than I arrived at the day before. I fancy in time I shall bring myself into that state which no man ever knew before me, in thinking I have enough. I really am afraid to be content with so little, lest my good friends should censure me for indolence, and the want of laudable ambition. So that it will be absolutely necessary for me to improve my fortunes to content them. How solicitous is mankind to please others!
> "Yours most affectionately."

Interesting to see how Gay's mind like a chameleon's took on the hues of whatever friend he happened to be writing to—and all in the best of faith. He knew it would please Swift if he talked of having a contempt for the world. Swift's own advice was "Once kick the world, and the world and you will live together at a reasonable good understanding." Well, he was going to kick the world all right in the *Fables*—he had talked in an earlier poem of Courtiers being "monkeys in action, paroquets in talk," and now he would show them to be a perfect menagerie of wild beasts as well. What could please Swift more? . . . And to indicate his poetic impartiality he was including himself in the menagerie as a Hare. Meanwhile Gay and Pope worked together on the tattered remnants of Scriblerus—those snacks of verses with which the various members of the defunct Club had enlivened their evenings, so long ago. Swift, Pope, Parnell, Arbuthnot, Gay—they were all included. Later Pope wrote to Swift:

> "Our Miscellany is now quite printed. I am prodigiously pleased with this joint volume, in which methinks we look like friends, side by side, serious and merry by turns, conversing interchangeably and walking down hand in hand to posterity."

Doubtless Swift was prodigiously pleased too. Scriblerus had hitherto been only a warm memory, as potent but as ephemeral as a gulp of wine: now that he was between two covers there was a permanent record of days long past.

The *Miscellany* was published in March: in the same month Gay's *Fables* made their first appearance—and leapt into popularity with such spirit that they almost put *Gulliver* out of countenance. Their success, says one Editor, was "great, immediate and unqualified." Defoe brought out in the same year a pamphlet with the astounding title *Uses and Abuses of the Marriage Bed*, and perhaps nothing could better indicate the selling power of the *Fables* than the fact that they survived, and triumphed, even in the face of a publication with a title like that. The Prince and Princess of Wales read them, the Court read them, the Town read them—and old illiterate ladies in obscure parishes ordered parcels from Watts and Tonson and opened them with trembling eager hands. Infants lisped the sedate absurdities as they sat in their go-carts or rode upon the shoulders of footmen. William, the young Duke of Cumberland, and the favourite child of the Royal Family, for whose amusement the *Fables* had been invented, may even have gone so far as to cast his eyes over the woodcuts accompanying each fable and read with some degree of approbation:

> Accept, young Prince, the moral lay,
> And in these tales mankind survey;
> With early virtues plant your breast,
> The specious arts of vice detest.
> Princes like Beautys, from their youth
> Are strangers to the voice of truth . . .
> To those in your exalted station
> Each courtier is a dedication;
> Must I too flatter like the rest,
> And turn my morals to a jest?

Echo, backed up by the Duke of Cumberland, answers No, No, No! But Gay has buckled his sword on. *Fear not*, he reminds himself, *all men—even infant princes—are dedication-proof.* He has written the *Fables* with one ideal ahead of him—a better pension than £150 a year, and a better position than that of Lottery Commissioner. He clears his throat bravely and continues:

> But shall I hide your real praise,
> Or tell you what a Nation says?
> They in your infant bosom trace
> The virtues of your Royal race,
> In the fair dawning of your mind
> Discern you gen'rous mild and kind . . .
> Go on, the height of good attain
> Nor let a nation hope in vain.

Could anything sound more genuine and disinterested—
except to those in the know? One of this number may
have been Edward Young—who failed as usual to join
in the general approbation and with most unclerical lack
of charity wrote to a friend in Ireland: "Gay has just
given us some Fables—50 in Number and about Five are
tolerable." Dr. Johnson in his life of Gay is kinder,
although he complains that from some of the fables "it
will be difficult to extract any moral principle." He
goes on: "They are, however, told with liveliness; the
versification is smooth; and the diction, though now and
then a little constrained by the measure or the rhyme,
is generally happy."

There is no doubt that the volume was a best-seller
and that people of all sorts bought it and read the first
edition with an enthusiasm never equalled in the reading
of the fourth or fifth or tenth or twentieth editions.
Altogether, they have been the most re-printed of all
Gay's works. It is not difficult to see why. They were
unique of their kind—they filled a cultural gap which
La Fontaine had filled in France and Aesop in Rome: it
was comparatively easy to be a classic when there were
no other claimants to that particular classical niche: the
Fables became a classic. The only one which need concern us, however, is the one chosen conspicuously to end
the volume and so—its author hoped—linger suggestively in the minds of its readers. This is (perhaps
because of its personal implication) the best of all.

The Hare and Many Friends

Friendship, like love, is but a name,
Unless to one you stint the flame.
The child, whom many fathers share,
Hath seldom known a father's care.

'Tis thus in friendships; who depend
On many, rarely find a friend.

   A Hare who, in a civil way,
Complied with everything, like *Gay*,
Was known by all the bestial train
Who haunt the wood or graze the plain;
Her care was never to offend,
And every creature was her friend.

   As forth she went at early dawn,
To taste the dew-besprinkled lawn,
Behind she hears the hunter's cries,
And from the deep-mouth'd thunder flies;
She starts, she stops, she pants for breath;
She hears the near advance of death;
She doubles to mislead the hound,
And measures back her mazy round,
Till, fainting in the public way,
Half-dead with fear she gasping lay.

   What transport in her bosom grew,
When first the Horse appear'd in view!

   'Let me, (says she) your back ascend,
And owe my safety to a friend.
You know my feet betray my flight;
To friendship every burdens light.'

   The horse replied, 'Poor honest puss,
It grieves my heart to see thee thus;
Be comforted, relief is near,
For all your friends are in the rear.'

   She next the stately Bull implor'd;
And thus replied the mighty lord:

   'Since every beast alive can tell
That I sincerely wish you well,
I may, without offence, pretend
To take the freedom of a friend.

Love calls me hence; a favourite cow
Expects me near yon barley-mow;
And when a lady's in the case,
You know all other things give place.
To leave you thus might seem unkind,
But see, the Goat is just behind.'
  The Goat remark'd her pulse was high,
Her languid head, her heavy eye:
' My back, (says he) may do you harm;
The Sheep's at hand, and wool is warm.'
  The Sheep was feeble, and complain'd
His sides a load of wool sustain'd;
Said he was slow; confess'd his fears;
For hounds eat sheep as well as Hares.
  She now the trotting Calf address'd:
' Shall I, (says he) of tender age,
In this important care engage?
Older and abler pass'd you by;
How strong are those! how weak am I!
Should I presume to bear you hence,
Those friends of mine may take offence.
Excuse me, then! you know my heart;
But dearest friends, alas! must part.
How shall we all lament! Adieu;
For see the hounds are just in view.'

If reproach has ever been cast in more gentle language, then I have not come across it. There is no record of the book's reception by others in high places, but the Princess of Wales was quick to feel the aspersion. She assured Gay—through the usual telephonic exchange of Mrs. Howard—that on that happy day when George I should breathe his last she would "take up the Hare." She had also promised, a year earlier, to send Dr. Swift some medals. . . . Yet when Swift arrived back in England at the end of April, he had not yet received the medals. Did they too hang, in some mysterious way, on the decease of George I? If so, then both he and Gay could kick their heels in idleness. The King, for all they knew to the contrary, might live to be a hundred.

It was at this stage that Mrs. Howard kept them happy; no one knew better how to sound a restrained and reasonable note of optimism that all was for the best in the best of all possible worlds. Her optimism cannot often have been justified, but on this occasion it was. George I, who was on one of his periodic trips to Hanover, died suddenly at Osnaburg. (Nobody took better advantage of the situation than Thackeray who in a magnificently purple passage describes Robert Walpole galloping through the night along the road from Kensington to Richmond to announce the news to the new King.) The Tories must have been jubilant that night: they were certain that Walpole carried along the road with him not only the news of George I's death, but his own political death-warrant.

Unfortunately even certainties sometimes fail to come off. Everybody knows the almost comic readjustment of affairs—in which Walpole after a period of turbulent uncertainty emerged again as triumphant as Mr. Punch at the end of a Punch and Judy show. Mrs. Walpole went to the new Court and was cold-shouldered by all the Tories on her way in; but as she came out, leaving a still omnipotent husband behind her, she declared she could have walked over their heads. It was all extremely entertaining for those who liked to catch the human monkey-house at a thoroughly lively moment. The Whigs therefore, entirely to their surprise, found themselves reinstated more firmly than before, all except Walpole who may have been shrewd enough to realise that the promise of an additional £100,000 a year to the royal purse from the Civil List had something to do with it. The Tories were as discomfited as ever. Almost the only person whose position was still unaffected, no matter which political party ruled the roost —was Mrs. Howard. George II moved with his Court to St. James's Palace and Mrs. Howard went with him, into a thoroughly comfortable suite. At this juncture that depression from Iceland, Mr. Howard, fades from the picture and is heard of little more. The triumph of near-virtue is supreme.

Although Walpole remained at the head of affairs, there was still a shred of hope for the place-hunters. Their new Majesties could not be expected to make any changes in official appointments until after the summer, but—at least in the smaller posts—they might be expected to please their own private inclinations. Swift, who had come over to England partly with the intention of going to Aix-les-Bains (on Arbuthnot's advice) and seeing what the waters there could do to cure his giddiness, was prevailed upon by Mrs. Howard to give up that idea. What actually passed in conversation is of course merely guesswork, but according to Swift we may gather that she gave some pretty strong hints that the men who stayed loyally on the spot were the ones who might hope to be remembered. It is also guesswork as to what precisely he hoped to achieve. But he took Mrs. Howard's advice, stayed in London and lived to regret it ever after.

Pope and Gay spent the late spring with Lord Harcourt in Oxfordshire acting, he described it, as his Merry Andrews, and chasing away those thoughts of depression which arose whenever he remembered the days of long ago. When they returned south Swift joined them at Twickenham. Lady Mary Wortley Montagu wrote to her sister:

"Both Dr. Swift and Johnny Gay are at Pope's, and their conjunction has produced a ballad . . . which, if nobody else has sent you, I will."

The ballad may have been the still popular *Molly Mog* or, more likely, that first song from *The Beggar's Opera* which was then in the middle of composition. If it was this song, then Lady Mary was exaggerating as usual when she put it down equally to the Twickenham Triumvirate. Gay wrote the major part of it, and Swift and Pope, it is known, 'tightened up' the last couplet. It was all that they ever gave to *The Beggar's Opera*, beyond the attention and encouragement during composition, without which Gay would probably never have written that work. The play was a pleasant preoccupation and somehow it is nice to think of two such essentially unmusical men as Pope and Swift controlled, for a few short months in their lives, by the notes from a flute—notes sounding impudently through the cloistered rooms of Pope's house, or echoing like another blackbird among the bird-filled trees which hung over the river's edge.

Others besides Lady Mary Wortley Montagu were extremely interested in the Dean's stay at Twickenham. The Duchess of Queensberry, who could claim to be as haughty and overbearing in her own right as Swift ever was—and who had heard ecstatic descriptions of him from Gay—came over one day from Petersham to beard the lion in his friend's den, but, says history, he was "out of humour, and would only peep at her from behind the curtains." She went away disappointed. A more important visitor than the Duchess was M. Voltaire, exiled from France on account of his heretical opinions, and determined to meet the man whose heresy had upset religious opinion in England almost as much as he had upset it in France. Various apocryphal stories of that assemblage of wits have come down to us, the chief story being the one in which Mrs. Pope, horrified by the freedoms of Voltaire's conversation, left the table in a hurry. As, however, Mrs. Pope spoke no French and Voltaire's oral English was nowhere near as good as his written English, this seems unlikely. Another story is that Gay read over to him, in manuscript, a large part of *The Beggar's Opera*: this is certainly possible, for the time and the place and Voltaire were all together, and what poet does not seize the opportunity to read his works out loud when he has a new and distinguished audience? A Major Broome, who kept a manuscript journal at the time, declared that Voltaire said he "admired Swift, and loved Gay vastly." The distinction has the air of being a familiar one.

Apparently the news of the composition of *The Beggar's Opera* was now public property. Mrs. Howard was certainly privy to it, and also the Queensberrys. Dr. Arbuthnot as the only other musical man in Gay's circle would certainly know, and for a long time there was a suspicion that his daughter—probably the one who was as good-natured and idle as Gay himself—provided the author with a number of the Scots airs to which the verses were set. The marvel is that Martha Blount and Mrs. Pope and Swift's servant Patrick did not also claim to have had a hand in its composition. Everybody who was told of the Opera was interested, but nobody was very sanguine of its success. Just as by now the general conviction was that Walpole could not make a mistake or ever suffer a setback, so (in a much smaller way) the general conviction was that whatever Gay attempted was bound—by the ill-luck which trailed him—to come off dubiously. And this in spite of the recent undeniable success of the *Fables*.

If ever a man could have been found to disagree with Stevenson that to travel hopefully is better than to arrive that man would have been Gay. He had been travelling hopefully for several years now—but in no sense could he be described as having arrived. Bolingbroke, when told of the Opera, was as encouraging as a mute at a funeral:

> "I wish John Gay success in his pursuit," he told Swift, "but I think he has some qualities that will keep him down in the world."

—a nasty back-hander from an expert in the art of giving back-handers. Gay was much too kind-hearted to reply but if he had thought of doing so there were several neat points to be made about Bolingbroke's *own* difficulty in rising out of a recumbent position.

But whatever Bolingbroke's opinion of the projected work—there was still immense fun to be got out of it at Twickenham, and beautiful memorable evenings in which the three friends would sit together—when Swift was at his most magnetic, Pope at his kindliest, and when Gay's own words were received with such instant appreciation that they sounded to him as if they were the wittiest words in the world. Doubtless there was the Dean's favourite claret to do honour to the situation: Pope may even have exceeded his usual thimbleful and risked the most excruciating headache in consequence: but that kind of evening does not require even the aid of wine to make it convivial. With such comradeship the glow comes from within: the wit is self-generated.

The house-party was split up, as before, by Swift's sudden departure for Ireland—unexplained but apparently inspired by his usual fears for Stella he left Pope a letter full of apologies and affection and Pope responded:

"It is a perfect trouble for me to write to you, and your kind letter left for me at Mr. Gay's affected me so much, that it made me like a Girl. I cannot tell what to say to you; I only feel that I wish you well in every circumstance of life."

Swift certainly needed good wishes. It seemed to him that he was prejudicing his last chance by leaving England at such a time, yet Stella still came first. The stars in their courses fought against him and he was detained at Holyhead nearly a week waiting to cross, during which time he worked off his spleen in a diary left behind him when he *did* sail and which was for some reason returned by the landlady to Pope and Gay—not to him. Simultaneously as they received it the great moment arrived. The new appointments at the Court of George II were announced—and Gay found himself offered a position as Gentleman-Usher to the two-years-old Princess Louisa.

Bitter blows are no less bitter for having been in some degree expected. Obviously before the actual appointments were made—and even while Swift was still in England—a rumour had been set about that Gay might expect something of the kind. Swift declared that while walking and talking with Gay that year, he had often found him preoccupied and when the Dean put a sharp question to him, Gay answered quite beside the point with "Well, I am determined not to accept the employment of Gentleman-Usher." He was as good as his word—and of all the acts of his life none has made his editors more impatient. Most of them take the Johnsonian view that, as he had written verses for one Royal child, there was really nothing particularly unsuitable in that he should have been offered a virtual sinecure concerning another: furthermore, if it was money he wanted, then another £200 a year was not to be sneezed at, and he was a fool to sneeze at it. Only one biographer has a good word to say for the poet—Walter Scott. In his edition of Swift he writes of Gay: "He, with proper spirit, refused the appointment, and in *The Beggar's Opera* took a most ample satisfaction upon King, Queen and Ministers." But it is easy to see that Scott was in the minority—and to feel the usual exasperation at any one being so foolhardy as to throw away a good opportunity when it came knocking at the door.

Two hundred years' lapse may make one dull-witted —but what precisely *did* Gay expect of the Court? If he would not take a sinecure, what position *would* he have taken, or did he feel qualified to fill? The answer, most likely, would have been of the negative kind: he didn't know what he wanted but he knew what he did *not* want. He did *not* want to be 'mortified,' as he felt mortified by the offer of the post of Gentleman-Usher. Useless, at such a juncture, to have reminded him that the great Molière's position as Valet-de-Chambre to Louis XIV involved far more indignity than a gentleman-usher could ever have been called upon to undergo in an English Court. Primed all the summer by the company of Swift and Pope—swelled up to an unusually large sense of his own capacities, this usually modest man was being offered his chance at the psychological moment when he felt too grand to take it. He turned it down, shook the dust of the Court off his heels for ever and went down into the country with the sympathetic Queensberrys. But before he went he wrote to Swift:

> "The Queen's family is at last settled, and in the list I was appointed gentleman-usher to the Princess Louisa, the youngest princess, which upon account that I am far advanced in life, I have

declined accepting; and have endeavoured in the best manner I could to make my excuses by a letter to Her Majesty. So now all my expectations are vanished, and I have no prospect but in depending wholly upon myself, and my own conduct. As I am used to disappointments, I can bear them; but as I can have no more hopes, I can no more be disappointed, so that I am in a blessed condition."

Swift did not reply immediately, but Pope being made aware of the same news accepted it like the philosopher he was.

"I have many years magnified in my own mind [he wrote to Gay] and repeated to you, a ninth beatitude, added to the eight in the Scripture, 'Blessed is he who expects nothing, for he shall never be disappointed!' I could find it in my heart to congratulate you on this happy dismission from all court-dependence; I dare say I shall find you the better and honester man for it many years hence; very probably the healthfuller and cheerfuller into the bargain. You are happily rid of many cursed ceremonies, as well as of many ill and vicious habits, of which few or no men escape the infection, who are hackneyed and trammelled in the way of a court. Princes indeed, and Peers (the Lackeys of Princes) and Ladies (the fools of Peers) will smile on you the less: but men of real worth and real friends will look on you the better. There is a thing, the only thing, which kings and queens cannot give you (for they have it not to give), liberty, and which is worth all they have; which, as I now thank God, Englishmen need not ask at their hands. You will enjoy that, and your own integrity, and the satisfactory consciousness of having *not* merited such graces from courts as are now bestowed on the mean, servile, flattering, interested and undeserving."

It is a wise and tender letter, and—a rarity in Pope's correspondence—a letter in which he meant every word he said. He commented to Swift on the situation:

> "Gay is a free-man, and I writ him a long congratulatory letter upon it. Do you the same: it will mend him, and make him a better man than a court could do."

It was not often that Swift took advice from other people but on this occasion he did just what Pope advised, and wrote to Gay:

> "I certainly approve your refusal of that Employment and your writing to the Queen. I am perfectly confident you have a keen enemy in the ministry. God forgive him, but not till he has put himself into a state to be forgiven. Upon reasoning with myself, I should hope they are gone too far to discard you quite, and that they will give you something which, although much less than they ought, will be (as far as it is worth) better circumstantiated. And since you already just live, a middling Help will make you just Tolerable."

But however well-intended, all this was cold comfort. Gay had turned down two hundred pounds a year which, although it was less than a royal groom drew, or a Maid of Honour, or a Lord of the Bedchamber, was still two hundred pounds a year. He had further shaken off the Court for ever: how then could he countenance, for a moment, Swift's deplorably-worded hope that he was not "discarded quite"—that he might still have something to make him "just Tolerable?" These were not the words of encouragement that he needed. He did his best, apparently, to make up on the swings what he had lost on the roundabouts by attempting to do a business deal on his own account—failed, and gave Arbuthnot matter for one of his best jokes. The Doctor wrote to Swift:

> "There is certainly a fatality upon poor Gay. As for hope of preferment, he has laid it aside. He had made a pretty good bargain (that is, a Smithfield one) for a little place in the Customhouse, which was to bring him in about a hundred a year. It was done as a favour to an old man, and not at all to Gay. When everything was concluded, the man repented and said he would not part with his place. I have begged Gay not to buy an annuity upon my life; I am sure I should not live a week."

Meanwhile Gay, looking desperately about him for some kind of friendly encouragement, remembered Mrs. Howard. As the hart pants for the water-brooks so he panted for a letter of explanation from the woman who had all along invited him to hope. There are those who absolve Mrs. Howard completely of even the appearance of complicity in the business of having led Gay up the garden path—but for an innocent person the letter she did write him has a curious guilty ring:

> "I hear you expect, and have a mind to have, a letter from me, and though I have little to say, I find I don't care that you be either disappointed

or displeased. Tell her Grace (the Duchess of Queensberry) I don't think she looked kindly upon me when I saw her last; she ought to have looked and thought very kindly, for I am much more her humble servant than those who tell her so every day . . . I suppose she always uses those worst who love her best, Mrs. Herbert excepted . . . I cannot help doing the woman this justice, that she can now and then distinguish merit."

But to talk of distinguishing merit to a man whose merit had just been insufficiently distinguished was too thin ice even for as experienced a skater as Mrs. Howard. She hastened to change the subject. Letting bygones be bygones, she rushes immediately into the less embarrassing prospect of the future:

"So much for her Grace: now for yourself, John. I desire you will mind the main chance, and be in town in time enough to let the opera have play enough for its life, and for your pockets. Your head is your best friend: it would clothe, lodge and wash you, but you neglect it and follow that false friend your heart, which is such a foolish, tender thing, that it makes others despise your head that have not half so good a one upon their own shoulders; in short, John, you may be a snail or a silkworm, but by my consent you shall never be a *hare* again.

"We go to town next week; try your interest and bring the duchess up by the birthday. I did not think to have named her any more in this letter; I find I am a little foolish about her; don't you be a great deal so; for if *she* will not come, do you come without her."

But blandishments and invitations were of no avail. Gay had made his decision to cut out Court life and—surprisingly stubborn when it came to the point—nothing would induce him to go back on it. Later he was able to take some gloomy comfort from Swift's lines celebrating the whole affair:

> "Thus *Gay*, the Hare with many friends,
> Twice seven long years the court attends,
> Who, under tales conveying truth
> To virtue formed a princely youth.
> Who paid his courtship with the crowd
> As far as modest pride allowed,
> Rejects a servile usher's place
> And leaves St. James's in disgrace."

Nobody could be more righteously angry on a friend's behalf than Swift—and his sojourn in Ireland convinced him, the more he thought about it, that Gay had been cruelly and abominably misused. The fact that his own interests had been completely overlooked in the recent appointments is not referred to but his warmth on behalf of Gay is significant: now, as before, he was expending wrath and disappointment on his friend's case instead of his own. This let off steam quite as well, and did not harm his reputation. But if Swift suspected Walpole to be the Keen Enemy in the ministry who had foiled Gay at every turn, he knew at whose door to lay the blame for the blighting of his *own* ambition; and if she had hurt him, then she had also hurt Gay. In some of the bitterest lines he ever wrote he subsequently summed up Mrs. Howard: "If she had never seen a Court it is possible she might have been a friend."

CHAPTER NINETEEN

1728. 'The Beggar's Opera.'

> "*I have been behind the scenes, both of pleasure and business. I have seen all the coarse pullies and dirty ropes, which exhibit and move all the gawdy machines; and I have seen and smelt the tallow candles which illuminate the whole decoration, to the astonishment and admiration of the ignorant audience.*"
> A LETTER FROM LORD CHESTERFIELD TO
> SOLOMON DAYROLLES, FEB. 23, 1748

EARLY in January 1728, Colley Cibber was approached to know if he would accept Gay's new play *The Beggar's Opera* for production at Drury Lane. Not entirely unnaturally, he refused it. He had been mauled once by Pope and Gay in their *Three Hours After Marriage*, and there was no reason why he should now turn the other cheek. For much the same reason probably Aaron Hill, still Master of the Queen's Theatre in the Haymarket, turned it down. The old school tie might account for much in the way of influence, but on this occasion it did not extend to making one old Barumite —not notably successful—give publicity to another old Barumite whose *Fables* had recently put him in the best-selling class. Aaron Hill was never a best-seller. Besides, some one had recently rubbed salt in the wounds by making the odious comparison:

"*Johnny*'s fine works at Court obtain renown.
Aaron writes trash. He ne'er collogues the town."

Impossible, after that, that Aaron should accept Johnny's

opera for production. The play was subsequently accepted by Mr. Rich of the Lincoln's Inn Fields Theatre, but without enthusiasm. It is safe to say, in fact, that no roaring success ever started its career with so many buckets of cold water poured over it, at the outset, by friends and enemies alike. Half-way through January we have Pope writing to Swift:

> "John Gay's Opera is on the point of delivery. It may be called, considering its subject, a Jail delivery. Mr. Congreve, with whom I have commemorated you, is anxious as to its success, and so am I. Whether it succeeds or not, it will make a great noise, but whether of claps or hisses I know not. At worst it is in its own nature a thing which he can lose no reputation by, as he lays none upon it."

Pope was not exaggerating when he related Congreve's apprehension about the play. That expert dramatist had remarked gloomily at rehearsal that "it would either make a great hit or be damned confoundedly." This attitude of extreme caution percolated through Gay's entire acquaintance. Even the Duke of Queensberry—not a literary critic as a rule—gave as his verdict after reading it: "This is a very odd thing, Gay. I am satisfied that it is either a very good thing or a very bad thing." Fortunately however one of Gay's friends was stubbornly convinced that it was a Good Thing, and she was the Duchess of Queensberry. That she 'pushed' the play for all it was worth is obvious; and it is not impossible that she may have crossed Mr. Rich's palm with silver before it was ever put on at all.

Rich was a queer customer; he had none of the prestige of the prolific Colley Cibber and the most that he could ever claim to have done for the English theatre was to introduce the Harlequinade to it. Colley Cibber was at least a pseudo-gentleman (no actor got nearer to gentility than that) but Rich, from what may be gathered, was not even pseudo. He was hasty, dirty, inaccurate, eccentric, and had a maddening habit of addressing every person as Mister. It was impossible that he should have discerned the potentialities of the piece he had just accepted, but he knew the Queensberrys to be wealthy and influential; he knew that the taste of the town was still entirely for "satires against the Government" and on this he probably decided to risk it.

There was no music to the play, in its original arrangement. It is even doubtful whether Gay meant the actors to do more than softly hum the airs of the songs. He had written them in song form because his natural taste ran to the neatness of lyric verse—and to make his task easier he had originally harnessed his inspiration to well-known tunes like *Packington's Pound* and *An Old Woman Clothed in Gray*. These were the ballad and country-dance tunes to which he had been brought up—tunes redolent of village-greens and tavern bars. They were to be found (by those who sought them there) in the tattered old Elizabethan and Stuart song-books still available. The solo singing of them on a bare and unlighted stage, without any sort of accompaniment, must have made other persons beside Congreve gloomy at rehearsals. Then Rich showed that the Harlequinade was not the only idea he could produce. In the Memoirs of Cooke the actor we read:

> "To this opera there was no music originally intended to accompany the songs, till Rich, the manager, suggested it in the second last rehearsal. The junto of wits, who regularly attended, one and

all objected to it; and it was given up till the Duchess of Queensberry, accidentally hearing of it, attended herself the next rehearsal, when it was tried, and universally approved of."

There is something that rings particularly true in that account: though many people are mentioned, including the anonymous junto of wits, nobody apparently dreamed of consulting the author. This piece of realism alone vouches for the veracity of the whole. Probably the Duchess of Queensberry, determined to have her own way in the matter, brought along with her to that almost final rehearsal the couple of fiddlers, the oboist and drummer who would, in all likelihood, have made up the orchestra. Dr. Pepusch, Rich's tame musical director, was called in at this point to take over the command of the musical side. In the short time at his disposal he "arranged the verses and wrote the overture" for the play. There his work ended. But the anxieties of production were not yet over. Mr. Quin, the principal actor and one of the few persons who, in Rich's opinion, could sing as well as act—suddenly turned down the part of Macheath. He had acted in other plays by Gay but throughout the rehearsals for this one he had felt that the gallant soap-bubble bravado of Captain Macheath did not come within his somewhat heavy range. The story is that just after he had decided to relinquish the part and struck producer and author and the Duchess of Queensberry dumb by this announcement—a voice was heard trolling some of the airs from one of the dressing-rooms. "There's your man," said Quin. The voice emerged as one Thomas Walker—an actor with the slightest of voices but with a most engaging personality. The exchange was made, and Walker took over the part which subsequently made him. After the heavy guns of Quin it was like having a mere catapult in action, but a catapult which succeeded in firing the highwayman's various points over into the auditorium with more ability and address than ever Mr. Quin's guns had done. Miss Lavinia Fenton, a young actress in her teens who had hitherto been entrusted with mere Abigail parts and walk-ons, at the salary of fifteen shillings a week, was given the part of Polly. She still had fifteen shillings a week. Rich could not have shown better how little he expected of the play.

The first night of the play was January 29, and *The Daily Journal* of February 1, describes it in these words:

> "On Monday was represented for the first Time, at the Theatre Royal in Lincoln's Inn Fields, Mr. Gay's new English opera, written in a manner wholly new, and very entertaining, there being introduced instead of Italian airs, above 60 of the most celebrated Old English and Scotch tunes. There was present then as well as last Night, a prodigious Concourse of Nobility and Gentry, and no Theatrical Performance for these many years has met with so much Applause."

This account, however, does not record how the play, before it turned into a *succès fou*, hung perilously in the balance. The manner was indeed so "wholly new" that neither the gallery nor the pit nor the nobility and gentry who had seats on the stage and in the side-boxes, knew quite how to take it. Add to this that the gallery and pit, always ill-mannered, began to boo and cat-call in the interval because no entr'acte (or 'second music' as it was called) was played. They were restored to good-humour temporarily by a 'bull' from the

Irishman amongst the actors who, sent on to apologise before the curtain, begged them to be patient and remember that there was "never any music at an opera." Things went better thereafter. Here at last was a chance for the Duke of Argyll, charmingly complimented by Gay in his ill-fated *Letter to a Lady*, to return the compliment. He was, says George Gilfillan, a playgoer "of taste and experience," and at this juncture he helped to restore confidence to the actors and the author's friends alike by exclaiming loudly (after a survey of the audience) "It will do. It *must* do! I see it in the eyes of them!"

Even so, it did not follow that what the eyes said the hands would reinforce. The applause did not begin until after the first eleven songs, when Polly's singing of the half-pathetic, half-comic lines:

> "O ponder well, be not severe;
> So save a wretched wife
> For on the rope that hangs my dear
> Depends poor Polly's life."

drew forth a spontaneous outburst of admiration. From then on, all was plain sailing. The play swept on to a triumphant conclusion. Mr. Walpole in a sidebox was observed to lead the applause. He was turning the tables on his enemies, as Bolingbroke had done at *Cato* so long ago—and by indicating his pleasure seeking to make the rest of the audience doubt their ears as to whether Gay had been 'getting at' the chief minister and his party all through the play or not. Bolingbroke had succeeded in misleading the audience as to which party Addison had intended to compliment by his couplet on Freedom in *Cato*. But *The Beggar's Opera* was very different stuff; no audience with even the smallest inkling of political opinion could fail to appreciate Gay's endless digs. It is a long worm that has no turning and the worm had turned at last.

Years earlier, Gay had written out a certain recipe for literary success:

> "Yet there are ways for authors to be great,
> With rancorous libels to reform the State."

Now, he was putting that recipe to the test. Gone was the 'squeamish' author who, because his natural friendliness forbade him to give offence to any man, wrote only harmless squibs. Mrs. Howard, time after time, had implored him to use his hard head, not his soft heart. Swift had asked his friends in their writings ever to give the world another lash on his account. Pope's whole doctrine was to attack dullness and hypocrisy by every weapon in one's armoury. His other friends Pulteney, Chesterfield, Bathurst, Bolingbroke and Burlington were all in league against the arch-enemy. Last—and up till then least in many estimates—now Gay, too, joined the fray, and the wit and audacity of his attack made all his other allies look silly.

Gay is, for most people, *The Beggar's Opera* and *The Beggar's Opera* alone. And *The Beggar's Opera* is one of those happy creations which needs no praise, no justification, no comparison with anything else. It triumphs because it *is*. Happy in the audacious hour of its birth, it remained the outstanding success in the eighteenth-century theatre—a play revived more frequently than any of its contemporaries and an almost unfailing 'mascot' in that it brought good luck and good audiences to every theatre in which it was played. William Hazlitt's review of a revival of the opera in 1815 contained the sentence, "All sense of humanity must be lost before *The Beggar's Opera* can cease to fill

the mind with delight and admiration." He then tells
an anecdote which, more than any of the superlatives
which have piled up successively since 1728, 'fixes'
The Beggar's Opera in character for ever. Apparently
at some stage of that performance in 1815 an old gentleman in the audience was so overcome with gratification
and excitement that he rose from his seat and roared
out: "Hogarth, by God!" He was an even better critic
than Hazlitt. For *The Beggar's Opera is* Hogarth: it
has Hogarth's accurate eye for detail, his susceptibility
and tenderness to beauty, his abhorrence—humorously
conveyed—of crime and stupidity, his ability to present,
with a few brilliantly sketched characters, an emotion
or a situation common to all. The play has none of
Swift's hurling angry rage—none of Pope's tittering
malice—nothing of any writer but Gay; but it has more
of Hogarth than any painter outside Hogarth ever had.
As he is the most English of all English painters, then
assuredly this is "the most English of all English
Operettas."

It is curious that, with such an obvious affinity of
spirit, Hogarth and Gay never seem to have "got
together." Hogarth himself was affected by the opera's
success as much as any one. He did a sketch in profile
of the author. He painted Lavinia Fenton as Polly
several times. He painted the scene on the stage where
Macheath is in chains and Polly kneeling before him
at least twice. He drew 'Benefit' tickets for Walker
and for another actor. He cartooned the whole cast in
the disguise of apes and donkeys and other creatures—
as Gay had cartooned mankind in his *Fables.* He
cartooned the triumphal entry of Rich (in Harlequin
costume) into Lincoln's Inn theatre, when it was rebuilt—in a carriage drawn by satyrs and with a ribbon
with the words GAY FOR EVER streaming victoriously

across the theatre's façade. But for all that the artist and the poet never made common ground. Hogarth had not dealt kindly with Pope in his cartoon the *Temple of Taste*, and just possibly this may have affected Gay's attitude towards the artist. Whatever the cause—a meeting between them is never recorded.

If it can never be known what Gay and Hogarth thought of each other, Gay's and Walpole's opinions of each other are well known. Walpole, never one to waste words, had summed up Gay as "the fat clown." But Gay, in return, was as little tender as his nature allowed him to be. Walpole might signify by his applause that he recognised the innocuousness of the whole performance, but it cannot have been pleasant to hear himself described as "Robin of Bagshot, alias Gorgon, alias Bluff Bob, alias Carbuncle, alias Bob Booty." Nor can he have appreciated overmuch being transformed into a highwayman and made to sing:

"How happy could I be with either
    Were t'other dear charmer away!"

It has already been said that Gay was nothing if not topical. Miss Molly Skerrit, Lady Mary Wortley Montagu's dear friend, had been living secretly with Walpole until 1728. During this year she began to live with him openly. Mrs. Walpole was still, however, alive—and *How happy could I be with either* had therefore tremendous point. But it was not the words so much as the whole implication of the opera which set Walpole by the ears. For years the press and the Opposition had been impotently belabouring both him and the Government with every opprobrious epithet they could lay hands on—but here came a man with a handful of popular songs and country dances and a fantastic tale about a handsome highwayman and laughingly exhibited his songs and his tale and said to the world *Behold the Government!* The thief-taker, modelled on Jonathan Wild, sang at the outset:

> "And the statesman because he's so great
> Thinks his trade as honest as mine."

The thief-taker's wife answered him patly:

> "My daughter to me should be, like a court lady to a Minister of State, a key to the whole gang."

This was bad enough, but worse followed. Polly the young heroine, looking as neat and innocent as a fresh-plucked daisy, remarked, two seconds after her entry, "a woman knows how to be mercenary, though she has never been to a court or an assembly." The same strain of cynicism and contempt runs through every character in the play. Highwaymen and whores, it might be supposed, were not in a position to discuss ethics but Gay made Captain Macheath declare that, as for tearing Polly from him "You might sooner tear a pension from the hands of a courtier." Even the Gang, in their haunt at Newgate, hammer the point home:

> *Matt Harry* Who is there here that would betray him for his interest?
> Show me a gang of courtiers that can say as much.

Peachum and *Lockit* return to the charge with—"In one respect indeed, our employment may be reckoned dishonest, because, like great statesmen, we encourage those who betray their friends" . . .

Lockit   "When you censure the age
           Be courteous and sage
           Lest the Courtiers offended should be:
           If you mention vice or bribe
           'Tis so pat to all the tribe
           Each cries 'That was levelled at me.'"

Small wonder that at this point the delighted house turned with one accord to see how Walpole was taking it in his side-box. He was smiling as imperturbably as ever, a villain, villain smiling damnèd villain to the assembled Tories. Not then, or at any time afterwards, was he incautious enough to betray any personal resentment at the criticism of himself and his *régime* in *The Beggar's Opera*. *The Craftsman* with joy might declare that the opera was "the most venomous *allegorical Libel* against the G——t that hath appeared for many years." Walpole still gave no sign of thinking so.

The criticism in the play was all the more effective since it was not overdone. If the satire had been laid on more heavily it must have failed through over-emphasis. But Gay had no more written *The Beggar's Opera* with the principal object of downing Walpole than he had written it, as many supposed, to make mock of the prevalent rage for Italian music. The Newgate subject had been in his head ever since Swift had first suggested it in 1715. Ten years later the exploits of Wild and Sheppard had made Newgate indubitable news, and in celebrating them in the *Newgate's Garland* that magnificent inspiration had come into Gay's head—of making comparisons between the corruption on Hounslow Heath and in prison and corruption in the Government. He might have illusions about highwaymen. He had none about the Government, or the Court where he had wasted so many years.

The *Beggar's Opera*, first and foremost, was an amplified *Newgate's Garland*. And, again like Hogarth, he had exhibited the vice and beastliness of some of his characters by setting their darkness against the light of the others. Students of Gay's technique will find a particularly interesting example in *Polly*, who makes her first entrance with all the brazen brisk impudence of a Restoration heroine, sings one thoroughly sophisticated song—and proceeds to change slowly thereafter into the natural lovely *Polly* that we know. In her the perpetual clash in Gay's nature between the pure lyric spirit he had been endowed with and the sophistication of the century he had inherited, fought a final battle. The lyric spirit won to the play's great advantage. Dryden had once declared with poetic insight of the work of that other poet Chaucer: "There is the rude sweetness of a Scots tune in it, which is natural and pleasing, though not perfect." So, had he been alive, might he have found in Gay's work not the rude but the tender, thready sweetness of an English flute. . . . No character of Gay's creation is so indubitably his— no one has songs fuller of poetry, than Polly with her *I like a ship in storm was tost, O Ponder well, be not severe, The turtle thus with plaintive crying, O what pain it is to feel, Thus when the Swallow, seeking prey, Cease your Funning*, and *No power on earth can e'en divide the Knot that sacred Love hath tied*.

Mr. Courthope, in his life of Pope, is one of the few who have esteemed Gay's work really justly. "Beyond all his contemporaries," he writes, "with the exception of Pope, he was by nature a poet, in the sense that he had an intuitive perception of the way in which whatever subject he selected ought to be treated in verse." I would go further and say that, because of his lyric gift, he could occasionally aspire to a buoyant melodic level which Pope never reached. Such occasions were admittedly rare, but in all Polly's songs the lyric note is sustained. Again, "Gay's happiest songs," says W. F. Bateson, "are pure poetry." The line *Over the Hills and Far Away* from one of the songs has been called the most characteristic line in English poetry. It has much of Gay in it, in that it is both effortless and simple—so simple that it is a line that seems to have developed itself naturally as it went along, as a stream develops, winding its way between the banks. Impossible, one would think, that any one ever deliberately *composed* such a line—and yet Gay was the first to put it into words. . . . In *Dione*, never published till after his death, fragments here and there again echo the true Gay—like a blackbird, wakened by a false warmth in October, suddenly essaying again the flute-notes with which he had filled the month of May:

> "May no rude winds the rustling branches move
> Breathe soft, ye silent gales, nor wake my love.
> Ye shepherds, piping homeward on the way,
> Let not the distant echoes harm your lay;
> Strain not, ye nightingales, your warbling throat,
> Make no loud shake prolong the shriller note
> Lest she awake; O sleep, secure her eyes
> That I may gaze, for if she wake, she flies."

Even from the heart of *Trivia*'s gentle tripping stanzas, pure poetry may be unearthed:

> "Let elegiac lay the woe relate,
> Soft as the breath of distant flutes, at hours
> When silent evening closes up the flowers;
> Lulling as falling water's hollow noise . . ."

In the *Shepherd's Week* is a song of praise, as simple and as natural as the song of a bird:

"My Blouzelinda is the blithest lass,
  Than primrose sweeter, or the clover-grass,
  Fair is the king-cup that in meadow blows,
  Fair is the daisie that beside her grows,
  Fair is the gilliflow'r, in gardens sweet,
  Fair is the mary-gold, for pottage meet.
  But Blouzelind's than gilliflow'r more fair,
  Than daisie, mary-gold, or king-cup rare."

Still more the songs in *Acis and Galatea*, "O Ruddier than the cherry" and the lesser-known but still lovelier:

  "Love in her eyes sits playing
    And sheds delicious Death
  Love on her lips sits straying
    And warbling in her breath."

No more interesting commentary on the times could be found than the fact that apart from taking Polly Peachum completely to their hearts the audiences had no comment to make on her—and that the character who *did* arouse comment and criticism was the dashing Captain Macheath. Everybody adored Polly, although they knew she was too good to be true. The trouble with Macheath, on the other hand, was that he was far too true to be good. Just as the best publicity for a *risqué* turn at a variety hall in these days is for a bishop to declare the whole thing to be disgusting, so *The Beggar's Opera* received the same 'lift' from a Dr. Herring, a cleric who, soon after the start of the Opera's run, devoted a whole sermon to preaching against it. Had the play needed any extra boosting this would have been the move most calculated to supply it: but it was splendidly, triumphantly self-sufficient. It laughed at Dr. Herring and did not need his censure. Nevertheless the question as to the morality of the Macheath character continued to occupy the public mind until the time of Dr. Johnson, when the Doctor after some such discussion "collecting himself as it were," says Boswell, "to give a heavy stroke, remarked: 'There is in it such a labefaction of all principles as may be injurious to morality!'" Labefaction or not, the stories as to the pernicious influence of Macheath upon young and plastic minds abounded in those early days. Young men with good homes who had gone to the Opera came out, it was said, transformed characters and made a bee-line immediately for Hounslow Heath and a highwayman's career. One young man could not even wait till he got there before beginning the life of a malefactor, but from a spirit of pure emulation took a gold watch off the first passer-by he encountered on leaving the theatre.

Gay's opera was singularly free of the dull smuttiness which marked contemporary plays, and to which virgins and grandmothers were accustomed to listen without batting an eyelid; but because Gay refused to be smug and sententious in his depicting of vice—and even made it humorous—the minority amongst his audience declared that he was a frightful danger to morality. A little controversy of this sort, helped on by Dr. Herring's diatribe, lent additional impetus to a play already progessing easily on its own momentum. As for the influence that Macheath and Polly between them exerted on the public—there are many anecdotes available. The best concerning Macheath has about it a certain nineteenth-century smugness completely missing from the character as drawn by Gay: "Walker, the original Macheath, was not a singer by profession, but his acting as the gallant highwayman was so excellent that his society was eagerly sought by all the dissipated young gentlemen of the day, *among whom he acquired habits of intemperance by no means favourable to the performance of his professional duties.*" (The italics are mine.) Concerning Polly, Lavinia Fenton woke, like Walker and Gay, to find herself famous overnight. If she had lived now she would have immediately been employed to advertise silk stockings and patent foods: as it was her portrait appeared instead on fans and miniature screens and her 'sayings,' genuine and apocryphal, were collected and published in book-form to divert the crowd. Very few voices were raised against the young actress but the Reverend Edward Young (never one for exercising the Christian virtue of charity in his letters, as we have seen) managed to comment less enthusiastically than the rest. Perhaps he was swollen just then with the importance of having been appointed Chaplain to the King. However that may be his comment, to his friend Tickell, was "Gay's *Beggar's Opera* has a Run, which is well for him. He might run, if his Play did not." He could also point out the mote in Miss Lavinia Fenton's eye.

> "Polly," he wrote to the same friend ". . . is the *publica cura* of our noble Youth; she plays her Newgate part well. It shows the Advantage of being born and bred in the Mint; which was really the case. She, 'tis said, had raised her Price from one Guinea to 100, tho' she cannot be a greater whore than she was before."

To turn to the musical aspect: nothing is more curious than that a play originally written as we know without any intention of an orchestral accompaniment, should have succeeded in killing the Italian opera so thoroughly that it was driven out of England for many years. This was the most astounding by-product of *The Beggar's Opera*. . . . Mrs. Pendarves, afterwards Swift's friend Mrs. Delany, gives us the best bird's-eye view of the whole affair. Handel's new opera had been put on almost simultaneously with *The Beggar's Opera*. Mrs. Pendarves, who had an unusually educated musical sense for an Englishwoman, wrote to her sister in January:

> "I like it extremely, but the taste of the town is so depraved, that nothing will be approved of but the burlesque. *The Beggar's Opera* entirely triumphs over the Italian one."

"Burlesque," had she known it at that early stage, was particularly applicable—for Gay had not confined himself entirely to old ballad-tunes and tunes of country dances. Handel himself had had rude hands laid upon him and his solemn march in *Rinaldo* was forced to accompany the impudent libretto of the tavern song:

> "Let us take the road
> Hark! I hear the sound of coaches."

That was another occasion, on the first night, when the audience, in the colloquial phrase, was 'bit.' Purcell, also, was made to do service, and his *Britons, Strike Home* marvellously changed into the less patriotic sentiment, "Since I must swing I scorn to wince or whine." But it was not so much the individual songs in *The Beggar's Opera* which killed the Italian opera as the overwhelming effect of a skilful collection of native music falling, with all its plaintive simplicity, upon ears weary of the rigidly traditional cadenzas of the Italian school. In February Mrs. Pendarves continued her Jeremiad to her sister. Only a month had passed since the first night of *The Beggar's Opera*; but it had done its work once for all. Mrs. Pendarves wrote:

> "The opera [meaning the Italian opera] will not survive after this winter: I wish I was a poet worthy the honour of writing its elegy. I am certain, excepting some few, the English have *no real taste for music*; for if they had, they could not neglect an entertainment so perfect of its kind for a parcel of ballad singers. I am so peevish about it that I have no patience."

A fortnight later, however, the spell overcame Mrs. Pendarves as it overcame practically all other opposition; by now she had seen Gay's play and she wrote:

> "I desire you will introduce *The Beggar's Opera* at Gloster; you must sing it everywhere *but at church*, if you have a mind to be *like the polite world*."

Meanwhile the exuberant author wrote to Swift:

> "I have deferred writing to you from time to time till I could give you an account of *The Beggar's Opera*. It is acted at the Playhouse at Lincoln's Inn Fields with such success, that the Playhouse has been crowded every night. To-night is the fifteenth time of acting and it is thought it will run a fortnight longer. I have ordered to send the play to you at the first opportunity. I made no interest either for approbation or money, nor has anybody been pressed to take tickets for my benefit; notwithstanding which I think I shall make an

addition to my fortune of between 6 and 7 hundred pounds. I know this account will give you pleasure, as I have pushed through this precarious affair without servility or flattery.

"As to my favours for great men, I am in the same state you left me, but I am a great deal happier as I have no expectations. The Duchess of Queensberry has signalised her friendship to me this season in such a conspicuous manner that I hope for her sake you will take care to put your fork to its proper uses, and suffer nobody for the future to put their knives into their mouths. . . . Lord Cobham says that I should have printed it in Italian over against the English, that the ladies might have understood what they read. The outlandish (as they call it) opera has been so thin of late that some have called that *The Beggar's Opera*, and if the run continues I fear I shall have remonstrances drawn up against me by the royal academy of music. As none of us has heard from you of late, every one of us are in concern about your health. I beg we may hear from you soon. By my constant attendance on this affair I have almost worried myself into an ill state of health, but I intend in five or six days to go to our country seat at Twickenham for a little air . . . I would write more but as to-night is my benefit I am in a hurry to go about my business."

The author's benefit night, in which all the evening's takings came to him, was commonly every third night of the run. As the usual run was anything from three days to a fortnight, but seldom longer, the manager and proprietors of the theatre found this an adequate arrangement. Rich, however, appears to have seen fairly early on that *The Beggar's Opera* was going far to exceed the usual run and that therefore the author would get more than what he considered a fair share of the takings. After the first two weeks, therefore, Gay stopped drawing a profit from every third night, and some other arrangement was come to. He was not a good manager of his own business affairs, however much he may have thought he was.

The man who *had* a good business head, without any doubt, was Jacob Tonson. Soon after the publication of *The Beggar's Opera* in book form in February, Messrs. Tonson and Watts, who were jointly responsible for publishing it, bought (for under a hundred pounds) the complete copyright of both *The Beggar's Opera* and the *Fables*, the two productions of Gay's which, above all his others, went on selling merrily well into the middle of the eighteenth century.

The news of Gay's success came to Swift at a time when he most sorely needed some brightening contact with his friends in London. Gay had written that none of the Dean's acquaintances had heard from him for a very long time. The reason was not far to seek. Stella had, ever since Swift's last return from London, been slowly sinking. She died the day before *The Beggar's Opera* was produced, and Swift in an agony of mind and spirit not often given to mortal man to bear had withdrawn himself out of sight of the windows through which the light from the church would come, when her funeral service was conducted. And as he withdrew his physical presence so he sought also to withdraw his mental one. In the "character" of Stella which he sat down to compose the night she died dispassion triumphed as it had always done over passion, and he wrote that she had every virtue but that she was "a little too fat." It is not the language of a lover or a priest;

it is a more terrible spectacle—the Dean being honest with himself and proving to himself that he could see the flaw even in Stella. The motive is transparent. Admit the flaw, and he knew that the memory could not hurt him so much; it was a trick familiar to him from his youth.

Upon the inevitable loneliness in which he found himself after Stella's death, Gay's letter with its cheerful chatter of success and happiness fell like a missive from another world. He grasped at it desperately: he dragged his mind back out of the dark recesses where it still went groping, aching after Stella, and forced it to concentrate, instead, on affairs in London. Stella was dearer to him far but she was dead. Let the dead bury their dead. He wrote to Gay mentioning no word of Stella, and congratulating him heartily upon his good fortune:

> "I beg you will be thrifty and learn to value a shilling . . . get a stronger fence about your £1,000, and throw the inner Fence into the Heap, and be advised by your Twickenham Landlord and me about an Annuity. You are the most refractory, honest, good-natured man I have ever known; I could argue out this Paper . . .
>
> "Will you desire my Lord Bolingbroke, Mr. Pulteney and Mr. Pope to command you to buy an annuity with the Thousand Pounds? . . . Ever preserve some spice of the Alderman and prepare against Age, and Dullness, and Sickness, and Coldness or death of Friends. A whore has a resource left, that she can turn bawd; but an old decayed Poet is a creature abandoned. . . . Lord, how the schoolboys at Westminster and university lads adore you at this juncture! have you made as many men laugh, as Ministers can make weep?"

And finally, paying the most generous compliment in his power:

"The Beggar's Opera has knocked down Gulliver; I hope to see Pope's dullness [the Dunciad] knock down the Beggar's Opera."

Swift could do more than give Gay good advice. He boosted *The Beggar's Opera* in *The Intelligencer*—a paper which he and Sheridan had recently started in Dublin. It was a congenial task:

"This comedy contains . . . a satire which, without enquiring whether it affects the present age, may possibly be useful in times to come; I mean where the author takes the occasion of comparing the common robbers of the public and their several stratagems for betraying, undermining and hanging each other, to the several arts of the politicians in times of corruption.
"This comedy likewise exposes, with great justice, that taste for Italian music among us, which is wholly unsuitable to a northern climate and the genius of the people, whereby we are overrun with Italian effeminacy and Italian manners. An old gentleman said to me, that many years ago, when the practice of an unnatural vice grew frequent in London, that many were persecuted for it, he was sure it would be the forerunner of Italian operas and singers; and then we should want nothing but stabbing, and poisoning, to make us perfect Italians."

Swift's article was typical of the eulogy of the time and Gay—who had never consciously intended it—must have been amused to find himself quite suddenly the champion of English music. True, he had asked in the *Epistle to Paul Methuen*:

> "Why must we climb the Alpine mountain's sides
> To find the seat where Harmony resides?
> Why touch we not so soft the silver lute,
> The cheerful haut-boy and the mellow flute?"

But the question had been merely rhetorical. Dozens of other wits, besides himself, had made mock of that so-essentially mockable thing, the Italian opera. Young and Gay did not often think alike on the same subjects but Young had written of the smart audiences:

> "Italian musick's sweet because 'tis dear,
> Their vanity is tickled, not their ear."

and earlier still, Steele and Addison had used every weapon of ridicule in vain against the musical seasons of Bononcini and Attilio. Hogarth had done in pencil what the rest had done in verse and prose. All to no avail. It had been left to John Gay to pelt the foreign opera out of England "with lumps of Pudding" as an Italian complained—*Lumps of Pudding* being the air to which the last song in *The Beggar's Opera* was set.

The triumph was as complete as it could well be. Even Colley Cibber (who had immediately set to and written *Love in a Riddle* in direct imitation of *The Beggar's Opera*, and seen it flop like a hamstrung elephant) gave credit where credit was due. He said handsomely that Gay was a good-natured, honest man, and added, "I will grant . . . that in his Beggar's Opera he hath more skilfully gratified the publick taste, than all the brightest authors that ever went before him." Not that every one was as large-minded as Colley Cibber. An anonymous—and obviously Whig—writer in the *Daily Post*, for instance, made a violent attack on what he described as *the Twickenham Hotch-Potch*. This article drew a sad contrast between virtue unrewarded in previous times, and vice triumphant in the present:

> "Thus have I set before the Readers' Eyes (it ran) in as short a Method as I could, the cruel Treatment that so many extraordinary Men have received from their countrymen for these last hundred Years. If I could now shift the scene and show them also the Penury and Avarice changed all at once into Riot and Profuseness, and more, squandered away upon four objects (an impertinent *Scotch*-Quack, a Profligate *Irish*-Dean, the Lacquey of a superannuated Dutchess, and a little virulent Papist) than would have satisfied the greater Part of those extraordinary Men, the Readers to whom these creatures should be altogether unknown, would fancy them prodigies of Art and Nature."

It is all very obscure and ungrammatical—and one is tempted to think that if it is true that Walpole paid out £50,000 a year to Whig press propagandists, then he might have got better value for his money. Such abuse, however, would not stop *The Beggar's Opera* or make people forget *Gulliver*, or rub out Pope's unfinished *Dunciad*. The stars in their courses may have fought against Scriblerus, but now despite Walpole and all he could do, the Scriblerians were coming into their own. Meanwhile the "Lacquey of a superannuated Dutchess" wrote jubilantly again to Swift:

> "I have got by all this success between seven and

eight hundred pounds and Rich (deducting the whole charge of the House) hath clear'd already near four thousand pounds. In about a month I am going to the Bath with the Dutchess of Marlborough and Mr. Congreve, for I have no expectations of receiving any favours from the court. I would not have talk'd so much upon this subject or upon anything that regards myself but to you; but as I know you interest yourself so sincerely in whatever concerns me, I believe you would have blamed me if I had said less. Your Singer owes Dr. Arbuthnot some money—I have forgot the sum but I think it is Two Guineas, the Dr. desired me to let you know it. I saw him last night with Mr. Lewis at Sir William Wyndham, who if he had not had the gout would have answered your letter you sent him a year and a half ago; he said this to me a week since, but he is now pretty well again and so may forget to write."

The Irish bull quality of the last sentence is Gay all over. He goes on hopefully:

"I have bought two pair of Sheets against your coming to town, so that we need not send any more to Jervas upon that account. I really miss you every day, and I would be content that you should have one whole window to yourself and shall long to have you again. I am, dear sir,
  "Yours most affectionately."

The underlying formality of the letters between Pope and Swift and Gay is important: throughout their lives they had a genuine respect for each other. Such formality contrasts oddly with Bolingbroke's assumption of easy

Prison Scene from "The Beggar's Opera."
After the painting by Hogarth

bonhomie:—" Adieu, dear Swift, with all thy faults I love thee entirely—make an effort and love me with all mine." This was not the way to the Dean's heart, but Bolingbroke never learnt it.

Pope, too, wrote to tell Swift of the opera's progress:

> "Mr. Gay's opera has been acted near Forty days running, and will certainly continue the whole season. So he has more than a Fence about his Thousand Pound. He will soon be thinking of a Fence about his Two Thousand." He seems, however, to have had an inkling that Gay was going to be as stubborn as usual about the matter of the annuity, for he adds:—"Shall no one of us live as we would wish each other to live? Shall he have no annuity, you no settlement on this side, and I no Prospect of getting to you on the other?"

If there was an answer to that, it was not in Swift's power to give it. He could not solve these conundrums, he could only wish, like Pope, that matters were otherwise. Meanwhile, London's Longest Run had come to an end (after taking in total receipts, close on ten thousand pounds) and the irresponsible author was off to Somerset again with Congreve and his young Duchess—thundering in a coach over the treacherous Hounslow Heath—clinging to his hat across the windy Wiltshire downs and so, after three days' travelling, to Bath. . . . Martha Blount, writing to Swift, was far less shrewish than usual when she said: "Mr. Gay's fame is increasing, but his riches are in a fair way of diminishing. He is gone to the Bath."

CHAPTER TWENTY

1728 (cont.). The Visit to Bath: writing 'Polly.' 'Polly' banned. Gay falls into a fever.

> "*You must forswear Courts, if you would not connive at Knaves, and Tolerate fools.*"
> LORD CHESTERFIELD IN LETTERS TO HIS SON

IT should be possible by now for a sympathetic reader to enter, to some degree, into the happiness which at this period filled the life of Gay. He had justified himself—and Pope's faith in him, and Swift's faith and Mrs. Howard's, and the Duchess of Queensberry's. He had shown himself a worthy Scriblerian. He was famous, once and for all. He had made a comfortable sum by the production of *The Beggar's Opera*, and he was in a fair way to becoming really independent for the first time. He had done nobody any harm at any time of his life, and he had contributed enormously to the gaiety of the nation. Completely untroubled personal happiness is as rare as a completely untroubled summer sea. It comes, in its perfection, swiftly and overwhelmingly. Now it had come to Gay.

He welcomed it with his usual modesty. His complaints of ill-usage at Court have led some of his editors to suppose that Gay fancied himself as a rare and unique being deserving of important appointments. This concept is completely at variance with all that we know of him. In 1727, as ever, all that Gay had wished to make clear to the world was not that he thought himself particularly important, but that, seeing that mediocrities were being rewarded every day he wished, as a rather higher than average mediocrity (who had also written the *Fables* and the *Letter to a Lady*), to register his claim also. There was nothing particularly overbearing about that. After the success of his opera he might well have become proud and overbearing. He never took advantage of the situation. As it was his nature to be "grovelling" (as Arbuthnot put it) in times of distress, it was also his nature to be amazingly sweet-tempered and unassuming in times of triumph. At the time of his departure for Bath he had every reason for acting the great man. His play had come off after the longest run on record (so long that Mr. (Macheath) Walker had grown careless of his words and, being reproved by Mr. Rich, had remarked "One can't remember the thing for *ever*"). Lavinia Fenton had become the favourite of the town and the passion of the Duke of Bolton ("that Great Booby," as Swift called him), who went frequently to feast his eyes on her plaintive, seductive rendering of Gay's Polly. The Royal Academy of Music had given up the unequal contest and resigned the season's honours to the theatre in Lincoln's Inn Fields. Gay (it is inevitable that the old tag should be brought out at this stage) had become Rich, and Rich Gay. He had, furthermore, the delightful presence of Congreve as travelling companion to Bath, and the doubtless stimulating company of Henrietta, Duchess of Marlborough.

In the company of worldly wits and women at Bath, and in the character of the author of *The Beggar's Opera*, it might be supposed that when Gay wrote to Swift from there some small touch of authority, of good opinion of himself reflected from the good opinion of others, might have found its way into his letters. On the contrary:

"The two hundred pounds you left with me are in the hands of Lord Bathurst, together with some money of mine, all of which he will repay at midsummer, so that we must think of some other way of employing it, as I cannot resolve what to do.

"I don't know how long I shall stay here, because I am now, as I have been all my life, at the disposal of others. I drink the waters and am in hopes to lay in a stock of health, some of which I wish to communicate to you. . . . *The Beggar's Opera* is acted here but our Polly here hath got no fame, but the actors have got money. I have sent by Mr. Delany the opera Polly Peachum and Captain Macheath [meaning engravings of the London Polly and Macheath]. I would have sent you my own head to make up the Gang, but it is not yet finished. I suppose you must have heard that I have had the honour to have had a sermon preached against my works by a Court Chaplain, which I look upon as no small addition to my fame. Direct to me here when you write and the sooner that is the sooner you will make me happy."

There is no doubt that for correspondence expressing utter helplessness and ineptitude none could do better than select a letter from Gay to Swift. Here he is the leaf drifting aimlessly upon the river, at the sport of every surge and eddy. The reception of it must have made Swift tremble in his shoes, to think he could ever have entrusted so poor a creature with two hundred pounds of his precious hard-earned money. Why he did so remains a mystery. True, Gay was that rare thing, completely honest—but then so was a box under the mattress, and both had about the same ability to turn the two hundred pounds into more. Yet, after all, Swift had only done what Pope had done so many years earlier, and at least the money formed a frequent excuse for correspondence. Meanwhile, a paragraph in *Brice's Weekly Journal* during July showed that Gay was not quite so inept and helpless as he liked to make out to Swift:

> "We hear from Bath that Mr. Gay, author of the celebrated *Beggar's Opera*, has been there these two months drinking the waters for his health, during which time he has taken more than ordinary pains with the Comedians of that city, in instructing them in the performance of his said opera, which has so good an effect that they have not only gain'd a great deal of Money by it, but universal applause."

About this time another paragraph, this time in a letter from Gay to Pope, is of particular significance for it concerns itself with a plan as yet rudimentary but which is to take on clearer and clearer outlines as time passes:

> "Is the Widow's house to be dispos'd of yet?" he asks Pope, "I have not given up my pretensions to the Dean; if it was to be parted with, I wish one of us had it; I hope you wish so too, and that Mrs. Blount and Mrs. Howard wish the same, and for the very same reason that I wish it. . . ."

The widow has been tracked down as a Mrs. Vernon, whose husband had been the largest land-owner in Twickenham and secretary, in his youth, to the ill-fated Monmouth. Her house is not so easily identifiable but it is supposed to have been one on Ham Walks. As it crops up again in the correspondence we may leave it here as Gay himself left it—somewhat in the air.

In August the warm weather forced a great many of the sojourners at Bath to move elsewhere. The town baked like an oven shut in by the shouldering hills. But Gay and Congreve and the Duchess of Marlborough stayed where they were. Gay wrote again to Swift:

> "The weather is extremely hot, the place is very empty, I have an inclination to study but the heat makes it impossible. The D. of Bolton I hear has run away with Polly Peachum, having settled 400 a year upon her during pleasure, and during disagreement 200 a year. Mr. Pope is in a state of persecution for his Dunciad. I wish to be witness to his fortitude but he writes but seldom. T'would be a consolation to me to hear from you."

The tender complaints trickled through, slowly, to Swift. Letters were long in transit. Sometimes the Dean was away from home; but when he thought of Gay his impatience bubbled over again. He let himself go to Pope:

> "I suppose *Mr. Gay* will return from *Bath* with twenty Pound more Flesh and two hundred less in Money: Providence never designed him to be above Two and Twenty, by his Thoughtlessness and Gullibility. He hath as little Foresight of Age, Sickness, Poverty or Loss of Admirers as a Girl of Fifteen."

Which is all extremely amusing but what it boils down to is that Gay, then as ever, refused to live in any time but the present. *Let's be Gay, while we may*—never did his own jingle fit the situation more aptly. He *would* live in the present and he would *not* plan for the future (except very vaguely) or repine the past—which seemed tragically silly to the Dean. If Swift himself had spent less time planning for the future—a future which never came within his grasp—and tearing his heart to tatters over the past, he too might have had, like Gay, his serene hour. . . . He wrote further to Pope:

> "You talk of the Dunciad, and I am impatient to have it *Volare per ora*. There is now a Vacancy for Fame, the Beggar's Opera has done its task, *discedat uti conviva satur*."

Gay also wrote to Pope to say, amongst other things, that he had heard from Mrs. Howard at Court and that she was in high health and spirits. He adds, with the nearest approach to sarcasm that he could compass:

> "Considering the multiplicity of pleasures and delights which one is overrun with in those places I wonder how anybody has health and spirits to support them."

Alice—a rather stout, jaded Alice of forty-two—had woken at last out of Wonderland and seen the Court for nothing but a pack of cards.

On the 28th May the "vacancy for fame" which Swift had perceived, was filled. *The Dunciad* was published, and fell like bursting shrapnel amongst the lesser scribes of literature. So the triad of the three cavaliers was completed. *Gulliver* with his sober matter-of-fact descriptions of amazing countries and their inhabitants had, by comparison, held up the civilisation that eighteenth-century London knew to ridicule and bitter shame: men had been described in that book first as pygmies and finally as Yahoos. But whatever the shape they took Swift's chief detestation, hypocrisy, was characteristic of them all. Gay, taking up the gauntlet in his *Beggar's Opera*, concentrated less on hypocrisy and more on the corruption of social life as all men knew it—and Newgate was his scene of action. Last but not least Pope (tolerant of either hypocrisy or corruption, except when they entered the world of letters), attacked stupidity, or "dullness" with all the vigour in his power. Not for him the mock-straightforwardness of a travel book which set out to describe an imaginary Lilliput and Brobdignag and turned the whole of Europe inside out in the process—nor the brisk engaging neatness of *revue intime* which purported to concern highwaymen in Newgate and made an Aunt Sally of the Government *en passant*; his way was the pillory—with chief Dunciad Mr. Theobald (later to give place to Colley Cibber)—and chief setting that Universal Darkness which was Dullness, or No-Knowledge, or half-Knowledge—or (regrettable as it may seem) Knowledge-employed-against-Pope.

The motive was elevated; the means employed were Pope's own not too nice ones. Dozens of persons who had irritated him in the past, intentionally or unintentionally, were dragged into the pillory and held up to the merciless crowd. Where their names were disguised by pseudonyms, cruel mocking "writer's notes" at the foot of the page denied them even that disguise. Swift had complained long before publication to Pope that such nomenclature was unimportant, and that in insisting on naming his enemies Pope was only giving them an immortality which they did not deserve and would not otherwise receive; but this wise counsel was of no avail.

Naturally bursting shrapnel is not received without

comment, and Dullness if it was not destroyed was at least temporarily stirred up by the publication of *The Dunciad*. If that was the kind of success that Pope wanted, then his new poem was supremely successful. Detached from its extreme felicity of execution and invention all that can be claimed for it, however, is that it is little Sawny Pope scrawling on the lavatory wall that Jacky Theobald and Colley Cibber are——and——and every other unprintable thing. Fortunately or unfortunately *The Dunciad* cannot be separated from the genius of the man who wrote it. The wall remains a lavatory wall but in a very exclusive lavatory upon the slopes of Parnassus—and the vile scrawlings are written upon it with the tip of an eagle's wing in Sawny Pope's own blood.

When the tumult and the shouting about *The Dunciad* had begun to die down, that is early in September, Pope and Arbuthnot, and probably Martha Blount, joined Gay at Bath. This would mean that for the remainder of the season Congreve and his duchess would be less in evidence; for Martha Blount was apt to be difficult in company where other women were concerned and, if Lady Mary Wortley Montagu is to be believed, Congreve found Pope's conversation and poetry "perpetual jokes, exceedingly despicable in his opinion." This is certainly an exaggeration—Congreve was the gentlest of all men in his criticisms—but it was nevertheless true that frequently people who were fond of Gay could not stomach Pope or Swift. Pope was that year in particularly poor health. He had not yet recovered from the shock of his coach accident and bile had gone out of him into the making of *The Dunciad*. But whatever his state of health to Gay he was still Pope, at the worst of times, and so better than Congreve, at the best of times.

Mrs. Howard, enjoying the country air at Hampton Court, wrote a round-robin of a letter to Bath and addressed it to Gay. One can almost hear her fan rap down on his shoulder in pretty reinforcement of authority:

> "I have made Mr. Nash governor to Lord Peterborough, and Lord Peterborough governor to Mr. Pope. If I should come to the Bath, I propose being governess to the Doctor and you. I know both to be so unruly, that nothing less than Lady P——'s spirit or mine could keep any authority over you . . ."

She adds, as it were in Gay's ear:

> "I have had two letters from Chesterfield, which I wanted you to answer for me; but upon my word I have not had one place to dispose of, or you should not be without one."

Gay, however, had had his fill of writing gallant letters for other people after that literary Marathon with Lord Peterborough. Doubtless he wriggled out of the new suggestion gracefully enough—at any rate he left her to tackle Lord Chesterfield herself. Altogether, Mrs. Howard needed, that year, all the health and spirits she could muster. Queen Caroline, usually the best and most compliant of wives where George's pleasure was concerned, had begun to find the perpetual presence of his mistress a little tiresome. The ritual of the royal dressing and undressing was established by long precedent but somehow the Queen saw to it that Mrs. Howard in her position as Woman of the Bedchamber had to perform a great many of the more menial tasks in that ritual. It was a poor sort of revenge, but the only sort the Queen could compass. The "incidents" that arose as a consequence made a deep impression on Mrs. Howard and successfully spoilt the year for her.

To those close to the event, such incidents may have seemed nothing more than the scrapping between two jealous women for the favours of the King, but they were symptomatic of much more. Before George II had succeeded his father, ambitious Courtiers had sought to reach him by two channels—the Princess of Wales or Mrs. Howard. Remembering the power of royal mistresses in the Stuart Courts and the French one (and even in the Court of George I) the foolish virgins amongst these had paid their court to Mrs. Howard; the wise ones, sensing the inherent power of the Princess of Wales, paid court to her, and were justified of their hopes. Of these by far the most important was Robert Walpole. From the first moment that Queen Caroline and Walpole came to an understanding England was ruled, not by a tetchy stubborn little King with cherub mouth and bulbous eyes, but by his wife and his chief Minister. The understanding had not been an immediate one. In conversation Walpole had been known to refer to the Queen in a friendly manner as that fat Bitch. But Queen Caroline had not made philosophy her favourite subject without imbibing a great deal of it herself. She found occasion to send a message to Walpole saying "Tell him that the Fat Bitch etc., etc." A woman who could give and take in such measure was a woman after Walpole's own heart. They may be said to have begun their long reign together from that moment.

But while Walpole's position was undisputed the length and breadth of the land the Queen had still to show, even inside St. James's, who ruled the roost. The

Court was a hive thronged with lookers-on, watching two Queen-bees sparring for the supremacy. Everything was conducted in the genteelest manner possible, and the stings were only administered in the privacy of the Royal Bedchamber. Moreover, the fight was not, as with bees, a fight to the death. At the end of it, however, Mrs. Howard's wings might be seen to be a little frayed and battered, while the Queen's remained spruce as usual. A political as well as a personal victory had been won, and the King (the only man in the Court who had remained sublimely oblivious of the whole circumstances) made the issue still more certain by such incidents as when he abused Mrs. Howard roundly in her rôle of dresser to the Queen by declaring, "You only try to hide the Queen's neck because you have an ugly one yourself." (At such times the patience of Griselda was essential. Mrs. Howard had that patience, as she had all the duller virtues.)

While the co-operation of the Queen and Walpole grew stronger every day—and while the news spread over the country in ballads and lampoons that George II was no more than a cipher in his own Court—Mr. Gay who despised politics and Courtiers and was a very pretty ballad-maker himself remained at Bath. He was not letting the grass grow under his feet even in that playground of a city. He had embarked on his second opera, *Polly*. Nor was he the only man to take advantage of the rage for English ballad-opera which *The Beggar's Opera* had initiated. England—that year and for many years after—was dotted all over with wits scribbling away feverishly at what they hoped would be similar successes. If accuracy in following the recipe were all that was required they might have been successes but it was not. They all had the recipe, but none of them could cook like Gay. They wrote the *Quaker's Opera*, and the *Prison-Breaker*; the *Beggar's Wedding* and the *Cobler's* and *Lovers'* and *Statesman's Opera*; the *Village Opera, Harliquin's* and the *Parson's Opera*; the *Fool's* and the *Sailor's Opera*; the *Beggar's Pantomime* and *Macheath in the Shades*; the *Schoolboy's* and the *Shepherds' Opera*—and hundreds more just like them. While the authors were busy cashing in, as they hoped, on the Newgate fashion, Gay, true to his talent, was a step ahead of them. He had left Newgate behind him and deported his whole company of characters to the West Indies.

Polly cannot here be discussed in detail, beyond saying that students of the theatre may be amused to discern how Gay's style has changed with his environment. *The Beggar's Opera*, written at Twickenham by an author sandwiched between the loved presences of Pope and Swift, has a cosy intimate atmosphere completely absent from *Polly*. Nor can this be ascribed simply to the fact that one play takes place in the cramped surroundings of Newgate and the other in the open spaces of the West Indies; for the sequel is far more sophisticated than the earlier play. The speeches in it are gracefuller and less crisp, and the atmosphere in the home of Mrs. Trapes and Ducat has much of the artificiality of *The Way of the World*; which is not surprising since Congreve must often have listened to, and advised on, extracts from *Polly*. But one feature from the original play remains unchanged—Polly Peachum is as enchanting as ever she was and her songs are almost as good.

It is not certain, but it is probable that after their stay at Bath that year Pope and Gay returned to town together. (Congreve, following later, was involved in a coach accident from which he never recovered.) In London the two parted ways again—Pope to return to Twickenham and Gay to his Whitehall lodgings to get in touch with Rich—tell him the good news about the new play and finish preparing a clear copy of it for rehearsals. Both of them wrote constantly to Swift telling him of the progress made. The Season was getting into swing again, the *beau monde* was clustering in again on London and Westminster, avid to have any news they could of the new ' bite ' which Mr. Gay had been preparing for Walpole and which had been part and parcel of the season's gossip at Bath. Prospects were rosy; Rich was obliging and much politer than he had been in the pre- *Beggar's Opera* days; all was for the best in the best of all possible worlds. It was not to remain so.

The blow fell with great suddenness—and we learn of it first in a letter from Swift dated November 12. In this he says to Pope:

> "I hear Mr. Gay's second Opera, which you mention, is forbid, and then he will be once more fit to be advised, and reject your advice."

Here was a clear case of bad news travelling fast. The unexpectedness of the blow bowled Gay—never very steady on his feet—quite over. It either coincided with or (I am more inclined to believe) induced another attack of colic. Even so, it appears that the author did not realise quite how irrevocable the decision was. He wrote to Swift:

> "I have been confined about ten days but never to my bed, so that I hope soon to get abroad about my business, which is the care of the second part of the Beggar's Opera, which was almost ready for rehearsal. But Rich received the Duke of Grafton's command (upon an information he was rehearsing a play improper to be performed) not to rehearse

my new play whatsoever till his Grace hath seen it; what will become of it I know not, but I am sure I have written nothing that can be legally supprest, unless the setting vices in general in an odious light, and virtue in an amiable one, may give offence. If it [the play] goes on I have taken care to make better bargains for myself, I tell you this, because I know you are so good to interest yourself so warmly in my affairs, that 'tis what you would wish to know."

Had the news of that ill-advised sale of copyright reached Swift's ears and resulted in a scolding of Gay? It looks like it. Not that Swift could claim to act as a good administrator in his own affairs. All he ever made, even out of *Gulliver*, was £300, and that, as he admitted, was chiefly owing to Pope.

If Gay remained ignorant of the real causes of the banning of *Polly*, the rest of London was not so. Lord Hervey in his Memoirs of the Court of George II puts the occasion clearly enough—and shows that the god in the car was not after all the Duke of Grafton but Robert Walpole. No man was more accustomed to or more tolerant of abuse: no man knew better that in a general way, bad abuse returned upon its sender. But *The Beggar's Opera* had done the job cleverly. Walpole had borne that well enough, but a sequel was, he no doubt considered, too much of a good thing. "He resolved," wrote Hervey, "rather than suffer himself to be produced for thirty nights together upon the stage in the person of a highwayman, to make use of his friend the Duke of Grafton's authority, as Lord Chamberlain, to put a stop to the representation of it. Consequently this theatrical *Craftsman* was prohibited at every Play-house." This censorship may have been arbitrary, but it was certainly effective. It was also, in a sense, fair enough in that it was meeting Gay on his own literary ground. A smaller man than Robert Walpole would have 'got back' at the author of *The Beggar's Opera* in a meaner, less direct, way—would have deprived him, for instance, of that last frail link with official life—his lodgings in Whitehall. But Walpole took away *Polly's* lodgings instead of Gay's. The history of the affair may be read in Gay's preface to his first edition:

"'*Twas on Saturday morning December 7th, 1728, that I waited upon the Lord Chamberlain; I desir'd to have the honour of reading the Opera to his Grace, but he order'd me to leave it with him, which I did upon expectation of having it returned on the Monday following, but I had it not 'till Thursday December 12, when I receiv'd it from his Grace with this answer; that it was not allow'd to be acted, but commanded to be supprest. This was told me in general without any reasons assign'd, or any charge against me of my having given any particular offence.*

"*Since this prohibition I have been told that I am accused, in general terms, of having written many disaffected libels and seditious pamphlets. As it hath ever been my utmost ambition (if that word may be us'd upon this occasion) to lead a quiet and inoffensive life, I thought my innocence in this particular would never have requir'd a justification; and as this kind of writing is, what I have ever detested and never practis'd, I am persuaded so groundless a calumny can never be believ'd but by those who do not know me. But when general aspersions of this sort have been cast upon me, I think my-self call'd upon to declare my principles; and I do with the strictest truth affirm, that I am as loyal a subject and as firmly attach'd to the present happy establishment as any of those who have the greatest places or pensions."*

As soon as it became apparent that the censorship of *Polly* was no threat but an accomplished fact, Gay's health broke down completely. He fell into a fever so bad that at times his life was despaired of. Once more the Duchess of Queensberry and Dr. Arbuthnot carried him off to Hampstead, hoping that the better air there might help him. But it was touch and go. It was not good air which the invalid needed so much as good news. He was a particularly poor subject for disease in that, when misery overcame him, it overcame also all his physical defences. He gave way utterly. Dr. Arbuthnot fought hard and when he won, took all the credit to himself: as he well might have, for certainly Gay was in no state of mind to give him any assistance. The phrase was not in existence then but doubtless that did not prevent the poor man from feeling that he did not care, at such a juncture, whether he lived or died. Mrs. Pope, who seems to have been sympathetically afflicted whenever Gay had an illness, was ill now—a circumstance which once more prevented Pope's presence at the sick-bed of his friend. Nevertheless he wrote:

"No words can tell you the great concern I feel for you ; I assure you it was not, and is not, lessened by the immediate apprehension I have now every day lain under of losing my mother. Be assured, no duty less than that should have kept me one day from attending your condition. I would come and take a room by you in Hampstead, to be with you daily, were she not still in danger of death. I have constantly had particular accounts of you from the Doctor, which have not ceased to alarm me yet. God preserve your life and restore your health! I really beg it for my own sake, for I feel I love you more than I thought in health, though I always loved you a great deal. If I am so unfortunate as to bury my poor mother, and yet have the good fortune to have my prayers heard for you, I hope we may live most of our remaining days together. If, as I believe, the air of a better clime, as the southern part of France, may be thought useful for your recovery, thither I would go with you infallibly; and it is very probable we might get the Dean with us, who is in that abandoned state already in which I shall shortly be; as to other cares and duties, Dear Gay, be as cheerful as your sufferings will permit; God is a better friend than a Court; even any honest man is a better. I promise you my entire friendship in all events."

All the letters which Pope wrote to Gay are pleasant letters, they are easily the cream of all his voluminous correspondence, and this is one of the best. The offer to go to France was indeed magnanimous beyond all words—for Pope dreaded above everything a sea journey (he declared that a doctor had once told him such a journey would kill him) and yet he was prepared to undergo it for his friend. How different the end of the story might have been if Mrs. Pope *had* died, at this juncture. Perhaps the impossible would then have happened and the three of them would have departed from England for ever—Swift to regain his health at Aix, Pope and Gay to shake off their migraines and fevers in the generous sunshine of the Mediterranean. There like three Bolingbrokes—only self-exiled—they would have cultivated their gardens and laughed at the follies they had left behind them. . . . But it was not to be. Mrs. Pope's life, like Gay's, hung in the balance for some time, and then she slowly climbed back to health again, as did Gay. Gay acknowledged Pope's kindness in the first shaky handwriting he could command, and Pope wrote back to him:

> "You need not call the few words I wrote you, either kind or good; that was, and is, nothing. But whatever I have in my nature of kindness, I really have for you, and whatever good I could do, I would, among the very first, be glad to do for you. . . ."

After three months' serious illness the convalescent returned from Hampstead—not to his lodgings in Whitehall, but to a suite in the Duke of Queensberry's house in Burlington Gardens, allotted to him from that time onwards. Dr. Arbuthnot had prohibited wine-drinking once more, but despite this drawback Gay slowly regained an interest in life: *Polly* might have been forbidden stage presentation but there was no ban against book presentation. He set about making a new copy, from his "first foul blotted papers," and superintended most of the details of the printing. Meanwhile, Court and country alike seized on the delicious new scandal, and the news flew round that here was the sequel to *The Beggar's Opera* banned by the Great Man, on account of all sort of palpable hits contained in it. Curiosity and speculation grew with every day that passed, until at last it became apparent to all Gay's friends that *Polly* was front-page news, and, whatever its merits or demerits, when it was printed it was going to sell like hot cakes.

Precisely because of this contemporary front-page

value, it has always been a problem to disentangle Gay's second play from the fuss and pother that then surrounded it. There is a tendency, when speaking of it, to bring in that complacent *cliché* that no sequel is ever as good as its first part. Granted, immediately, that *Polly* is not as perfect a piece of work as is *The Beggar's Opera* —but if it is not as good it is at least one of the best sequels in history; and if it had ever had the chance to come to the stage as *The Beggar's Opera* did, there is no reason why it should not have reaped nearly as rich a reward. It might have had even more important results. It might, just conceivably, have laughed Walpole out of office. For despite his disarming preface, in which he declared that his intention had only been to "lash vice in general," it is perfectly certain that Gay was getting at Walpole in it as he had got at him in *The Beggar's Opera*. If Walpole was Macheath in the first play, then he was certainly intended for Morano—or Macheath disguised as Morano—in the second. And in that case the dialogue in *Polly* between the high-minded barbarian Indian Pohetohee and the civilised scoundrel Morano would have been embarrassing hearing for the chief Minister in any theatre.

In the character of Morano, Captain Macheath's heart has grown blacker as well as his face. There is a touch of Petruchio, of Raffles, of the Scarlet Pimpernel, about the captain in the first play—but with the second the charm has departed. Only the scoundrelism remains:

Pohetohee	Have ye notions of property?
Morano	Of my own.
Pohetohee	Would not your honest industry have suffic'd to support you?
Morano	Honest Industry! I have heard talk of it indeed among the common

	people, but all great genius's are above it.
Pohetohee	Have you no respect for virtue?
Morano	As a good phrase, Sir. But the practisers of it are so insignificant and poor, that they are seldom found in the best company.
Pohetohee	Is not wisdom esteem'd among you?
Morano	Yes, Sir: But only as a step to riches and power; a step that raises ourselves, and trips up our neighbours.
Pohetohee	Honour, and honesty, are not those distinguish'd?
Morano	As incapacities and follies. How ignorant are these *Indians*! But indeed I think honour is of some use; it serves to swear upon.
Pohetohee	Have you no consciousness? Have you no shame?
Morano	Of being poor . . .

In the general application of *Polly*, as apart from the particular, Gay was, as often, ahead of his time. His comparison in *Polly* between the native honesty of the Indian and the treacherous duplicity of every European in the play (except Polly herself) might not have " gone over" well in 1728. But the criticism—slightly modified —is still applicable to-day. Much of the dialogue given to Prince Cawwawkee might come equally well from the lips of the Ex-Emperor of Abyssinia—or of the Chinese Generalissimo, after their betrayal by the white nations. From the moment when the noble Prince

Cawwawkee is captured, and Vanderbluff declares of the rest of the Indians "We must beat civilizing into 'em, to make 'em capable of common society, and common conversation" to when Polly, disguised as a boy, encounters Cawwawkee "in chains" in a poor cottage:

> *Polly*   Unfortunate prince! I cannot blame your disbelief, when I tell you that I admire your virtues, and share in your misfortunes.
>
> *Cawwawkee*   To be oppressed by an *European* implies merit. Yet you are an *European.* Are you fools? Do you believe one another? Sure, speech can be of no use among you. . . . You are asham'd of your hearts, you can lie. How can you bear to look into yourselves?
>
> *Polly*   My sincerity would bear even your examination
>
> *Cawwawkee*   You have cancell'd faith. How can I believe you? You are cowards too, for you are cruel. . . . You can be avaricious. That is a complication of all vices. It comprehends them all. Heaven guard our country from the infection.

Such satire is still applicable though the fact that it is so is incidental. What cannot be repeated too often is that Gay did not write for posterity. He was a topical writer. He wrote *The Beggar's Opera* not as a classic but as a *revue intime* of the years 1720-28. Subsequent judgment has reversed the titles and chosen it to be a classic: but *Polly* too was written as *revue intime*; and should be judged primarily as such, and not as a classic. If it had been produced then, as hot on the trail of the Government as ever *The Beggar's Opera* had been, and with the Jessie Matthews of the times tricked out in the additional attraction of men's clothes (as every audience expected to see and adored to see its favourite actress) there is no reason whatever why *Polly* should not have succeeded as the first play had done, and been received with as much acclaim. As it was, it had to wait for production until 1777, when everybody concerned, except the aged indomitable Duchess of Queensberry, was dead.

According to his nephew, Gay had plans for visiting his native county again about this time. "It was his intention," writes the Reverend Joseph Baller, "to pass some months in Devonshire, and apartments were accordingly provided for him in a house near Landkey in the vicinity of Barnstaple, but his friends were disappointed of their expectations of seeing him." It seems a pity that the opportunity was missed. Barnstaple would no doubt have prepared a civic reception fit for such a hero, and the hero would have been able to admire the statue of Queen Anne (which had been set up, since his time, on the quay-side) and the Palladian proportions of the charming little colonnade which it surmounted. Such relatives as survived would also have been able to take back, in person, the various unkind judgments they had passed on the idle apprentice of so long ago. But some other plan intervened: and there is every likelihood that, whatever it was, it was inspired by the Duchess of Queensberry.

CHAPTER TWENTY-ONE

1729. The Publication of 'Polly.' The Visit to Scotland. Living at Amesbury.

> "*Every Porter in Politics can padlock the door against Satire, and teach Power to keep all wit at a distance.*"
> AARON HILL IN A LETTER TO LORD BOLINGBROKE, SEPTEMBER, 1733.

UP to this time in her acquaintance with Gay, the Duchess of Queensberry had held a somewhat nebulous position. She had been confined to the position of an admirer and kind patron of a deserving poet. But there had been no active part which she could play, and this to a person of her temperament was undoubtedly unsatisfactory. Now the moment had come. Walpole's banning of *Polly*, via the Lord Chancellor, gave her the chance she had been waiting for. She was twenty-nine and extremely good-looking. She had been married nine years and had produced two sons to perpetuate the family name. She had tasted Court life and found it full of that insincerity which was, to her, one of the most odious of vices. No one, it is certain, ever read Gay's comments on Court life with more emphatic agreement than the Duchess. No one despised more the gentle middle path to which Mrs. Howard kept in her Swiss canyons. . . . There was never a *via media* for the Duchess. Things were either bad to her, tremendously bad—or else tremendously good. The treatment of John Gay was, she considered, atrocious—and that being so, she set out to right it.

Most people are familiar with the steps she took—how she began soliciting subscriptions for the published *Polly*, even, relates a horrified historian, in the presence of Majesty itself. The King is supposed to have contained his temper moderately well for him but no sooner was the Duchess out of the drawing-room than Lord Stanhope—as Chamberlain—was sent after her to request that she should not again attend the Court. This might have depressed a less buoyant woman: it merely invigorated the Duchess of Queensberry. She sat down and dashed off a letter which she desired Lord Stanhope to carry back to the King. Lord Stanhope, having read it, temporised. He suggested that she should consider again, and let her judgment dictate a wiser letter. The Duchess, nothing loth, promptly wrote a second and far worse one. Whereupon Lord Stanhope hastily took up the first and departed with it. Unless his fingers were asbestos they must have shrivelled a little from the heat of so much righteous anger.

"The Duchess of Queensberry," the letter ran, "is surprised and well pleased that the King has given her so agreeable a command as to stay from Court, where she never came for diversion, but to bestow a civility on the King and Queen; she hopes by so unprecedented an order as this that the King will see so few as he wishes at his Court, particularly such as dare to think or speak the truth. I dare not do otherwise, and would not have imagined that it would not have been the very highest compliment I could possibly pay the King to endeavour to support mirth and innocence in his house, particularly when the King and Queen both told me they had not read Mr. Gay's play. I have certainly done right then to stand by my own words

2 A

rather than his Grace of Grafton's, who has neither made use of truth, judgment or honour, through this whole affair, either for himself or his friends.

"C. QUEENSBERRY."

It is difficult not to admire such brisk wrath, bestowed so salutarily on such exalted personages. But lest it should all seem slightly over-stated there is a story of Horace Walpole's which, if it is true (and certainly no story ever sounded truer), fully justifies the edge to the Duchess's temper. The tale is that she not only solicited subscriptions in the presence of majesty but actually tackled the King on the subject himself, assuring him at the same time (as she had declared in her letter) that as he hadn't read the play he couldn't possibly know what it was about or condemn it off-hand—and offering even to go up to his closet to read it to him. George made a thoroughly Hanoverian reply: he said he would be delighted to receive her Grace in his closet but that he hoped he knew how to amuse her better than by reading plays. Did he catch Queen Caroline's eye as he made his little joke? If he did, she certainly smiled dutifully. She knew how to appreciate the King's jokes, if few others did. But the Duchess of Queensberry was not of that number. She made her exit with proper spirit, and upon Lady Hervey remarking—either sincerely or sarcastically—that the Court would be losing its greatest ornament, replied rudely: "Madam, I am entirely of *your* opinion." No little chit of a Molly Lepell was going to score off a Hyde with Monmouth and Clarendon and Burlington and Rochester relations, and more royal blood in her little finger than the whole of the Hanoverians between them.

What one would give for an account of the whole affair in some contemporary copy of the American magazine, *Time*! Imagine the treatment it would have received. The Duchess on the cover in the milkmaid portrait by Jervas, and underneath in italics—*She put royalty right on censorship and closets*. Inside, a story that would stream out for pages—and yet more pictures—George in his robes (*No highbrow, he*) the Duke of Grafton's knee and shoulder very large, getting out of a coach ("*neither truth, judgment nor honour*") and Gay in his round velvet cap as ever, looking thoroughly bewildered and labelled (*His present—a brickbat for Walpole*). Imagine the horde of adjectives wrapped round the personalities—Socialite, for the Duchess of Queensberry, Square-chopped for the Chief Minister, Frog-eyed for the King, Bumbling for Gay. Even Molly Lepell (*Youth's youngest daughter, she*) and Mr. Rich might make an entrance. (*He made Gay Rich (see cut)*).

Alas for posterity, there was no *Time* then—and we have to take our records from the vaguer, more desultory but just as inaccurate recollections of people like Hervey and Horace Walpole.

Early in March Swift wrote to Pope somewhat puzzlingly:

> "Mr. Gay is a scandal to all lusty young men with healthy countenances, and, I think, he is not intemperate in a physical sense. I am told he has an asthma, which is a disease I commiserate more than deafness, because it will not leave a man quiet either sleeping or waking. I hope he does not intend to publish his opera before it is acted; for I defy all your subscriptions to amount to eight hundred pounds. And yet, I believe he lost much more, for want of human prudence."

Here Swift is referring, without doubt, to that

unlucky sale of the copyright of *The Beggar's Opera* and the *Fables*, both of which were still selling merrily, but without advantage to Gay. Whether it was the asthma, or the colic, certainly Gay was in a particularly distressed condition early in 1729. Congreve had just died, from the after-effects of his coach accident, and it may have been the loss of yet another Scriblerian which added to his depression. Whatever it was, it gave rise to a letter to Pope which exhibits him in most miserable mood:

"DEAR MR. POPE,—My melancholy increases, and every hour threatens me with some return of my distemper, nay I think I may rather say I have it on me. Not the divine looks, the kind favours and expressions of the divine Duchess, who hereafter shall be in place of a queen to me—nay, she shall be my queen—nor the inexpressible goodness of the duke, can in the least cheer me. The drawing-room no more receives light from those two stars. There is now what Milton says is in hell, darkness visible. Dear Pope, what a barren soil (to me so) have I been striving to produce something out of! Why did I not take your advice before my writing fables for the duke, not to write them? or rather to write them for some young nobleman? It is my very hard fate I must get nothing, write for them, or against them . . . I find myself in such a strange confusion and depression of spirits that I have not strength even to make my will, though I perceive by many warnings that I have no continuing city here. I begin to look upon myself as one already dead and desire, my dear Mr. Pope, whom I love as my own soul, if you survive me, as you certainly will, if a stone should mark the place of my grave, see these words put upon it:

> Life is a jest, and all things show it
> I thought so once, and now I know it.

with what more you may think proper. . . . What the bearer brings besides this letter, should I die without a will, which I am the likelier to do as the law will settle my small estate much as I should myself, let it remain with you, as it has long done with me, the remembrance of a dead friend [Parnell?] but there is none like you, living or dead."

To the same period, undoubtedly, belongs the *Elegiac Epistle to a Friend, written by Mr. Gay when he laboured under a Dejection of Spirits*. It is, as G. C. Faber says, entirely unlike any other poem of Gay's, and consists of twenty-eight four-line stanzas with alternating rhyme-endings, slightly reminiscent of Cowper or Goldsmith or Gray—those later eighteenth-century poets who were not afraid to let feeling, as opposed to reason, have principal place in the scheme. It was addressed, as was the letter, to Pope and deserves a place here precisely because it does show, for once, Gay in elegiac instead of lyric mood:

> "Friend of my youth, sheddst thou the pitying tear
> O'er the sad relics of my happier days?
> Of nature tender, as of soul sincere,
> Pour'st thou for me the melancholy lays?
>
> O! truly said!—the distant landscape bright
> Whose vivid colours glitter'd on the eye
> Is faded now, and sunk in shades of night
> As on some chilly eve, the closing flow'rets die.

Yet had I hop'd, when first, in happier times,
    I trod the magic paths where Fancy led
The Muse to foster in more friendly climes,
    Where never Misery rear'd its hated head.

How vain the thought! Hope after hope expires!
    Friend after friend, joy after joy, is lost;
My dearest wishes feed the funeral fires
    And Life is purchas'd at too dear a cost.

    *   *   *   *   *   *

Full well I know, in life's uncertain road
    The thorns of misery are profusely sown;
Full well I know, in this low vile abode
    Beneath the chastening rod what numbers groan.

    *   *   *   *   *   *

Me not such themes delight—I more rejoice
    When chance some happier, better change I see,
Though no such change await *my* luckless choice,
    And mountains rise between my hopes and me.

    *   *   *   *   *   *

Long has my bark in rudest tempest toss'd
    Buffetted seas, and stemm'd life's hostile wave;
Suffice it now, in all my wishes cross'd,
    To seek a peaceful harbour in the grave.

And when that hour shall come (as come it must)
    Ere many moons their waning horns increase,
When this frail frame shall mix with kindred dust,
    And all its fond pursuits and troubles cease:

When those black gates that ever open stand
    Receive me on th' irremeable shore,
When Life's frail glass has run its latest sand
    And the dull jest repeated charms no more:

Then may my friend weep o'er the fun'ral
   hearse,
Then may his presence gild the awful gloom,
And his last tribute be some mournful verse
   To mark the spot that holds my silent tomb."

Odd that a man who could express such sentiments was at the same time being fêted and honoured as the author of a play which had scared the Ministry into imposing a censorship, and who was, undoubtedly, the man of the hour! But Gay's thoughts were turning inward, not outward, even while his friends and acquaintances rallied round him. The Queensberry affair at Court was having wide repercussions. Arbuthnot, writing to Swift, summed up the situation better than anybody else:

"John Gay is now become one of the obstructors of the peace of Europe, the terror of Ministers, the chief author of *The Craftsman*, and all the seditious pamphlets which have been published against the Government. He has got several turned out of their places; the greatest ornament of the Court banned from it for his sake; another great lady is in danger of being chassée likewise; about seven or eight great duchesses pushing like the ancient circumvalliones in the church, who shall suffer martyrdom on his account first. He is the darling of the city. If he should travel about the country he would have hectacombs of roasted oxen sacrificed to him, since he became so conspicuous. . . . I hope he will get a good deal of money for printing his play, but I really believe he would get more by showing his person, and can assure you this is the self-same John Gay

whom you knew and lodged with in Whitehall
2 years ago."

Arbuthnot was, with his customary exuberance, exaggerating a little to enliven the letter—but it is true that if Gay could have spared time from thinking of tombs he would have realised that he had become something much better than a corpse—and that was a martyr. It is also true that his women friends rushed to assist him, and to show themselves the protectors of neglected genius. Pope hints even at an unseemly scuffle to retain or gain the ball. "I can give you no account of Gay," he writes curiously to Swift, "since he was raffled for and won back by his Duchess." There is the smallest hint of jealousy in such phrasing, but Pope should have come down to brass-tacks. The whole point was that when it came to real action, the Duchess of Queensberry had not an ailing mother to hold her back, and Pope had. Pope might have had the right of precedence over her concerning Gay—since he was an older friend, but as he did not come forward, then the Duchess of Queensberry was certainly not going to resign the prize to any lesser combatants. The crowd was so noticeable that verses entitled *The Female Faction, or the Gay Subscribers* came out in earnest celebration:

"Then Gay, all future Trophies wisely scorn
And Glory, thou'rt to *present* Status born.
By Nations Deify'd be Homer's shade
He smiles unconscious of the Honours paid;
Thy Works, whilst *Here*, sublimest columns raise
From Women's Bounty, and from Women's
    Praise
The *Brightest Sex* thy worth in rev'rence hold
And load the *living* with *Renown* and *Gold*."

Another poem, *The Banish'd Beauty, or a Fair Face in Disgrace*, celebrated the event in enthusiastic but somewhat obscure couplets, and urged Gay to take the foil off his rapier—in other words to drop all the romantic hyperbole about Macheath, come out into the open and attack Walpole as a statesman instead of a stage highwayman. In the midst of all the to-do and fuss Gay sat down and wrote to Swift from Burlington Gardens:

"I must acquaint you (because I know it will please you) that during my sickness I had many of the kindest proofs of friendship, particularly from the Duke and Duchess of Queensberry; who, if I had been their nearest relation and dearest friend, could not have treated me with more constant attendance then; and they continue the same to me now. . . ." [Obviously being ill in the Queensberrys' house was a very different affair from being ill in the Burlingtons' house. He continues with some pride]: "For writing on the cause of virtue and against the fashionable vices, I am looked upon at present as the most obnoxious person almost in England. Mr. Pulteney tells me, I have the start of him. Mr. Pope tells me, that I am dead, and that this obnoxiousness is the reward for my inoffensiveness in my former life. I wish I had a book ready to send you; but I believe I shall not be able to complete the work till the latter end of next week. Your money is still in Lord Bathurst's hands; but I believe I shall receive it soon. I wish to receive your orders how to dispose of it. I am impatient to finish my work, for I want the country air; not that I am ill, but to reserve my strength; and I cannot leave my work till it is finished. While I am writing this,

I am in the room next our dining-room, with sheets all round it, and two people from the binder folding sheets. I print the book at my own expense, in quarto, which is to be sold for six shillings, with the music. You see I do not want industry and I hope you will allow that I have not the worst economy ... Mrs. Howard has declared herself strongly, both to the Queen and the King, as my advocate. The Duchess of Queensberry is allowed to have shown more spirit, more honour and more goodness, than was thought possible in our time. I should have added, too, more understanding and good sense. You see my fortune (as I hope my virtue will) increases by oppression. I go to no courts, I drink no wine, and am calumniated even by ministers of State; and yet am in good spirits. Most of the courtiers, though otherwise my friends, refused to contribute to the undertaking, but the city, and the people of England, take my part very warmly, and, I am told, the best of the citizens will give me proof of it by their contributions."

Before, however, Swift had had time to receive this, a reply from him to an earlier letter of Gay's crossed with the letter from Burlington Gardens. The Dean began in answer to an obvious complaint:

"I deny it. I do write to you according to the old Stipulation, for when you kept your old company, when I writ to one I writ to all. But I am ready to enter into a new Bargain, since you are got into a new World, and will answer all your letters. You are first to present my most humble Respect to the Duchess of Queensberry and let her know that I never dine without thinking of her, altho' it be with some difficulty that I can obey her when I dine with Forks that have but two Prongs, and when the Sauce is not very consistent ... I will leave my Money in Lord Bathurst's hands, and the management of it (for want of better) in yours, and pray keep the Interest Money in a Bag and sealed by itself, for fear of your own Fingers under your Carelessness."

After this fond teasing he returns again to the thought of that "old company" which Gay used to keep. It makes him sigh as the thought of Martin Scriblerus used to make him sigh:

"Mr. Pope talks of you as a perfect Stranger; but the different Pursuits and Manners, and Interests of Life, as Fortune has pleased to dispose them, will never suffer those to live together, who by their Inclinations ought never to part."

This is the bitterest drop in the whole cup. In deploring the separation of Pope and Gay he is deploring also his own separation from them and echoing again in his heart those anguished earlier cries, wrung out from him by circumstance: "But I am condemned to another Scene ..." and "If I had my way I know very well who should have my affections, *but they are not in the way* ..." It is easier to turn from the general to the particular:

"I hope when you are rich enough, you will have some little Œconomy of your own in Town or Country, and be able to give your Friend a Pint of Port; for the domestic season of life will come on . . . I writ lately to Mr. Pope. I wish you had a little Villakin in his Neighbourhood, but you are yet too volatile, and any Lady with a Coach and Six Horses could carry you to Japan."

Soon after this, though the ban on the public presentation of *Polly* remained in full force, she appeared in book form, and sold all the better for the notoriety which had accumulated about her.

The publication of *Polly* was the only time Gay ever undertook publication on his own behalf. This time he was taking care of himself, as he had told Swift he would, with a vengeance. The edition had a sale of ten thousand copies—a reputable number not to be sneezed at even to-day, and he succeeded in making twelve hundred pounds out of it. The 'Female Faction' still stood loyally by him, and gave generously for their copy. The young Duchess of Marlborough gave £100 for her first edition; but this was presumably due less to her interest in the play than in memory of Congreve, in whose presence so many of Polly's lines had been quoted or composed. Congreve's death, as has been seen, made a deep impression upon Gay, and Pope wrote of it, "Every year carries away something dear with it, till we outlive all our tendernesses, and become wretched individuals again, as we began." As he saw it, the bond of friendship which had warmed and vitalized the members of the Scriblerus Club was fast dissolving. There was no longer any entity—only wretched individuals, crying alone in a wilderness that all was vanity and vexation of spirit to a world that would not heed them.

One interesting conclusion arises at this point. It is that satire, when employed as ferociously and wholeheartedly as Swift and Pope (and later even Gay) applied it, has a curiously devitalizing effect upon its author. It seems to thin the blood and slow down the circulation and harden the very arteries of the heart. It was not as if any of these poets was remembering the rule of Juvenal—that as soon as ill-temper becomes visible in satire, the satire becomes mere spleen. Neither Swift nor Pope saw it as spleen. And since their mental factories were perpetually employed in turning out gibes and lampoons—since they were stoked only with the sevenfold fires of disgust and wrath, it is not surprising that the effect upon their physique was finally deleterious. Love acts as an emollient and restorative—it is beneficent in all its aspects. Hatred, fear, or rage, each in its separate channel, can poison the digestive juices, short-circuit the nervous system, alter the glandular distribution, and deaden or retard circulation. Certainly in the exercise of their satirical genius these three men, in greater or lesser degree, suffered in physique as a consequence. It is customary to attribute Swift's misanthropy, in some part, to deafness and giddiness—and Pope's to the fact that he was an invalid from a child—and Gay's to indolence and colic. But which was the cause—and which the effect? Whatever the truth of the matter it is worth emphasising that this year, when all three were separated, Pope was polishing his attack on Dullness (*Lo, thy dread empire, Chaos, is restor'd: Light dies before thy uncreating word*), Swift was publishing the most nauseating of all his pamphlets —his *Modest Proposal for preventing the children of Poor People from being a Burden to their Parents or Country, and for making them beneficial to the Publick*, and Gay was busy formulating, under continual pressure from his admirers, less 'Squeamish' and more direct attacks upon Walpole. Bearing in mind these occupations, Wordsworth's words—"The poet . . . is the rock of defence of human virtue; an upholder and preserver, carrying everywhere with him relationship and love" —sound strangely inapplicable. These men were not preservers but destroyers, and in their occupation they partly destroyed themselves.

There is another consideration. Precisely because of their misanthropic occupations these writers were doubly as dependent as other men on friendship. Because they could hate so desperately, they needed love even more desperately. Born to a cold, corrupt and ungrateful age (as they saw it), they clung together intermittently for warmth—and when they had derived heat from such friendly contact—rose up and denounced what they saw around them. . . . Congreve had been one of them: now he was gone with Parnell and Oxford into the shades. All that was left of Parnell was his letters and his verse—no more warm humanity. And all that was left of Lord Oxford was a son and heir who wrote extremely polite letters and continually plagued Pope with presents of collars of brawn from Wimpole.

Naturally enough Gay's triumph with *Polly* was observed by pirate booksellers, who seized upon this new prize with delight, and rushed out their own editions. The law of copyright was not clearly defined enough as yet to help the author much, though by taking legal action it was possible to obtain some compensation; but the process was tedious and expensive and it was part of the wits' credo to detest law and lawyers almost as much as they detested war and soldiers. Gay had endured piracy of his work before; but so sudden and concerted was the attack upon his new book *Polly* that he resolved to bear it no longer—even though not to do so meant the hateful and expensive process of going to law. He gave his affairs into the hands of justice and left London. Dr. Arbuthnot wrote to Swift:

"Mr. Gay is gone to Scotland with the Duke of Queensberry, he has about twenty law-suits with the booksellers, for printing his book."

(It is not known whether the notorious Mr. Curll, chief Captain Hook of all the piratical crew, was one of the *Polly*-snatchers; but he appears upon the scene later.)

From this time until the time of his death Gay's life was spent, willy-nilly, in an atmosphere of comfortable splendour. If in the past he had dreamed that he dwelt in marble halls, his dream was now turned into solid fact. One sees him forever jolting in huge coaches across England, at the side of the Duchess of Queensberry—ever approaching, or driving away from, small model palaces (each with a grateful pediment over the front door and four Palladian arches to support it) through decorous avenues of lime or elm or oak or chestnut. The Queensberry family had a variety of these country seats and Gay grew to know them all almost as well as their owners did—Middleton Stoney in Oxfordshire, Petersham in Surrey, Amesbury in Wiltshire, and Drumlanrig Castle in Scotland. To these they added town houses in London and in Edinburgh; and in May, 1728, it was for Drumlanrig that they were bound—first calling in at Edinburgh on the way.

It was at Edinburgh that Gay met the first Scottish poet of his acquaintance—Allan Ramsay. That hatmaker-wig-maker-farmer-poet held the same sort of position in the intellectual society of Edinburgh as Pope held in London. He was a pretty good versifier himself, and edited Scots miscellanies of poetry, sprinkling them liberally with verses from the Twickenham school of poetry, which he greatly admired. He seems to have been a genial, enthusiastic kind of person, and when he heard that Mr. Gay was in Edinburgh he seized upon the visitor with both hands. John Gay, in consequence, was made free of Allan Ramsay's residence, where life immediately resolved itself into a cheerful crowded fugginess and where drinks and smokes and song and other revelry by night may almost have made the visitor think momentarily that he was back at Twickenham, especially when ballads from *The Beggar's Opera* were sung in his honour. From all accounts the Gay-Ramsay *entente* was a happy one, and they both enjoyed each other's company. Indeed, after Gay had crammed his fat body into the coach again and jolted on with the Queensberrys to Drumlanrig, Allan Ramsay sat down and indited an enthusiastic Epistle to him, lest auld—or comparatively new—acquaintance be forgot:

> "Now lend thy lug and tent me, Gay,
> Thy Fate appears like flow'rs in May
> Fresh, flourishing, and lasting ay
>   Firm as the aik,
> Which envious winds, when critics bray
>   Shall never shaik.
>
> Come, show your loof. Ay, there's the line
> Foretells thy verse shall ever shine,
> Dowted, while living, by the nine
>   And a' the best,
> And be, when past the mortal line,
>   Of fame possest.
>
> Immortal Pope and skilfu' John
> The learned leech from Caledon
> With mony a witty dame and don
>   Owre long to name
> Are of your verses very fon'
>   And sound your fame."

Are of your verses very fon'. A man whose ear was attuned to the graceful compliments of Immortal Pope might be forgiven for finding this a little crude—especially as there seemed to be no happy ending to the story, except the assurance that, after death, Gay would like Homer receive his due of praise. But crude or not, it sprang from genuine feeling, and since Gay was also genuine it is possible that the Gentle Shepherd's *Epistle* was received more gratefully than many better-written eulogies.

After Edinburgh, Drumlanrig Castle opened its gates to greet the three fugitives from Court life. Gay, who imagined he had just turned his back on palaces for ever, now found that life was just one darned palace after another, with Drumlanrig the culminating palace of all. G. A. Jellicoe in his *Gardens of Europe* writes:

> "The approach to Drumlanrig Castle is itself dramatic. The drive leads towards and over a mighty bridge, winds through a wild park and suddenly enters a broad avenue finished at the end by the great building bristling with towers. . . . You must imagine the sun lighting up the pink stone, and all around a tumbling, conifer-crowned landscape, penetrating at times as far as the building itself."

A great rosy-red building "bristling with towers" . . . If Gay ever climbed to the top of its six stories, and entered one of the many pepper-pot turrets on its roof, or traced his way amongst the tall stacked chimney-pots to lean over the balustrades, he would have looked down upon a landscape as wild and stormy and unfamiliar as any he had ever seen. This was the Queensberry inheritance, when for a casual month at a time they woke the fortress to activity. From the sternness and strength and wide, clean sweep of moors they in turn drew their sternness and strength and independent outlook. There they were monarchs of all they surveyed. As far as eye could see the earth existed for their pleasure. Deer browsed on the mountains, hawks hovered in the shrill blue sky over the heather, pheasants and partridges glided through the seeding grass, gamekeepers shot poachers, coachmen polished harness, oiled wheels, examined horses, blacksmiths shoed them and made window-hinges and door-handles and fire-screens, housemaids dusted, kitchenmaids scrubbed, cooks conferred with gardeners and keepers, game hung spicily in the sheds, wine grew sleekly old in the cellars, swallows thundered in the chimneys, cuckoos filled the woods with shouting, lizards basked, corn grew, under-gardeners cut down shrubberies and rolled lawns, beaters fed ferrets and kept down vermin, fires crackled in the hearth, cows gave milk, hens eggs, and the sun warmth—all, it might appear, for the Duke and Duchess, and their sons and heirs. The wonder is that amidst such halcyon delights, a month should have been enough to enjoy them. Gay spent the greater part of his time in the library, "putting together books" for the Duke's library in Burlington Gardens, and doubtless annotating and adding to the index as he worked. Each to his own taste, and the tastes of the Duke and Duchess were for other things than the library.

After Drumlanrig there was the smaller but just as elegant country seat at Amesbury in Wiltshire—the house with which, of all the Queensberry seats, Gay was to grow most closely acquainted. On the way there the entourage stopped to rest at London, and Gay learned the happy news that the profits from the sale of *Polly* were still rolling in. Pope was as glad to learn it as the author was, but Swift could, as ever, look on the dark side of things.

"I hope," he wrote gloomily to Pope, "Mr. Gay will keep his £3,000 and live on the interest without decreasing the Principal one Penny; but I do not like your seldom seeing him. I hope he is grown more disengaged from the Intentness on his own affairs, which I ever disliked."

How true that we are always most intolerant of those faults in others which, we are conscious, also exist in ourselves!—Swift was no exception. He is acting the heavy father here, carping at the waywardness of his son; and Pope in a maternal, protecting character (a boy's best friend is his mother) writes back:

"Mr. Gay assures me his £3,000 is kept entire and sacred; he seems to languish after a Line from you, and complains tenderly."

The Queensberrys took some time to settle down into their character of rural hermits. For some months they flitted from seat to seat—as if uncertain where to take up permanent residence. And wheresoever they went Gay and the two children went too. After Amesbury, Middleton Stoney. There they paused long enough in August for Gay to sit down at a table and write to Mrs. Howard; and from the tone of the letter it is obvious that constant travelling agrees with him:

"I desire you will send word whether white currants are proper to make tarts; it is a point that we dispute upon every day, and will never be ended unless you decide it.

"The Duchess will be extremely glad if you could come here this day sen'night; but if you cannot, come this day fortnight at farthest, and bring as many unlikely people as you can to keep you company. Have you lain at Marble Hill since we left Petersham? Hath the Duchess an Aunt Thanet alive again? She says that there are but two people in the world that love and fear me—and those are Lord Drum [Drumlanrig] and Lord Charles [Douglas]. If they were awake I would make them love those that I love, and say something civil to you. The Duchess hath left off taking snuff ever since you have. I have not left it off, and yet take none; my resolution not being so strong. Though you are a water-drinker yourself, I dare say you will be sorry to hear that your friends have strickly adhered to that liquor, for you may be sure their heads cannot be affected with that.

"General Dormer refused to eat a wheat-ear, because they call it here a fern-knacker; but since he knew it was a wheat-ear, he is extremely concerned. . . . The Duke hath rung the bell for supper and says How can you write such stuff?"

Others besides the Duke might echo the question; but Mrs. Howard was less critical. To hear from Gay at all was pleasant, since it showed her that he bore no malice for the unfortunate affair of the gentleman-ushership. She replied in the same cheerful gossipy manner. Since Chesterfield and Bathurst had been made distinctly unwelcome at Court by her jealous royal lover, since Swift now detested her, Peterborough was more than ever the property of Mrs. Robinson, and Pope busy with his new venture the *Grub Street Journal*, even letters from a strayed poet such as Gay were welcome to Mrs. Howard. Besides, she was genuinely fond of him—as she was, indeed, of the Duchess of Queensberry. She delighted to write jointly to both.

Swift was not nearly so obliging. In his heart of hearts he still deprecated that Gay should be spending any time away from Pope. Only in the homely atmosphere at Twickenham and in the company of another poet, he imagined, could Gay feel really safe. Life with the great ones was not all jam; or, if it was, it was like the Burlington menu—jam to-morrow, and jam yesterday, but never jam to-day. Whenever he was more low-spirited than usual sudden remembrance of humiliations endured at Moor Park—was it centuries ago?—wrung groans from the Dean and made the sweat stand out upon his brow. If he could suffer so from mere memory—if he could be conscious, so long after, of the miserable insecurity of tenure there—how must Gay suffer now in similar circumstances with the Queensberrys! In his blackest moments Swift fancied that he saw Gay turned adrift suddenly—homeless, forlorn, starving. It was not unheard of for authors to starve to death—far from it.

All these conjectures, though well-meant, were somewhat inconsistent, since Swift knew quite well by this time that Gay had made a small fortune by his two operas, and was not, as far as he knew, put to the labour of spending a penny of it. Yet still his prevailing sentiment was that "An old decay'd poet is a creature abandoned." And at the same time that Swift deplored the conditions in which Gay lived he felt a kind of envy like toothache gnawing him spasmodically—that Gay should be so loved and sheltered while he was left friendless on a starved promontory, a child of thunder and of thunderbolts, a gaunt, dreadful orphan of the storm.

Three-quarters at least of his apprehensions on Gay's behalf were groundless. Since Gay was not proud, so he could never be humiliated. He could indeed occasionally be 'mortified,' but that was a very desiccated emotion compared to humiliation: a budgerigar in a cage does not wonder how it can repay a handful of bird-seed a day—or dash its brains out against the bars at the humiliation of being kept—no more did Gay. Why should he? He sang for his supper as well as any budgerigar ever did, and remarked more than once that he was enjoying his 'independence,' which showed that *he* regarded himself as quite independent and not at all humiliated, whatever any one else might suppose. Meanwhile he went on pouring letters to Swift into the void:

"I have long known you to be my friend upon several occasions and particularly by your reproofs and admonitions. There is one thing you have often put me in mind of, the over-running you with an answer before you had spoken. You find I am not a bit the better for it; for I still write and write on, without having a word of an answer."

After this he is proud to tell Swift that he is not entirely a gentleman of leisure. He is busy "new writing a damned play," *The Wife of Bath*.

"The ridicule turns upon superstition, and I have avoided the very words bribery and corruption. . . . You have often twitted me in the past with hankering after the Court. In that you mistook me, for I know by experience that there is no dependence that can be sure but a dependence upon oneself. I will take care of the little fortune I have got. I know you will take this resolution kindly; and you see my inclinations will make me write to you whether you will write to me or no. I am, dear sir, your most sincerely and most affectionately."

Even so, he cannot yet fold the letter up, seal it and address it to the Dean in Dublin. Writing to Swift is so like speaking to him, one becomes voluble at the mere thought of so heartening a listener. He adds a postscript:

> "To the lady I live with I owe my Life and fortune. Think of her with respect and value and esteem her as I do; and never more despise a Fork with three prongs. I wish too that you would not eat from the point of your knife. She hath so much goodness, virtue and generosity that if you knew her you would have a pleasure in obeying her as I do. She often wishes she had known you."

So tempting a bait as that last sentence would have roused the Dean from almost any lethargy. The Duchess's reputation had already gone as far as Dublin and he knew her by repute for a woman of dignity and spirit. Once long ago, when she had been a mere girl, he had caught a glimpse of her in the Mall—but it had been dusk, and so he could not judge whether Prior's estimate of her beauty was just or not—and once he had seen her through the curtains of the Twickenham window. But what was beauty, after all? Something for the worms to eat, no more. Besides, there was something a little disturbing in the elegiac tone of that conclusion: "She often wishes she had known you"—almost as if he were already dead—gone beyond recall. Was he conscious of this? Whether or not, he chose to answer it in the same elegiac strain:

"I wish for her own sake I had known the Duchess of Queensberry, because I should be a more impartial judge than you; but it was her own fault, she never made me any advances. [Something of the old arrogance here.] However, as to you, I think the obligation lies on her side, by giving her the opportunity of acting so generous and honourable a part, and so well becoming her dignity and spirit."

All this, of course, was meant to be read out loud to the Duchess, as assuredly it was, and just as assuredly the Duchess was flattered by this favourite pretence (on Swift's part) of refusing to flatter and of merely speaking the truth. At first she merely talked about the Dean—and Gay was quick to pass on the conversation. Later the third person singular was dropped, and without further pretence the Duchess joined naturally in the correspondence. After that letters written jointly by Gay and the Duchess of Queensberry—letters which sometimes puzzled Swift to know who had written what, as much as the older Pope-Gay correspondence has puzzled other people—were sparks of light that came to illumine the ever-growing darkness that was settling down about him more deeply every year. Letters from him in his exquisitely neat, beautiful manuscript were red-letter days for Gay and the Duchess. All exiles, they prattled across hundreds of miles to each other of every subject but the country and the Court. This was wise, since an arbitrary sort of post-office spy system had been in force on letters from Gay since his *Beggar's Opera*, and Swift's correspondence had been suspect from days as long ago as *The Tale of a Tub*. Even so, they corresponded, and due either to the inefficiency or the broadmindedness of the censorship their letters were usually allowed through (though frequently they showed signs of having been tampered with in transit). This, however, was the kind of melancholy price one paid for acting as unofficial national critic and, after all, it was not much. Voltaire had been imprisoned for less.

Only in one way was it brought home to Gay that his position as "the terror of Ministers" was unpopular with the Government. Towards the end of the year, and without explanation, his lodgings in Whitehall were taken from him. His commissionership, however, remained—as if to show that Walpole could temper the wind to the shorn lamb as well as to the black sheep and be magnanimous to a beaten foe.

As for the Duchess of Queensberry, who had been ruder to the royal family than anybody else since Cromwell, nobody bothered to impose a censorship upon her. She was only a misguided woman, and in any case *her* situation had been neatly summed up years earlier by Addison in his essay on *Pretty Disaffection.* What happened, in Addison's essay, to the ladies who were ill-advised enough to venture into politics—and who took the wrong side?

> "They are forced to live in the country and feed their chickens; at the same time that they might show themselves at Court, and appear in brocade, if they behaved themselves well. In short, what must go to the heart of every fine woman, they throw themselves quite out of the fashion."

Alas for Addison, the Duchess of Queensberry was not a fine woman, she was Rosalind, exiled like Rosalind from the Court and returned with her Touchstone into Arden, far from the madding crowd's ignoble strife; and she wished no more to return to that strife than Touchstone did.

The most noticeable thing about the Duke of Queensberry is that, though doubtless he was a worthy man, it is so seldom that anybody notices him at all.

CHAPTER TWENTY-TWO

1730. 'The Wife of Bath.' 'Trivia,' third edition. Correspondence with Swift.

> "*Let the necessitous and sycophants haunt levees, and seek to sponge upon the Publick; 'tis a pursuit beneath a freeborn country gentleman.*"
> GAY: 'THE DISTRESS'D WIFE'

TWENTY-SEVEN years after its first appearance *The Wife of Bath*, much refurbished, took the boards again in January 1730. This time the theatre was the one in Lincoln's Inn Fields instead of Drury Lane, but the net result was the same, and the play failed as it had failed on the previous occasion. Gay took the result with equanimity. He was by now experienced enough in the theatre world to know that the reception of any play, however good or however bad, is absolutely unpredictable, and has no bearing on intrinsic merit, if any. Possibly Rich was more disappointed in the failure than the author was. While in London he stayed once more in Burlington Gardens, but a very short sojourn there was enough for him and his host and hostess. He wrote to Swift:

> "I am going very soon into Wiltshire with the Duke of Queensberry, with an intention to stay there till the winter. Since I had that severe fit of sickness I find my health requires it; for I cannot bear the town as I could formerly. I hope another summer's air and exercise will reinstate

me. I continue to drink water, so you cannot require any poetry from me. I have been very seldom abroad since I came to town, and not once to Court. This is no restraint upon me, for I have grown old enough to wish for retirement. [Old enough, at 43! Here surely is the most specious of arguments—and yet it was one that Gay had not been ashamed to employ before. Had he not told the Queen, at the age of 42, that naturally with one foot in the grave he could not undertake the task of being gentleman-usher to the Princess Louisa? True his expectation of life was at least ten years less then than it would have been now; even so, forty-five was not senility may perhaps be argued in Gay's favour that he had caught the trick from Pope, for ever since the age of 30 Pope off and on had been treading the sere and yellow path.] I saw Mr. Pope a day or two ago in good spirits, and with good wishes for you. . . . For we always talk of you. The doctor does the same. I have left off all grand folks but our own family. . . . I do not hate the world, but I laugh at it; for none but fools can be in earnest about a trifle. I am, dear sir, yours most affectionately."

Once safe again in Wiltshire Gay was quick to resume correspondence with the rest of his friends, and they with him. It was, in his wineless condition, the only kind of writing he felt equal to. Mrs. Howard, writing to him of *her* country engagements at Hampton Court, remarked:

"We hunt with great violence, and have every day a very tolerable chance to have a neck broken."

But that was just her fun; she still liked to indicate that with her life went merrily, and all was for the best in the best of all possible worlds. Gay, replying in the same mood, intimated that the amusements at Amesbury were just as satisfying: "We do not play cards, and yet the days are too short for us." It suggests a charming picture of domesticity, something like, at a later time, Dr. Johnson taking tea with his Miss Williams or Cowper sitting in the twilight with his Mary Unwin. Despite the Darby-and-Joan atmosphere, however, it is clear that Gay had no real thoughts of declining slowly into the grave in a local churchyard, or even of ultimately inhabiting part of a Queensberry mausoleum. He was enjoying life mightily with the duchess and duke—but only for the time being. (Had he not said he would be at Amesbury until the winter?) Still deep down in his heart was that other exciting plan, the day-dream of the "snug little house" first referred to, two years earlier, in a letter from him to Pope. It was (needless to say) Swift who had originally advised the purchase of the little Villakin. Gay now set about carrying the advice into action and wrote to Mrs. Howard:

> "As soon as you are settled at Marble Hill, I beg you will take the Widow's House for me and persuade the Duchess to come to Petersham."

It was a day-dream promising the most delightful prospects—Gay, Swift and Pope, the Twickenham Triumvirate, reunited once more under the roof of Gay's own little Villakin, with the sweet Thames to run gently beside them until they had ended their song. But, perhaps naturally, Mrs. Howard did not take the inquiry very seriously, and as ever Gay needed a strong hand behind him to prod him into action. Had Swift written to him at this stage: "I am coming over on such and such a date. Have a house ready to receive me in," Gay would have been a perfect little Mrs. Tittlemouse of energy in preparing his Ideal Home. The sheets would have been ready washed, mended and aired; the curtains would have been hung in the windows, the wine would have been decanted, the Bolingbroke recipe for stewed veal in casserole, in all its glory, would have graced the shining table-cloth, and the lamp would have been hanging in the window to welcome the returned exile home. But no such definite command was given and the Villakin, for the nonce, remained a mere ambition.

If such a plan *had* come to pass, there is nobody to whom it would have been more welcome than to Pope. He had been immersed up to the neck in quarrels ever since the publication of *The Dunciad*, and every fresh issue of the *Grub Street Journal* added vigour to the fight. Bolingbroke, his only close companion in the absence of Swift and Gay, was as gracious and agreeable to him as ever, but we may guess that the ex-minister's preoccupation with political matters was sometimes irritating to a man who considered all politics to be boring beyond words. Philosophy, from Pope's point of view, was far preferable to politics, and almost to his surprise he began to find himself engaged in deep philosophical discussions with Bolingbroke. At Twickenham from that time onwards the proper study of mankind was man. This was all very well, but neither Pope's constitution nor his religion was really adapted to deep philosophical discussions. The proper study of man, from the true Pope perspective, was a study so close that half a brick could be heaved at him. And if, as he himself averred, *whatever is is right*, then it was wrong of him to wish, as he *did* wish continually, that the Dean would come over to end his days at Twickenham, and that Gay once more would make up the three. Even while entangled in labyrinthian discussions with Lord Bolingbroke he would still write the most charming rallying letters to Gay:

"How comes it that Providence has been so unkind to me (who am a greater object of compassion than any fat man alive) that I am forced to drink wine, while you riot in water, prepared with oranges by the hand of the Duchess of Queensberry, that I am condemned to live on a highway side, like an old patriarch receiving all guests . . . while you are rapt into the Idalian groves, sprinkled with rose-water and live on burrage, balm and burnet up to the chin, with the Duchess of Queensberry?"

It might never be guessed from this easy banter that, amongst other quarrels, Pope was still busy with his campaign against Lady Mary Wortley Montagu. Still not yet in print, his lines on Sappho had yet managed to achieve a quite successful hand-to-hand and mouth-to-mouth circulation amongst both the friends and the enemies of that lady, and she returned the criticism with interest. It is an odd contrast this, in Pope's life—at one moment reclining under the haycocks at Dawley with his beloved St. John, and having all sorts of good intentions towards mankind in the abstract, writing to Swift and Gay in the same affectionately-disposed character—at another, attacking Lady Mary Wortley Montagu about her linen, her friends, her complexion, her avarice, her husband. After Lady Mary there was the author of *A Pop upon Pope* still to be carved up in little pieces and all the flapping bugs, the mere mayflies of literature, to be squashed and trapped and beaten out of existence. It was a Jekyll-and-Hyde life that few besides Pope could have sustained so easily over so large a space of years. True, Swift had done much the same thing at an earlier time—all day the blustering, capable, brutal Dean, servant of his own conjured spirit, at night in his letters to Stella the tenderly domineering Presto of the "Little Language." But Stella was dead, and the best of Presto had gone with her. Sometimes, it is true, a shadow of the former Presto emerged—usually at a woman's instigation—Lady Betty Germaine, Mrs. Howard, Mrs. Delany, later Mrs. Pilkington. Soon it was to be the sight of the Duchess of Queensberry's handwriting at the foot of a letter from Gay which roused Swift to most animation. The Dean side was in abeyance, the Presto side in full emergence, in all that correspondence. Only Gay never veered from being Gay. "He is," wrote Pope in answer to an inquiry from Swift, "60 miles off, and has been all the summer, with the Duke and Duchess of Queensberry. He is the same man." Which was as much as to say, although we are separated, and I deplore it as heartily as you do, our minds and hearts are still one. He has not changed, nor I—no matter what appears—nor you. This stability, in an unstable and unfriendly world, still remains to us.

Meanwhile down at Amesbury life had many compensations for a disinherited poet. Gay was with his adored Duchess—that monument to his mind of honesty and sincerity. He could walk with her and talk with her to their mutual improvement and enjoyment. There were two boys who were fond of him at home in the holidays and a Duke somewhat nonplussed by having a live poet about the house but extremely gracious nevertheless. There were occasional shopping excursions to the market town of Salisbury. Bath, the queen of cities, lay only a day's journey to the west, and Swift (lured on, it is possible to conjecture, mainly by the postscripts from the Duchess) beginning to enter at last into a correspondence as regular as the post-office spies, his own activities, and the inconveniences of mails allowed it to be. . . .

It is clear from Gay's next letter that he has by no means given up the scheme of the Widow's House at Twickenham. Swift has twitted him before now, with building castles in the air. Very well then:

> "My ambition," he writes to Swift, "is levelled to the same point that you direct me to, for I am every day building Villakins, and have given over that of Castles. [Nevertheless, he hastens to point out—sure that Swift will approve—we must make haste slowly, even in so delightful a plan.] If I were to undertake it in my present Circumstances I should in the most thrifty scheme soon be straitened, and I hate to be in debt, for I cannot bear to pawn five pounds worth of my liberty to a Taylor or a Butcher. I grant you this is not having the true spirit of modern Nobility, but 'tis hard to cure the prejudice of education. . . . I have been extremely taken up of late in settling a steward's account. I am endeavouring to do all the service I can for a friend, so I am sure you will think I am well employed. . . . The Duchess wishes she had seen you and thinks you were in the wrong to hide yourself and peep through the window that day she came to Mr. Pope's. . . . I will not imbezzle your interest money, though by looking upon accounts I see how money may be imbezzled."

Sancta Simplicitas! Here is the man that the parsimonious, ever-careful Dean had entrusted years earlier with two hundred precious pounds—and the same man whose business acumen had led him to lose an entire fortune in the South Sea Bubble—and he has just discovered "by looking upon accounts" how money may be "imbezzled." None of this augured well for the two hundred pounds. Nor yet did his style, usually so simple and straightforward, seem well adapted to the discussion of money matters. Certainly a sentence from one of his letters on the subject of the eternal two hundred: "My Lord Bathurst is still our cashier. When I see him I intend to settle our accounts, and repay myself the five pounds out of the two hundred I owe you," is not a model of clarity. It savours of nothing so much as the verse from *Alice*:

> "*I gave her one, they gave him two*
> *You gave us three or more;*
> *They all returned from him to you,*
> *Though they were mine before.*"

Swift, however, was much more interested in Gay's remark that he was settling somebody else's accounts (however topsy-turvily) than in news of his own. The news filled him with enthusiasm, and he was immediately convinced—heaven knows why—that Gay was being employed as a sort of secretarial bailiff by the Duke of Queensberry, and that in that capacity he would be far safer than in the one of non-paying guest. The Duke of Queensberry has not come down to posterity as brilliant in any particular respect, but he seems to have realised (better than Swift did) that it was not wise to entrust Gay with business matters. Nevertheless, Swift later was to be so carried away by the image of his friend riding round the Queensberry estates and preparing the ducal accounts that he burst into verse on the subject— a pleasant little piece of flattery concerning Gay's honesty and the Duke's percipience. Meanwhile the misunderstanding persisted, and Gay wanted, more than ever, Swift's advice about what to do with his *own* 'revenues,' and *still* could get no definite statement out of the Dean. He wrote and wrote—but Swift seemed suddenly to have lost interest. Nothing daunted, he tried his luck again in July:

> "If you won't write to me for my own sake you might write for your own. How do you know what is become of your money? . . ."

But underneath the raillery he is plaintive. In the long, hot days of summer he sees himself suddenly at a standstill. The wheat and the rye grow up, and the ears fill with corn, and are harvested. And after that there is threshing and ploughing, manuring and seed-time again. Nature has a calendar of its own which proceeds with a serene unconsciousness. Only human beings stand still, and have neither seed-time nor harvest:

> "I have left off wine and writing. . . . I took your advice and some time ago took to Love, and made some advances to the Lady you sent me to in Soho. [Truly the functions of a Dean are extensive ones!] But I met no return, so I have given up all thoughts of it and have now no pursuit or amusement. A state of Indolence is what I don't like and would not choose; I am not thinking of a Court preferment, for I think the Lady I live with is my friend, so that I am at the height of my ambition. You have often told me there is a time of life when every one wishes for a settlement of his own; I have frequently that feeling about me; but I fancy it will hardly ever be my lot. [*Not unless you come*

to England, is here written between the lines. *Answer my incapacity with your capacity, my passive desires with your triumphant activity.* But he must not depress the Dean too much. Again and again he has declared that he is too old, too poor, too busy, too ill, to come to England. The fact that the Villakin seems doomed to remain a castle in the air shall not be laid at *his* door.] So that I will endeavour to pass away my Life as agreeably as I can in the Way I am. I often wish to be with you, or you with me, and I believe you think I say true. I am determined to write to you though those dirty fellows at the post office do read my Letters, for since I saw you I am grown of that consequence to be obnoxious to the men I despise; so that it is very probable in their hearts they think me an honest man. I have heard from Mr. Pope but once since I left London. I was sorry I saw him so seldom but I had business that kept me from him. I often wish we were together again. If you will not write, come."

Continually, from the depths of his retirement, one is reminded that although Gay was cut off from actual conversation with his other friends, this did not affect the closeness of their relationship. Thus we have Mrs. Howard writing to him (in his old profession of cementer of friendships) about the Duchess of Queensberry: "Do not let her forget me, and do not think I ever will forget you. Mr. Pope is well; Mrs. Blount says she will write to you. I have not seen the Doctor since I left London." Apparently there was still a lack of cordiality between both ladies—especially on the part of the Duchess. It may have been that she, together with Dr. Swift, was of the opinion that in the old Court days Mrs. Howard had led Gay up the garden path once too often. If this were so, then it is really rather comic that Mrs. Howard should have spent her time pleading with the man she had, however unconsciously, injured, and begging him to make her peace with the Duchess, who was annoyed with her precisely because she *had* injured him! Even civil enquiries concerning the Duchess's health were not always welcome to that most autocratic of women. Gay deplored the fact, and wrote back to Mrs. Howard:

> "It is what the Duchess never would tell me— *how she does*; but I cannot take it ill, for I really believe it is what she never really and truly did to anybody in her life. As I am no physician and cannot do her any good, one would wonder she could refuse to answer this question out of common civility, and so I am determined never to ask her again. If you have a mind to know what she hath done since she came here, the most material things that I know of are, that she hath worked a rose [in embroidery] and milked a cow, and these two things I assure you are of more consequence, I verily believe, than hath been done by anybody else."

What with the Duchess refusing to answer enquiries concerning her health, and Swift refusing to answer any letters at all (as it seemed to Gay), life was not entirely happy. Swift, as a matter of fact, was not as idle and uninterested as he seemed. He was conducting an argument by correspondence with Mrs. Howard, in which all the vinegar came from his side and all the oil on troubled waters from hers. He was still harping on the treatment of poor Gay, still fuming over the blunders of Walpole, still intolerant of majesty.

"I am angry with the queen for sacrificing my friend Gay to the mistaken piques of Sir Robert Walpole, although he was convinced at the same time of Mr. Gay's innocence, and though, as I said before, I told her the whole story."

This acrimony continued slowly over some months, but since oil and vinegar will never mix, and since Mrs. Howard was not quite as silly as she seemed and knew well enough that Swift was not above using Gay as an excuse for working off his own spleen and disappointment, no useful conclusion was ever reached. Only Gay, the object of dispute, still with that steadfast sweetness of temper which was the foundation of his nature, remained the friend of both parties. Obedient to Swift's latent rather than declared wish he was doing his best this year to keep in touch with Pope. He wrote a letter to him which must have been a very pleasant one, but which has since been lost to us. Pope's mother was again ill, and a great anxiety to him, but he found time to reply to it with a surface formality that is most moving:

"DEAR SIR,—I may with great truth return your speech, that I think of you daily—oftener, indeed, than is consistent with the character of a reasonable man, which is rather to make himself easy with things and men that are about him, than uneasy for those which he wants. . . ."

In other words, if Pope has not yet found the philosopher's stone, he is getting, as children say, 'warm' to it. Always the most equable of the three poets, he has come finally, he fancies, through the purifying fires of persecution and attack—so that he is now immune. True, he has in turn poured boiling oil on the heads of the attackers, and flung little poisoned darts and mud that sticks and that all the perfumes of Arabia cannot wash away—but as soon as his ammunition is exhausted he has scampered up again into that Ivory Tower where St. John sits, waiting for the tumult to die down so that pleasant abstract discussions about mankind and the government of mankind and the purpose of Creation may be resumed. But downstairs on the floor of hard fact Mrs. Pope is still ill; and constant anxiety concerning her wears out even the "reasonable man" that Pope is now fast becoming. At such unguarded moments his letters to Gay have a quality of emotion peculiar to that correspondence alone: "Are we never to live together more, as once we did? I find my life ebbing apace, and my affections strengthening as my age increases." Again:

> "Your letter is a very kind one, but I can't say so pleasing to me as many of yours have been, thro' the account you give of the dejection of your spirits. I wish the too constant use of waters does not contribute to it. . . . I also wish you were not so totally immersed in the country; I hope your return to town will be a prevalent remedy against the evil of too much recollection—I wish it partly for my own sake. We have lived little together of late, and we want to be physicians to one another. It is a remedy that agreed very well with us both, for many years."

It is no use: Patty Blount is pleasant company sometimes—Bolingbroke is pleasant company sometimes—but Patty Blount has fits of peevishness and sulkiness which tire an already easily-tired man, and the rarefied air which St. John breathes occasionally seems thin and insufficient to a wit who has known and enjoyed the odours of a coffee-house. Besides, the attacks upon the little man have scarified him, and put him on the rack of most exquisite torment. "What?" says Patty Blount, when discussing such attacks. "Even if he *did* say it of you, it is not nearly so bad as what Mrs X. said of *me* last Sunday. . . ." "What?" says St. John. "Will you really take notice of such abuse? You should ignore it as a statesman does; and as *I* used to. Turn, my dear friend, to page 3 of *A Patriot King*." His mother, when she had been well, had been more understanding. Every attack upon her son was resented as bitterly as he himself resented it, and the comfort given had been both bounteous and sustaining. As for those others—Swift and Gay and Arbuthnot—their very presence had been sufficient of old to drive away the bogeys and hobgoblins sent to torment him. "Are we never to live together more, as once we did? When shall we three meet again?" There could be no answer to those questions so long as Swift remained in Ireland.

At Amesbury the free-born country gentleman continued his country occupations. He was taking, for the first time in his life, a great deal of exercise each day, riding all the morning, walking and talking with the Duchess in the afternoon. Even rural sports (which he had celebrated in that first epistle of his to Pope) were now receiving his attention. In September a joking reference is made in a letter to Mrs. Howard, about "a quarrel about a fishing-rod." In November he has taken to the gun. But still, whatever his occupations, he keeps up the old appeals to Swift:

> "DEAR Sir,—So you are determin'd never to write to me again, but for all that, you shall not make me hold my tongue—you shall hear from me (the post office willing) whether you will or

not. I see none of the folks you correspond with, so that I am forced to pick up intelligence concerning you as I can; which has been so very little, that I am resolved to make my complaint to you as a friend, who I know loves to relieve the distressed; and in the circumstances I am in, where should I apply, but to my best friend? Mr. Pope indeed, upon my frequent inquiries, has told me that the letters which are directed to him concern me as much as himself; but what you say of yourself, or of me, or to me, I know nothing at all. . . . Pray, do you come to England this year? . . . I wish you would; and so does the Duchess of Queensberry. What would you have more to induce you? Your money cries, Come, spend me; and your friends cry, Come, see me. I have been treated barbarously by you. If you know how often I talk of you, how often I think of you, you would now and then direct a letter to me, and I would allow Mr. Pope to have his share in it. In short I do not care to keep any man's money; that serves me so. Love or money I must have; and if you will not let me have the comfort of the one, I think I must endeavour to get a little comfort by spending some of the other. I must beg that you will call at Amesbury, on your way to London; for I have many things to say to you; and I can assure you, you will be welcome to a three-pronged fork. I remember your prescription, and I do ride upon the Downs, and at present I have no asthma. I have killed five brace of partridge, and four brace and a half of quails; and I do not envy Sir Robert or Stephen Duck, who is the favourite poet of the Court. I hear sometimes from Pope, and from scarce anybody else.

Were I to live ever so long, I believe I should never think of London, but I cannot help thinking of you. Were you here I could talk to you, but I would not; for you shall have all your share of talk, which was never allowed you at Twickenham. You know this was a grievance you often complain'd of and so in revenge you make me write all, and say nothing . . . Both the Duke and Duchess would be very glad if you would come to Amesbury, and you must be persuaded. I say this without the least private view—for what is it to me whether you come or no? for I can write to you, you know."

To this extremely ingenious appeal the Duchess of Queensberry adds a footnote as brusque and to the point as a communication from that earlier autocrat, Queen Elizabeth:

"I would fain have you come. I cannot say you will be welcome; for I do not know you, and perhaps I shall not like you, but if I do not (unless you are a very vain person), you shall know my thoughts as soon as I do myself.
"C. Q."

This directness aroused the Dean from his lethargy: he shook it off as a great shaggy dog shakes the water off his back, in a glittering thunder-shower. Almost by return of post he replied to her obliquely, by way of Gay:

"I desire you will tell her Grace, that the ill-management of forks is not to be helped when they are only Bidential, which happens in all poor Houses, especially those of Poets; upon which

Account a knife was absolutely necessary at Mr. Pope's, where it was morally impossible with a bidential fork to convey a morsel of Beef, with incumbrance of mustard and Turnips, into your mouth at once. . . ."

This is not perhaps of itself anything to make the angels weep, but taken in conjunction with all that we know of Swift he is seen here at a pathetically abandoned moment. Remember, this is the man who was the self-appointed autocrat of the breakfast-table of his time— and of the dinner and supper-table as well. His guests knew perfectly well that to eat with the Dean meant to submit themselves entirely to his direction—however humiliating the procedure. William III had first taught the young Swift to eat asparagus. (It was all he had ever done for him, Swift might have added.) And years later Swift's Irish publisher, on dining with the Dean, was compelled to eat even the stalks—because King William had done so. When asked if he were fool enough really to do such a thing the publisher had replied to his questioner: "Yes, and let me tell you if you had been dining tête-à-tête with Dean Swift *you* would have eaten your stalks, too." Yet this was the man who was putting up excuses to the Duchess of Queensberry for using that anachronism, the three-pronged fork, and for eating peas off the point of his knife! "When the sauce is not very consistent," he had pleaded earlier; and now, that it was "morally impossible" at Mr. Pope's house to manage otherwise. If this spectacle is not a spectacle of one of the mighty fallen, then nothing is. From this he turns to matters which concern Gay personally:

"Mr. Pope complains of seldom seeing you; but the Evil is unavoidable, for different Circumstances of Life have always separated those whom Friendships would join. . . . I hope you have now one Advantage which you always wanted before, and the Want of which made your Friends as uneasy as it did yourself; I mean, the Removal of that Solicitude about your own affairs, which perpetually filled your Thoughts and disturbed your conversation. For if it be true what Mr. Pope seriously tells me, you will have Opportunity of saving every Groat of the Interest you receive; and so by the Time he and you grow weary of each other, you will be able to pass the rest of your wine-less life in Ease and Plenty, with the additional Triumphal Comfort of never having received a penny from those tasteless, ungrateful People from whom you deserved so much, and who deserve no better Genius's, than those by whom they are celebrated."

It was not often that any of Swift's friends resented the chastening rod which, when he saw fit, he liked to lay about their shoulders—and Gay was usually as unresentful as the rest. At the same time, something in the last letter about his solicitude about his own affairs seems to have got him, for once, under the skin. It appears that he did not resent the imputation that he was apt to be preoccupied with his own affairs—how should he?—but the further imputation that he was preoccupied to the point of remaining silent during conversation. Over this misapprehension Swift soon put him right:

"I never charged you with not talking," he wrote, "but the dubious State of your Affairs in those Days was too much the Subject . . ."

But whether it was reproof or admonition or useful advice which came over from the Deanery at Dublin, the recurring theme which bound all the letters together was what to do with the money which Swift had given Gay to take care of. It is, of course, typical that since Gay had himself lost a fortune in the earlier subscriptions of the South Sea Company, he should have bought bonds in the same (now sadder and wiser) Company for Swift. He does not appear to think highly of their prospects; at the same time he does not like to sell out until Swift tells him what to do about it. As to the rest of the money, sometimes plaintively, sometimes jokingly, he is ever at Swift to know what is to be done about that. But Swift would much rather fence with Her Grace about matters concerning his proposed visit to Amesbury. Can she look after him if he is ill? Will she let him have his own way? Will she be able (preposterous doubt) to put up his horses? Badgered at last into reply by Gay's persistence, he replies guardedly:

"I will send for the money when you put me into the way."

It is not much, but at least it is something. Gay writes back enthusiastically, forgetting to put Swift "into the way" of collecting the two hundred pounds, unless the ever-reiterated plea to come to England may be so interpreted. The Wiltshire air is splendidly bracing; there are endless opportunities for exercise. Swift could, as he puts it, "ride upon the downs and write conjectures upon Stonehenge." In view of such a happy prospect, the rather remoter prospect of the Villakin fades back into the clouds where it first appeared. How did Horace put it: "Let the mind be joyfull of the present (or nearly present), good, nor be sollicitous for what is to come." As he himself had written: "*Let us drink and sport to-day, ours is not to-morrow.*" Again he writes to Swift, this time making clear that just as there is only one reigning divinity at Amesbury, so there is also only one Chancellor of the Exchequer:

"The Duchess is a more severe check upon my finances than ever you were; and I submit, as I did to you, to comply with my own good. I was a long time before I could prevail with her to let me allow myself a pair of shoes with two heels; for I had lost one, and the shoes were so decay'd they were not worth mending. . . . The lady you mention, that dislikes you, hath no discernment. I really think you may safely venture to Amesbury, though indeed the lady here likes to have her own way as well as you, which may sometimes occasion disputes: and I tell you beforehand that I cannot take your part."

Here the pen is snatched from his hand by the Duchess of Queensberry:

"I do in the first place [she writes] contradict most things Mr. Gay says of me to deter you from coming here, which if you ever do, I hereby assure you, that unless I like my own way better, you shall have yours;—and in all disputes you shall convince me if you can. . . . I would fain know you; for I often hear more good likeable things than it is possible any one can deserve. Pray come, that I may find out something wrong; for I, and I believe most women, have an inconceivable pleasure to find out any faults except their own. Mr. Cibber is made poet-laureate.

"I am, sir, as much your humble servant as I can be to any person I do not know.—C. Q."

"PS. Mr. Gay is very peevish that I spell and write ill, but I do not care; for neither the pen nor I can do better. Besides, I think you have flattered me, and such people ought to be put to trouble."

To which Gay adds the PPS.:

"Now I hope you are pleas'd, and that you will allow that for so small a sum as £200 you have a lumping penniworth."

It is a good pennyworth, certainly. It assures Swift, as he must have been glad to be assured, that Gay is in an atmosphere very different from the deplorably degenerate atmosphere at the Court and he is glad that his friend should be so. The news of the appointment of Colley Cibber to the position of Poet Laureate rouses him to a new outburst of cynicism. Stephen Duck was bad enough, but Colley Cibber—a mere actor, a gross, vain, strutting booby who had dared to set himself up against Pope, in past days, and who has won his present position by writing propaganda for Walpole in the shape of his play, *The Non-Juror!* Things were come to a pretty pass when with Dryden's laureateship still a living memory such people were exalted to poetry's highest position! A *Rhapsody on Poetry* was the result—with the Court scarified by Swift for its behaviour, the Court:

> "Whence Gay was banished in disgrace
> Where Pope will never show his face
> Where Young must torture his invention
> To flatter knaves, or lose his pension.

> Attend, ye Popes and Youngs and Gays
> And tune your harps and strew your lays;
> Your panegyrics here provide
> You cannot err on flattery's side. . . ."

In his condemnation of the Court and all its works, the Dean, covertly if not openly, included Mrs. Howard. His correspondence with her had at last petered out. Somewhere in his heart of hearts he had still hoped, still believed, that she would have been able to reinstate Gay with glory, possibly even have engineered some sort of apology for him. At least he clung to such imaginations with his subconscious mind. Even to such a convinced pessimist justice is sometimes achieved, if only accidentally. Not for him, of course. For him to rot away in Ireland and, in his own words, die "like a poisoned rat in a hole." His last hold on English life and English things had gone with the departure of Lord Carteret. In the future loomed up the ' Sunday Spongers,' the coteries of small people whom he should rule like a King and despise as he ruled—in future only the friendship of the Delanys, of Sheridan and of later "pennyworth" friendships—for those to whom he delighted to give himself were not "in the way." In future petty clerical occupation, scolding of servants and vergers in lieu of better men. In future the small jokes, epigrams, riddles, writing the long, long day, ever writing because the mind *must* be occupied, it must never be still. It is a prisoner in solitary confinement, no contact with the outside world, and must be occupied. Sacks were once given to prisoners to sew, and at the end of the day, unpicked and the labour all to do again to-morrow. So Swift, all too soon, was to set his prisoner-mind to making verses as futile and useless as the sacks in gaol, and at the end of the day, too, they were destroyed in their turn—torn up and thrown into the fire. With some inkling, therefore, of what was to be his own position, before him—and with certain knowledge that Pope, though he had achieved much, had never achieved and would never achieve State recognition—it had still remained with Swift to hope that the least of the three of them should yet arrive at this crowning glory. The appointment of Colley Cibber showed that even that hope was fruitless. The Court " whence Gay was banished in disgrace" (though Gay, quite reasonably, might prefer to put it otherwise) would never welcome him back again. There was spiritual wickedness in high places, and the meek were never further, in the Dean's opinion, from inheriting the earth. There remained an honourable retirement, a retirement in which Pope and Gay, living in their Villakins side by side at Twickenham, should grow old together, and upon which the Dean should make occasional raids, for the cheering of their spirits and the betterment of their souls. Scriblerus in Villakins—a sort of intellectual garden suburb for oppressed genius—it was, as it remained, an enchanting idea.

Amidst rural sports and friendly correspondence the second year of Gay's retirement to the position of a country gentleman drew slowly to an end. He was still obedient enough to Swift's commands to exercise furiously, despite the shorter days and colder weather. Unfortunately exercise was not the cure-all that Swift and Dryden fancied it to be. Giving up his beloved wine and bumping about on horseback with the fervour of a man employing flagellation may have helped Gay's health a little but it did not lessen the occasional attacks of colic, and—if the Duchess is to be believed —other indispositions. In November she wrote to Mrs. Howard:

"Mr. Gay is such a dotterel that he constantly catches every complaint I have, and I am enough his mimic to go about as much as I can; but I do not think I look so well as he does."

Gay had bemused himself into a hare in his *Fables*, and now the Duchess saw him as a dotterel, which in plain English is a species of plover which runs to meet the trappers and bird-nesters with happy cries and is therefore nicknamed dotterel from such foolish behaviour. . . . It was a nickname as apt for Gay as for the plover. We may despise this behaviour of the dotterel as optimism entirely unjustified by instinct or experience: the fact remains that in a world governed largely by fear and suspicion it is pleasant sometimes to meet trust and faith—even if the end, for the dotterel, is still a wrung neck and a rifled nest.

CHAPTER TWENTY-THREE

1731. 'Acis and Galatea,' first public performance. 'Poems on Several Occasions,' published in a second edition. Working on the second 'Fables.' Living with Pope at Twickenham. The Post of Lottery Commissioner goes from him.

> *What's a mistress and a wife?*
> *Joy for moments: plague for life.*
> GAY: ' ACHILLES '

EARLY in the new year Gay came up to London. He had his old friends at Twickenham to see, and new schemes to discuss. There was the scheme for sharing a house with Swift; there were—in all probability—projected tours to France and Italy—to all those places which he knew so well in his Horace and which still demanded personal investigation. Then there was the scheme of Pope's for living in "a warmer clime." All these things were, if not probable, still possible. He had saved money; they had all saved money. What more natural than that Gay should indulge, at this stage, his earlier desires "to see foreign lands?"

It is not known what originally called him up to London but since Handel's cantata *Acis and Galatea* for which he had written the words some fifteen years earlier was to receive its first public performance on March 26, it is likely that this may have had something to do with it. The cantata was put on "as a stage performance, without choruses" by Rich at his Lincoln's Inn Fields' theatre. The extremely loose law of copyright from which the wits and men of letters already suffered, afforded as scant protection to musicians. Handel does not appear to have been consulted over this production at all, and since the composer was cold-shouldered so in all probability was the librettist. The affair was entirely in the hands of Mr. Rich who, if he hoped he had another potential *Beggar's Opera* on his hands, was doomed to be disappointed. The slight, charming *Acis* has always been popular but it is no more than a curtain-raiser to some bigger piece. Records of the performance and the reception are both missing. Yet at least, if excuse were needed, the performance *was* an excuse for Gay to come up to London once more. Now that his lodgings in Whitehall were gone, London meant either the rooms allotted to him at Burlington House, or Pope's house at Twickenham. He seems to have chosen Twickenham. The problem of what to do with Swift's money and his own is still pressing heavily on him, however, and a few days before the performance of *Acis and Galatea* he sits down and writes to the Dean from Pope's address:

> "I had a scheme of buying two lottery tickets for you, and keeping your principal entire, and as all my good fortune is to come, to show you that I consult your advantage, I will buy two more for myself, and you and I will go halves in the ten thousand pounds. (If this is not pure Dotterelism, then what is?) That there will be a Lottery is certain, the scheme is not yet declar'd, but I hear it will not be the most advantageous one for we are to have but 3 per cent. I sollicit for no Court favours so that I propose to buy the tickets at the market price, when they come out. . . . I have nothing at the time of writing but my Frock that was made at Salisbury and a Bob periwig. I persuade myself that it is shilling weather as

seldom as possible. I am very happy in my present independency, I envy no man but have the due contempt for the voluntary slaves of Birth and Fortune. I have such a spite against you that I wish you may long for my company as I do for yours, though you never write to me you cannot make me forget you. So if it is not out of friendship you write so seldom to me it doth not answer the purpose. Those, who you would like should remember you, do so, whenever I see 'em."

Although the principal Old Boy of the Twickenham coterie was not available there was a minor sort of Old Boys' Reunion during Gay's visit to Pope this month, and we are told they dined together at Barnes one evening in the company of old Jacob Tonson (who gave the party), Lord Bathurst and young Lord Oxford. Despite this temporary conviviality it must have been a little depressing for the returned exile to see how sternly time had marched on during his absence. Pope was always occupied, of course, with some scheme or other, Tonson was equally busy, Lord Bathurst and the other relict lords of Queen Anne's *régime* were completely absorbed with political work for the Opposition and their own family affairs. Only the unattached country gentleman, come up to town for diversion, found himself a little idle. There was Mr. Hoare to be seen at his Fleet Street bank, of course, about money affairs—and the much-discussed cash to be collected from Bathurst. After this visit had been paid Bathurst wrote typically to Swift:

"Should any man but you think of trusting John Gay with his money? None of his friends would even trust him with his own whenever they could avoid it. He has called in the £200 I had of yours: I paid him both principal and interest. I suppose by this time he has lost it. I give you notice, you must look on it as annihilated."

Lord Bathurst was accurate about the transaction but not quite accurate about Gay's losing it. Like most good letter-writers (and he was easily the best letter-writer of any lord of his time) he had the gift of exaggeration to perfection.

Apart from doing his little bit of financial business Gay spent the rest of his time in London in paying a round of visits to all his old acquaintances. Apart from the actual Court, he seems to have lost only one friend in the course of his life and that was Lord Burlington. Gay himself could not (or would not) account for the reason of the rupture. It is possible, of course, that Dr. Arbuthnot's retailing of the poultice incident would lose nothing in repetition. Whatever it was, Gay accepted the loss without complaint; and when Swift charged him with a commission to Lord Burlington, merely pointed out gently that Pope had better take it as he himself was no longer *persona grata* in that quarter. Certainly he must have got into touch again with Mrs. Howard—because Swift censured him severely for still keeping up with that lady. In a month, however, he was back at Amesbury, little changed except that Arbuthnot, on account of his improved health, had allowed him a partial return to wine-drinking. This he hastened to celebrate in a letter to Swift—after talking once more on the topic of money. Since the rolling stone had settled down at Amesbury for a while, the financial moss had accumulated in the most gratifying manner. On his leaving town, he told Swift, he left the sum of £3,400 in Mr. Hoare's hands. After that:

"Since I have got over the impediment to a writer of water-drinking, if I can persuade myself that I have any wit, and find that I have inclination, I intend to write, though at present I have another impediment, for I have not provided myself with a scheme. [Such a confession, as Gay must have known, was an irresistible temptation to Swift—and a sure producer of a Thousand easy Schemes and Inventions from that generous and universal provider.] I have always found myself of no consequence and am now of less than ever; but I have found a way in one respect of making myself of more consequence, which is by considering other people of less. Those who have given me up, *I* have given up, and in short I seek after no friendships, but am content with what I have in this house. . . . Your last letter was more to the Duchess . . . than to me so I now leave off to offer her the paper."

The Duchess is concise and more to the point:

"It was Mr. Gay's fault that I did not write sooner, which if I had I hope you would have been here by this time, for I have to tell you that all your articles are agreed to, and that I only love to have my own way when I meet not with others whose ways I like better. I am in great hopes that I shall approve of yours for to tell you the truth I am a little tir'd of my own. Pray sett out the first fair wind and stay with us as long as ever you please."

But so determined an invitation made things much too easy for the Dean who, maddeningly like Penelope in some of his moods, liked to unpick all the good work of the day during the night. He would show the Duchess that he could not be captured by fine ladies as easily as that. His heart tells him to go—that from Dublin to Amesbury is an easy trip, that he will see Gay and an intelligent woman again, and that Pope and Bolingbroke and Bathurst and Arbuthnot are all within visiting distance—no more cursed sea between him and his friends—but still his mind keeps him back. The letter is no longer extant but it appears that as well as prevaricating once more over the proposed trip, he, according to his practice, hastened to supply Gay with half a dozen promising "Schemes" to write on. Out of every one of them might there not grow up another success like *The Beggar's Opera?* But *The Beggar's Opera* by now was so old-established a success and its Swiftian origin (perhaps) so forgotten by Gay that he was not as grateful for this as he should have been. Indeed, he reproved the Dean gently:

> "You and I are alike in one particular—I mean, that we hate to write upon other folks' hints. I love to have my own scheme, and to treat it in my own way. This, perhaps, may be taking too much upon myself, and I may make a bad choice; but I can always enter into a scheme of my own with more ease and pleasure, than into that of any other body. I long to see you. I long to hear from you."

At this point the gaps in a correspondence already full of holes are particularly frequent. From references in what letters do exist, dating from a time when they passed briskly to and fro between Dublin and Wiltshire, it is clear that a great many subjects were touched on as well as schemes for a visit to England and possible schemes for Gay's next work. A reference to Mrs. Howard in a lost letter from Gay obviously calls down the vials of wrath on that lady in a lost reply from the Dean.

Again the ameliorative influence comes into play, and Gay writes:

> "You should consider circumstances before you censure; 'twill be too long for a letter to make an Apology; but when I see you I believe I shall convince you that you mistake her."

We come now to one of the most baffling references in all the correspondence, and one which seems completely detached from anything which came either before or after it. The previous year, it will be recalled, Gay had written in one of his more depressed letters to Swift that, on the Dean's advice, he had taken to love (much as if he had said he had engaged on a course of Phosphorine to soothe his nerves), but that, "not meeting with any return" from the lady in Soho further recommended by Swift, he had given up all thought of it—and so had "no pursuit or amusement." If ever it were necessary to make it clear that there was no suspicion of a love-affair between Gay and the Duchess of Queensberry or Mrs. Howard surely these ingenuous confessions should dispel that illusion for ever. He now returns to the subject—admitting that a similar incident had occurred on his recent visit to London:

> "When I was in town, after a bashful fit for having writ something like a love-letter, and in two years making one visit, I writ to Mrs. Drelincourt to apologise for my behaviour, and

received a civil answer but had not time to see her. They are naturally very civil—so that I am not so sanguine as to interpret this as an encouragement. I find by Mrs. Barber that she very much interests herself in her affair; and indeed, from everybody else who knows her, she answers the character you first gave me."

—Or, to paraphrase once more from the verse in *Alice*:

> *They told me you had been to her*
> *And mentioned me to him:*
> *She gave me a good character*
> *But said I could not swim.*

... The letter continues:

"Whenever you come to England, if you will put that confidence in me to give me notice, I will meet you at your landing-place and conduct you hither. . . . I look upon you as my best friend and counsellor. I long for the time when we shall meet and converse together."

In this letter, for the only time vouchsafed to us, Swift may be observed in the capacity of match-maker—and in it, for the only time in Gay's life as far as we know, does that extraordinarily simple man play with the idea of marriage. The tortuously-recorded reference to Mrs. Drelincourt, with its perfect maze of a corollary about Mrs. Barber is, however, easier to comprehend if it is taken (as I think it should be) in conjunction with the earlier visit to Soho. Whether "They" were Mrs. Drelincourt and Mrs. Barber, or, as I am more inclined to think, Mrs. and Miss Drelincourt, cannot now be known, but the Drelincourts themselves are easier to run to earth. A Peter Drelincourt was the Dean of Armagh and had long been an Irish acquaintance of Swift's. Mrs. and Miss Drelincourt were his wife and daughter who had, through Swift's agency, been introduced at least three years earlier to Gay. (There is a passage in a letter from the Dean to Mrs. Drelincourt, dated 1727, which links up both ladies and Gay, i.e., "my humble servant to Miss Drelincourt. I assure you she makes a good figure in the Mall; and I could, in consequence, do no less than distinguish her. I have desired Mr. Gay to show you this letter.") It is surely not straining credulity to deduce that the Drelincourts referred to there and in Gay's letter were one and the same people, and—in view of the fact that the custom of the times gave even unmarried women the title of Mrs.—that he was therefore paying court to Miss Drelincourt.

The extreme meekness and mildness of Gay's assault upon the Drelincourt citadel succeeded, when he read of it, in infuriating Swift. This was not the way in which *he*, in his hey-day, had handled women. He wrote back, commenting briskly on the affair:

> "You are the silliest lover in Christendom. If you like Mrs. D. why do you not command her to take you? If she does not, she is not worth Pursuing; you do her too much Honour; she hath neither Sense nor Taste if she dares to refuse you, though she had ten thousand pounds. I do not remember to have told you of thanks you have not given, nor do I understand your meaning, and I am sure I had never the least thoughts of any myself. If I am your Friend it is for my own

Reputation, and from a Principle of Self-Love, and
I do sometimes reproach you for not honouring
me by letting the world know we are Friends."

This seems a little unfair. We have it on the Duchess
of Queensberry's evidence that Gay was never tired of
singing Swift's praises and of basking in remembrance
of their hours spent together. It was not in his nature
to boast of anything but if it had been then he would
certainly have boasted of his friendship with Swift
whom, in his most recent letter, he had elevated to the
position of "best friend"—over even Pope whom he
loved, as he put it, as his "own soul." But then Swift
longed at this period for nothing as much as for friendship, and might have spoken of his heart as did the
Duke in *Twelfth Night*:

> But mine is all as hungry as the sea
> And can digest as much . . .

When he could not, or would not, come over to see his
friends, he still did his best to bring Pope and Gay
together. He wrote to Pope:

> "Learn to play at cards, or tables, or bones . . .
> or when you are able to, go down to Amesbury
> and forget yourself for a fortnight with our friend
> Gay and the Duchess."

Pope was a permanence in Gay's life, the Drelincourts
a mere flash-in-the-pan. The Drelincourts thus dismissed
and Gay informed that he had approached the matter
from the wrong angle altogether, Swift returned to
more important considerations—what Gay is to do
with his life in future. Obviously he has forgotten that

he ever attempted any match-making at all, on behalf of his friend. The Villakin is still what matters—and the money to keep the Villakin afloat:

> "I cannot allow you rich enough until you are worth 7000 L., which will bring you L300 per annum, and this will maintain you, with the Perquisite of Sponging while you are young, and when you are old will afford you a Pint of Port at night, two Servants and an old maid, a little Garden and Pen and Ink—provided you live in the Country. Have you no Scheme either in Prose or in Verse? The Duchess should keep you at Hard Meat, and by that means force you to write."

And here ends the somewhat abortive Drelincourt episode. No more is heard of either lady and later Miss Drelincourt did the right thing and married into the peerage. . . . As for Gay, his temporary vision of himself as husband and lover was easily dispelled.

Towards the end of June an event occurred which was of great interest to Gay as well as to other friends of Mrs. Howard. By a succession of accidents which neither husband nor wife can ever have foreseen the Hon. Charles Howard inherited the earldom of Suffolk—and Mrs. Howard was consequently elevated, all in a day, to the position of Countess of Suffolk. Her husband had done peculiarly little for her all his life, and doubtless if the title had been his for bestowal his long-estranged wife would not have received it. Nevertheless she became the Countess of Suffolk and the elaborately-contrived grades of work of the women engaged in the Queen's bed-chamber had consequently to be readjusted. Although a mere Honourable might kneel and hold the wash-basin for the royal ablutions obviously a Countess needed promotion. Soon after becoming Countess, therefore, Mrs. Howard relinquished her position as Woman of the bed-chamber in the Queen's room and became Mistress of the Robes. She was still, of course, Woman of the bed-chamber—in the more literal sense —to the King, though lately some pressure was required, both from the Queen and from Walpole, to keep up this arrangement. Unfortunately the King was as stubborn in his love-affairs as he was in affairs of ordinary palace procedure, and his 9 o'clock visits to his mistress's room, it may be imagined, became more and more perfunctory, his manner more and more parade-ground and less and less lover-like. Because of this the two promotions she had received may have been some consolation to the lady. Gay wrote of her to Swift—though he knew that to mention her name was to invite an outburst of scorn or abuse:

> "Your friend Mrs. Howard is now Countess of Suffolk. I am still so much a dupe, that I think you mistake her. Come to Amesbury, and you and I will dispute the matter; and the duchess shall be judge. . . . I have heard from her; Mr. Pope has seen her; I beg you would suspend your judgment till we talk over the affair together; for I fancy, by your letter, you have neither heard from her nor seen her; so you cannot at present be as good a judge as we are."

He adds comically but rather touchingly:

> "I will be a dupe for you at any time: therefore I beg it of you, that you would let me be a dupe in quiet."

—and then turns to explain away the episode of his having looked after the Queensberry accounts. He had been mortified rather than flattered by Swift's celebration of this episode in verse—and now he sets matters out in their true light:

" . . . As to my being manager to the Duke, you have been misinformed. Upon the discharge of an unjust steward he took the administration into his own hands. I own I was called into his assistance, when the state of affairs was in the greatest confusion. Like an ancient Roman I came, put my helping hand to set affairs right, and as soon as it was done, I am retired again as a private man."

The Duchess adds a characteristic foot-note:

"By your letter I cannot guess whether we are to see you or not. Why might not the Amesbury downs make you better? C.Q."

It was little use: Swift could not escape from so stern a realist as his would-be hostess was. Whatever excuse he mustered to prevent direct action, she cleared it away with a puff of breath as if it were no more than a cobweb. Health, or lawsuits, money or weather or policy—they were all brought up in turn as excuses to avoid the journey, and all confuted. It was flattering, but a little disturbing as well. If ever Swift was embarrassed in his life then he was surely embarrassed by this boldest of approaches. And yet, too, he revelled in it— as he always enjoyed the rare opportunity of contact with a mind as direct and fearless as his own. Nevertheless he could not make up his mind to enlarge that contact. He could, on occasion, be just as lacking in resolution as his friend Gay. The excuses of money, lawsuits, health, weather and policy having been offered and rejected he bethought himself belatedly of the Duke, and wrote a letter saying that conscious though he was of the honour done him by the Duchess's invitation, etc., etc., and much as he would enjoy reorganising Gay's life for him, etc., etc.—he had heard no word from the Duke. He could not accept an invitation from which the Duke so conspicuously refrained. Even that last card failed him—and the result was a most charming letter from the Duke of Queensberry pointing out that whatever the Duchess wanted was law at Amesbury—and that what "our friend John" wanted was also most agreeable to the Duke. It was difficult to know how to acknowledge such graciousness—even by a master of prose. He returned for the time being into cautious silence—and Dublin occupations.

The withdrawal of each of the three cavaliers from the turmoil of London life did not mean that, in consequence, life forgot them. A second edition of Gay's *Poems on Several Occasions*, in two volumes, was published by Tonson, during the year—and *Newgate's Garland* was reprinted in a musical miscellany. Pope's prose activities were keeping him busy—especially with Aaron Hill, who had been brave enough to resent the comparatively harmless lines in which he had been celebrated in *The Dunciad*. If Pope had ever known the stamina and staying-power of that confirmed letter-writer it is doubtful if he would ever have embarked on the correspondence. Yet, however wearisome, the work had its reward—and fully to appreciate Pope's patience and forbearance and gift for seeing the silver lining readers are referred, without question, to his correspondence with Aaron Hill. There is, strange to say, a distinct likeness between the Swift-Queensberry correspondence and the Hill-Pope one—apart from the fact that, chronologically, they coincided. In both, the great men are a little uneasy, a little at bay, and at their most evasive; in both, their opposite numbers are tenacious, flattering by implication and very much to the point. We have seen how the Swift-Queensberry correspondence ran. The Hill-Pope began with a complaint from Aaron Hill concerning the offensive lines—and followed up with a typical piece of Pope in which the reasoning is somewhat as follows: (*a*) that Hill is making it all up and the lines do not exist outside his imagination; (*b*) that if they are there then obviously they bear a meaning quite different from the one Hill imagines—that they are, in fact, somewhat flattering. This tergiversation did not suit Hill at all. He could play round-the-mulberry-bush with any one on less painful occasions—but just now he would not budge from the point. He stuck to it, daring even to reprove Pope for hypocrisy when Pope said he cared little for the world's opinion of his poetry—and he was, in fact, so pugnacious and persistent that Pope ended by having a kind of admiration for the man.

It was, in a sense, courageous of Hill to go on scolding Pope like a governess when Pope with a stroke of his pen could have annihilated his adversary. Something of this Pope may have felt, or he may have felt a horticultural sympathy for a man who owned a grotto even bigger and better than his was. Or, still more, he may have sensed that Aaron Hill, whatever his shortcomings, was the sort of man who might be trusted implicitly to treasure up any correspondence he had with famous people. In that sense, writing to him would be like writing to the strong-room in the British Museum. Apart from these, there are no explanations of how he came to endure Hill's attentions. His work in these later years indeed might be divided up into walking and talking with Bolingbroke, doing a little gardening, writing his *Essay on Man*, avoiding the occasionally flattering attentions of the Court—and corresponding with Aaron Hill. In the year of grace 1731 the correspondence was still in its early stages and consisted largely of Pope's justifying himself, with senatorial dignity, to Aaron Hill and to posterity. Thus we have him writing, after being told that he was too careless of his literary position:

"If it be any deviation from greatness of mind to prefer friendships to fame, or the honest enjoyments of life to noisy praises; I freely confess that meanness."

Yes, it is easy to laugh at, if Pope is here just *poseur*; but only too often what Pope happened to write to posterity was also what, in his heart of hearts, was his own conviction. And no man in the world knew better the meaning of friendship, or placed it on a higher pinnacle of estimation. It was he who said that he wished to show what friends wits might be, "in spite of all the fools in the world." . . . It was he who wrote, at a much later stage, to Swift: "I am a man of desperate fortunes, that is, a man whose friends are dead: for I never aimed at any other fortune than friends." On his death-bed he added a postscript to that declaration: "There is nothing that is meritorious but virtue and friendship, and indeed friendship itself is only a part of virtue."

At about the same time that Pope was blotting one of the first of his many replies to Aaron Hill, Swift was composing his satirical verses *On the Death of Dr. Swift*. Years earlier he had prophesied the death of poor

Partridge the almanac-maker; now he prophesied and recorded his own demise, and the news of its reception. There is no gentle senatorial dignity about the verses but a half-savage, half-laughing caricature of all his friends and acquaintances in which, by implication, Swift seems to be saying: "There, but for the grace of God, go you, and YOU, and YOU!" Pope might remain as sure of the infallibility of friendship as he was of the infallibility of the dogmas of Holy Church. Swift knew better. It was not for nothing that every birthday he read as suitable Scriptural accompaniment the chapter from Job in which that patriarch cursed the day when his mother conceived him. For Job had friends once—and what use were they when the hour of need came? In the same way Swift believed, or affected to believe, that his friends too would show that their feeling for him was ephemeral and insincere.

> Here shift the scene, to represent
> How those I love my death lament.
> Poor Pope will grieve a month, and Gay
> A week, and Arbuthnot a day.
> St. John himself will scarce forbear
> To bite his pen and drop a tear.
> The rest will give a shrug and cry
> "I'm sorry—but we all must die!"

These lines have often been held up to show by their degrees of comparison, exactly at what worth Swift estimated the friendship of the men named. But a very little examination will show that Swift never intended them to be taken so seriously—would, indeed, have been much disturbed had he been able to learn how his light couplets have successively blown upon the reputation of his brother-poets. Did he mean us to believe that

Pope would love him longest? If Arbuthnot's name had scanned in that line is it not possible that *he* would have received that portion instead of Pope? As to Gay, his name was far too valuable for rhyming-purposes to allow him to be shifted about over-much. No, in general outline and implication Swift was certainly debunking friendship here, because he detested hypocrisy and feared too that if too implicit a trust were placed in so precious a quality as friendship it would ultimately fail him. He could not bear that it should fail him. Mainly to reassure himself, to reaffirm that he was independent of *any* man, he wrote the verses. But despite the general implications of *Lines on the Death of Dr. Swift* the particular implications were not deliberate. He did not intend really to distinguish between the degrees of warmth of the friendship felt for him by Arbuthnot, Pope and Gay. He was devoted to them all as they to him and had written, in a brighter hour, that violent friendship was "much more lasting and as engaging as violent love." Yet it amused him now, to scandalise them by pretending to be convinced that none of them cared a hoot for him—and that, incidentally, he did not *care* that none of them cared a hoot for him. . . .

At Amesbury Gay spent the summer, growing ever fatter in retirement, fighting down recurrent attacks of depression and colic, riding upon the downs, meditating—not upon Stonehenge, as he had suggested Swift should—but on a "scheme" to occupy his indolent brain and satisfy honour. His resolute retirement from London life did not go unnoticed in Court circles. Possibly on Walpole's advice, the sinecure post of Lottery Commissioner "went from him"—in the discreet and evasive language of history—about this time. It was his last link with those early days when he had first held a small Government appointment and as such he must have been sorry to see it go—more for the sake of its association than for the income to be derived from it—though of course the loss of that was serious too. It may have been the additional spur to his activities which led him to embark about this time on a second book of fables. Once before, riding with Swift and Pope, he had found the ambling gait of a horse conducive to composing fables. At Amesbury he could please himself with the same conditions; and in the evening the audience, though small, was most appreciative. Even so, it was difficult for him, then as ever, to concentrate. So many pleasant things offered themselves to be done instead. Life was, so obviously for this man, something to be *lived*—and not just a breathing-space for working in. He had none of Swift's turbulent energy—none of Pope's bee-like application. *What is this life if, full of care, there is no time to stand and stare?*—or better still—ride and stare?

The autumn was drawing on, but as long as it was good riding-weather Gay postponed the task of working seriously at the *Fables* and pleased himself instead by paying a round of visits in the Thames valley. In September he wrote to Swift:

"For about this month or 6 weeks past I have been rambling from home, or have been at what may not improperly be called other homes, at Dawley and at Twickenham; and I really think at every one of my homes you have as good a pretension as myself; for I find them all exceedingly disappointed by the lawsuit that has kept you this summer from us. . . . I wish you had your own money; for I wish you free from every engagement that keeps us one from another. . . . You may make your own conditions at Amesbury, where I am at present. You may do the same at Dawley; and Twickenham you know is your own. But if you rather choose to live with me—that is to say if you will give up your right and title [meaning the Deanship]—I will purchase the house you and I used to dispute about once against Ham Walk, on purpose to entertain you. Name your day, and it shall be done. I have lived with you, and I wish to do so again in any place and upon any terms."

Had this noble offer been accepted the last years in the lives of both Swift and Gay might have been very different. But Swift would not commit himself to it. England had never been kind to him, and for this Prospero on his desert island no rescue party was to come and take him off to end his days in peace and honour. Because the offer was not accepted it was, of course, as if it had never been. Gay, however, patiently went on expecting a favourable answer. Swift had said, more than once, that he and Pope and Gay should all live together in Twickenham. He had said that the Domestic Season of Life would come on. Well, it had come—now was the time, Gay reasoned, and that being so surely Swift would agree.

But when Swift ultimately wrote he characteristically ignored the one question to which Gay wanted an answer:

"If your Ramble was on horseback," he wrote, "I am glad of it on account of your Health; but I know your Art of patching up a Journey between Stage-coaches and Friends' coaches; for you are as arrant a Cockney as any Hosier in Cheapside. One clean shirt with two cravats, and as many

Handkerchiefs, make up your Equipage; and as for a night-gown it is clear from Homer, that Agamemnon rose without one. I have often had it in my head to put it into Your's, that you ought to have some great Work in scheme, which will take up seven years to finish, besides two or three under-ones, that may add another Thousand Pounds to your Stock; and then I shall be in less Pain about you. I know you can find Dinners, but you love Twelve-penny Coaches too well, without considering that the Interest of a Whole Thousand Pounds brings you but half a crown a day. I find a greater longing than ever to come amongst you. . . ."

Was there ever such a maddening man? He says he wants to come, and yet he will not come. He advises Gay to look about for a Villakin and then when Gay tells him he has found a Villakin and is prepared to buy it—says that he must earn more money first and talk about such sordid details as rates of interest and twelve-penny coaches. Nor is this the only scolding that Gay receives. In one of his more recent letters he had mentioned Mrs. Howard just once too often. Now Swift turns on him:

"I will have nothing to do with that Lady; I have long hated her on your account, and the more because you are so forgiving as not to hate her . . . and I heartily wish you joy of your scurvy treatment at Court, which hath given you leisure to cultivate both public and private Virtue, neither of them likely to be soon met with within the Walls of St. James's or Westminster."

As an example, of how little Gay could be influenced —even by Swift—when he was fond of some one, there is nothing better than the concluding paragraph of a letter to Mrs. Howard from him, written in the very same month that Swift had reviled her. It runs:

"If ever you thought well of me; if ever you believed I wished you well, and wanted to be of service to you, think the same of me; for I am the same, and shall always be so."

He never spoke a truer word. If there was anything to forgive in her treatment of him, then he had freely forgiven her, and in the best way of all, by forgetting that there had ever been anything to forgive. Such magnanimity lay completely outside Swift's compass. . . . He might have been right to wish that Gay had some piece of "great work" in hand with "two or three under-ones," but even apart from meditating upon the new *Fables* Gay was not idle this year. With the return of wine-drinking he had embarked upon at least three new pieces—*The Distressed Wife*, a comedy modelled somewhat on the Congreve pattern, but without his brilliance or finish; *Achilles*, which was, like *Polly* and *The Beggar's Opera*, in prose with songs interspersed; and *The Rehearsal at Goatham*, a really witty little curtain-raiser which mocks the plights of a poor puppet-showman who, when he arrives to give his performance in a small country town, finds that every word that he ventriloquises out of the mouth of his puppets is taken to have a personal application to some village pomposity. It was the old story:

> If you mention vice or bribe
> Tis so pat to all the tribe
> Each cries—That was levell'd at me.

A contemporary broadsheet with portrait of Mr. Gay by Aikman.

Jack Oaf early in the scene declares with owlish solemnity that he is quite sure that the play—which needless to say he has neither read nor seen—is "a heavy, biting, stupid, malignant satire upon the whole corporation" of the town of Goatham. To this charge stands up *Broach*, who declares "I know there are idle reports about master *Peter* and his show—But have you seen it, Mr. Oaf? Have you read it, Mr. Gosling?

Oaf:	I cannot say that.
Gosling:	But we know enough of the thing in general.
Oaf:	There are things quoted.
Gosling:	Passages, very obnoxious passages.

Here Gay is ridiculing, with the utmost good-humour, exactly the sort of obstacles which were put in the way of the production of his *Polly*. The obstructions pile up as the action proceeds. No sooner has the unfortunate Peter begun his play than there is an outburst amongst the Big Noises of the town—*Sir Headstrong Bustle, Sir Nathaniel Ninny,* and *Sir Humphrey Humdrum*—because they suspect the before-referred-to obnoxious passages.

Peter:	But I hope, sirs, you will not disappoint the audience: consider, sirs, it will be a great loss to me.
Cackle:	And so much the better.
Sir Headstrong:	Such audacious wretches should starve, who, because they are poor, are so insolently honest in everything they say, that a rich man cannot

	enjoy his property in quiet for 'em.
Pother :	We must keep these wretches down. 'Tis right to keep mankind in dependence.
Sir Headstrong :	'Tis the rascals who live by their industry, who are so impertinent to us.

After a good deal of this sort of thing the puppet-showman, under difficulties, is allowed to begin the play. Even so his troubles are not over. Because he makes the very harmless statement that the town where the action of his play is set is in Spain another burst of suspicion breaks out.

Cudden :	Why in *Spain*? Why must it be in *Spain*? Did not you, Mr. *Drone*, sell serges formerly to some merchant or other who traded to *Spain*. . . . He'll be about some of us presently; that I can see.

Every sentence, after that, is seen by the alderman to contain "a most bitter innuendo." *Sir Headstrong*, for instance, on hearing that the heroine "appears at the window in a *Moorish* habit, expecting her spouse from *Paris*," expostulates:

Sir Headstrong :	*Paris!* That now is at me.
Bray :	No, 'tis at me.
Sir Headstrong :	I won't have *Paris* mention'd.
Bray :	All the world must apply it to me. Do but consider, Sir

> *Headstrong*, I had a relation once there who was bubbled, and bubbled me too to that most conspicuous degree, that we were both look'd upon as fools. . . .

and when *Pickle* describing yet more of the play's action remarks that the hero "meets accidentally with some of his own countrymen and neighbours" the low-water-mark of nonsense is reached:

Drawle : Hold, hold, sir. My ears very much deceive me, or he mention'd neighbours.
Cackle : Ay, there he is at us all. For you know all of us are neighbours to somebody or other.
Sir H. Humdrum : We'll have no more of this impertinence.

And the outraged aldermen walk out in a body, presumably to call in the watch to stop the performance, followed by the booing and catcalls of the rest of the audience; while *Peter* the puppet-showman remarks:

> "There is nothing to be done here; they have the power and we must submit—so to-morrow we'll leave the town."

It was exactly the comment Gay might have made himself after the banning of *Polly*. For the Government had the power and he had to submit; and he *did* leave the town. Slight though this one-acter is, it has many extremely good lines. In it Gay was no doubt merely letting off steam about censorship in general but the result is a crisp and amusing little play—much more effective than either of the two longer pieces. It has the fresh air of an impromptu and may well have been written for private performance before a house-party at Amesbury. However that may be, at the end of November Gay had left Amesbury behind him and was once more staying at Twickenham with Pope. Swift was once more importuned by Pope to join them and once more wrote back to him putting obstacles in the way. Gay wrote again to him on December 1st:

"You used to complain that Mr. Pope and I would not let you speak; you may now be even with me, and take it out in writing. If you do not send to me now and then, the Post-office will think me of no consequence, for I have no Correspondent but you. You may keep as far from us as you please, you cannot be forgotten by those who ever knew you, and therefore please me by sometimes showing that I am not forgot by you. I have nothing to take me off from my Friendship to you; I seek no new Acquaintance, and court no Favour; I spend no shillings in coaches or chairs to Levees or Great Visits, and as I do not want the assistance of some I formerly conversed with, I will not so much as seem to seek to be dependant . . ."

This statement of Gay's confutes once more the popular conception of him as a perpetual parasite on other people—especially in his latter relationships. Certainly neither the Queensberrys nor he himself considered matters so to stand. True, he had spent months with them at Amesbury and other places but still, he considered, the position was an honourable one, and he was giving as good as he got. It might safely be said, in fact, that at no time did he feel more independent—less "grovelling," than at this time. He had left the Queensberrys. He was staying with Pope. He was rich. He was ready, at the first word from Swift, to rush over to Ham Walks and pay down the first instalment on the little house there in which—vain hope!—they were to end their days together. Why on earth should he feel dependant? Precisely how little he *did* feel dependant is shown by the almost patronising style of the next paragraph:

> "You have the good wishes of those I converse with, they know they gratify me when they remember you; but I really think they do it purely for your own sake. I am satisfied with the Love and Friendship of Good men, and envy not the Demerits of those who are conspicuously distinguished."

After which Pope takes up the pen with a brusqueness unusual to him but born it may well be of the Dean's interminable indecisions:

> "For God's sake why all this Scruple about Lord Bolingbroke's keeping your Horses, who has a Park, or about my keeping you on a Pint of wine a Day? We are infinitely richer than you imagine; John Gay shall help me to entertain you, though you come like King *Lear*, with fifty Knights."

As to work, when the Dean *did* come he should see that Gay had not been idle. He was busy, he wrote, "in the way of those *Fables* I have already published."

CHAPTER TWENTY-FOUR

1732. Finishing writing 'Achilles' and the 'Fables.' A visit to Sir William Wyndham in Somerset. Another visit to London. Illness and death

> *" Fear no more the frown o' the great*
>   *Thou art past the tyrant's stroke;*
> *Care no more to clothe and eat;*
>   *To thee the reed is as the oak:*
> *The sceptre, learning, physic, must*
> *All follow this, and come to dust.*
>
> *Fear no more the lightning-flash*
> *Nor the all-dreaded thunder-stone;*
> *Fear not slander, censure rash,*
>   *Thou hast finished joy and moan . . ."*
>   'CYMBELINE,' ACT IV, SCENE II

IT is significant that once Gay had rejoined Pope at Twickenham he should have dropped work, for the time being, on the plays (for plays never interested Pope) and have renewed work on the *Fables*. But they were Fables with a difference. This time there is practically no attempt at turning out a story in the manner of La Fontaine or of Æsop. The prevailing thought in his mind is still the corruption of the Government (which has, incidentally, treated him so badly) and therefore corruption shall be his quarry. No doubt the flame of inspiration, burning weakly at first, was skilfully blown upon by Pope. Not from malice aforethought so much as from a conviction as profound as ever Gay's was (but more personal in application) that corruption was multiplying apace and that certain Great Names were at the head of it. Once more it was not a lampooning campaign that a Scriblerian was embarking on but a crusade in the name of all sorts of high-sounding virtues. According to one of Spence's anecdotes Pope's conviction that the pillars of his contemporary society were all but falling is made plain. He quotes him as saying of Government malpractice: "It will never hold: it may last our time, but our posterity must be totally undone if we are not. Look into other States, and see how they have fallen round about us; the same cause will produce the same effects: and God will hardly go out of his way, for the first time, in favouring us."

Though not all Spence's anecdotes are to be trusted this one has the real senatorial ring about it. Pope *did* believe that the country's affairs were being mismanaged and he had as is already shown, an inner prophetic sense of disaster to come unless affairs could be straightened out. He sincerely believed that his friend Gay was performing a valuable public service by having another go at Walpole in his *Fables*.

Meanwhile propaganda on the other side was far from mute, and Colley Cibber as Poet Laureate started the year well for the King by a New Year's Ode which made up in fulsomeness what it lacked in literary merit. The subject would doubtless have been a trying one for even the good writers of the day, but as the good writers were all in disgrace and so did not have to tackle the task they found great pleasure in reading Colley Cibber's effort aloud to each other and suffering from the most exquisite attacks of laughing-stitch as a result. The Ode is too long to quote in full but as a sample these two verses are adequate:

"Awake, with joyous songs, the Day!
The day that leads the opening year
The year adorning, to prolong
Augustus' sway
Demands our song
And calls for universal cheer.

But ah! the sweets his sway bestows
Are greater far than greatness knows;
With various pensive cares opprest
Unseen alas! the Royal breast
Endures its many, many a weight
Unfelt by swains of humble state."

A reply to these loyal sentiments was not long forthcoming—and, since Gay was at that time at Twickenham, and had been hoisted willy-nilly, into the place of Chief Poet of the Opposition, it has been ascribed to him. All that can be said of it is that though the technical excellence of the verses are up to Gay's standard the extreme viciousness of the sentiments is utterly unlike him. That is not to say that Gay had no hand in it—when pressed thereto by his friends—or that some of the Opposition Lords such as Bathurst, Chesterfield, and Bolingbroke, together with Pope, may not have made themselves responsible for the rest. As a specimen of anti-Hanoverian feeling it is certainly worth quoting:

"God prosper long our gracious King
    Now sitting on the throne;
Who leads this nation on a *string*
    And governs all but *One*.

This is the day when, right or wrong,
    I, Colley Bays, Esquire,
Must for my sack indite a song
    And thrum my venal lyre.

Not he who ruled great Judah's realm
  Y-clepèd Solomon
Was wiser than Our's at the helm,
  Or had a wiser son.

He raked up wealth to glut his till
  In drinking, w——s and houses;
Which wiser G——e can save to fill
  His pocket and his spouse's.

The Q——n I also pray, God save!
  His consort plump and dear
Who, just as he is *wise* and *brave*,
  Is *pious* and *sincere*.

O! may she always meet success
  In every scheme and job
And still continue to caress
  That honest statesman, Bob.

God send the P——, that babe of grace,
  A little w—— and horse;
A little meaning in his face;
  And money in his purse . . ."

While it is not certain that Gay had anything to do with the ode that mocked Colley Cibber it is certain that while he was at Pope's he busied himself for a while with the new *Fables*. Whether this grew beyond outlining the structure of them and discussing with Pope individual lines which were to be embedded in them, like gems in a ring, is not discoverable. After January he returned to Amesbury—and the bosom of the Queensberry household; and there, once more, he temporarily dropped his writing:

> "I find myself dispirited," he wrote to Swift, "for want of having some pursuit. Indolence and idleness are the most tiresome things in the world, and I begin to find a dislike to society. I think I ought to break myself of it but I cannot resolve to set about it. . . . If you would advise the Duchess to confine me four hours a day to my own room when I am in the country, I will write, for I cannot confine myself as I ought."

This pathetic plea must have produced a great deal of tut-tutting in the Dean as he paced endlessly to and fro in the Deanery or along the Dublin streets. Yet he had not so much to feel superior over, after all. If Gay could not confine himself as he ought, then Swift could not stir himself as he ought. When Gay wrote that he was dispirited for want of some pursuit he could write back blusteringly:

> "I wonder you will doubt of your genius. The world is wider to a poet than to any other man, and new follies and vices will never be wanting, any more than new fashions."

Yet he wrote of himself in the same year, to Pope: "My poetical fountain is drained . . ." Also he refused, out of kindness or caprice, even to answer Gay's often-repeated question about the house at Ham Walks. Winter passed: spring began again to touch with colour the outlines of the Salisbury plains. Swift left Gay kicking his heels in indecision until early May, when he wrote to him:

> "I find by the whole cast of your letter you are as giddy and volatile as ever, just the Reverse of

Mr. Pope, who hath always loved a domestick life from his Youth."

If this was cool, then what came after it was insult added to injury. It appeared that Gay might just as well have saved his Post Office fee as ever have *mentioned* the matter of the Villakin:

> "I was going to wish you had some little place you could call your own, but I profess I do not know you well enough to contrive any one system of life that would please you. You pretend to preach up riding and walking to the Duchess, yet from my knowledge of you after Twenty Years, you always joined a violent desire of perpetually changing Places and Company, with a rooted Laziness, and an utter impatience of Fatigue. . . . You mortally hate writing, only because it is the thing you chiefly ought to do, as well to keep up the Vogue you have in the World, as to make you easy in your Fortune. You are merciful to everything but money, your best Friend, whom you treat with Inhumanity. . . . Tell me, have you cured your absence of mind? Can you attend to Trifles? Can you at Amesbury write domestic Libels to divert the Family and neighbouring Squires for five miles around? or venture so far on Horseback, without apprehending a stumble at every step? Can you set the Footmen a laughing as they wait at Dinner? and do the Duchess's women admire your wit? In what esteem are you with the Vicar of the Parish? Can you play with him at backgammon? Have the Farmers found out that you cannot distinguish Rye from Barley, or an Oak from a crab-tree? You are

sensible that I know that the full extent of your Country Skill is in fishing for Roaches, or Gudgeon at the highest."

That was the veritable Swift. He need never have signed his letters, they bore the imprint of his personality in every line. The rhetorical catechising of Gay about his activities is typical. Again (having discovered that Gay is back with the Queensberrys), he is anxious to make his friend's place there secure. The questions he put to him are, nearly all of them, questions he could himself have answered in the affirmative at that time, long, long ago, when he was a mere chaplain to my Lord Berkeley. To be able to make the footmen laugh, to play backgammon with the Vicar—to be on good terms with the Duchess's women, these are the things which matter. That is the text he is preaching to-day. Seek ye first these things, he is advising Gay, and security of tenure shall be added unto you. Never did a man take so much trouble with such little need. The Duchess had already assured him that she and Gay found each other's company invaluable. She had gone further: she had almost pleaded with the Dean not to advise Gay to leave her, or to build up visions of little houses at Ham Walks. The only time she was ever jealous of the Dean was when he tried, as she fancied, to take Gay from her, and from time to time in their correspondence there is an amusing sparring match between the two of them, over the apparently unconscious head of Gay himself.

Despite the fact that the Duchess never went so far as actually to lock Gay up in his room to make him write, work with the *Fables* continued.

"Though this is the kind of writing that appears very easy," he wrote to Swift early in the new year, "I find it is the most difficult of any I undertook. After I had invented and finished one Fable, I despaired of finding another."

He wrote again in May:

"I have a moral or two more which I wish to write upon. I have also a sort of a scheme to raise my finances by doing something for the stage, with this and some reading and a great deal of exercise [the gibe about "utter impatience of fatigue" had evidently gone home] I propose to pass my summer; I am sorry it must be without you. Why can't you come, and saunter about the Downs on horseback in the autumn to mark the partridge for me to shoot for your dinner? . . ."

His extraordinary percipience over business matters holds to the end:

"The Premium of the Bonds is fallen a great deal since I bought yours; I gave very near six pounds for each Bond and they are now sold for about fifty shillings. Everything is very precarious, and I have no opinion of any of their Publick Securitys. . . . Mr. Pope's state of health is much the same way as when you left him. As for myself I am often troubled with the cholick: I have as much inattention and have, I think, lower spirits than usual, which I impute to my having no one pursuit in life."

The second series of *Fables* are sixteen in number as against fifty in the first series. As is usual with sequels, they are considered to be much less successful. Whether this is so or not is debatable. Certainly the general effect is one of chagrin and disappointment. In the earlier *Fables* there had been a certain delight traceable in the formation of each story, in its felicitous phrasing and apt turns of speech. These second *Fables* are, as their first editor wrote: "on subjects of a graver and more Political turn." They are obsessed with Politics—and are, moreover, self-conscious. How could they be anything else, since Gay knew that when they were read all sorts of meanings would be dug out of them that he had never put there in the first place? Well, this time, when the courtiers and ministers came to dig and delve they should find what they looked for. He would not be blamed a second time for faults he had not consciously committed. The first Fable is addressed to a lawyer—possibly William Fortescue, now risen to heights of glory as Master of the Rolls. In it the author avows:

> "All private slander I detest
> I judge not of my neighbour's breast;
> Party and prejudice I hate,
> And write no libels on the State.
> Brutes are my theme. Am I to blame,
> If men in morals are the same?"

If there was not something in *that* to make men sit up, then the age was sunk into degeneracy indeed. In the same jaunty yet bitter manner (a bitterness which has grown upon him in his later years and which now flowers here like a nettle, for the first time) he addresses his second Fable "to a friend in the Country"—possibly Pope:

> "E'er I begin, I must premise
> Our ministers are good and wise;

> So, though malicious tongues apply,
> Pray, what care they, or what care I?
> If I am free with Courts, be't known
> I ne'er presume to mean our own."

After much rhyming abuse of Walpole, with every i dotted and every t crossed, he concludes:

> "Give me, kind heav'n, a private station,
> A mind serene for contemplation,
> Title and profit I resign,
> The post of honour shall be mine. . . ."

While, after publication, these rhymed attacks might well wring the withers of ministers, it does not require much imagination to see how much they would be appreciated in that democratic, almost republican household at Amesbury. Indeed throughout the *Fables* a certain democratic strain runs, which has never before been featured so prominently in Gay's writings. Being of ordinary birth himself, it was of course easier for him than for lords to see that all titles were a hollow mockery. Pope, if he ever felt this—as he did on occasion —never felt it for long. He had an inherent respect for titles—even though he could fall asleep when the Prince of Wales was reading poetry at his own table. And Swift, though he affected to despise them as much as any man, had the same inherent respect. They were both Tories by instinct. But Gay was a Liberal by instinct. Years earlier he had written that there was little between a lord and a common man except their different modes of expression. The Duchess of Queensberry, within limitations, seems to have held much the same opinions. . . . This did not prevent her (on an occasion when a sentry of the battalion her husband was commanding had refused to allow her to pass because he had not recognised her) from insisting that the whole battalion should be flogged. Unfortunately there is always an occasion when our principles forsake us—especially when the person that holds them is both wilful and passionate. Nevertheless that was one incident only, and since Gay and the Duchess still fundamentally felt the same about things he expressed himself strongly. Some of the lines that touch on this subject are amongst the best in the *Fables*:

> "With partial eye we're apt to see
> The men of noble pedigree.
> We're prepossest my lord inherits
> In some degrees his grandsire's merits;
> For these we find upon record,
> But find *him* nothing but—my lord."

Again, in advice "to a young nobleman," he writes:

> "By birth the name alone descends;
> Your honour on yourself depends.
> Think not your coronet can hide
> Assuming ignorance and pride."

Amongst all the sixteen fables, far and away the most interesting is the one called *The Countryman and Jupiter*, which Gay addressed to himself. It has an intimate, living, breathing quality which is completely lacking in all the others. It is Gay, sitting astride a chair in the old position, addressing himself in the glass before him —and this time without any semblance of the *poseur*:

> "Have you a friend (look round and spy)
> So fond, so prepossess'd as I?

Your faults, so obvious to mankind,
My partial eyes could never find.
When by the breath of fortune blown,
Your airy castle were o'er-thrown,
Have I been over prone to blame,
Or mortified your hours of shame?
Was I e'er known to damp your spirit
Or twit you with the want of merit?

Think Gay (whate'er may be the case),
Should fortune take you into grace,
Would that your happiness augment?
What can she give besides content?"

    Fortune in that last couplet means, of course, good fortune—in other words that recognition by the Court which was the only public recognition Gay's contemporaries knew or valued. This was far more precious to the wits than money—and Gay, in his heart of hearts, still craved it. Because he could not hate, himself, he disliked being hated. It was little use assuring himself that lots of better men than he would ever be were under a cloud. Swift, too, as he wrote in the Fable addressed to the Dean, had "many foes." Pope was loathed most heartily. But somehow this realisation did not help matters—especially when he was away from them. Fundamentally, below all the childish I-don't-mind-in-the-least-if-I'm-sent-out-of-the-room attitude and the moralising and the chagrin visible in the second *Fables*, Gay still did not give up hope, in the far distant future, that all would come right. Meanwhile he addressed himself, without much conviction, to Content.

    In June, *Acis and Galatea* was put on for the second time in London—this time not at Lincoln's Inn, but at the King's Theatre in the Haymarket, and under the irritable direction of the great Handel himself. This time, too, the choruses were not missing; furthermore, "scenery, machines and other decorations" were advertised as an additional lure. Since Handel had also added numbers from the much earlier Italian version of *Acis* the script as Gay had written it must have been much altered. But whoever respects the whims of a mere librettist? Gay was in town again for a short time in May, but not, apparently, because of anything to do with *Acis and Galatea*. *Acis* was performed; the King and Queen presumably went to it (since Handel was under the royal patronage), and the Prince of Wales's party as presumably stayed away from it. That is to say, the Whigs attended, and the Tories did not. Soon after that the Season broke up, and Gay, like the rest of society, left London for the country. Back in Amesbury he still went on writing to Swift, begging him to come and live with him. He had been striving to improve himself, at odd moments, so that he might be worthy of that honour:

> "As to my eating and drinking," he wrote, "I live as when you left me, so that in that point we shall agree very well in living together, and the Duchess will answer for me that I am cur'd of inattention for I never forget anything she says to me."

But this was asking too much of the Duchess. She was certainly not going to corroborate a statement which might result in Gay's leaving her once and for all. She picked up the pen and continued without even a capital letter:

> "for he never hears what I say and so cannot forget . . . Pray don't persuade Mr. Gay that he

is discreet enough to live alone; for I do assure you he is not, or I either. We are of great use to one another for we never flatter or contradict but when 'tis absolutely necessary: if ever we quarrel 'twill be about a piece of bread-and-butter for somebody is never sick except he eats too much of it. He will not quarrel with you for a Glass or so for by that means he hopes to be able to Gulp down one of those forty millions of schemes that hindered him from being good Company. I would fain see you here; there is so fair a chance that one of us must be pleased, perhaps both, you with an old acquaintance and I with a new one, 'tis so well taking a journey for, that if the Mountain will not come to Mohamet Mohamet must come to the Mountain. But before either of our journeys are settled I desire you would resolve me one question whether a man who thinks himself well where he is should look out for his house and servants before 'tis convenient, before he grows old, or before a person with whom he lives pulls him by the sleeve in private (according to plan) and tells him they have enough of his company."

To which Swift replied first in his best oracular manner to Gay about his continued ill-health:

"Your cholic is owing to intemperance of a philosophical kind; you eat without care, and if you drink less than I, you drink too little."

And also oracularly to the Duchess:

"I will answer your Question. Mr. Gay is not discreet enough to live alone, but he is too discreet to live alone. . . . Your quarrelling with each other upon the Subject of Bread and Butter, is the most usual thing in the world; Parliaments, Courts, Cities and Kingdoms quarrel for no other cause. . . ."

But the Duchess still clung to her point and would not be put off by oracles about discretion.

"I believe," she wrote back to him, "for all you gave Mr. Gay much advice, that you are a very indiscreet person yourself, or else you would come here and take care of your own affairs; and not be so indiscreet as to send for your money over to a place where there is none. Mr. Gay is a very rich man; for I really think he does not wish to be richer; but he will, for he is doing what you bid him. . . . When he began to be a sportsman he had like to have killed a dog and now every day I expect he will kill himself, and then the bread-and-butter affair can never be brought before you, it is really an affair of too great consequence to be trusted to a letter . . . He stands over me and is very peevish (and sleepy) that I do not give him up the pen for he has yawned for it a thousand times. . . ."

There was something else to do besides shooting, that August. That was sitting for a portrait to Jonathan Richardson, Kneller's pupil. This, the last picture that was done of him, has the date August 12th. It shows him to be, though a little older, what Pope had called "still the same man." It is not likely that Gay himself would have commissioned the work, but it *is* likely that the Duchess, apprehensive as ever of that villainous

Villakin just round the corner, wished to have, in the traditional phrase, something to remember him by. Actually, however, the Villakin was losing even the nebulous outline it had achieved in the past. Swift had suggested it, Gay had endeavoured to get Swift to agree to come and share it with him—because then, as always, he needed somebody else to make up his mind for him—and, since Swift ignored the subject whenever it cropped up, Gay turned instead to the other task to which his best friend and counsellor had urged him. He wrote:

"I have an intention to get more money next winter; but am prepared for disappointments, which I think it is very likely I shall meet with. Yet as you think it convenient and necessary that I should have more than I have, you see I resolve to do what I can to oblige you." [There follows a courageous and particularly charming sentence:] "If my designs should not take effect I desire you will be easy under it as I shall be; for I find you so solicitous about me, that you cannot bear my disappointments as well as I can. If I do not write intelligently to you it is because I would not have the clerks of the post office know everything I am doing. If you would have come here this summer, you might with me have helped to drink up the Duke's wine, and saved your money. I am grown so saving of late, that I very often reproach myself with being covetous; and I am very often afraid that I shall have the trouble of having money and never have the pleasure of making use of it."

What premonitory shadow of death fell across the page and inspired him to write those last lines—even in joke, as he probably intended them—we shall never know. A shadow, however, did pass, and he was momentarily depressed under it, and then—since he was Gay and being Gay, lived in the moment, the shadow passed and the sunlight flowed down again serenely. The "scheme" by which he hoped to get more money next winter was *Achilles*, a full-length play formed, like *The Beggar's Opera* and *Polly*, of prose with songs interspersed. Its chief originality is that it inverts the favourite masquerade of dressing a woman up in men's clothes, and dressed up a man in woman's clothes instead. *Achilles*, however, turned out subsequently to be no *Charley's Aunt*, but a rather dull play redeemed by songs as technically neat as the earlier operas, but with none of their naive charm. He had finished his *Fables* and (feverishly industrious for him) was working to finish *Achilles* before going off visiting again.

In October he was ready for relaxation, and this time Sir William Wyndham was the host. This was consistent at least: all his life, as Gay had himself remarked much earlier, he seemed to spend with people out of favour. Now that he was highly out of favour himself, he went off to visit a Jacobite and ex-Chancellor of the Exchequer at Orchard Wyndham in Somerset, where, he wrote to Swift, he ate a lot of fish, visited and was impressed with Dunster Castle at Minehead, and was "entertained with sea-views." Pope had once eulogised Sir William in:

> "Wyndham, just to freedom and the throne;
> The master of our passions and his own."

But it was all very old history now. Sir William, in fact, was a left-over from an earlier period; it was therefore fitting that a poet whose turns of thought and speech were also reminiscent of an earlier period should be his guest. It was while Gay was staying with Wyndham that the fourth volume of the Miscellanies of the Scriblerus Club was published. If this was the swan song of the wits, certainly they themselves were not conscious of it, for most of them were still busy with schemes. Gay had completed his new series of fables, and as soon as he returned from Somerset to Wiltshire he began putting the finishing touches to *Achilles*, before bringing it up to town to arrange for its production. Whilst thus occupied, he heard from Pope:

> "Sir Clem. Cotterell tells me you will shortly come to town. We begin to want comfort in a few friends about us, while the winds whistle and the waters roar. The sun gives us a parting look, but it is but a cold one. . . . I wish you could be here till your family come to town. You will live more innocently, and kill fewer harmless creatures, nay none, except by your proper deputy, the butcher. [This gentle dig was a comment on the fact that Gay had recently been preening himself in a letter to Pope because he had succeeded in getting a bag of nineteen brace of partridges that season. Such sport was too childish for Pope, and he continued with a characteristic piece of advice.] I advise you to make men your game, hunt and beat about here for coxcombs, and truss up rogues in satire."

To which Gay might have replied that he had already done so in his *Fables*, and that bringing down partridges was mere relaxation—a sort of exercise to keep his hand in—after bringing down ministers and courtiers in verse. Pope continues:

"Here is a dead vacation at present, no politics at court, no trade in town, nothing stirring but poetry. Every man, and every boy, is writing verses on the royal hermitage; I hear the queen is at a loss which to prefer. . . . You would oblige my lady Suffolk if you tried your hand on this occasion. I am sure I would do as much for the Duchess of Queensberry if she desired it. Several of your friends assure me it is expected of you."

Pope has been much criticised for this paragraph in the last letter that has been traced from him to Gay. It shows certainly a lack of consistency, since in one part of it he urges Gay to make men his game—that is, to satirise them—and in the next recommends panegyric. Gay had never been a happy panegyrist, and his resolution in neglecting the Court and all its works during the past four years should have been sufficient of itself to demonstrate to Pope that any suggestion of writing verses about the new royal hermitage at Richmond—or the royal anything else, for that matter—would be waste of time. No doubt Pope excused his own attitude to himself by reasoning that, since any event at Court, however insignificant, was the signal for an outburst of versification from all 'loyal' writers, then an event as earth-shaking as the one of the queen laying out her new gardens at Richmond was sufficient excuse for even Gay to celebrate it. Nor should he alone be blamed for the advice; as the letter shows, Lady Suffolk was also keen that Gay should try his hand. The Queen had said she would "take up the hare." Well, the chase had been a long one and the harriers had succeeded in driving the quarry far afield. Now that he was no longer in his first flush, when his coat was a little moth-eaten and his ears creased like parchment, could he not be tempted to come hopping back, poor puss, lured with the easily-spared crumbs of praise and encouragement right up to the royal doorstep? And might not the Queen (granted that she passed at the right psychological moment) *still* "take up the hare?" Some such reasoning must have passed through Lady Suffolk's mind. She had apparently forgotten, though Gay had not, that earlier flop, the *Letter to a Lady*. . . . Whatever the actual distribution of blame between them, Pope and Lady Suffolk together shared it. Gay received their well-meant but nevertheless insulting advice with his usual good temper. A less equable man might have seized the occasion to blow up with righteous indignation, and to turn out seventy derisive couplets entitled *To Mr. P. and Lady S. on their late advice to me to write Panegyric,* or some such. But that was not Gay's way to the friends who loved him, even while they grossly misunderstood him. He replied gently:

> "As to your advice about writing panegyric, it is what I have not frequently done. I have indeed done it sometimes against my judgment and inclination and I heartily repent of it. And at present, as I have no desire of reward, and see no just reason for praise, I think I had better let it alone. There are flatterers good enough to be found, and I would not interfere in any gentleman's profession."

From now until the end events follow fast upon each others' heels. One of the dearest wishes of individual human beings is that, when death shall come, it shall come swiftly and painlessly. The latter half of this prayer was not to be granted to Gay, but at least there was no long-drawn-out period of misery and decay. He was volatile in death as in life, busy until the end with his beloved schemes and inventions. Certainly he had no premonitions, unless the sudden serious tenderness of the closing lines of a letter to Swift, written on November 15th, may be counted as such: "Believe me, as I am, unchangeable in the regard, love and esteem which I have for you. . . ." Ten days later Swift heard from him again—this time from his rooms in Burlington Gardens, whence, he wrote, he had come in advance of the Queensberrys, to follow his own inclinations. It is typical that Pope's last letter to Gay should have described with beauty the end of a dying year: "We begin to want comfort in a few friends about us, while the winds whistle and the waters roar. The sun gives us a parting look, but it is but a cold one." And that Gay's last letter to Swift should be still looking ahead, forgetting the winter, remembering the spring: "Why won't you come among us at the beginning of the New Year?" On this so often reiterated enquiry the correspondence closes down; the affectionate question has been asked for the last time.

The "own inclinations" which Gay had come to town to follow have been quite reasonably concluded to be arrangements for the putting on of *Achilles*, under Rich's direction, at the newly-built theatre in Covent Garden. It may be supposed either that he brought the seeds of serious illness up to town with him or else that, away from the Duchess's vigilant supervision, he took too little care of himself—did not wrap himself up enough from the November weather, or over-ate again from pure excitement at being once more in the intoxicating bustle which was the atmosphere of the theatre that he knew and loved. Added to this, he was suffering undeniably from a certain tenseness and apprehension. He had generously warned Swift not to mind if *Achilles* were a flop as *The Wife of Bath* had been, but he needed constantly to warn himself. He was still so incurably a dotterel, still so ready to run to meet the bird-nesters with happy cries of look-at-my-fine-clutch-of-new-eggs! *Achilles* was his newest and brightest. *Achilles* might (he could not—being Gay—help hoping) reinstate him in public esteem much more effectively and honestly than any toadying piece of panegyric could ever do. True, one of the refrains of a song in the very same play ran:

> "Reputations hack'd and Hew'd
> Can never be mended again."

But for an optimist it was always possible that the impossible might happen. With wild hopeful fancies such as these, and rashly inattentive to his own health, Gay signed, folded up and sealed his last letter to Swift, and went out to walk in the Mall, sit and drink in a coffee-house, meet Rich or Pope or Bolingbroke or Bathurst, and so engage in one or other of the countless enjoyments which went to make up his life in town. A week later, from some intestinal trouble and in his forty-seventh year, he was dead.

No details are known of the development of the fatal illness, but Pope and Arbuthnot attended him continually whilst he lay at Queensberry House. He died on December 4th. On December 5th Pope wrote to Swift:

> "One of the nearest and longest ties I have ever had is broken all on a sudden by the unexpected death of poor Mr. Gay. An inflammatory fever hurried him out of life in three days. He died last night at nine o'clock, not deprived of his senses entirely at last, and possessing them perfectly till

within five hours. He asked of you a few hours before, when in acute torment by the inflammation in his bowels and heart. His effects are in the Duke of Queensberry's custody. His sisters, we suppose, will be his heirs, who are two widows. As yet it is not known whether or not he left a will. Good God! How often are we to die before we go off this Stage? . . . I shall never see you now, I believe; one of your principal calls to England is at an end. Indeed he was the most amiable by far, his qualities were the gentlest; but I love you as well and as firmly. Would to God the man we have lost had not been so amiable nor so good; but that is a wish for our sakes, not his. Sure if innocence and Integrity can deserve Happiness, it must be his. Adieu, I can add nothing to what you will feel, and diminish nothing from it. Yet write to me, and soon. Believe no man now living loves you better, I believe no man ever did, than

"A. Pope."

Enclosed with this was a brief paragraph from Dr. Arbuthnot:

"I am sorry that the renewal of our correspondence should be upon such a melancholy occasion. Poor Mr. Gay died of an inflammation, and, I believe, at the last a mortification of the bowels; it was the most precipitate case I ever knew, having cut him off in three days. He was attended by two physicians besides myself. I believed the distemper mortal from the beginning. I have not had the pleasure of a line from you these two years."

The tone of this last is as 'professional' and dry as the tone of Pope's is emotional. It takes, one would suppose, a judicious mixture of cripple, Catholic and poet to produce a letter quite so 'un-English' in its exhibition of naked feeling as Pope's was. That Gay should have been able to evoke such a letter from the most bitterly-hated and hating man of his time is the best epitaph his life has ever had. Swift's reply to it is as deliberately restrained and casual in tone as Pope's had been emphasised and unrestrained. Pope was visibly beating his bosom at the loss of Gay. Swift merely set his jaw and then spoke in his ordinary voice—only a little more harshly than usual. The terror was still behind him that some day some one should see through the surface-Swift, through the Dean's clothes and the careful phrases, and probe beneath to the palpable defenceless human frame. Not even God, if he could help it, should catch him at such a disadvantage.

Sentiment remained, to the end, an implacable enemy of Swift's. To relax, to give way to an engulfing tenderness was a far more shattering experience for him than to give way to rage or fear or disgust. Any of these might be disciplined, but tenderness was like a flood. Even to think of it opened the heart's gates and drowned that reasonable creature, man. Death of any sort was the final test. If he could stand up to death with nonchalance he could be accounted strong. A strange credo, perhaps, for a dean of the Established Church, but the only one, to his way of thinking, that gave him self-possession. The fact that this dread gave him some sort of premonition is borne out by the sentence with which he endorsed Pope's letter: "On my dear friend Mr. Gay's death; received December 15th, but not read till the 20th, by an impulse foreboding some misfortune."

It was an impulse only too true. When after the lapse

of five days he had brought himself to open and read the letter, he replied to Pope:

"I received yours with a few lines from the Doctor and the account of our losing Mr. Gay; upon which Event I shall say nothing. I am only concerned that long living hath not hardened me. . . . If you are acquainted with the Duchess of Queensberry I desire you will present her my most humble service; I think she is a greater loser by the Death of a Friend than either of us. She seems a lady of excellent Sense and spirit. I had often Postscripts from her in our Friend's letters to me, and her Part was sometimes longer than his, and they made up a great part of the little happiness I could have here. . . ."

But this was by no means all. Swift succeeded in withdrawing himself so thoroughly from the situation that he was able to continue the letter for several pages more and to discuss quite different topics. There was no artificiality about this: he really felt, as his letter indicated, quite normal and matter-of-fact about the whole thing. Only to those in possession of the earlier facts is it possible to guess from such a document that there had ever been a bond of real feeling between the dead man and Swift. Again there is the typical shuffling-off of responsibility, the self-induced delusion that the Duchess was a greater loser by Gay's death than either him or Pope. He would lend his common-sense to advise on Gay's obsequies as he had advised on many actions of his life, but he would not lend his heart. No one, not even Pope, should see that.

Nineteen days elapsed between the death of Gay and his burial; there was nothing singular about such delay then, and since the Duke and Duchess naturally wished to do everything they could in the way of last sad offices for the man they had both loved, and since they were not in London at the time he died, no other explanation seems necessary. Pope, meanwhile, fell into a fever—brought on, said Martha Blount, by the death of his friend. Even so he continued to correspond with Swift, anxious that nothing the two of them could suggest should be lacking on this, the last of all occasions on which they could do Gay honour. They discussed the work he had had in hand when he died, and how Pope should edit it. Swift was immediately very insistent that only the best should be allowed to appear. He knew that the tendency would be to publish every scrap of scribbled paper found in every commode drawer from Amesbury to Drumlanrig. Gay's sisters would, of course, get the proceeds (as well as the six hundred pounds odd that he had left). The thought of it made his blood boil. He would rather the sisters were hanged, he said, than that anything below Gay's best level should appear in print. Gay had too often tried to repeat past successes, he said. He seemed to derive as much comfort from dwelling on the flaws in Gay's work as Pope derived from dwelling on the innocence and sweetness of the dead man's character.

Since Pope was the premier epitaph-writer of his time, it naturally fell to him to compose the verses for Gay's memorial. It was known by now that he was to receive that last of honours—burial in the Poets' Corner in Westminster Abbey—and Pope had the Abbey in mind when he wrote. When he had finished he sent the epitaph off, with some temerity, to Swift:

> "Of manners gentle, of affections mild;
> In wit a man—simplicity, a child;

With native humour temp'ring virtuous rage;
Form'd to delight at once and lash the age;
Above temptation in a low estate,
And uncorrupted e'en among the great,
A safe companion and an easy friend,
Unblam'd through life, lamented in thy end,
These are thy honours, not that here thy bust
Is mixed with heroes, or with kings thy dust;
But that the worthy and the good shall say,
Striking their aching bosoms, ' *Here* lies Gay.'"

It is evidence of Pope's sincerity that, though he was the prince of plagiarists just as he was of epitaph-writers, in these dozen lines he has stolen only one line from anybody else, and since that one came from his great master, Dryden, it might be accounted a loan rather than a theft. In the year of Gay's birth Dryden had written *Lines to the Pious memory of the accomplished young lady Mrs. Anne Killigrew*, who had died of smallpox in that same year. Of her he had written: "Her wit was more than man, her innocence a child." Forty-seven years later Pope readapted the line to fit Gay. Swift, however, when he read the epitaph, was concerned more with assonance than with plagiarisms. He objected to the double *ing* sounds in the line: "Striking their aching bosoms . . ." and suggested pensive bosoms instead. Pope incorporated pensive with gratitude, and spoilt his epitaph. No, Swift could never be a poet, but he remained a Dublin School of Journalism to the end of his days.

Two days before Christmas the body of John Gay was taken to lie in state at Exeter Change. At nine o'clock the same evening it was borne with appropriate honours to Westminster Abbey and interred in the South Transept, whence, in his own lifetime, Addison, Congreve and

Prior had all preceded him. The burial service was conducted by the Dean of Westminster. The pall-bearers were Pope, Lord Chesterfield, Lord Cornbury (a brother of the Duchess of Queensberry), General Dormer, Mr. Berkeley and Mr. Gore. Of this service Dr. Arbuthnot wrote to Swift:

> "It was some alleviation of my grief to see him so universally lamented by almost everybody, even by those who knew him only by reputation. He was interred at Westminster Abbey, as if he had been a peer of the realm; and the good Duke of Queensberry, who lamented him as a brother, will set up a handsome monument upon him. . . . I believe the *Beggar's Opera*, and what he had to come upon the stage, will make the sum of the diversions of the town for some time to come. Curll (who is one of the new terrors of death) has been writing letters to everybody for memoirs of his life."

The handsome monument of which Dr. Arbuthnot spoke was in due course set up. It is a platform surmounted by an obelisk decorated with such symbols as pipes, masks and trumpets, against which stands a despondent Cupid engaged in unveiling a medallion on which is engraved a bust of Gay. He is in profile, still in the familiar velvet cap, and looking unnaturally grave and wise. Pope's epitaph is carved in the place of honour, and under it is an eulogy which for sonority of effect and skilful arrangement of periods suggests that Pope may also have had a hand in its conception. It deserves its position at the end of a chapter as well as at the end of the life of a poet:

"Here lye the ashes of Mr. JOHN GAY;
The warmest friend;
The most benevolent man;
Who maintained
Independency
In low circumstances of fortune;
Integrity
In the midst of a corrupt age;
And that equal serenity of mind
Which conscious goodness alone can give
Through the whole course of his life.

Favourite of the Muses,
He was led by them to every elegant art;
Refined in taste
And fraught with graces all his own.
In various kinds of poetry
Superior to many,
Inferior to none,
His works continue to inspire
What his example taught
Contempt of folly, however disguised
Detestation of vice, however adorned
Reverence for virtue, however disgraced.

CHARLES and CATHERINE, Duke and Duchess of QUEENSBERRY, who loved this excellent Person living, and regret him dead, have caused this Monument to be erected to his memory."

CHAPTER TWENTY-FIVE

Conclusion

On meurt deux fois, je le vois bien;
Cesser d'aimer et d'être aimable
C'est un mort insupportable;
Cesser de vivre, ce n'est rien.
    VOLTAIRE: 'LINES TO MADAME DU CHATELET'

IT would only be fair, at this stage, to allow that great debunker, Dr. Johnson, to remove the atmosphere of qualified appreciation which has accumulated round our subject. Sixty years after Gay's death the Doctor happened to be writing in *The Idler* on the subject of Pope's epitaphs. He made ponderous sport of the one on Gay. Using a pair of colossal literary pincers, he lifted every line, turn by turn, out of its context, and exhibited it, wriggling like an eel. By the time he has reached the end there is, needless to say, precious little epitaph left, and his verdict is: "The eight first lines have no grammar, the adjectives are without any substantives, and the epithets without a subject. The thought in the last line, that Gay is buried in the bosoms of the worthy and good, who are distinguished only to lengthen the line [a nasty hit, that], is so dark that few understand it; and so harsh, when it is explained to them, that still fewer approve."

There were, however, other verdicts than Dr. Johnson's. Lord Orrery wrote in a very different manner of Pope's epitaph:

> "Entombed with Kings though Gay's cold ashes lie
> A nobler monument thy strains supply,
> Thy matchless muse, still faithful to thy friend,
> By courts unawed his virtues dares commend.
> Lamented Gay, forget thy treatment past,
> Look down—and see thy merit crowned at last!
> A destiny more glorious who can hope,
> In life beloved, in death bemoaned by Pope."

As they had dealt differently during Gay's lifetime, so after his death Pope and Swift still pursued their characteristic ways. Pope soothed as he talked, recalling the beloved now vanished presence. Swift laid about him with a flail, accusing people of not caring in the least that he had died. Lady Betty Germaine was one correspondent prepared, on occasion, to give as good as she got. Swift, who was an old friend of hers had approached her early the year before, recommending Gay to her in the warmest possible manner and obviously hoping that, since the Countess of Suffolk had proved such a broken reed, he might be able to depend on her instead. "Mr. Gay," he had written, "is as honest and sincere a man as ever I knew. . . ." But Lady Betty Germaine could no more reinstate Gay than she could make pigs fly. Dean Swift, she probably thought resentfully, really did ask one to do the most impossible things. Besides, Lady Suffolk was a friend of hers, and, she was quite sure, was innocent of any crime. After Gay's death she wrote on the subject to Swift:

> "As to the Countess of Suffolk . . . I wish with all my heart, as a judgment upon you, that you had seen her, as I did, when the news of your friend's death came; for though you are a proud person, yet (give you, devil, your due) you are a sincere, good-natured, honest one."

But beyond wishing that Swift *had* seen Lady Suffolk on this occasion, Lady Betty Germaine diplomatically divulged nothing; and it is somehow fitting that the reactions of that discreetest and most correct of women should remain a mystery.

It would have been easier to guess how the Duchess of Queensberry took the news, even if we had not had her letters to confirm it. Whether deliberately or accidentally, Gay had so arranged his second series of Fables that the last one was the one entitled, appropriately enough, *The Raven, the Sexton and the Earth-worm*. Its preamble was addressed "To Laura"—still the Duchess's poetic pet-name. Reading over and rereading this last personal address from Gay must have been for her the most poignant of pleasures. He had loved and admired her beyond all other women; and chiefly, as she knew, for her freedom from all the smaller vices—vanity, gossip, back-biting, hypocrisy, and those other faults which Swift, Prior, Pope, Addison and Gay himself had all had occasion to castigate in their work. The Duchess of Queensberry, a feminist in embryo, seems to have concurred in the wits' opinions. She despised her own sex because the average rich woman of her acquaintance presented women in so poor a light. But not even the worst enemy of the Duchess of Queensberry could have accused her of preoccupation with scandals or with her personal appearance. Her nonchalance over the latter point had impressed Gay—himself by no means above being interested in such fal-lals as coats with silver buttons or blue knots—almost more than anything else about her. For him she had every possible virtue. Had he not written, from the bottom of his heart:

> "But ev'ry beauty I can trace
> In *Laura's* mind, in *Laura's* face;

> My stars are in this brighter sphere;
> My Lilly and my Rose is here."

And in his last Fable he still laid tributes at her feet, borrowing the method from Swift to do it, and flattering most astutely even while pretending to abstain from flattering:

> ". . . Since then I dare not speak my mind,
> A truth conspicuous to mankind;
> Though in full lustre ev'ry grace
> Distinguish your celestial face,
> Though beauties of inferior ray
> (Like stars before the orb of day)
> Turn pale and fade: I check my lays,
> Admiring what I dare not praise.
> If you the tribute due disdain,
> The muse's mortifying strain
> Shall, like a woman, in meer spight
> Set beauty in a moral light.
> Though such revenge might shock the ear
> Of many a celebrated fair;
> I mean that superficial race
> Whose thought ne'er reach beyond their face,
> What's that to you? I but displease
> Such ever-girlish ears as these.
> Virtue can brook the thought of age,
> That lasts the same through ev'ry stage."

Now again, as before, his mind has turned to the Elizabethan preoccupation with age and death. Then he had written:

> "Love, *Laura*, love, while youth is warm,
> For each new winter breaks a charm."

That was seven years earlier. Between the time of writing that and writing this last Fable he had grown to know her at least seven times as well. He had learnt that she could endure (by virtue of that ever-to-be-admired virtue, Reason) thoughts which would make a weaker woman recoil in horror:

"Were you by Antoninus taught,
 Or is it native strength of thought,
 That thus, without concern or fright,
 You view yourself by reason's light?"

And again, whilst he is commemorating Laura, the lyric touch returns for a moment to gild something extremely difficult to gild—the commonplace metre of the rhymed couplet:

"Those eyes of so divine a ray,
 What are they? Mould'ring, mortal clay.
 Those features, cast in heav'nly mould,
 Shall, like my coarser earth, grow old:
 Like common grass, the fairest flow'r
 Must feel the hoary season's pow'r.
 Dust form'd us all. Each breathes his day,
 Then sinks into his native clay.

Shall like my coarser earth, grow old. . . . Less than a year after writing those lines Gay had discovered that he was never to grow old; and the Duchess of Queensberry herself, whilst in time she was to grow old, and to feel the hoary season's power as much as the rest, lived on with a beauty which lingered well into her old age. Thirty years after, Horace Walpole reported of her attendance at a royal reception: "The Duchess of Queensberry and Lady Westmoreland were in the procession, and did credit to the ancient nobility." Further: "The Duchess of Queensberry looked well, though her locks milk-white."

But these coming events had not cast even their shadows before, at the close of the year 1732. Reading over the last of Gay's poems addressed to her (he had been remarkably sparing of addresses, and perhaps for that reason they were the more precious), how should his friend and companion have any inkling of what was to come? As he had been, she was concerned with the present. The hot tears falling upon the page, and dimpling it as rain dimples a river, were the present. Of the future just then she knew nothing, and cared still less. Early in the new year she wrote to Swift:

"SIR,—Soon after the death of our friend Mr. Gay, I found myself more inclined to write to you, than to allow myself any other entertainment. But, considering this might draw you into a correspondence, that most likely might be disagreeable, I left off all thoughts of this kind, till Mr. Pope showed me your letter to him . . . which encourages me to hope that we may converse together as usual, by which advantage I will not despair to obtain in reality some of those qualities you say I *seem* to have. I am conscious of only one, that is, being an apt scholar; and if I have any good in me I certainly learnt it insensibly of our poor friend, as children do any strange language. It is not possible to imagine the loss his death is to me; but so long as I have any memory, the happiness of ever having such a friend can never be lost to me. . . . While I had that very sincere, good friend I could sometimes lay open all my rambling thoughts, and he and I would often view and dissect them, but now they come and go, and I seldom find out whether they be wrong or right, or if there be anything to them. Poor man, he was most truly everything you say of him. I have lost in him the usefullest limb of my mind."

This tribute came only a few months after the death of Gay. The curiously simple phraseology of the sentence about the laying open of her rambling thoughts, with its pathetic close, demonstrates more clearly than anything else could ever have done what Gay had meant to her. Nor did her sense of loss evaporate. Once she had gone walking with him through the corridors of trees or of houses: now she walked alone, and the rambling thoughts accompanied her alone, blundering like white moths about her head, inexplicable, intangible—perhaps even (worst of all) unnecessary. Gay was no longer there to catch those thoughts for her, and to elucidate them into something more comforting than moths. He could no longer enjoy her pleasures and commiserate in her griefs. Two years later the sense of loss was still acute:

"I often want poor Mr. Gay," she wrote to the Duchess of Suffolk. "Nothing evaporates sooner than joy untold, or even told, unless to one so entirely to your interest as he was, who bore an equal share in any satisfaction or dissatisfaction that attended us. I am not in the spleen, though I write thus; on the contrary, it is a sort of pleasure to think over his good qualities. His loss was really great, but it is a satisfaction to have once known so good a man. As you were his friend as much as I, it is needless to ask your pardon for dwelling so long on this subject."

If the Duchess's imperiousness had not been so ineradicable, and if Gay in his lifetime had not deliberately encouraged and enjoyed such imperiousness, it might have been possible to resent on his behalf the somewhat selfish attitude inherent in her letters to both Swift and Lady Suffolk. It would have been possible to employ much the same language about an accident far less serious than the death of a friend, and *I often want poor Mr. Gay* might read just as well: *I often miss the central heating of our town house, you have no idea what a difference it made to the atmosphere; an always equal temperature, night and day, and no fumes whatever. One touch of my fingers, and I could turn it hot or cold as I pleased.* But where would be the sense in resenting an attitude which Gay himself would by no means have resented? If central heating might have warmed and invigorated her body, certainly he had warmed and invigorated her mind. He would have liked to have been missed with such melancholy petulance, and for such deliciously selfish ends. At least there was no possibility of any posing *there*. Happy in most things, he had been happy even in the hour of his going. He might have echoed with Voltaire that merely to cease to live was nothing. The real death would have been to have survived the love of his friends and the sensation of loving them. His was a happy ghost, and more often than may be supposed it is the happy ghosts which survive and hang like a perfume or an echo around their former habitations.

At first the sense of loss was acute. The Duchess of Queensberry felt as if a limb had been lopped off. Pope told Martha Blount that when he stayed with Lord Bathurst he could "hardly bear the memories of poor Gay." He wrote further to her: "Let us comfort one another, and if possible, study to add as much more friendship to each other, as death has deprived us of in him." Again, in his lines to Dr. Arbuthnot which occur in the *Prologue to the Satires*, and which contain some of the most vitriolic lines which even Pope ever wrote, he changed his cursing to blessing when he spoke of Gay:

> "Blest be the Great! for those they take away,
>   And those they left me, for they left me Gay;
>   Left me to see neglected Genius bloom,
>   Neglected die, and tell it on his tomb:
>   Of all thy blameless life the sole return
>   My verse, and Queensb'ry weeping o'er thy urn."

The other references in the *Epistle* were very different. While the shafts of anger released by readers of them were still whirling about his head, he could sit down at Twickenham and cultivate instead the inward eye, which showed him things far less evanescent than the vices of contemporary society. Whilst so occupied he wrote to Swift:

> "There is nothing of late of which I think more than Mortality, and what you mention, of collecting the best Monuments we can of our Friends, their own Images in their writings. (For these are the best, when their Minds are such as Mr. Gay's was, and as yours is. . . .)"

Again:

> "I have felt more (I fancy) in the loss of Mr. Gay than I shall suffer in going away myself into a state that can feel none of this sort of losses. I wished vehemently to have seen him in a condition of living Independence, and to have

lived in perfect indolence the rest of our Days together, the two most idle, most innocent, undesigning Poets of our age. I now as vehemently wish you and I might walk into the grave together, by as slow steps as you please, but contentedly and cheerfully . . ."

To which Swift answered, characteristically:

"I cannot affirm that I pity our friend Gay, but I pity his Friends. I pity you and would at least equally pity myself, if I lived amongst you, for I should have seen him oftener than you did."

The detachment here is all but perfect. Almost it might be supposed that Gay was a stranger whose pleasant face he had once glimpsed on the Mall and whom, if Swift had had time, he might have become acquainted with. But he did not always succeed in attaining such remoteness. Three years later, writing to Pope on the death of Dr. Arbuthnot, he was more revealing:

"The deaths of Mr. Gay and the Doctor have been terrible wounds near my heart. Their living would have been a great comfort to me, although I should never have seen them; like a sum of money in a bank, upon which I should have drawn at least annual interest, as I did from you, and have done from my Lord Bolingbroke."

In 1739 Pope was still vividly recalling those halcyon days when, for a brief moment, the poets *had* been as they were in the time of Augustus:

"In the summer I generally ramble for a month to Lord Cobham's, the Bath or elsewhere.

In all these Rambles my mind is full of the images of you and poor Gay, with whom I travelled so delightfully two summers."

The remembrance of those summers still warmed him; but no reminiscent shaft of sunlight from them could ever penetrate the windows of Swift's Castle of Despair. As time passed he was to lock himself up in it ever more and more securely, separate himself ever farther and farther from his friends; until finally the only other creature left to share his confinement was one whose coming he had long dreaded, and who wore the faceless face of madness.

The rest of the world remained unmoved by an event as unimportant as the death of a minor poet. Once more the unrestrainable Mr. Aaron Hill must be quoted, in a letter written to the great Mr. Handel on the day after Gay's death. It begins by offering profuse thanks for the tickets which Mr. Handel has so kindly sent him and continues by begging Mr. Handel to try the experiment, once again, of using an English libretto for his music:

> "I am of opinion that male and female voices may be found in the Kingdom capable of everything that is requisite; and, I am sure, a species of dramatic opera might be invented, that by reconciling reason and dignity with musick and fine machinery, would charm the ear and hold fast the heart together . . ."

In a sense Handel may be said to have taken Mr. Hill's advice—if the later oratorios, that is, may be accounted a "species of dramatic opera"; but the interesting point about the letter is that it should have been written just at the moment when the man who, above all others, had succeeded in dislodging Italian opera from the English stage, and in demonstrating the entire suitability of the English language for setting to music, had breathed his last. *The Beggar's Opera* admittedly was not at all the sort of wedding of English verse and music that Aaron Hill envisaged. It was, for all that, the immortal part of John Gay. If the latter half of the eighteenth century belongs musically to what has been called the golden certainties of Handel and to the organ and large orchestra, then just as surely the first part of it belongs to the silver impudence of the flutes and trumpets accompanying the old English and Scots airs—to the ever-triumphant *Beggar's Opera*.

Three days after Gay's death John Rich, taking the tide of publicity at full flood, revived *The Beggar's Opera* at the new theatre at Covent Garden. It ran, then as ever, with resounding success. Conceived at a period of great happiness in the life of its author, it has proved to have a vitality that no amount of maltreatment and alteration has ever seriously affected. It may be added that *Achilles* appeared on the stage, according to plan, in the early part of 1733 and though Pope reported to Swift that it succeeded very well, being "another original of its kind," that it proved to be of no more than passing interest. It may also be added that nearly fifty years after Gay's death, when even the seemingly-immortal Robert Walpole had gone the way of all flesh, *Polly* was finally 'released' for public performance. The aged Duchess of Queensberry, who had long survived husband and both sons, was present, but she was the only link with *Polly's* past and a tenuous one at that, for she died soon afterwards, from eating a surfeit of either strawberries or cherries, in Savile Row. There would have been poetic justice if it had been cherries, for it might well have been her of whom Gay had written with a touch of Herrick in his youth:

> O ruddier than the Cherry
> O sweeter than the Berry
> O Nymph more bright
> Than moonshine Night
> Or Kidlings blithe and merry!
> Ripe as the melting cluster,
> No Lilly hath such lustre
> Yet hard to tame
> As raging flame
> And fierce as storms that bluster!

But the incident on which one would like to close a life of Gay is neither the eventual production of *Polly* nor the continual revivals of *The Beggar's Opera*. It is one described by J. R. Chanter in *The Western Antiquary*, and concerns the tenor Thomas Incledon who was, in his day, a popular singer and a more than popular Macheath:

> "Half a century after Gay's death, Incledon the celebrated vocalist, during a professional tour of the West, visited Barnstaple as a pilgrimage to the birthplace of Gay, and on being shown the house in which the poet had passed his early days, astonished and delighted the neighbours by breaking out into song in the open street in front of the house, and in the stillness of a bright moonlight evening, warbled several of his songs and ballads, as a tribute to Gay's memory. I had this from an ancient inhabitant, an eye-witness of the scene."

So many scenes in the lives of poets are apocryphal, but there is a ring of truth about this one, for it has the brief, bird-like spontaneity of *All in the Downs*, of the *Shepherd's Lament*, of any of Macheath's songs. It is fitting too, to close as we began in Joy Street, leaving Incledon standing bareheaded in the moonlight, his serenade soaring easily up into the astonished stillness of the soft west-country air. Somewhere in the realms of outer space one seems to see Gay's familiar face leaning down over an eighteenth-century cloud, asking, delighted, surprised, still unbelieving, "What? For *me*?" Yes, for you.

THE END

INDEX.

Acis and Galatea, 161, 201, 210, 333, 419, 420, 457, 458
Addison, 34, 35, 37, 38, 40-45, 47, 51, 53, 54, 57, 58, 67, 72, 77, 80, 88, 95, 103, 108-111, 114, 117, 119, 120, 124, 130, 131, 135, 136, 155-157, 163, 170, 173, 189, 195-197, 224, 325, 342, 393, 472, 477
Aix-les-Bains, 179, 180, 309, 362
Alliance, the Triple, 176
Amesbury, 383, 386, 387, 395-397, 400, 408-410, 413, 414, 422, 424, 428, 430-432, 436, 437, 444, 449, 451, 455, 458, 463, 471
Anne, Queen, 22, 31, 33-36, 51, 52, 62, 67, 71, 87, 102, 107, 110, 113, 114, 117, 123, 124, 145, 147, 207, 252
Arbuthnot, Dr., 36, 48, 77-80, 82, 83, 85, 87, 89, 99-101, 104, 105, 112, 114, 115, 117, 118, 121, 136, 143, 144, 153, 154, 165, 167, 169, 170-172, 201, 205, 217, 219, 220, 223, 229, 236, 244, 255, 264, 265, 273, 282, 285, 295, 296, 303, 309, 311, 317, 344, 347, 353, 361, 363, 375, 376, 382, 408, 422, 424, 435, 436, 467, 468, 470, 473, 483, 484
Argyll, Duke of, 325
Assiento, the, 202, 203
Atterbury, Bishop, 80, 81, 86, 88, 114, 121, 224, 243
Attilio, 233, 342

Bacon, 89
Baller, Rev. Joseph, 20, 367
Banck, John van der, 49
Bank of England, 17, 202
Barber, Mrs., 426
Barn Elms, 76
Barnes, F. E., 217
Barnstaple, 11, 13-15, 17, 28-32, 277, 367, 487
Barnstaple Grammar School, 17, 31
Bath, 141, 144, 165, 166, 191, 223, 225, 226, 236, 251, 253-255, 278, 344, 345, 347, 349, 350, 353, 354, 356, 358, 400, 484
Bathurst, Lord, 77, 126, 139, 154, 187, 192, 200, 204, 220, 253, 273, 274, 326, 348, 377, 379, 388, 402, 422, 424, 448, 467, 482
Battle of the Books, 34
Beggar's Opera, The, 18, 25, 310-312, 314,
321-331, 348, 349, 351, 352, 356, 359, 360, 363, 364, 366, 367, 372, 384, 392, 420, 424, 473, 486, 487
Behn, Mrs. Aphra, 248
Bellenden, Miss, 167, 179
Berkeley, George, 95, 473
Berkeley, Lord, 64, 452
Besant, Sir Walter, on the Mississippi and South Sea schemes, 212
Bill of Rights, 17
Binfield, 32, 54, 59, 61, 97, 116, 121
Birrell, Augustine, 35
Blackheath, 251
Blake, Joseph, *alias* Blueskin, 256-259
Blenheim, 31
Blount, Sir John, 202, 203, 211, 213, 216
Blount, Martha, 138, 162, 167, 173, 201, 255, 289, 311, 345, 353, 407, 408, 471, 482
Blount, Teresa, 138, 162, 173, 201
Blueskin's Ballad, 258
Boileau, 24, 145
Bolingbroke, Lady, 282
Bolingbroke, Lord, 35, 39, 41-43, 48, 52, 71, 77, 80, 81, 96, 98, 102, 113, 114, 117, 121, 125, 126, 139, 148, 154, 156, 175-177, 179, 180, 186, 192, 194, 201, 225, 232, 237, 243, 273, 274, 280, 281, 296, 300, 312, 325, 326, 340, 344, 345, 398, 399, 407, 408, 424, 434, 435, 445, 448, 467, 484
Bolton, Duke of, 347, 350
Bononcini, 210, 233, 234, 342
Boyne, Battle of the, 17
Bradshaw, Lady Margaret, 223
Bristol, 32
Broome, 152, 311
Brothers' Club, 77, 78, 80
Buckingham, 57, 139
Budgell, 47
Burlington Gardens, 221, 363, 377, 378, 386, 395, 466, 467
Burlington House, 132, 133, 157-160, 187, 221, 225, 226, 228, 230, 302, 420
Burlington, Lady, 159, 160, 167, 210, 221, 229, 238, 251
Burlington, Lord, 132, 139, 141, 143, 145, 154, 157, 159-162, 165, 167, 193, 200, 210, 220, 221, 229, 238, 251, 276, 326, 422
Burnet, Bishop, 83, 130, 131, 192
Button's Coffee-house, 38, 163

INDEX

Campaign, the, 34
Canons, 193, 210
Caroline, Princess, of Hanover, *see also* WALES, PRINCESS OF, 111, 120
Carteret, Lord, 260, 272, 416
Caryll, John, 131, 141, 193
Chandos, Duke of, 193, 210, 214
Charles II, 7-9, 62
Chatenay, Madame de, 163
Chaucer, 8
Chelsea, 60, 64, 73, 97, 282
Chester, 285
Chesterfield, Lord, 10, 108, 109, 154, 175, 177, 192, 204, 220, 238, 253, 326, 354, 388, 448, 473
Cheyne, Mr., 143, 144
Chiswick, 162-164, 209
Cibber, Colley, 170, 171, 248, 320-322, 342, 343, 352, 353, 414, 415, 417, 447-449
Clarendon, Lord, 98, 99, 102, 104-106, 112, 114
Cobbett, *Rural Rides*, 141
Cobham, Lord, 274, 338, 484
Cockthorpe, 191, 193
Coffee-houses, their importance, 40, 41, 88, 131, 168, 177, 213
Collins, Churton, 82
Compton, Mr. Spencer, 67
Conduct of the Allies, The, 51, 52, 249
Congreve, 38, 44, 77, 80-82, 86, 88, 118, 139, 144, 201, 222, 223, 225, 248, 251, 280, 321, 322, 344, 345, 347, 350, 353, 357, 372, 380, 382, 472
Constantinople, 31, 37, 193
Cooke, Thomas, *Battle of the Poets*, 263, 264
Cornbury, Lord, 473
Cornwall, 15
Cornwallis, Lord, 63
Cotterell, Sir Clement, 463
Country Post, The, 84
Coward, Dr., 46
Craggs, James, 110, 139, 197, 201, 206, 215, 216, 224
Crashaw, 95
Croker, 236
Cromwell, Oliver, 7, 35, 393
Cromwell (the writer), 54, 127
Curll, 383, 473

Daily Courant, 41
Daily Gazetteer, 41
Dawley, 399, 437, 438
Defoe, Daniel, 18, 23, 35, 41, 103, 141, 227, 269, 303

Delany, 348, 416
Dennis, John, 50, 53, 55, 169, 173, 184
Devon, 13, 15-17, 28, 59, 141, 144, 165, 367
Dijon, 197, 198
Disney, Duke, 114, 226
Dobson, Austin, 36, 40
Dodington, Mr. Bubb, 67
Donne, 95
Don Saltero's Coffee-house, 163
Dorchester, 144
Dormer, General, 473
Dorset, Duke of, 67, 118
Drapier's Letters, 249, 255, 256, 260, 282
Drelincourt, Dean, of Armagh, 427, 428
Drelincourt, Miss, 427-429
Drelincourt, Mrs., 425-428
Drumlanrig, 383-386, 471
Dryden, 7, 38, 43, 44, 261, 331, 417, 472
Dublin, 32, 391, 413, 424, 450
Duck, Stephen, 409, 415
Dunciad, 350-353, 398, 432
Dunster Castle, 462

Edinburgh, 383, 385
Elizabeth, Queen, 16
Essay on Criticism, 50
Essay on Man, 434
Essex, Earl of, 201
Etherege, 10
Exeter, 141, 144
Exeter Change, 472

Faber, Professor George, 28, 29, 137, 272, 373
Fables, The, 25, 303-307, 311, 320, 327, 347, 372, 418; *Fables*, second series of, 453-457, 462, 463, 477-479
Female Faction, the, 376
Fenton, Lavinia, 324, 327, 335, 347
Fitzwilliam, Lady, 251, 252
Fitzwilliam, Lord, 251
Flett, Phineas, 19
Ford, Charles, 54, 227, 228
Fortescue, William, 31, 59, 80, 82, 85, 86, 121, 154, 192, 252, 273, 454
France, 51, 180, 181, 197, 200, 311, 419

Gains, Earl of Anjou, 13
Garth, Dr., 77
Gay, Elizabeth, 14
Gay, Joanna, 14, 20, 59, 471
Gay, John, the musical year, 9-11; pedigree, 12-15; schooldays, 17-20; apprenticed, 22, 23; distaste for apprenticeship, 24, 25; back in Devon,

INDEX

28; gap in life's history, 28-31; in London, 36, 37; secretarial work, coffee-houses, 38; booksellers' hack, becomes author, 39, 40; *The Present State of Wit*, 43-46, 53; goes to Court, 48; popularity, 49; acquaintance with Swift and Pope, 54; *The Mohocks*, 55; *Epistle to Mr. Lintot*, 56-58, 136; secretary to the Duchess of Monmouth, 59, 60; thanks Pope for recommendation, 61; life in the Monmouth household, 64; *Rural Sports*, 64, 67-70; *The Wife of Bath*, 73, 74, 390, 467; Swift's opinion of his age, 79, 80; the Scriblerus Club, 80, 82, 83, 85; *The Country Post*, 84; literary friendships, 88, 90, 91; *The Fan*, 93, 94; *Araminta, Penthesilea, A Contemplation on Night, A Thought on Eternity*, 94-96; *The Shepherd's Week*, 96, 97, 145; secretary to Lord Clarendon, 98, 102, 103; fitness for the post, 103, 104; friendship with Mrs. Howard, 107, 108, 110, 111; asked for a copy of his poems, 111, 112; recalled from Hanover, 114; Pope's advice to write something on the King, 117; *Epistle to a Lady*, 118-120, 347, 465; invited to Binfield, 121; *The What D'Ye Call It*, 124-130, 166; a visitor to Burlington House, 132; *Mr. Pope's Welcome from Greece*, 137-140, 152; *The Journey to Exeter*, 141-143, 145; working hard, 144; never in love, 145; edition of Horace, 145-147; *Trivia*, 150-153; high society, 154; *Toilette, God's Revenge Against Punning*, 155; at Burlington House, 158-161; at Chiswick with Pope and Swift, 162, 163; Swift's hint to Gay, 164, 258; *The Espousal, Three Hours after Marriage*, 165, 169-171, 180, 247, 320; life in Bath, 166, 167; failure of plays, 172, 173; trip to Aix-les-Bains, 179, 180; *Epistle* to Pulteney, 180-182; *The Despairing Shepherd*, 182, 183; *Epistle* to Lowndes, 185, 186; trying to help Prior, 187; The Birth of the Squire, 189; *Epistle* to Methuen, 190, 342; stays at Cockthorpe, 191, 192; at Addison's death-bed, 195, 196; visit to France, 197; *Poems on Several Occasions*, 200, 205, 432; South Sea stock, 206, 210-212; Duchess of Queensberry's friendship, 207; ill and depressed, 217, 219-221; *Epistle to Mr,*

Thomas Snow, 218, 225; eulogy on the dead Marlborough, 223; hears bad news, 224; neglected by patrons, obtains small post, 227-229; feelings for Mrs. Howard, 236; advised to write a satire, 241, 242; *The Captives*, 243-245; a failure, 247-249; at Bath, 251; invites Pope, 254; *Newgate's Garland*, 257-260, 330, 331, 432; helps Pope on Shakespeare, 261, 262; composes *Fables*, 269, 271, 274, 290; with Pope and Swift at Twickenham, 273, 274, 280, 281; visits Marble Hill, 276-279; Walpole angry, 283; Swift's censure, 284, 285; who was Laura, 290-292; at Twickenham, 294; Court preferment, 294, 295; Gay's tribute to Gulliver, 297-299; *Fables* nearly finished, 300, 302; printed, 303; promise of royal patronage, 307; with Pope at Lord Harcourt's, 309; with Swift at Pope's, 310; refuses appointment, 313, 314, 316, 317, 319; *The Beggar's Opera*, 321-331; appreciations of Gay, 331-333; Italian opera hard hit, 335-337, 342, 486; profits of play, 339; Swift's congratulations, 340; newspaper praise, 341; and abuse, 343; at Bath, 345, 350; joined by Pope, 353; composing *Polly* at Bath, 356; returns to London, 357; *Polly* banned, 358-360, 368; serious illness, 361; *Polly* in book form, 360, 363-366; plans to visit Devon, 367; the Duchess intervenes, 368-371; elegiac poem, 373, 374; notoriety, 375, 376; at Burlington Gardens, 377, 378; *Polly* published, 380, 486, 487; pirate editions, 382; meets Allan Ramsay, 384; living with the Queensberrys, 387; correspondence censored, 392, 393, 404, 408, 461; *Wife of Bath* revived, 395; the Villakin, 397, 398, 401, 404, 413, 417, 429, 439, 451, 461; talks of accounts, 402; question of Swift's money, 413, 420; the country gentleman, 413, 417, 421; a dotterel, 418; Swift's schemes, 423-425, 429, 439, 440; gap in correspondence, 424; love affairs, 425-429; loses his appointment, 436; a second book of *Fables*, 437, 440, 445-447, 449, 462, 463; offer to live with Swift, 438; *The Distressed Wife, Achilles*, The Rehearsal at Goatham, 440-443, 486; at Twickenham with Pope, 444; a skit on

INDEX

Cibber, 448; his liberal views, 455, 456; portrait painted, 460; scheme of *Achilles*, 462, 463, 466, 467; death, 467; grief of Pope and Swift, 467, 468, 470, 471; Poets' Corner, 471; Pope's epitaph, 471; monument and eulogy, 473, 474; eulogy of Laura, 477-479; tributes to Gay's memory, 480-485, 487, 488
Gay, Jonathan, 14, 20, 22, 27, 31, 47
Gay, Katherine, 14, 20, 471
Gay, Phillip, 13
Gay's Chair, 28-30
Gay, Thomas, 19, 20, 28
Gay, William, 11, 13, 14, 19
George, of Denmark, 36
George Augustus, Elector of Hanover, later, George I, 102, 105-107, 110, 111, 113, 114, 176, 181, 188, 193, 201, 204, 211, 214, 227, 234, 237, 242, 250, 253, 283, 300, 307, 308, 355
Germaine, Lady Betty, 400, 476, 477
Germany, 16
Gilbert le Gay, 13
Gilfillan, George, 325
Glencoe, Massacre of, 17
Godolphin, Lord, 34, 51, 114
Goldsmith, 10, 82, 83, 91
Goldsworthy, Manor of, 13
Gore, Mr., 473
Grafton, Duke of, 358, 359, 369
Great Storm of 1703, 31, 32
Gulliver's Travels, 271, 272, 274, 282, 293, 295-301, 303, 341, 343, 351, 352, 359

Halifax, Lord, 111, 139
Hampstead, 217, 361, 363
Hampstead Heath, 77, 78
Hampton Court, 31, 71, 133, 154, 162, 172, 354, 396
Ham Walks, 438, 445, 450, 452
Handel, 157-161, 193, 201, 210, 227, 233, 234, 336, 419, 420, 458, 485, 486
Hanmer, Rev. Jonathan, 28-30
Hanover, 99, 105-107, 111, 114, 133, 158, 176, 211, 308
Harcourt, Hon. Simon, 202
Harcourt, Lord, 114, 126, 140, 154, 191-193, 309
Harley, Lady Elizabeth, 222
Harley, Robert, later Lord Oxford, 35, 48, 52, 80-82, 85, 87, 98, 102, 103, 113, 114, 121, 126, 178, 187, 194, 202, 242, 255, 382
Harrison, 54

Hazlitt, William, 326, 327
Herbert, 95
Herbert, Mrs., 318
Herrenhausen, 105-107, 111
Herring, Dr., 333, 334
Hervey, Lord, 138, 154, 178, 201, 204, 224, 250, 359, 371
Hill, Aaron, 31, 36-40, 46, 59, 159, 160, 248, 320, 432-434, 485, 486
Hills, R. H. (printer), 40
Hitler, 16
Hoare, 421, 422
Hogarth, 23, 129, 189, 327, 328, 331, 342
Holland House, 163, 164, 195
Horace, 17, 24, 30, 145, 161, 189, 212, 419
Hounslow Heath, 35
Howard, Charles, later Earl of Suffolk, 106, 107, 133, 234, 235, 309, 429
Howard, Henrietta, later Countess of Suffolk, 106, 107, 110, 111, 117, 119, 120, 133-135, 138, 152, 154, 178, 181, 183, 188, 197, 199, 204, 206, 210, 220, 221, 223-225, 234-238, 240-245, 247, 251-254, 268, 274-279, 282, 284, 287-289, 296, 300, 301, 307-309, 311, 317-319, 326, 346, 351, 353-356, 368, 378, 387, 388, 396, 397, 400, 404-406, 408, 416, 417, 422, 425, 429, 430, 439, 440, 464, 465, 476, 477, 481, 482
Howe, Miss, 167

Incledon, Thomas, 487, 488
Indies, 14
Ireland, 33, 164, 177, 283, 285, 301, 305, 312, 319, 408, 416
Irwin, Lord, 214
Italy, 419

James II, 11, 16, 31, 35, 63, 76
Jeffreys, Judge, 15
Jennings, Mary, 240
Jervas, 54, 59, 72, 74, 87, 131, 140, 144, 157, 167, 179, 208, 283, 344, 371
Johnson, Dr., 13, 18, 23-25, 49, 80, 93, 150, 175, 177, 185, 188, 207, 216, 305, 334, 397, 475
Journalism, Rise of, 41-43
Joy Street, 11, 15, 19, 20, 488

Kendal, Duchess of, 188, 193, 204, 214, 288
Kensington, 64, 308
Kensington Palace, 16, 105
Kent, 159
Keynsham Abbey, 13
King Arthur, 12, 13

INDEX 493

Kirke's Lambs, 15
Kitkat Club, 76-78, 275
Kneller, Sir Godfrey, 11, 77, 114, 140, 179, 201, 214

La Hogue, Battle of, 17
Lansdowne, Lord, 68, 77, 140, 154
Laracor, 32, 34
Law, John, 202
Leeds, Duke of, 200
Leicester Fields, 154, 188, 234, 236, 273, 282, 284, 285
Lepell, Mary, later Lady Hervey, 138, 167, 179, 209, 370
Letters:
  Arbuthnot to Pope, 115; to Swift, 264, 265; 317; 375, 376; 383; 468; 473
  Bathurst to Swift, 421, 422
  Bolingbroke to Swift, Pope and Gay, 280, 281
  Gay to Addison, 155, 156; to Caryll, 131, 132; to Henrietta Howard, 197, 198, 199; 238, 239, 240; 243; 251; 277, 278; 387, 388; 397, 405; 440; to Parnell, 130; 167, 168; to Pope, 349; 351; 372, 373; 465; to Swift, 99, 100; to Swift and Arbuthnot, 105, 106; to Swift, 226; 233; 287; 294, 295; Gay and Pope to Swift, 302; Gay to Swift, 314, 315; 337, 338; 343, 344; 348; 350; 358; 377, 378; 390, 391; 395, 396; 401; 403, 404; 408-410; 414, 415; 420, 421; 423; 424; 425, 426; 430, 431; 437, 438; 444, 445; 450; 452, 453; 458, 459; 461; to Tonson, 215
  Germaine, Lady Betty, to Swift, 476
  Hill to Handel, 485
  Howard, Henrietta, to Gay, 237, 238; 240, 241; 317, 318; 354; 396
  Pope to Gay, 55; 61; 115-117; 225; 237; 315, 316; 361, 362; 363; 399; 406; 407; 463, 464; to Swift, 74, 75; 265; 266; 268; 286; 294, 295; 303; 313; 321; 345; 387; 467, 468; 483, 484; to Arbuthnot, 115
  Pulteney to Swift, 281
  Queensberry, Duchess of, to George II, 369, 370; to Henrietta Howard, 418; 481; to Swift, 460; 480, 481
  Swift to Arbuthnot, 79; to Gay, 100, 101; 230-233; 316; 340, 341; 378-380; 392; 410-412; 427, 428; 429; 438, 439; 450-452; 459, 460; to

Henrietta Howard, 406; to Pope, 164; 243; 266; 286; 300; 350, 351; 358; 371; 387; 428; 470; 484; to Tickell, 273
Lewis, Erasmus, 48, 100, 101, 126, 205, 294, 344
Lincoln, Earl of, 229
Lines on the Death of Dr. Swift, 434-436
Lintot, Bernard, 38, 55, 56, 58, 64, 66, 127, 131, 136, 156, 172, 180, 200, 215
Literary Clubs, 76-90
Locke, John, 95
London, 15, 16, 22, 25; life in, 26-29; ravages of storm, 32; 34-36; life in coffee-houses, 38; 80, 91, 115, 121, 141, 150, 166, 172, 191, 233, 234, 258, 273, 383, 410, 419, 422, 425, 432, 436, 471
Lonsdale, Lord, 201, 214
Louis XIV, 16, 17, 52, 105
Louisa, Princess, 313, 314, 396
Lowndes, William, 185, 186
Luck, Mr., 17, 18, 30
Lympne, 11

Macaulay, 195
Macheath, Captain, 258, 296, 323, 327, 329, 333, 334, 248, 377, 487, 488
Mar, Countess of, 296
Marble Hill, 238, 242, 276, 278, 280, 388, 397
Marlborough, Henrietta, Duchess of, 222, 223, 225, 251, 344, 345, 347, 350, 353, 380
Marlborough, Sarah, Duchess of, 34, 51, 52, 214, 227, 242
Marlborough, Duke of, 15, 22, 35, 51, 52, 67, 76, 111, 114, 123, 128, 222, 227, 252
Masham, Lord, 201
Masham, Mrs., 51, 52, 282
Mattaire, 145, 146
Mawson's Buildings, 162
Methuen, Paul, 190
Middleton Stoney, 383, 387
Milton, 95
Minehead, 462
Miscellany, The, 303
Mitchell, Joseph, 227
Mohocks, The — Gay's play, 55
Moliere, 184, 185
Molly Mogg, or the fair maid of the Inn, 275, 310
Monmouth, Duchess of, 59-65, 75, 96, 98, 99, 102, 104, 170

INDEX

Monmouth, Duke of, 11, 12, 15, 62, 63, 349
Montagu, Charles, 44
Montagu, Edward Wortley, 250
Montagu, Lady Mary Wortley, 61, 107, 138, 153-155, 162, 181, 192, 193, 201, 207, 210, 221, 222, 235, 242, 250, 251, 255, 289-292, 296, 309, 310, 328, 353, 399
Moore-Smyth, James, 173
Moor Park, 32, 389

Nantes, Edict of, 16
Nash, 253, 354
Newcastle, Duke of, 67
Newmarket, 36
Newton, Sir Isaac, 35, 95, 214

Oldfield, Mrs., 244, 247
Orange, Prince of, 16
Orchard Wyndham, 462
Orrery, Lord, 77, 199, 475, 476
Ottoman Empire, A Full Account of the, 37
Ovid, 17, 161
Oxford, Lord (the younger), 273, 421
Ozinda's Chocolate House, 78

Paget, Lord, 37, 99
Parker, E, 172
Parnell, 47, 52, 54, 77, 79, 80, 82, 85, 92, 97, 98, 101, 102, 115, 117, 121, 130, 137, 141, 154, 167, 180, 187, 192, 194, 195, 219, 224, 225, 303, 373, 382
Parson's Green, 253
Partridge, 435
Paston, 39
Patrons and Poets, 60, 61, 64-67, 141
Pelham, Mr., 201
Pendarves, Mrs., 336, 337, 400
Pepusch, Dr., 323
Peterborough, Lord, 114, 134, 154, 187, 224, 252-254, 274, 282, 354, 388
Petersham, 290, 299, 310, 383, 388, 397
Phillips, Ambrose, 97, 173, 184, 269
Pilkington, Mrs., 400
Politics under Queen Anne, 51-53, 58, 72, 76, 113; under George I, 123, 124, 147, 148, 174-177, 179, 223; under George II, 354-356
Polly Peachum, 258, 325, 327, 329, 331-334, 348, 350
Pope, Alexander, 9, 18, 32-34, 38, 47, 48, 50-54, 57-61, 67-69, 71, 72, 74, 79-83, 85-88, 90, 93, 94, 97-99, 101-104, 109-112, 114-117, 121, 126-128, 130-136, 140, 141, 144, 145, 151-157, 159-165, 167-174, 180, 181, 183-185, 187-189, 191-194, 196, 197, 199-201, 206-209, 217, 219-222, 224, 225, 233-235, 237, 242-246, 249-251, 254, 255, 261-269, 271-274, 276, 278-282, 284-287, 289, 291-294, 296, 297, 299-303, 309, 310, 312-316, 320, 326-328, 331, 332, 340, 343-346, 349-354, 357-359, 361-363, 371-373, 376, 377, 379-382, 385-389, 396-401, 404, 406-409, 411, 412, 415-417, 419-422, 424, 428, 430, 432-437, 445-451, 453-455, 457, 460, 462-467, 469-473, 475-477, 480, 482-486
Pope, Mrs., 162, 163, 217, 237, 254, 311, 361-363, 406-408
Portland, Duke of, 214
Portugal, 14
Pretender, The Young, 148
Prior, Matthew, 10, 35, 37, 38, 40, 51, 57, 71, 72, 77, 88, 94, 103, 114, 118, 139, 178, 187, 193-195, 200, 205, 208, 210, 222, 224, 290, 391, 473, 477
Pulteney, Lord, 147, 154, 175, 192, 273, 281, 300, 326
Pulteney, Mr. William, 177-182, 184, 185, 188, 200, 223, 251, 340, 377
Purcell, 336

Queensberry, Duchess of, 206-209, 217, 219-224, 236, 251, 284, 289-291, 293, 295, 310, 311, 314, 318, 321-323, 338, 346, 361, 367-372, 376-378, 383, 385, 386, 389, 392, 393, 397, 399-401, 404, 405, 408-411, 414, 417, 418, 423-425, 428-432, 444, 445, 449-452, 455, 456, 458-460, 464, 466, 470, 471, 473, 474, 477, 479-482, 486
Queensberry, Duke of, 201, 206, 207, 209, 219-221, 223, 251, 289, 311, 314, 321, 322, 363, 372, 377, 383, 385, 386, 394, 395, 400, 402, 410, 431, 432, 444, 445, 449, 452, 461, 466, 468, 471, 473, 474, 483
Queen Sophia, 284, 301
Quin, 323, 324

Radcliffe, Dr., 214, 216
Ramsay, Allan, 383, 384
Rape of the Lock, 56, 59, 93, 94, 135, 136
Red Cross, 12, 17
Review, The, 41
Rich, 321-324, 327, 338, 344, 347, 358, 395, 419, 420, 466, 467, 486
Richardson, 179, 460
Richmond, 188, 225, 236, 238, 240, 273, 276, 279, 281, 284, 290, 308, 464

INDEX

Robinson, Mrs. Anastatia, 253, 254
Rochester, 10, 140
Rural Sports, 64, 67, 68, 75, 93, 169, 200

Satire, its effect on the Satirist, 380-382, 454
St. Germains, 31, 35, 51, 52
St. James's Palace, 82, 83, 85, 87, 115, 188, 210, 309, 319, 355, 439
St. John, Henry, see BOLINGBROKE, LORD
Salisbury, 145, 400, 420
Savage, 88
Schulenberg, Duchess of, 214
Scotland, 76
Scott, Jane, 29
Scott, Walter, 314
Scriblerus Club, 78-89, 91, 92, 98, 99, 104, 114, 115, 121, 154, 194, 232, 275, 301, 303, 343, 346, 372, 379, 380, 417, 447, 463
Scudamore, Lady, 139
Sedgemoor, 11, 12, 15
Sedley, 151
Senesino, 253
Shepherd's Week, The, 39, 181, 225, 333
Sheppard, Jack, 256-258, 330
Sheridan, 272, 341, 416
Sitwell, Edith, 109
Skerrit, Miss Molly, 250, 328
Smyrna Coffee-house, 38
Snow, Thomas, 217
Soho, 403, 425, 426
Somerset, 345, 462, 463
Sophia, Electress of Hanover, 102
Southey, 23
South Sea Company, 177, 193, 201-206, 209-211, 213, 214, 217, 222, 223, 402, 413
Spain, 51, 193, 252
Spenser, 8, 97
Stair, Earl of, 201
Stanhope, Lord, 123, 176, 177, 216, 369
Stanton Harcourt, 191, 192
Steele, Richard, 9, 35, 38, 41-43, 46, 51, 53, 54, 66, 72-74, 77, 88, 93, 94, 103, 108, 124, 130, 140, 170, 171, 217, 342
Stella, 109, 161-164, 205, 246, 272, 282, 285, 288, 293, 312, 313, 339, 340, 400
Sunderland, Lord, 123, 175-177
Swift, Dean, 14, 18, 32-34, 38, 41, 42, 44, 47, 48, 51-53, 58, 64, 72-74, 77-83, 85, 87-92, 97-105, 108-114, 118, 121, 125-128, 140, 144, 145, 149-151, 153-156, 158, 161-165, 168, 180, 181, 185, 187, 189, 193, 194, 196, 205, 206, 218, 220, 222-227, 229-234, 236, 242, 245, 246, 248, 249, 253, 255-258, 260, 262-269, 271-275, 277, 280-288, 290, 293-303, 307, 309-317, 319, 321, 326, 327, 330, 337, 339-341, 344-353, 357-359, 362, 371, 375-378, 380-382, 386-389, 392, 397, 399-406, 408, 410, 411, 413-417, 419, 420, 422, 423, 426-431, 434-440, 444, 445, 450, 452, 455, 457-460, 462, 466, 467, 469-472, 476-478, 480, 482-486

Tale of a Tub, 34, 301, 392
Tatler, 41, 42
Taw, 15, 30, 277
Temple, Sir William, 64
Thackeray, 10, 49, 272, 308
Theatre, The English, 247, 248
The Chapter, 38
Theobald, 262, 274, 352, 353
Tickell, 47, 51, 54, 67, 117, 119, 120, 135, 136, 140, 170, 273, 335
Tonbridge, 191, 238
Tonson, Jacob, 38, 44, 66, 76, 136, 145, 156, 200, 214-216, 225, 303, 339, 421, 432
Torquay, 16
Tower Hill, 11, 21, 63
Townshend, Lord, 123, 176, 177
Trevelyan, G. M., 22
Trivia, 25, 40, 150-153, 160, 166, 169, 200
Trumbull, Sir William, 32
Tunbridge Wells, 141, 236-238, 240
Twickenham, 193, 209, 217, 221, 238, 243, 246, 251, 254, 261, 273, 276, 282, 284, 294, 297, 309, 310, 312, 338, 349, 357, 284, 389, 391, 398, 401, 410, 417, 419, 420, 437, 438, 444, 446, 448, 483
Twyford, 18

Underhill, 97
Upper Flask Inn, 77
Utrecht, Treaty of, 71, 195, 202

Vanbrugh, Sir John, 77, 248
Vanessa, 58, 109, 162, 205, 218, 222, 246, 282
Van Loo, 179
Vernon, Mrs., 349
Virgil, 17
Voltaire, 81, 163, 185, 310, 311, 393, 482

Wales, Prince of, later George II, 154, 175, 176, 181, 188, 204, 210, 214, 234-236, 247, 250, 253, 269, 274, 283, 288, 300, 303, 309, 313, 355, 356, 369, 378, 430

Wales, Princess of, later Queen Caroline, 175, 188, 196, 210, 214, 220, 227, 244, 247, 269, 274, 275, 282, 289, 296, 303, 307, 354-356, 369, 370, 378, 406, 430, 464, 465
Walker, Thomas, 323, 327, 334, 347
Walpole, Horace, 127, 132, 175, 224, 290, 370, 371, 479
Walpole, Mrs., 308, 328
Walpole, Robert, 36, 67, 123, 147, 154, 156, 174-178, 193, 201, 203, 204, 220, 223, 227
Warton, Joseph, 30, 195, 196
Warwick, Countess of, 163
Warwick, Earl of, 139, 200
Watts, 95
Welsted, Leonard, 173
West Indies, 357
Westminster, 31, 439
Westminster Abbey, 471-473
Westmoreland, Lady, 479
Wharton, Duke of, 67, 156, 214

Whitehall, 230, 231, 244, 282, 285, 357, 360, 363, 393, 420
Wild, Jonathan, 256-259, 329, 330
William III, 17, 31, 51, 71, 76, 103, 411
William, Prince, Duke of Cumberland, 269, 290, 304
Will's Coffee-house, 38, 163
Wimpole, 382
Winchelsea, Countess of, 139, 153, 170
Windsor, 32
Windsor Forest, 68
Wine, 39
Women, Estimate of, 108-110, 116, 129, 134, 135, 153, 237, 239, 275, 370, 393
Wood's Pence, 249, 255
Wren, Christopher, 35
Wycherley, 32, 33, 248
Wyndham, Sir William, 148, 344, 446, 462, 463

Young, Edward, 37, 67, 95, 117, 120, 214, 227, 228, 305, 335, 342, 415, 416